CRIME AND MEDIA STUDIES

Diversity of Method, Medium, and Communication

First Edition

Edited by Franklin T. Wilson

Indiana State University

Bassim Hamadeh, CEO and Publisher
Michael Simpson, Vice President of Acquisitions
Jamie Giganti, Managing Editor
Jess Busch, Senior Graphic Designer
Angela Kozlowski, Acquisitions Editor
Michelle Piehl, Project Editor
Alexa Lucido, Licensing Coordinator
Kaela Martin, Interior Designer

First published in the United States of America in 2015 by Cognella, Inc.

Trademark Notice: Product or corporate names may be trademarks or registered trademarks, and are used only for identification and explanation without intent to infringe.

Cover Image: Copyright © 2013 iStockphoto LP/Vertigo3d.

Back Cover Image: Edited by Brenda Thompson Photography

Printed in the United States of America

ISBN: 978-1-62661-768-1 (pbk)/ 978-1-62661-769-8 (br)

www.cognella.com   800-200-3908

CONTENTS

SECTION ONE: INTRODUCTION

SECTION TWO: CRIME

SECTION THREE: LAW ENFORCEMENT

SECTION FOUR: COURTS

SECTION FIVE: CORRECTIONS AND PUNISHMENT

SECTION SIX: JUSTICE SYSTEM

This book is dedicated to my mother, Elizabeth Burns Wilson French (Libby), who taught me through example that you should always try to help people if you can. Whether it was raising me as single mother on a secretary's salary, leading female employees to unionize, donating time to charities, or serving as a role model for females and males of all ages, I will always cherish the example you have provided.

ACKNOWLEDGEMENTS

I would, first and foremost, like to thank Dr. Howard Henderson from the Administration of Justice Department at Texas Southern University and Dr. Ashley Blackburn from the Department of Criminal Justice at the University of Houston Downtown for all of your encouragement and support. Second, I would like to thank the staff at Cognella, especially Angela Kozlowski, Michelle Piehl, Jamie Giganti, Chelsey Rogers, Jess Busch, Luiz Ferreira, Alexa Lucido, and Mike Simpson, among others for all of your help in preparing this text for publication.

PREFACE

With the publication of *Crime and Media Studies: Diversity of Method, Medium, and Communication*, it is my hope that this book will, first and foremost, help to introduce a new generation of students and practitioners to crime and media studies and its endless potential for impacting public perception and policy. Moreover, it is my hope that the discussion sessions, writing exercises (blogs and press releases), public consumption exercises, and the brownbag or roundtable session contained in this text will help bolster the communication of criminological research, crime and media studies in particular, to the media and to all members of society in the future. And, finally, it is my hope that a major first step toward a more informed citizenry has begun.

Divided into six distinct sections, the book first tackles the ramifications of the communication disconnect that has long existed between those who study issues surrounding the criminal justice system and that of the media and the average citizen. Specifically, the first section explores the role of literacy rates in the United States and the need for criminologists and other social scientists to recognize the large gap between the writing level of their peer-reviewed research and the 8th to 9th grade literacy level of the average American. More importantly, it documents the role literacy rates have played since the 1950s in how information is disseminated to the public through various media outlets. It emphasizes how the responsibility falls upon criminologists and other social scientists to learn how to communicate both their expertise and research findings concisely and at the average literacy level, or below, of the audience they wish to educate. Section 1 also emphasizes the need for future practitioners to ensure that their personal literacy levels remain high enough to not only fully comprehend the findings of the latest peer-reviewed research but to subsequently use those findings in their day-to-day decision making and in policy construction and implementation.

The remaining five sections of the text are divided into the key aspects of the criminal justice system: crime, law enforcement, courts, corrections and punishment, and the justice system as a whole. Each section features articles that address major issues facing the criminal justice system such as crack vs. powder cocaine sentencing policies, methamphetamines, domestic violence, race, gender, juror perceptions, culture of punishment, and the death penalty, among others. These critical topics are explored through the examination of a variety of media, including print news, broadcast news, movies, court TV, television crime dramas, comic books, and hip-hop and bluegrass music, among others.

The book as a whole is intended to reveal to students the sheer breadth of venues across multiple disciplines that are publishing crime and media research. Specifically, the book contains 14 peer-reviewed journal articles from 11 different journals and a list of over 200 different peer-reviewed journals in which crime and media research has appeared over the past decade (Appendix A). Most importantly, this book emphasizes the need to ignore old ideological divides, be they methodological or theoretical, and encourages, instead, a grassroots united front of researchers and practitioners using whatever methodology is needed to help society. The articles in this text provide students with examples of crime and media studies that have used quantitative, qualitative, and mixed methodologies to explore pivotal issues facing the criminal justice system and point to how this research can be used to inform the public and improve criminal justice policies.

SECTION ONE

Introduction

STOP THE HUMBLE MUMBLE

Bringing Criminology to the People

by Franklin T. Wilson
Department of Criminology and Criminal Justice, Indiana State University

"Speeches only reaches those who already know about it."

OutKast featuring Erykah Badu "Humble Mumble"

The United States represents only 5% of the world's population, but accounts for more than 25% of the world's incarcerated population (Talvi, 2007; American Civil Liberties Union, 2014). Incarcerating at a rate of 716 for every 100,000 citizens, the United States dwarfs its nearest competitors, Rwanda (492), Russia (475), Brazil (274), Spain (147), Australia (130), China (121), and Canada (118) (Wamsley, 2013; Sentencing Project, 2014). With 2.2 million people incarcerated in prisons and jails (Glaze and Herberman, 2013) and an additional 4.7 million under probation or parole supervision (Maruschak and Bonczar, 2013), one might think the United States is a society that is prone to crime, when, in fact, the high incarceration and correctional supervision rates are largely due to changes in sentencing policies and laws since the 1970s (Sentencing Project, 2014). While these statistics may surprise the common person on the street, to criminologists and other social scientists, this is common knowledge. These sentencing policies and laws, as well as a variety of social issues, have been allowed to exist largely because the expertise of and research conducted by criminologists and other social scientists do not reach the general public. This is, arguably, due to such experts being denied media platforms and/or failing to reach out to the media in a manner that is concise and matches the literacy level of the average citizen.

Criminologists have long known about increasing rates of correctional supervision. They have also known that this growth, as well as the crimes that are committed, are largely due to a complex web of social issues that, if properly addressed, could serve as more effective crime prevention and control measures than have traditional "tough on crime" measures. And yet, addressing these issues is rarely presented as viable solutions to the general public (Sacco, 2006; Surette, 2011; Tunnell, 1998; Welch, Fenwick, and Roberts, 1998). These social issues can be compressed into broad categorizations such as socioeconomic class, race, gender, and culture, among others, each comprised of its own set of equally intricate sub-issues. Meanwhile, the general public's understanding of the criminal justice system continues to be far less informed than those who study the system. This lack of a properly informed society, arguably, leads to public support of policies and laws that target individual failings and ignore the social issues that are more appropriately to blame. While it is easy to criticize those who make or enforce the aforementioned policies and laws, these individuals are often the end product of a process of approval that began long before they were elected or appointed. In the end, it all originates with what the general public perceives as a problem and what solutions they support. These perceived problems and supported solutions are most often rooted in highly simplistic beliefs such as "an eye for an eye and a tooth for a tooth," "the death penalty deters crime," and "hiring more police officers will stop crime," among other beliefs that criminologists and other social scientists have proven to be counterproductive and/or completely inaccurate. These belief systems are passed on generation to generation while the social science findings that dismantle them rarely reach the general public.

These comfortably simplistic beliefs have continued, despite the large percentage of the population being imprisoned or otherwise involved with the criminal justice system, due to the fact that the majority of United States citizens have no personal experience with the criminal justice system. This personal experience is referred to in crime and media studies as "experienced reality" (Surette, 2011). The knowledge most people have of the system, its inner workings, and, most importantly, how social issues feed its growth is largely informed by secondhand knowledge. This secondhand knowledge is what crime and media researchers refer to as "symbolic knowledge," the knowledge one has acquired from other people, institutions, and the media (Surette, 2011). Given the lack of interaction most people have with the criminal justice system, the symbolic knowledge attained from other people and institutions can most often be traced back to some form of media. Therefore, the majority of what most people believe they know about crime and the criminal justice system comes from the media (Robinson, 2011; Surette, 2011).

Informing the public about crime and justice issues through media is nothing new. With the rise of the penny press in the 1830s, daily print media became the first form of media to mass market information to the public (Surette, 2011). Crime stories quickly became a basic feature of the daily newspapers of the time. However, while modern media depictions focus primarily on the individual (Sacco, 2006; Surette, 2011; Tunnell, 1998; Welch, Fenwick, and Roberts, 1998), these early depictions placed the blame on class inequality and discussed crime as the fault of social and political failings of society at large (Surrette, 2011). No matter what the message, print media in the 1830s as well as today relies on an audience that is literate. So, when discussing what information is passed on to the general public regarding criminal justice issues in our modern society, the question that must be raised is just how literate, or illiterate, has our society become? Are members of our modern and technologically advanced society capable of looking up peer-reviewed research findings of those who study the complexities of criminal justice issues? If they have access to such research, are they capable of interpreting and applying the findings to their own lives? If research is presented in the news media, are they capable of understanding it in its original format? Are they capable of determining the difference between rigorous study findings and that of personal opinion pieces? The answer, and stark reality, to each of these questions is no.

The Reality of Literacy in the United States

The first surveys of adult literacy in the United States revealed that in 1935 the average reader had limited reading abilities, reading somewhere between a 7th and 8th grade level (Gray and Leary, 1935). More recently, the National Adult Literacy Survey (NALS) in 1992 and its follow up study, the 2003 National Assessment of Adult Literacy (NAAL), the largest study of its kind, revealed that the average adult reads at approximately an 8th grade reading level (Dubay, 2007).

The NAAL study measured functional English literacy of adults in the United States. Specifically, it measured three types of literacy:

- **Prose Literacy**—The ability to search, comprehend, and use information from continuous texts such as news articles and instructional materials (National Center for Education Statistics, 2014a). Examples include editorials, news stories, brochures, and instructional materials (American Library Association, 2014).
- **Document Literacy**—The ability to search, comprehend, and use information from noncontinuous texts such as job applications, maps, and food labels (National Center for Education Statistics, 2014a). Examples include job applications, payroll forms, transportation schedules, maps, tables, drug labels, and food labels (American Library Association, 2014).
- **Quantitative Literacy**—The ability to identify and perform computations using numbers embedded in printed materials (National Center for Education Statistics, 2014a). Examples include balancing a checkbook, calculating a tip, and completing an order form (American Library Association, 2014).

In each of the literacy categories participant's scores placed them into one of four categories (National Center for Education Statistics, 2014a):

- **Below Basic**—"indicates no more than the most simple and concrete literacy skills."
- **Basic**—"indicates skills necessary to perform simple and everyday literacy activities."
- **Intermediate**—"indicates skills necessary to perform moderately challenging literacy activities."
- **Proficient**— "indicates skills necessary to perform more complex and challenging literacy activities."

The 2003 NAAL results showed virtually no change since the 1992 NALS study in regard to prose and document literacy, while quantitative literacy showed a slight increase (National Center for Education Statistics, 2014b). The 2003 study revealed:

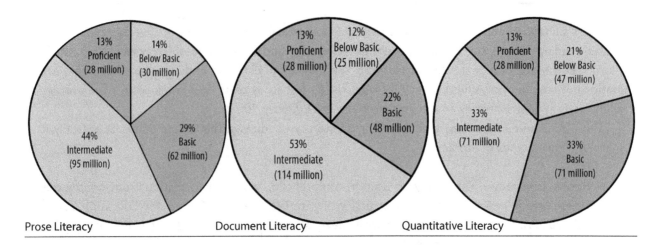

Prose Literacy   Document Literacy   Quantitative Literacy

Based on these findings, 14% (30 million) of United States citizens cannot understand medication instructions, read stories to their children, assist their children with their homework, read newspaper articles, determine a location on a map, read communications from financial or government institutions, complete job applications, or perform in any other way that requires more than basic literacy skills (American Library Association, 2014; "Impact of Illiteracy," 2014). It is estimated that of these 30 million citizens, some 11 million are completely nonliterate (National Center for Education Statistics, 2014b). Most importantly to this text is the fact that 87% (187 million) of citizens are functioning at or below a literacy level that, at best, allows them to perform moderately challenging literacy activities, well below the writing level of most peer-reviewed research studies. So, criminologists and other social scientists who wish their research to impact policy and laws must be able to reduce their research down to the essential findings. Further, they must be able to communicate these findings concisely and at a literacy level that, at a minimum, matches the average citizen. Likewise, any practitioner who wishes to draw from the most up-to-date research regarding the issues impacting the citizens which they serve must know how to look up the appropriate peer-reviewed research, understand it, and subsequently translate it to the citizens they serve. It is also important to keep in mind that, while an increased number of people are graduating from high school and earning college degrees, this does not necessarily translate into higher literacy rates.

While increasing one's education level has been found to help increase literacy, it does not help as much as many might think. In 2006, The National Survey of America's College Students, which used the same methodology as the NAAL study, showed that literacy scores for college students was significantly higher in all three categories than the average score for adults in the NAAL study (Baer et al., 2006; Dubay, 2007). However, the study also showed that "over half of college students nearing graduation cannot perform complex reading tasks such as understanding the arguments of newspaper editorials" and that "most students cannot perform complex but common mathematical tasks" (Dubay, 2007, p. 24). The 2003 NAAL study revealed that, as with the 1992 NALS study, individual scores rose with each level of education attained. However, the study also revealed that scores fell for each level of education when compared to the scores from the 1992 study. Specifically, prose scores dropped nine points between 1992 and 2003 for those with some high school or less education while high school graduates dropped six points. College graduates dropped 11 points in prose and 14 points in document literacy while those classified as graduate studies/degree dropped 13 points in prose and 17 points in document literacy (National Center for Education Statistics, 2014c).

While drops in literacy scores across all education levels are alarming, even more alarming is the fact that reading levels do not match one's level of education attained in the United States. More often than not, individual reading levels fall well below one's educational attainment. High school graduates still read comfortably at an 8th grade level and college graduates at a 10th grade level (Dubay, 2007). Given that most readers only find reading enjoyable if the material is written two grade levels below their reading level, the majority of popular print media such as novels are written at a 7th grade reading level (Dubay, 2007; "Flesch and Gunning," 2005, Klare and Buck, 1954). This is further reflected by the findings of a report by Renaissance Learning, Inc. (2014) that examined book-reading habits of students in grades 1–12 in the United States. The study revealed that high school students (grades 9–12) are reading books somewhere between the 5th and 6th grade reading levels (Renaissance Learning, Inc., 2014). So, while 76% of Americans over the age of 18 claimed to have read at least one book in the past year (Zickuhr, 2014), it is most likely the reading level of those books fell below the 7th grade level. The need to understand literacy levels has long been recognized not just by publishers of books/ novels but by publishers of newspapers and television news programs as well.

Newspapers and Literacy

While newspapers have a long history of providing the literate public with information regarding crime and the criminal justice system, the reading level of the papers did not always match the average reading comprehension level of society. In the 1950s, Rudolph Flesch and Robert Gunning proposed the idea that newspapers should be written at the same reading level as the reading comprehension level of the average American adult (Chall, 1958; Klare, 1963; Macris, 2010). Until that point, newspapers were generally written at a 12th grade level (Macris, 2010; "Flesch and Gunning," 2005). Their research revealed that if the writing levels of newspapers and wire services were lowered, the number of people reading the papers increased (Davies, 2006; Dubay, 2004; "Flesch and Gunning," 2005). With the average American reading between an 8th and 9th grade level at that time, newspapers chose to move from a 12th to a 9th grade reading level and newswires moved from a 16th to an 11th grade reading level (Fry, 2009; Marcris, 2010; Dubay, 2004; "Flesch and Gunning," 2005). While reading level estimates of newspapers vary today depending on the subject of the article analyzed, William H. Dubay's estimate of reading levels of newspapers and magazines serves as a good representation of most estimates. He estimated that the top U.S. newspapers and magazines are written between a 9th and 12th grade reading level (Dubay, 2007). He also found that a correlation continues to exist between the reading level and the circulation numbers of newspapers. Specifically, the lower the reading level, the larger the circulation numbers (i.e., the more people reached). For example, according to Dubays' (2007) analysis, *TV Guide* and *Readers Digest*, the two magazines with the largest circulation in the world, were written at a 9th grade level. Similarly, the two newspapers with the largest circulation numbers in the study, the *New York Times* and *USA Today*, were written at a 10th grade level.

This can further be demonstrated by looking at the education levels of those who read certain newspapers. As most college graduates read comfortably at a 10th grade level and high school graduates at an 8th grade level, and given Dubay's estimate that most top U.S. newspapers and magazines are written between a 9th and 12th grade reading level, the readership of such publications should have higher levels of education when compared to the readership of local newspapers. According to a report by Pew Research Center on the demographics of news audiences, those who are college graduates comprised 56% of the *Wall Street Journal* and the *New York Times* readership, while those with some college accounted for 24–27%, and those with a high school education or less only comprised 16–18% (Kohut, Doherty, Dimock, and Keeter, 2012). Similarly, college graduates accounted for 45% of *USA Today*'s readership, while those with some college education accounted for 31%, and those with a high school education or less made up 24%. Daily newspaper (local newspapers) readers, on the other hand, are made up of 37% college graduates, 30% with some college, and 33% with a high school education or less (Kohut, Doherty, Dimock, and Keeter, 2012). Therefore, larger newspapers like the *Wall Street Journal* and the *New York Times* write for an audience with a higher education level, and local newspapers write for an audience that is more evenly divided among education levels.

This said, if criminologists and other social scientists are trying to reach the largest audience possible, instinctively, one might think that publishing information in the *New York Times* or *USA Today* might be the best approach given their wide distribution. But, if one considers that in 2013 only 31% (65 million) of Americans had graduated with a bachelor's degree or greater, 27% (55 million) had some college education, and 42% (86 million) had a high school education or less (U.S. Census Bureau, 2013) then local newspapers may be the more effective medium given that their readership reaches more of those with some college education and below. This is the group that accounts for approximately 69% of the United States population. While the information may not reach the sheer number that larger newspapers do, it will reach a larger percentage of those who fall into the 87% (187 million) of United States citizens who are functioning at or below literacy levels that, at best, allow them to perform moderately challenging literacy activities. One sees similar trends in television news as well.

Television and Literacy

Nielsen (2012) revealed that television viewing by the average American has doubled over the past 20 years. As of 2012, the average American watched 34 hours of television per week, not including recorded programs that could increase this number even further. Therefore, the average American will spend over two years for every ten years of his or her life watching television (Wilson and Henderson, 2014). In the 1990s the estimation was only one year for every ten years of life (Surrette, 2007). With this exponential increase in television viewing, it becomes more and more important for those who wish to invoke legal or policy improvements to understand what television platforms either reach the most people and/or reach the audience that needs the information most.

Olmstead, Jurkowitz, Mitchell, and Enda (2013) revealed that 71% of Americans get their TV news from local TV news, 65% from network TV news (e.g., ABC, CBS, NBC), and 38% from cable TV news (e.g., CNN, Fox News, MSNBC). The crossover rates, those who watch more than one format, are highest between local and network news. According to Olmstead and colleagues (2013), "90% of network news viewers also watch local news, and 82% of local news viewers also tune in to network news" (p. 4). However, only 44% of network and local news viewers watch cable news. The lower percentage of citizens who watch cable news is most likely tied to politics. According to The Pew Research Center, trends in news consumption between 1991 and 2012 indicate that the majority of news viewers prefer news that does not have a specific political viewpoint (Kohut, Doherty, Dimock, and Keeter, 2012). Given that many of the cable news stations tend to lean toward a specific political party, either through their news broadcasts or individual shows on the network, it is not surprising that many viewers choose more neutral platforms in comparison (Kohut, Doherty, Dimock, and Keeter, 2012).

Unlike newspapers, the education levels of viewers across all three platforms are distributed relatively evenly. The 2012 Pew Research Center report on "Trends in News Consumption: 1991–2012" revealed that network evening news, CNN, local TV news, MSNBC, and Fox News viewer education levels are 24–31% college graduates (network evening news ranking the highest and Fox News the lowest), 30–35% some college (MSNBC ranking the highest and network evening news the lowest), and 38–43% high school education or less (Fox News ranking the highest and CNN and MSNBC tied for the lowest) (Kohut, Doherty, Dimock, and Keeter, 2012). And while the "literacy" rates for television broadcasts are harder to grasp, some indications might be gathered by examining the reading level scores for their websites. In 2010, Adam Sherk examined news websites to determine which contained the most advanced and least advanced content. Using Google reading level scores, which determine what percent of a website is at a basic, intermediate, or advanced reading level, he determined that none of the network or cable TV news websites contained more than 2% advanced reading material. Network news websites contained 28–41% basic reading level material and 57–70% intermediate reading level material. Cable news websites contained 23–27% basic reading level material and 69–73% intermediate reading level material (Sherk, 2010).

If one is trying to reach the largest audience possible, instinctively, one might think that appearing on cable television news stations, such as CNN, Fox News, or MSNBC, or a network nightly news program might be the best approach given their wide viewership. But, again, a local news platform may be the more effective medium given that its viewership reaches more of those with some college education and below; the group that accounts for approximately 69% of the United States population. While the information may not reach the sheer number that cable or network news programs do, it will reach a larger percentage of those who fall into the 87% (187 million) of United States citizens who are functioning at or below literacy levels that, at best, allow them to perform moderately challenging literacy activities.

No matter what platform one chooses, the general public's knowledge of the criminal justice system and, more importantly, the role of issues that the general public may not instinctively recognize as connected to "crime," are informed by print media and visual media. Both of these tailor their publications and broadcasts to those who read at the most basic levels (Dubay, 2007). Consequently, it is highly unlikely that we will see criminologists and other social scientists used as experts on most television platforms or in most newspaper articles unless they learn how to communicate their research findings and/or convey their expertise at the literacy level of the audience they need to reach.

Why No Criminologists as Experts?

Be it old or new media, visual or print media, entertainment or news media, or some combination of media formats, the information conveyed regarding the criminal justice system and the social issues that drive the system are rarely informed by those who actually study the highly complex nature of crime and the criminal justice system. Instead, research has shown that the media regularly utilize prosecutors, police officials, and politicians, among others who are working within the criminal justice system as expert commentators (Barak, 2007; Beckett and Sasson, 2004; Chermak, 1995; Frost and Phillips, 2011; Tunnell, 1998; Welch, Fenwick, and Roberts, 1997; Welch, Fenwick, and Roberts, 1998). These individuals are experts, but much of their expertise comes from working within the day-to-day policy and legal limitations of the criminal justice system. They are generally not afforded the time to think abstractly about crime, the corresponding societal response, or to conduct complex research studies that can be used to educate the general public and policy makers. Rather, they are forced to work within the restricted confines of the current system and public expectations—expectations that are often based in the simplistic beliefs mentioned earlier. Consequently, it "should" fall to criminologists and other social scientists to provide the expertise and research findings to help create a more informed citizenry.

The lack of criminology and criminal justice researchers used as experts by the media was officially recognized as early as 1988 with Gregg Barak's article "Newsmaking Criminology: Reflections on the Media, Intellectuals, and Crime," published in *Justice Quarterly*, the flagship journal of the Academy of Criminal Justice Sciences. Barak (1988) called on criminologists to insert themselves into the media coverage of crime and criminal justice issues and, as a result, better inform media coverage and the general public (Frost and Phillips, 2011). Very few studies have tested newsmaking criminology, but in one of the most recent tests by Frost and Phillips (2011), the absence of criminologists in news coverage appears to have continued more than 25 years after Barak's article. This lack of presence should not be surprising if one considers that the majority of those who have examined newsmaking criminology have predominantly focused on appearances in national newspapers, cable news, national news, or newsmagazines. This, arguably, reflects an assumption that the best way to distribute one's expertise and research findings is through network news, cable news, or large newspapers. However, as was demonstrated above, cable news is the television news platform where the lowest percentages of Americans receive their news. Additionally, as was mentioned above, national newspapers focus primarily on those with higher literacy rates and likely exclude a significant portion of society.

Little attention has been given to local newspapers or television stations, arguably, the more accessible platforms for criminologists and other social scientists to introduce themselves, their research, and their expertise to the public. Few, if any, have ever posited the idea that the majority of society and the news media, in particular, may have no idea what those who hold a Ph.D. in criminology or criminal justice actually do. As a result, they would never think to use them as experts. Nor has anyone posited the idea that criminologists should market their research findings to the media in a format that is readable at a 6th–8th grade level like their counterparts in the medical field and other hard sciences (Fry, 2009; Kunz and Osborne, 2010). Lastly, perhaps criminologists could inform a larger portion of society by becoming consistent voices in the local news media rather than waiting to be called on as experts by network news, cable news, or larger newspapers.

This author would propose that studies of newsmaking criminology should not just be looking at how often criminologists are appearing in the media but also exploring how often criminologists reach out to reporters regarding their research findings, how efficiently they communicate with the media, and whether or not they are listed as experts with the press release companies their universities utilize. A more revealing study might be to survey news reporters and simply ask four questions: 1) What do you believe criminology and criminal justice professors (those with a Ph.D.) do? 2) How many times have you been approached by a criminology or criminal justice professor about reporting the findings of their research? 3) Have you ever asked to use a criminology or criminal justice professor, who has a Ph.D., to comment on a news piece? and 4) If you answered yes to Question 3, what was your experience and if you answered no, why not? This book is designed to help bridge this communications gap both for criminologists who wish to create a more informed citizenry towards policy change and improvement and progressive practitioners who wish to inform their individual decision making, their agencies, and their communities with the most up-to-date peer-reviewed research.

Facing Reality and the Need for Better Communication

It is unlikely in the near future that average literacy levels in the United States, levels that have changed very little since 1935, are going to reach the proficiency level needed for the general populace to 1) know how to access peer-reviewed research, 2) read and completely comprehend the research, and 3) tie the research findings to policy and legal issues. Nor is it likely that the profit-driven media will risk alienating, at a minimum, 87% of its readers and viewers by presenting information at a literacy level that exceeds that of the general populace's capabilities—a populace that includes reporters and media executives who must understand the research and its significance before it potentially goes to print or on the air. Therefore, the responsibility falls upon those who possess the knowledge to learn to effectively communicate with the media and the public.

In 2011, great attention was given to the Occupy Wall Street movement. The movement's slogan, "We are the 99%," referenced the economic disparity in the United States where the majority of wealth is held by less than 1% of society. Similarly, according to the United States Census Bureau (2013), across all disciplines, less than 1.6% of the population attain Ph.D.s, arguably, the highest level of intellectual capital. Additionally, only a fraction of the elite population who attain Ph.D.s, the terminal (highest) level of education attainable in the field of criminology and criminal justice, actually go on to study crime and the criminal justice system. Even smaller percentages of this elite population actively conduct research and publish in peer-reviewed outlets. Therefore, much like those who took part in the Occupy Wall Street movement believed that the 1% of society who hold the majority of economic wealth should give back to society, it is argued here that the 1% of the educated elite who hold the majority of intellectual capital should give back in a similar fashion. This book takes the stance that those who study the complexities of crime and criminal justice, including the social ills that feed its growth, have a moral and ethical obligation to give back to society by communicating their research and expertise concisely and at a literacy level that the majority can understand. Specifically, this book contends that the most important peer-reviewed research that must reach practitioners, and the general public alike, is that body of research that exposes the myths and mistakes regularly depicted in the media.

The collection of articles in this book focuses on the three traditional forms of media: print, sound, and visual, what Surette (2011) collectively refers to as "legacy media." However, today we also have "new media," which is "made up of devices and capabilities encompassing digital and Internet technology that are characterized by interactive social media and multimedia content" (Surette, 2011, p. 14). The digital format of the new media can meld print, sound, and visual media and allows for faster communication and news looping. With this ever-increasing speed of communication, the need for criminologists and other social scientists to perfect their ability to concisely communicate their expertise and peer-reviewed research findings in a manner that meets with the literacy level of the average member of society has never been so great.

The title of this piece draws from the song "Humble Mumble" written and performed by the group OutKast and Erykah Badu (Benjamin, Patton, Sheats, and Wright, 2000). The song addresses how speeches are not an effective way to promote change, namely because those who listen to the speeches already agree with what is being said. While the song promotes hip-hop as a way to mobilize the oppressed communities, this book promotes literacy awareness and effective communication with the media as a better method to improve society. It is time to stop our own humble mumble and start reaching out.

Therefore, this book is designed to serve several functions. First, it is designed to demonstrate to the reader how crime and media research can be applied to all aspects of the criminal justice system: crime, law enforcement, courts, corrections and punishment, and to the system as a whole. Second, this book contains 14 peer-reviewed journal articles from 11 different journals to demonstrate how crime and media studies have been published in a wide variety of journals across multiple disciplines. This is also emphasized by providing the reader with a list of over 200 different peer-reviewed journals in which crime and media research has appeared over that past decade. Third, this book, much like Brent and Kraska (2010), encourages a tearing down of the walls of the methodological divide between qualitative and quantitative researchers. The articles in this text provide examples of crime and media studies that have used quantitative, qualitative, and mixed methodologies to address key issues such as sentencing policies, race, gender, and domestic violence, among others. This books calls for, and provides tools for, the development of a grassroots united front of researchers using whatever methodology is needed to help members of society. Subsequently, it calls on criminologists and other social scientists to actively communicate their expertise and research findings to both the media and the general public at an effective literacy level.

References

American Civil Liberties Union [ACLU]. (2014, July 31). The prison crisis. Retrieved from: https://www.aclu.org/safe-communities-fair-sentences/prison-crisis.

American Library Association [ALA]. (2014, July 31). Outreach resources for services to adult new and non-readers. Retrieved from: http://www.ala.org/advocacy/literacy/adultliteracy.

Baer, J. D., Cook, A. L., and Baldi, S. (2006). *The literacy of America's college students.* Washington, D. C.: American Institute of Research.

Barak, G. (1988). Newsmaking criminology: Reflections on the media, intellectuals, and crime. *Justice Quarterly, 5*(4), 565–587.

Barak, G. (2007). Doing newsmaking criminology from within the academy. *Theoretical Criminology, 11*(2), 191–207.

Beckett, K., and Sasson, T. (2004). *The politics of injustice: Crime and punishment in America.* Thousand Oaks, CA: Sage.

Benjamin, A., Patton, A., Sheats, D., and Wright, E. (2000). Humble mumble. On Stankonia [CD]. New York, New York: Arista Records.

Brent, J. J., and Kraska, P. B. (2010). Moving beyond our methodological default: A case for mixed methods. *Journal of Criminal Justice Education, 21*(4), 412–430.

Chall, J. S. (1958). *Readability: An appraisal of research and application.* Columbus, OH: Bureau of Educational Research, Ohio State University.

Chermak, S. (1995). Crime in the news media: A refined understanding of how crimes become news. In G. Barak (Ed.), *Media, process, and the social construction of crime: Studies in newsmaking criminology* (pp. 95–130). New York: Garland.

Davies, D. R. (2006). *The Postwar Decline of American Newspapers, 1945–1965,* Issue 6. Westport, CT: Praeger.

DuBay, W. H. (2004). *The Principles of Readability.* Costa Mesa, CA: Impact Information.

DuBay, W. H. (2007). *Smart language: Readers, readability, and the grading of text.* Costa Mesa, CA: Impact Information.

Flesch and Gunning—the fog busters (2005, May 15). *Plain Language at Work Newsletter* (15). Retrieved from http://www.impact-information.com/impactinfo/newsletter/plwork15.htm.

Frost, N. A. and Phillips, N. D. (2011). Talking heads: Crime reporting on cable news. *Justice Quarterly, 28*(1), 87–112.

Glaze, L. E., and Herberman, E. J. (2013). Correctional populations in the United States, 2012. Washington, D.C.: Bureau of Justice Statistics.

Gray, W. S., and Leary, B. (1935). *What makes a book readable.* Chicago: Chicago University Press.

Impact of Illiteracy. (n.d.) *Plain Language at Work Newsletter.* Retrieved from http://www.impact-information.com/impactinfo/literacy.htm.

Klare, G. R., and B. Buck. (1954). *Know Your Reader: The scientific approach to readability.* New York: Heritage House.

Klare, G. R. 1963. *The measurement of readability.* Ames, Iowa: University of Iowa Press.

Kohut, A., Doherty, C., Dimock, M., and Keeter, S. (2012, September 27). *Trends in news consumption: 1991–2012: In changing news landscape, even television is vulnerable.* Washington, D.C.: The Pew Research Center.

Kunz, M. B., and Osborne, P. (2010). A Preliminary Examination of the Readability of Consumer Pharmaceutical Web Pages. *Journal of Marketing Development and Competitiveness, 5*(1), 33–41.

Macris, A. (May 2010). What grade is your content comprehension? *The Escapist Magazine.* Retrieved from http://www.escapistmagazine.com/articles/view/video-games/columns/publishers-note/7536-What-Grade-is-Your-Content-Comprehension.

Maruschak, L. M., and Bonczar, T. T. (2013). *Probation and parole in the United States, 2012.* Washington, D.C.: Bureau of Justice Statistics.

National Center for Education Statistics (2014a). *National assessment of adult literacy (NAAL): Performance Levels.* Retrieved from http://nces.ed.gov/naal/perf_levels.asp.

National Center for Education Statistics (2014b). *National assessment of adult literacy (NAAL): Demographics-overall.* Retrieved from http://nces.ed.gov/naal/kf_demographics.asp.

National Center for Education Statistics (2014c). *National assessment of adult literacy (NAAL): Demographics-education.* Retrieved from http://nces.ed.gov/naal/kf_dem_edu.asp.

Nielsen. (2011). *State of the media: Trends in TV viewing—2011 TV Upfronts.* Retrieved from http://www.nielsen.com/content/dam/corporate/us/en/newswire/uploads/2011/04/State-of-the-Media-2011-TV-Upfronts.pdf.

Olmstead, K., Jurkowitz, M., Mitchell, A., and Enda, J. (2013, October 11). *How Americans get tv news at home.* Washington, DC: Pew Research Center. Retrieved from http://www.journalism.org/2013/10/11/how-americans-get-tv-news-at-home/.

Renaissance Learning Inc. (2014). *What kids are reading: The book-reading habits of students in American schools.* Wisconsin Rapids, WI: Renaissance Learning.

Robinson, M. B. (2011). *Media coverage of crime and criminal justice.* Durham, NC: Carolina Academic Press.

Sacco, V. (2006). Media constructions of crime. In G. Potter, and V. Kappeler (Eds.), *Constructing crime: Perspectives on making news and social problems* (2nd ed., p. 29–41). Long Grove, IL: Waveland Press.

Sentencing Project (2014). Fact Sheet: Trends in U.S. corrections. Retrieved from http://sentencingproject.org/doc/publications/inc_Trends_in_Corrections_Fact_sheet.pdf.

Sherk, A. (2010, December 2014). Which news sites have the highest reading levels according to Google? [Blog] Retrieved from http://www.adamsherk.com/publishing/news-sites-google-reading-level/.

Surette, R. (2007). *Media, crime, and criminal justice: Images, realities, and policies* (3rd ed.). Belmont, CA: Thomson/Wadsworth.

Surette, R. (2011). *Media, crime, and criminal justice: Images, realities, and policies* (5th ed). Stamford, CT: Cengage Learning.

Talvi, Silja J.A. (2007). *Women Behind Bars: The Crisis of Women in the U.S. Prison System.* Emeryville, CA: Seal Press.

Tunnell, K. (1998). Reflections on crime, criminals, and control in newsmagazine television programs. In F. Bailey, and D. Hale (Eds.), *Popular culture, crime, & justice* (pp. 111–122). Belmont, CA: Wadsworth.

U.S. Census Bureau. (2013). Table 2. Educational Attainment of the Population 25 Years and Over, by Selected Characteristics: 2013. *Educational Attainment in the United States: 2013—Detailed Tables.* [Table 2]. Retrieved from https://www.census.gov/hhes/socdemo/education/data/cps/2013/tables.html.

Walmsley, R. (2013). *World Prison Population List,* (10th ed.). London: UK: International Center for Prison Studies and University of Essex.

Welch, M., Fenwick, M., and Roberts, M. (1997). Primary definitions of crime and moral panic: A content analysis of experts' quotes in feature newspaper articles on crime. *Journal of Research in Crime & Delinquency, 34*(4), 474–494.

Welch, M., Fenwick, M., and Roberts, M. (1998). State managers, intellectuals and the media: A content analysis of ideology in experts' quotes in feature newspaper articles on crime. *Justice Quarterly, 15*(2), 219–241.

Wilson, F. T. and Henderson, H. (2014). The criminological cultivation of African American municipal police officers: Sambo or sellout. *Race and Justice, 4*(1), 45–67.

Zickuhr, K. (2014, January 16). A snapshot of reading in America in 2013. Retrieved from http://www.pewinternet.org/2014/01/16/a-snapshot-of-reading-in-america-in-2013/.

SECTION ONE SUMMARY

Key Discussion Sessions

1. Remember that the majority of the research conducted regarding crime and the criminal justice system is conducted by Ph.D.s and when published, the research is often written at a higher literacy level than the average American who reads comfortably at an 8th to 9th grade level.

   Given the discussion and data provided in Section 1 regarding the large gap between the general public's literacy levels and that of the experts regarding crime and the criminal justice system, "how do you believe the experts should communicate their knowledge to most citizens?" What would be the best method of communication to use for your hometown? What would be the best method for you and your friends?

2. Do you believe that the general public is aware of how low the literacy rates are in the United States? Do you believe that most people realize their personal literacy scores most likely fall well below their acquired education level? What impact do you believe these issues have on policy and lawmakers' abilities to propose alternatives to the "get tough on crime" crime control measures currently utilized in the United States?

Public Consumption Exercises

The public consumption exercises in this text build upon each other. Information gathered in this section will be utilized in future section exercises. Therefore, it is important for you to complete the following exercises, but save the information gathered so that you can quickly reference the information in later exercises. Your professor may ask you to turn in each assignment separately and/or as a portfolio assignment at the end of the semester/term. In each exercise make sure to use the designated bolded headings to divide the paper properly.

Exercise 1: Know Your Writing Level

Whether you want to work within the field or to pursue a Ph.D. it is important for you to determine your current writing level. By writing level this author means at what literacy level do you currently write? Remember, you should always strive to be able to write and read at the highest level possible. This can be accomplished by reading material that may not be comfortable for you but stretches your limits on a regular basis.

To determine your current writing level, write a 400-word essay about your hometown. Do not perform extensive edits or have people proof this paper; it is important to understand your true writing level. Then follow the instructions in Appendix C to calculate your writing level. Provide your score following your 400-word essay to complete this assignment. Depending on your current level, you will be able to determine what steps you may need to take to improve your writing capabilities and/or ability to communicate more efficiently with the media and the general public.

Exercise 2: Know Your Audience

In this exercise you will identify four audiences. These audiences are to differ considerably from one another. This information will help guide you in determining the importance of specific research information and the best way to communicate that information to different populations and the media in future section exercises.

Home County: Your home county is the county in which you have spent most of your life. If your university county is the same, then choose a different county from within your state with considerably different demographic characteristics (i.e., much larger population size, different racial characteristics, and different literacy rates, etc.).

County from Different Region: Choose a county from a different region of the United States than your Home County and University County. For example, if your Home County is in the Southwest and you are attending school in the Midwest, choose a county from the South, West, or Northeast. Make sure this county has different demographic characteristics (i.e. population size, different racial characteristics, education levels, literacy rates, etc.) than your Home County and University County.

University County: This is the county in which your university is located. If you are using this book as part of an organizational training program, utilize the county in which your organization is located.

University: This refers to the student population of your university or members of your organization. If you are using this book as part of an organizational training program, substitute your organization population for student population.

In this exercise you are to determine the demographic information and literacy information (**number and percent**) for each of the sections in the chart on the next page. If your professor does not provide you with a copy of the chart, you may want to make a copy of the chart and record both the number and percentage next to each category for quick reference in future exercises.

To gather the required information use the United States Census Bureau website provided below to look up the basic demographic information for counties. Utilize your university website to determine the basic demographics of your university student population. Utilize the National Center for Education Statistics website provided below or other sources to determine the average literacy level for the required counties. To determine the average literacy level for your university population, determine what counties the majority of students are from, and utilize the National Centre for Education Statistics website data for those counties to determine an average literacy level. For example, if the majority of students come from three different counties, determine the average literacy level for each county. Then add the three scores together and divide by three to determine the university average.

Quick Facts United States Census Bureau

http://quickfacts.census.gov/qfd/index.html#

National Center for Education Statistics—State and County Estimates of Low Literacy

http://nces.ed.gov/NAAL/estimates/StateEstimates.aspx

Home County Audience	County from Different Region Audience
Name of County _____ Population _____ Gender • Male • Female Race • White alone • Black or African American alone • American Indian and Alaska Native alone • Asian alone • Native Hawaiian and Other Pacific Islander alone • Two or more races • Hispanic or Latino • White alone, not Hispanic or Latino Education • High school graduate or higher • Bachelor's degree or higher Literacy Rate • Lacking basic prose literacy skills • Lower Bound • Upper Bound • Average (add upper and lower and divide by 2)	Name of County _____ Population _____ Gender • Male • Female Race • White alone • Black or African American alone • American Indian and Alaska Native alone • Asian alone • Native Hawaiian and Other Pacific Islander alone • Two or more races • Hispanic or Latino • White alone, not Hispanic or Latino Education • High school graduate or higher • Bachelor's degree or higher Literacy Rate • Percent lacking basic prose literacy skills • Lower Bound • Upper Bound • Average (add upper and lower and divide by 2)
County of University Audience	**University Audience**
Name of County _____ Population _____ Gender • Male • Female Race • White alone • Black or African American alone • American Indian and Alaska Native alone • Asian alone • Native Hawaiian and Other Pacific Islander alone • Two or more races • Hispanic or Latino • White alone, not Hispanic or Latino Education • High school graduate or higher • Bachelor's degree or higher Literacy Rate • Percent lacking basic prose literacy skills • Lower Bound • Upper Bound • Average (add upper and lower and divide by 2)	Name of University _____ Population _____ Gender • Male • Female Race • White alone • Black or African American alone • American Indian and Alaska Native alone • Asian alone • Native Hawaiian and Other Pacific Islander alone • Two or more races • Hispanic or Latino • White alone, not Hispanic or Latino Education • High school graduate or higher • Bachelor's degree or higher Literacy Rate • Percent lacking basic prose literacy skills • Lower Bound • Upper Bound • Average (add upper and lower and divide by 2)

SECTION TWO

Crime

CRACK-ING THE MEDIA MYTH

Reconsidering Sentencing Severity for Cocaine Offenders by Drug Type

by Richard D. Hartley and J. Mitchell Miller[1]

A wide range of critics have called for reform of federal cocaine sentencing policy in recent years. The criticism centers on charges that sentencing for cocaine offenses are unfair and inefficient, concerns seemingly validated directly by racially disparate sentencing outcomes and the failure of the drug war generally (Gray, 2001; Jensen, Gerber, & Mosher, 2004; Tonry, 1995). A legislative effort to "get tough" on narcotics offenders anchored a crime control outlook popularized during and since the Reagan administration. This effort has been frequently portrayed as responsive to a mediaincited moral panic about cocaine and specifically the crack cocaine epidemic of the 1980s, which was characterized as extremely socially threatening and crime inducing (The Sentencing Project, 2008).

The risks of drug use received national attention in 1986 after college basketball star Len Bias died from an apparent cocaine overdose, with resultant media-led moral panic focusing on crack in the inner city (Inciardi, Pottieger, & Surrat, 1996). In response, Congress enacted numerous mandatory minimum penalties specifically targeting various narcotics and violent offenses under the Anti Drug Abuse Act of 1986 (Pub. L. No. 99-570, 100 Stat. 3207 (1986)) and the Omnibus Anti Drug Abuse Act of 1988 (Pub. L. No. 100-690, 102 Stat. 4181 (1988)).

These mandatory minimum statutes increased the number of individuals receiving lengthy prison sentences by subjecting mid- or low-level participants to the same penalties as major distributors of narcotics and by setting the mandatory minimum trigger for crack cocaine at an especially low level—5 g. The passage of

---

1   Department of Criminal Justice, College of Public Policy, University of Texas at San Antonio, San Antonio, Texas

these comprehensive and wide-ranging mandatory minimum statutes coupled with low-level minimum trigger thresholds for crack cocaine offenses increased the number of cocaine, and especially crack cocaine, offenders being prosecuted, convicted, and sent to federal prison. The sentence lengths of narcotics offenders under these statutes increased and made most offenders ineligible for parole. In 1992, 74% of the 8,972 cocaine cases in federal district court were powder cocaine offenses, by 1996, the number of cocaine cases in federal district court decreased overall (8, 705) but half of the cases were now powder offenses and the other half involved crack (United States Sentencing Commission [USSC], 2007). In 2000, the composition was similar; there were 5,241 powder cases and 4,706 crack cases (USSC, 2002).

According to the United States Department of Justice (USDOJ, 1992), cocaine use peaked around 1985 and has been declining since. The National Household Survey on Drug Abuse (NHSDA) reports 14 million illicit drug users in 2000, 1.2 million of which were users of cocaine. This accounts for roughly 0.5% of the U.S. population—265,000 of which were identified crack users. In addition, according to the NHSDA (2000), illicit drug use was highly convergent across racial and ethnic categories (6.4% of Whites and Blacks and 5.3% of Hispanics report use in the past month). According to the USDOJ (2006), however, nearly 60% of the current prison population are racial or ethnic minorities.

Racial disparity in federal imprisonment rates may have to do with the fact that minorities comprise a disproportionate share of federal narcotics inmates convicted for crack cocaine. Some argue this can be explained by the nature of the crack versus powder cocaine markets (Fagen & Chin, 1990). Crack tends to be an urban phenomenon, sold out in the open at the street level, whereas cocaine tends to be sold in closed, private settings (Inciardi et al., 1996; The Sentencing Project, 2002). In addition, crack is far cheaper than powder cocaine and minorities who use or sell crack are more likely to be detected by police (Lockwood, Pottieger, & Inciardi, 1995). An alternative argument is that the mandatory minimum trigger for crack is 100 times lower than that for powder cocaine; in other words, those using or selling crack, as opposed to powder cocaine, are singled out for increasingly harsh punishments. Crack was touted by politicians and the media as physiologically and psychotropically more dangerous than powder cocaine (The Sentencing Project, 2008). News reporters described the addictive qualities of crack cocaine as leading to a national crisis (Chiricos, 2004; Inciardi et al., 1996). Unit dosing, however, is similar for both forms of cocaine and both are "now widely acknowledged as pharmacologically identical" (The Sentencing Project, 2008, p. 5). Therefore, under the statutory minimum ratio, powder cocaine "represents a 100 fold increase over the crack cocaine form in the number of doses available for use" (Hatsukami and Fischman, 1996, p. 1581).

Regardless of the explanation, mandatory minimums targeting narcotics offenses have helped to drive one of the largest imprisonment binges in U.S. history. The U.S. prison population in the last 20 years has tripled and the number of inmates sent to prison on narcotics offenses has increased eightfold (Reinarman & Levine, 2004).

Less than 10 years after this legislative mandatory minimum binge, the United States Sentencing Commission issued the first of a series of reports regarding federal cocaine sentencing policy. Each of these reports cited statistics contrary to the idea of crack offenders as more threatening or dangerous than users of cocaine or other illicit narcotics (USSC, 1995, 1997, 2002, 2007). The 1995 report, for instance, stated that "there is little empirical evidence … to suggest that either crack or powder cocaine users commit large numbers of violent acts to raise money to buy drugs" (p. ix). Regarding media reports about crack users as more crime prone than their powder counterparts, the report specified that

The Commission finds no research to suggest, however, that powder cocaine users are any less likely to commit crimes to support their habits. Studies report that neither powder nor crack cocaine excite or agitate users to commit criminal acts and that the stereotype of a drug-crazed addict committing heinous crimes is not true for either form of cocaine. (USSC, 1995, p. ix-x)

The most recent report reiterates the initial reports regarding violence by these offenders; the incidence of use of a weapon by cocaine offenders is very low, occurring in only "0.8 percent of powder cases and 2.9 percent of crack cases" (USSC, 2007, p. 33).

Sample (2001) has argued that legislative responses to moral panics follow a process wherein media portrayals of phenomenon have an influence on legislators' behavior, in the form of crime control-oriented policy reform and intensified law enforcement practices. Statistics on arrests for these offenses can then be used to judge popular perceptions of these offenses. To the extent that law and policy are affected by a moral panic over crack and cocaine, the media is a significant change agent effecting "get tough" legislation. Law enforcement practices suggest such an intensification process transpired; crack cocaine offenses went from comprising one quarter of federal cocaine drug cases to making up one half in less than 4 years even though the number of cocaine cases overall was declining. Because the mandatory minimum trigger for crack (a drug more often bought and sold in urban, minority markets) was set at a threshold 100 times lower than for cocaine, minority overrepresentation in imprisonment statistics began to rise (Tonry, 1995).

Questions have surfaced regarding whether media portrayals influence criminal justice practices, particularly where discretion is involved. To the extent negative media portrayals are linked to extra-legal factors such as race, ethnicity, gender, or age, disparities in sentencing practices must necessarily be considered in a broader context. Some research has deemed the media an important influence on the decision-making practices of criminal justice officials as well as criminal justice policy (see generally, Duffee, 1990; Feld, 2003; Stroman & Seltzer, 1985; Surette, 2007, 1990), although there are numerous methodological problems as well as causal difficulties (see Surette, 1992) in examining media effects on criminal justice outcomes (for instance, are outcomes caused by the media, another confounding event receiving media coverage, or both events acting interactively). Some research has shown causal effects on the discretion of certain courtroom actors such as jurors (Greene and Loftus, 1984; Greene and Wade, 1988) and prosecutors (Pritchard, 1986; Pritchard, Dilts, & Berkowitz, 1987), and scholars have also examined media portrayals of child abusers and their effect of judicial sentencing (Surette, 1999) and sex offenders and their effect on legislative policy making (Sample, 2001).

The effect of media portrayals of drug offenders on judicial sentencing decisions, however, has not been empirically examined. Furthermore, current studies on media effects largely ignore how decision-making practices are affected after a moral panic diminishes. This issue is especially salient to the extant literature due to the media induced crack-cocaine epidemic of the 1980s and 1990s and the subsequent rapid increase in cocaine offenders sent to prison. Therefore, the purpose of this study is to explain the effects of media portrayals of narcotics offenders on judicial sentencing practices, specifically, as well as augment the current literature on media influences of crime and justice, generally. We do this by (a) examining media portrayals of powder and crack cocaine offenders in a nationally distributed newspaper and (b) analyzing judicial sentencing decisions for federal powder and crack cocaine offenders.

Surette (1999) has used the term "echo effect" to describe the influence of the media on court decision-making. He argues that, for courtroom actors, these echo effects become a "media- induced reconstruction of reality concerning the importance of a set of cases" (p. 628). The Congressional enactment of numerous mandatory minimums specifically targeting federal cocaine offenders may have reconstructed the sentencing reality of certain defendants. Judges likewise may be influenced by negative media portrayals of certain groups of offenders and adjust their decisions for these set of cases. McCain (1992) also believes that media influences lead to discriminatory practices by the court system and argues that unfair decisions will continue to affect those negatively portrayed by the media no matter the extent of future negative media portrayals. Chiricos (1996) argues that the specific consequence of the moral panic over drugs has been a disproportionate number of African American males being sent to prison.

Moral Panic and the Media

The ability of the media to disseminate large amounts of sensational information to a sizeable audience profoundly shapes public opinion of crime types and criminals (Sample, 2001). Coverage becomes especially injurious when reporting is not representative of typical offenses or offenders. Both television and newspapers consistently have been observed as distorting crime information (Durham, Elrod, & Kincaid, 1995). At certain times, these misleading portrayals of offenders and events have been pointed enough to instigate moral panic. Cohen (1972) coined the term *moral panic* to describe a condition when certain ideas or phenomena are characterized as particularly threatening to the norms of a society. Pettit (2002) argues that when crime is exposed negatively in the media, it produces outrage in the public. He further argues that a process usually occurs where we see "exposure of the crime in the media, the emergence of popular outrage, and the political reaction of calling for a return to earlier tougher policies" (p. 437). Chiricos (2004) asserts that the United States has encountered at least two moral panics in the last 20 years, one centered on violence and the other on crack cocaine. These phenomena have frequently been linked, with crack depicted as the causal, and thus more important, threat.

The moral panic surrounding crack cocaine surfaced in mid 1986 (Chiricos, 2004) and continued into the 1990s (Reinarman & Levine, 1997a). It was during this period that politicians and the media engaged in antidrug campaigns specifically targeting crack cocaine. Numerous television and newspaper headlines demonized crack as a new plague that was both dangerous and highly addictive—a challenge to the moral fabric of American society (Reinarman & Levine, 1997a, 2004). Crack was targeted as especially threatening because of its availability to a broader spectrum of classes due to its cheap price relative to other illicit drugs (The Sentencing Project, 2008). The "crack baby" phenomenon also emerged out of this epidemic with the media reporting that crack was being delivered in utero to the unborn fetuses of pregnant crack users. Curiously, statistics did not show that crack use was more prevalent than powder cocaine or that crack was America's drug of choice (Reinarman & Levine, 1997b). In fact, the extent of crack use at this time was not well known and measures of powder cocaine use revealed declining numbers. The Drug Enforcement Administration for example regarded crack cocaine as a "secondary rather than primary problem" (Inciardi, 1987, p. 482).

Although cocaine use while pregnant can cause harmful fetal effects, the USSC (1995) observes that dependable information comparing the babies of mothers using crack versus those born to powder users is not available. Furthermore, medical tests cannot distinguish between crack and powder in mother or child. The 1995 report states that crack users do tend to use higher quantities of cocaine than powder users making blood concentrations of the drug greater, which could expose unborn babies to higher amounts of narcotics. Statistics, however, showed "that 7.5 percent to 17 percent of all pregnant women use illicit drugs during their pregnancy, resulting in 100,000 to 740,000 drug-exposed babies each year" and that of those, only "30, 000 to 160, 000" were exposed to cocaine (USSC, 1995, p. x). These findings suggest that cocaine-exposed babies comprise a very small portion of the overall number of fetuses exposed to narcotics. Nonetheless, fueled by the media-frenzied idea of a super dangerous crack offender and an increase in the number of cocaine-exposed babies born with severe mental and developmental defects, politicians jumped on the opportunity to pass new and enhanced legislation against narcotics overall and for cocaine particularly.

Implementation of Mandatory Minimums

These new mandatory minimum statutes passed by Congress enhanced sentences for certain offenses. If a case meets the criteria for a minimum, the judge must impose the minimum sentence length. Mandatory minimum statutes are by no means new, having been implemented at various times in the United States since 1790 (Tonry, 1995). Until recently, however, these laws were not "comprehensively aimed at whole classes of offenses" (USSC, 1991b, p. 6). Specifically, these minimums targeted narcotics offending near schools (Pub. L. No. 98-473, §503(a), 98 Stat. 2069 (1984), use or possession of a weapon during the commission of a violent (Pub. L. No. 98-473, §1005(2), 98 Stat. 2138 (1984) or drug crime (Pub. L. No. 99-308, §104(a) (2) (A-E), 100 Stat. 456 (1986), Pub. L. No. 99-570, §1402(a), 100 Stat. 3207-39 (1986), the sale of narcotics to a person under 21 years of age (Pub. L. No. 99-570, §1105(a), 100 Stat. 3207-11 (1986), and employing someone under age 18 in a drug offense (Pub. L. No. 99-570, §1102, 100 Stat. 3207-11 (1986)).

Probably the most significant minimum statutes, however, were enacted under the Anti Drug Abuse Act of 1986 (Pub. L. No. 99-570, 100 Stat. 3207 (1986)) and the Omnibus Anti Drug Abuse Act of 1988 (Pub. L. No. 100-690, 102 Stat. 4181 (1988)). The 1986 act fixed the statutory minimums to the amount or weight of the drugs involved (USSC, 1991a). It also made those sentenced under them ineligible for parole. This act was specifically targeted at mid-level players in drug distribution networks, mandating a 5-year minimum for possession of 100 g of heroin or 500 g of cocaine.

Under the 1988 Act, Congress specifically targeted crack users by establishing a 5-year statutory minimum for possession of only 5 g of crack cocaine—creating the 100-to-1 disparity ratio trigger between cocaine forms. The 1988 act also expanded all minimums formerly applicable only to distribution and importation/exportation cases to conspiracies to commit these offenses (USSC, 1991a). Surprisingly, just a decade earlier through the Comprehensive Drug Abuse Prevention and Control Act of 1970 (Pub. L. No. 91-513, 84 Stat. 1236 (1970)), Congress effectively repealed most of the mandatory minimums for narcotics offenses. The stated reasons for the repeal of the minimums included that they hindered rehabilitation, fettered the ability of judges to use their discretion in individual cases, diminished the deterrent effect of drug laws already in place, and caused prosecutors to circumvent the minimums in many cases on the grounds of their excessive severity (USSC, 1991b).

Yet just 15 years after these drug minimums were repealed, Congress would enact new mandatory minimums for narcotics violations. The new drug minimum statutes were passed using some of the exact same arguments under which they had been repealed, as if Congress had legal amnesia. The enactment of additional mandatory minimums covering a wide variety of offenses continued well into the 1990s and to date there are over 60 federal mandatory minimum statutes that cover 100 plus offenses (Tonry, 1995).

The controversy over mandatory minimums is not only due to their excessive severity but also the disproportionate focus on low-level offenders, especially regarding the 5 g threshold for crack. African Americans have also been disproportionately arrested for crack offenses and received lengthier sentences than other racial groups (Caulkins, Rydell, Schwabe, & Chiesa, 1998), creating disparity in terms of race and social class. Eighty-five percent of crack offenders who are subject to minimums are Black (USSC, 2002) and between "1986 and 1990 both the rate and average length of imprisonment for federal offenders increased for blacks compared to whites ... caused largely by the mandatory minimum penalty for drug offenses and more specifically by the 100-to-1 quantity ratio of powder to crack cocaine" (Angeli, 1997, p. 1214).

An obvious result of mandatory minimums then has been race- and class-based disproportionate confinement. The United States prison population has tripled since the 1980s and the influx of narcotics offenders has heavily contributed to prison overcrowding and the current demographic composition of the prison population (Reinarman & Levine, 2004; USDOJ, 2001). The United States Sentencing Commission since 1995 has recommended equalizing or conflating the 100-to-1 mandatory minimum ratio trigger between crack and powder cocaine. Congress has failed to act on such proposals although did implement a safety valve provision exempting low-level and first-time narcotics offenders in 1994. If the criteria for the safety valve are met, a judge may ignore the drug minimum at sentencing. The exemption criteria include little or no criminal history, no weapon use, not a leader, manager, or supervisor in the offense, no resultant serious injury or death, and truthful testimony to law enforcement officials (USSC, 1999).

In 2008, the USSC itself made an amendment to decrease the sentencing guidelines' ranges for crack cocaine offenders and to apply this amendment retroactively. By the middle of 2008, almost 6,000 inmates convicted on crack cocaine charges applied for a sentence reduction under the new amendment; 80% of these were granted resulting in an average sentence reduction of 22 months (USSC, 2008). The Supreme Court has also issued rulings regarding narcotics sentencing policy in general and crack cocaine in particular. In *Booker v. United States* (543 US 220 (2005)), the court made the Federal Sentencing Guidelines only advisory and not presumptive in nature; judges were now only required to consult the guidelines when determining sentences. In *Kimbrough v. United States* (552 US _ (2007)), the Supreme Court ruled that a federal district judge could sentence a crack cocaine offender below the applicable guideline range citing the unfairness of the 100-to-1-trigger disparity. Criticisms of mandatory minimums and the introduction of amendments to decrease some of the sentences under these laws imply that although they may not be repealed, there is a good possibility of further reform.[1]

Empirical Research on Mandatory Minimums

Objection to mandatory minimums has centered on severity and inflexibility (Zimring, Hawkins, & Kamin, 2001). This case outcome rigidity has spawned other issues, specifically noncompliance by prosecutors who, whether intentionally or not, inject discretion into the process. Some research finds that mandatory minimums have not worked as expected; the unintended consequence has been a shift of discretion from judges to prosecutors that has resulted in widespread circumvention. These studies indicate that prosecutors sometimes opt not to file charges carrying mandatory minimum penalties even when evidence indicated that such charges were warranted (Meierhofer, 1992; Schulhofer & Nagel, 1997; United States General Accounting Office (USGAO), 1993; USSC, 1991b; Wilmot & Spohn, 2004). This circumvention reduces the deterrent impact that mandatory minimums intended to have on sentencing severity (Caulkins et al., 1998). In fact, most studies examining mandatory minimums generally cite findings similar to those Congress noted when repealing them in 1970: that they do not work as intended, they hinder the ability of other laws to provide uniformity, and result in widespread circumvention (see for instance Tonry, 1995; USSC, 1991a, b).

In sentencing offenders at the federal level, the form plus the amount of an illicit drug equals the sentence (Beckett and Sasson, 2000). However, many drug offenders who are sentenced under the mandatory minimums are low-level offenders who ostensibly present little threat to society (Meierhofer, 1992; USDOJ, 1992). In fact, of the 25,184 drug offenders convicted in 1999, about half had no prior convictions and of those that did only 13% were for violent offenses (Scalia, 2001). Yet 92% of first-time offenders and 94% of those with one prior were sentenced to prison. In addition, in 1999, 62% of drug defendants had a statutory minimum apply, and those facing crack charges received the longest average sentences at 114 months (Scalia, 2001). These average sentence lengths approximate those served by violent and weapons offenders. Other postminimum era studies conclude that minorities and the poor have been disproportionately affected by mandatory drug minimums (see, for instance, Bushway & Piehl, 2007; Caulkins et al., 1998; Mauer, 1999; Ogletree, 2006; Tonry, 1995).

Drug control policy in the United States has traditionally focused on various population segments in a cyclical fashion. Reinarman and Levine (1997a), for example, contend that the United States appears to continually suffer from historical amnesia: "For over a hundred years, U.S. drug policy has been forged by symbolic politics and special interests, by moral entrepreneurs and media magnification, and by efforts of dominant groups to control threatening others from different races and lower classes" (p. 8). As the outcomes produced by these laws have been realized, drug war failure has become more obvious (Tonry, 1995) and political focus has been redirected from narcotics and toward the more imminent threat of terrorism.

Theoretical Underpinnings

Several explanations have been crafted for explaining judicial decision making. Although legal factors such as crime seriousness and prior record continue to be the most primary case outcome determinants, race, ethnicity, and gender influence decisions in certain contexts (for a comprehensive review of research on the legal and extralegal factors affecting judicial decision making, see Spohn, 2000). The focal concerns perspective has facilitated the study of judicial decision making through the examination of three main concepts (*blameworthiness, protection of the community, and organization implications*) to postulate that "judges may rely not only on the defendant's present offense and prior criminal conduct, but also on attributions linked to the defendant's gender, race, social class or other social positions" (Steffensmeier & Demuth, 2001, p. 151). Due to limited time and information, judges use a perceptual shorthand to make decisions about offenders' dangerousness and risk for recidivism based on stereotypes and attributions linked to personal characteristics. Negative media portrayals, if linked to offender characteristics, therefore, could influence judicial perception regarding various attributes as proxies for dangerousness and risk. These attributions in turn "become informal norms, routines, and guides as mechanisms to reduce uncertainty in sentencing" (Steffensmeier, Ulmer, & Kramer, 1998, p. 769).

Criminal justice decision makers, especially judges, often do not have complete knowledge about a certain case. Lack of information can lead judges to base their decisions on experience, stereotypes, and prejudice (Albonetti, 1991). For instance, some researchers argue that judicial decisions are not solely based on legally relevant factors but also perceptions of threat and dangerousness (Eisenstein & Jacob, 1977; Feeley, 1983; Nardulli, 1978). Some studies show extralegal factors such as age (Spohn & Holleran, 2000; Steffensmeier et al., 1998; Steffensmeier & Motivans, 2000), gender (Daly, 1987; Spohn

& Beichner, 2000; Steffensmeier, Kramer, & Streifel, 1993), race or ethnicity (Spohn & Holleran, 2001; Steffensmeier & Demuth, 2000; Steffensmeier et al., 1998), and social status (Chiricos & Bales, 1991) also exert influence under certain contexts. Previous research has also shown departures to be an intervening mechanism through which both racial and gender effects emerge (Albonetti, 1997; Farrell, 2004; Hartley, Maddan, & Spohn, 2007a; Kramer & Ulmer, 1996). To date, most research has shown at least partial support for the focal concerns perspective of judicial decision making; however, it has been argued that this theoretical framework has not been widely tested (Hartley, Madden, & Spohn, 2007b).

Media portrayals of cocaine offenders and the implications of this coverage for sentencing decisions of actual narcotics offenders constitute the focus of this analysis. The attributions of crack and powder cocaine offenders, as well as the extent to which extralegal factors affect federal sentencing outcomes for cocaine, are examined by a focal concerns and mixed-methods theoretical- methodological symmetry. To date, no research has specifically examined the effect of media portrayals of cocaine offenders on judicial sentencing practices. The focal concerns perspective argues that judges may use stereotypical information about dangerousness and risk of certain offenders when sentencing. The focal concerns perspective maintains that this stereotypical information may cause extralegal factors to influence sentencing outcomes. This study thus examines media influence on judicial discretion by testing the focal concerns perspective through examination of media portrayals of powder and crack cocaine offenders in the *USA Today* and a regression analysis of sentencing decisions for federal powder and crack cocaine offenders for the year 2000.

A two phase sequential mixed-methods design (Creswell, 1995; Tashakkori and Teddlie, 1998) enables analysis of three related research questions. First, we explore both the extent to which media portrayals depict cocaine offenders as threatening, dangerous or otherwise negative and the extent to which these accounts differ across crack and powder cocaine incidents. Second, we examine whether disparities exist in federal sentencing statistics regarding demographics of crack and powder cocaine offenders. Finally, we explore media portrayal potential to influence judicial sentencing decisions.

A mixed-methods design using data from two sources facilitates exploration of the above research questions. A content analysis of *USA Today* articles on cocaine explores media reporting of crack cocaine versus powder cocaine offenders and offending. A regression analysis partitioned by cocaine type provides insight into federal sentencing practices. Although studies examining media influence on decision-making practices have limitations with regard to causal ordering and an ability to account for all relevant extraneous variables, media effects on criminal justice discretion is nonetheless an important topic in today's cyber and hypermedia worlds.

If media portrayals of cocaine offenders are not negative, and/or extralegal disparities are not present in judicial sentencing decisions, we hypothesize that this may, in part, be due to the fact that the media-reported moral panic surrounding cocaine has been institutionalized through harsh legislation whereby the media no longer needs to report negatively.

Methods

Data and Variables

Content analysis of newspaper accounts. Weber (1990) defines content analysis as "procedures to make valid inferences from text" (p. 9). Researchers use content analysis whenever their interest is to "examine artifacts of social communication" (Berg, 2004, p. 267). Content analysis is most often used where the medium is written or transcribed or can be transformed into text. Abrahamson (1983), however, argues that any type of communication can be examined using content analysis. The content analysis here seeks to explore media portrayals of crack versus powder offenders and the degree to which they are negative. Data for the content analysis were gathered from the *USA Today* for the dates October 1, 1999, through September 30, 2000 (these dates comport with the USSC federal sentencing statistics for fiscal year 2000). The *USA Today* covers issues of national concern and is distributed in all 50 states, the District of Columbia, Puerto Rico, and Guam and has the largest average daily circulation of any newspaper in the United States (daily circulation of 2.3 million in 2008 and just over 1.8 million in the year corresponding with the content analysis for this study [Jesdanun, 2008; Sutel, 2000]). The *USA Today* was therefore chosen for content analysis as it may have the most potential for media influence of crime and criminals.

Individual articles from the newspaper were analyzed according to type of language used (negative or pejorative), article focus (specific crime, location of offending, offending in general, offender legislation), emphasis (use of statistics or a description of event), amount of space (word count), as well as page placement (section and page number). Observations were then formulated into sociological constructs (Berg, 2004) representing broader content themes. The individual newspaper articles therefore are the units of analysis in this portion of the study. Several key words (crack, cocaine and war on drugs) were used as criteria of selection to gather articles for content analysis; the first two are specific to crack and cocaine content and the latter is more narcotics general. These terms were explored using the search engine LexisNexis. Although content analysis is typically seen as a quantitative method, and some of the data collected were indeed operationalized, latent content analysis was also conducted to gather qualitative information such as adjectives used to describe the offenders and similar opinionative language characterizing crime, criminals, or the criminal justice system. Smith (1975) believes that both manifest and latent content analysis should be used, and Berg (2004) notes that excerpts of text should be included to support the researcher's interpretations or to provide context to the manifest content.

The themes will be categorized according to what Abrahamson (1983) labels a combination inductive/deductive approach where the articles are analyzed and content is coded based on derived elements but then themes are identified from content through analytic induction (Glaser & Strauss, 1967) to provide postfactum explanation (Merton, 1968). Berg (2004) notes that using "both inductive and deductive reasoning may provide fruitful findings" (p. 275-276). Huberman and Miles (1994) and Tashakkori and Teddlie (1998) further that the essence of qualitative content analysis is to begin with some conceptually specified categories and deductively and inductively arrive at themes. Previous content analytic studies have used these methods on a variety of crime topics using various medium and found interesting results (see for instance, Berg, 1986; Dabney, 1993; Miller, Wright, & Smith, 2000; Wright, Miller, & Britz, 2001).

The content analysis instrument used here was adapted from an instrument used by Sample (2001) to gather content from newspapers regarding media portrayals of sex offenders. Sample's content analysis revealed that media reporting on sex offending had steadily increased. She argued that this increased media reporting had impressed upon the public the idea that sex offenses were a rising crime problem even though official statistics did not support this. Sample (2001) concluded that the media portrayals "indirectly influenced the enactment of sex offender legislation by affecting the public's perceptions" (p. 99). Her interviews with politicians supported the idea that legislators respond to public outrage with increased legislation. The content analysis for the current study is similar in that data are gathered directly from newspaper accounts regarding media reports of crack and powder offenders. Opinions, adjectives, and other descriptive information used to describe the offense or offender were also collected with attention to intercoder reliability (Weber, 1990). To minimize unreliability in coding, we developed a random sample of articles to compare coded information with the original sample.[2] The content analytic approach used here allowed consideration of how cocaine form-specific actors and events are portrayed in a print medium for 1 year through thematic construction of categories of content. These content analytic findings and the results from the official sentencing statistics will be used to draw inference about the influence of media reporting on decision-making practices of judges regarding the sentencing of these offenders.

Quantitative analysis of federal sentencing statistics. Data for statistical analysis come from the USSC's *Monitoring of Federal Criminal Offenses 2000.* These data were chosen for two reasons. First, it predates the terrorist attacks in New York on September 11, 2001; narcotics media coverage may have taken a back seat to terrorism after September 2001. Second, data for both the regression and content analyses are from the same year. The federal sentencing data contain information on cases reported to the USSC, and, as such, some limitations exist.[3] The original data set contained documentation on a total of 10,107 crack and powder cocaine defendants, which comprise the sample for this analysis.

The dependent variable for this portion of the study is sentence length in months.[4] Control variables include those that according to the USSC are legally relevant predictors of sentence length, including offense type (*trafficking* = 1; *possession* = 0), drug type (partitioned by crack and powder cocaine), mandatory drug minimum (*drug minimum applied* = 1; *drug minimum not applied* = 0), number of conviction counts, final offense level, acceptance of responsibility (*defendant accepted responsibility* = 1; *no acceptance of responsibility* = 0), use of a weapon during offense (*defendant received a weapon enhancement* = 1; *no weapon enhancement applied* = 0), and criminal history. The presence of various process variables are also legally accepted predictors of sentence length and are thus included (i.e., whether the defendant received a downward departure from the guidelines, whether the defendant received a substantial assistance departure for assisting the prosecutor in another case, and whether the defendant received a safety valve adjustment for being a first-time, low-level offender).

Extra legal factors known to be relevant to sentence are also included as controls. These include the offender's race/ethnicity, sex (*female* = 1; *male* = 0), age, education (*high school degree* = 1; *no high school degree* = 0), disposition (*trial* = 1; *plea* = 0), pretrial detention status (*detained* = 1; *released* = 0), and citizenship status (*noncitizen* = 1; *citizen* = 0). The offender's race/ethnicity is measured using three dummy variables (White, Black, Hispanic), with White offenders as the reference category. Age is a continuous variable.

The data are partitioned by cocaine type, and ordinary least squares (OLS) regression was used to analyze sentence length.[5] Kautt and Spohn (2002) argue that data partitioning is superior to dummy coding when, as is the case here, effects of the case and offender characteristics are expected to vary across the categories of the variable of interest. This analysis allows for exploration of interaction effects between the independent variables and type of drug on sentence lengths. Because the media newspaper accounts were extracted from the *USA Today* for the same time period, these data reflect national accounts and characterizations of cocaine offenders in 2000.

Results

Content Analysis

A search of the key terms for the content analysis portion of this study initially produced 139 articles. After articles that were not related to narcotics offending (movie reviews, book reviews, etc.) and articles that were repeats under two or more key words were removed, 78 articles remained for analysis. This result alone seems to suggest that the media (*USA Today*) was not that concerned with reporting on crack and powder cocaine offenses or offenders in the year 2000.[6] This is somewhat surprising considering that there were over 10,000 crack and powder cocaine cases processed in Federal District Court in fiscal year 2000. The fact that only 12 of those 78 articles focused on crack cocaine specifically lends further credence to the belief that the media, in 2000, did not consider crack cocaine an alarming epidemic worthy of a large quantity of reporting. This minimal focus on drugs generally and crack cocaine specifically could be initial evidence consistent with the assertion of Reinarman and Levine (1997b) that through the implementation of legislative mandatory minimums and harsher punishments, the threat of crack has been institutionalized.

The majority of the *USA Today* articles (31) focused on the specific crime, 13 addressed offending in general, 8 highlighted drug legislation, 10 focused on the location of the offense, and

Table 1. Frequencies and Means of Content Analysis for the *USA Today* in 2000 Variable

Variable		Crack	Cocaine	Combination of key words	War on drugs
Number of Articles		12	53	9	4
Section/page	A	6	24	8	3
	First Page	2	3	1	2
	B	1	2	0	0
	First Page	1	1	0	0
	C	4	19	0	0
	First Page	0	6	1	1
	D	1	7	1	0
	First Page	0	1	1	0
	E	0	1	0	0
	First Page	0	0	0	0
Number of words	Minimum	333	103	339	329
	Maximum	3,470	2,204	1,571	962
	Mean	850	683	957	645
	Median	652	571	877	643
Focus of article	Specific crime	3	27	1	0
	Location of offending	0	9	1	0
	Offending in general	7	8	2	0
	Offender legislation	0	0	4	2
	Combination	2	4	1	2
How point is made	Use of statistics	2	10	3	3
	Description of events	7	31	3	0
	Both	3	12	3	1
Gender	Male	4	20	0	1
	Female	0	5	1	1
Age		3	4	NA	NA
Race		1	0	4	2
Ethnicity		0	8	1	0

16 reported on a combination of the above. Most of the newspaper articles made characterized situations with a description of either the offenders or the event and a number of them also made use of statistics to back up the characterizations. Generally, articles did not report information on the gender of the offender, but gender could be intuited in 32 of the articles by the name of the offender. Eleven of the articles mentioned the age of the offender, 9 mentioned ethnicity, and 7 mentioned race. These references to race and ethnicity, however, were not focused on specific offenders but rather on aggregate statistics about drug users arrested, prosecuted, and incarcerated. These articles were more focused on narcotics legislation and cited statistics on how narcotics laws were unfair or biased against minority offenders. A few articles, however, did mention that the countries of Mexico and Colombia were the major source of narcotics flowing into the United States and included descriptions of the high-profile arrests of drug traffickers from these countries.

Table 1 reports the frequencies and means from the content analysis of the USA Today articles. Although only two crack and three powder articles made the front page, 50% of the crack articles and roughly 45% of the powder articles were in section A of the newspaper. Furthermore, eight of the nine articles that mentioned two or more of the key words in combination were in section A of the USA Today; however, only one was on the front page. Finally, although only 4 of the 78 articles specifically mentioned the war on drugs, 3 were in section A of the newspaper and 2 were on the front page.

The majority of articles (53) focused on powder offenders, and ranged from 103 to 2,204 words with an average of 683 words. Crack articles, in comparison, ranged from 333 to 3,470 words with an average of 850 words. Although there were fewer articles on crack, they had both mean and median word lengths that were longer than the articles on powder. Despite less coverage of crack, it appears the media allocated greater page space to these articles. Also fewer in number were articles mentioning a combination of key words. These articles, however, had a larger average word count than those on crack or powder alone. A majority of the USA Today articles provided descriptions of events (41) as emphasis, some contained statistics (18), and others (19) used both statistics and a description of the event.

Extralegal factors. Very few articles mentioned the age of the offender (7). In 32 of the articles, gender was mentioned or deciphered by names, confirming that the majority of narcotics offenders reported in the USA Today were male. A few, however, mentioned that females were increasingly the targets of narcotics laws. One article, for instance, mentioned that "the number of women in state and federal prisons rose 573% in 17 years, and much of that increase was due to drug convictions" (Fields, 1999, p. A3). Another stated "drug abuse level among girls is now essentially the same as it is with boys" (Fields, 2000a, p. A4) and two other articles focused on the arrests of pregnant females who tested positive for cocaine. One discussed a Supreme Court case on whether hospitals should be required to notify authorities if a patient who is pregnant tests positive for cocaine, emphasizing that doing so would damage the "patient-doctor bond" and deter "women from seeking prenatal care" (Willing, 2000, p. A4). The other sent mixed messages to readers by stating some of the consequences of drug use and pregnancy, specifically that "maternal cocaine use can cause premature labor, low birth weight and serious birth defects"; somewhat balanced, it also stated that the "crack baby crisis was overblown" and that the hospital targeted only low-income women, most of whom were African-American (Biskupic, 2000, p. A3).

Only 7 of the 78 newspaper articles actually mentioned race. Race in these articles, however, was not used in relation to a particular offender but rather in discussing aggregate statistics or current legislation. One discussed the disparate penalties between crack and powder offenders stating that the harsher punishments for "selling different forms of the same illegal substance disproportionately target blacks" (Wickham, 1999, p. A19). Another mentioned that "a generation of African Americans are ending up in prison" due to the disparity in crack and powder cocaine sentencing (Shapiro, 2000a, p. A2). A third reported that "according to the U.S. Sentencing Commission, 65% of crack cocaine users are white, yet more than 90% of those prosecuted for crack crimes in federal court are black" (Cole, 2000, p. A17). Finally, another cited that African Americans "are being jailed at a much higher rate than whites even though five times as many whites use drugs" (Fields, 2000b, p. A3).

Most of the articles mentioning ethnicity focused on powder cocaine. These articles mentioned both the narcotics trade on the U.S. Mexican border and the gang activity associated with drug cartels in addition to statistics on the disproportionate number of Hispanics represented in cocaine arrest and sentencing statistics. For example, one article stated "48.5% of defendants in powder cocaine cases were Hispanic" (Cauchon, 1999, p. A4) and another reported that "Mexicans, whose country is a key juncture in the contraband pipeline that stretches from Colombia to Canada, increasingly are succumbing to drug abuse" (Smith, 2000, p. A22). Another discussed a mass gravesite, the result of "50 years of fierce drug gang activity on the border between Texas and Mexico" and stated that "Mexican drug traffickers are sending larger quantities of drugs into the USA" (Garcia, 1999, p. A3).

Violence. Most of the newspaper articles we examined discussed possible charges, the majority of which were either possession or trafficking; very few focused on violence associated with cocaine. In the late 1980s, the crack cocaine epidemic was portrayed as the cause of violent crime in the United States. The majority of newspaper articles examined here do not portray cocaine offenders as violent. A few articles did discuss amounts of drugs or money confiscated and one described a Drug Enforcement Administration (DEA) drug bust that netted "4, 640 kilograms of cocaine, 55.6 kilograms of heroin, 14.3 kilograms of morphine base, 362.5 metric tons of marijuana ... 159 vehicles, 77 weapons, 17, 235 rounds of ammunition and $75, 072 in U.S. currency" (Fields, 2000c, p. A3). Another article relayed the "record amounts of cocaine" that the US Coast Guard had seized; "125, 904 pounds ... worth about $4 billion" (Leinwand, 2000a, p. A3).

One article also described the arrests of 40 members of a Puerto Rican drug ring who ran 20 plus distribution centers and netted "$20, 000 to $50, 000 a day in sales" and who were charged with "killing dozens of people" (Fields, 2000d, p. A3). Finally, another accounted the arrest of "the third-highest-ranked member of the most violent cartel in the Western Hemisphere" who was the head of a drug cartel responsible "for as many as 100 murders" and whose arrest was a "major victory for both Mexican and U.S. law enforcement" (Fields, 2000e, p. A4). The articles that mentioned violence in relation to the narcotics trade generally described how ruthless the drug cartels were by chronicling their intimidation of citizens in Mexico or Puerto Rico and the torture and murder of rival gang members and Mexican law enforcement officials.

Nonetheless, a majority of the articles did not represent narcotics offenders in this negative way and most did not discuss weapons or mention any violence in relation to narcotics offenders. No articles specifically mentioned crack cocaine offenders in relation to weapons or violent behavior.

Overall, these content analysis findings contradict the perception of cocaine, and particularly, crack cocaine offenders as dangerous and threatening.

Specific criminal offenses. Most of the media depictions focused on a specific crime. These articles, however, centered attention on offenders whom the public would probably not associate with narcotics offending. Almost half (38) of the 78 articles found in the *USA Today* focused on atypical or celebrity offenders. These offenders included National Basketball Association (NBA), National Football League (NFL), Major League Baseball (MLB), and National Hockey League (NHL) players, a Cuban high jumper, a boxer, Dennis Quaid, Bobby Brown, Shoe mogul Steve Madden, the son of Michael Douglas, 30 American Airlines employees, and several Los Angeles Police Department (LAPD) police officers. Nine of the 78 articles alone were written about baseball star Darryl Strawberry's cocaine addiction and legal problems.

The adjectives used in the descriptions of these "atypical" cocaine offenders were not pejorative and provided more information about the individual and their unblemished past rather than focusing on the negative aspects of cocaine or narcotics use. For example, one article spoke of corruption within the Los Angeles Police Department citing that an officer had been charged with stealing eight pounds of cocaine from the evidence room. The article described the officer as being "a former member of an elite gang unit" (Kasindorf, 2000, p. A5). The article furthered that the officer had received only a 5-year prison sentence, instead of the 12-year maximum, for offering the names of other LAPD officers involved in criminal activity. The article also mentioned that chief of the LAPD had ordered detectives from the force not to cooperate with the district attorney. Another article reporting on the same story said that the officer testified against "cops who planted evidence, beat suspects, lied in court, and sold drugs," but went on to say that within the LAPD "there's probably a rogue cop or two, but 99% of the cops ... believe in doing their job" (Leinwand, 2000b, p. A3). Other articles cited the accolades that the "atypical" narcotics offender had achieved in sport, television or fashion. These 38 articles provide evidence that the *USA Today* in 2000 focused largely on atypical or celebrity offenders and their noncriminal past than on offenders who generally wind up in federal district court facing severe narcotics charges and penalties.

Legislation. Articles focusing on offender legislation spoke mostly about the harshness of current laws. Some also discussed politicians' opinions of the war on drugs. These opinions ranged from calling the drug war a complete failure to quoting some who were hesitant to publicly admit narcotics legislation needed to be amended for fear that they would appear soft on crime. A majority of the articles that emphasized the harshness of drug laws cited statistics naming them as the major cause for disparities in imprisonment. One article cited Hillary Clinton as hinting that Congress "ought to look at the disparity in punishment between crack and powdered cocaine" (Shapiro, 2000b, p. A10).

One article reported that the governor of New Mexico publicly stated that the war on drugs is a failure and that drugs should be "a controlled substance like alcohol ... Legalize it, control it, regulate it, tax it" (Jones, 1999, p. A4). An article quoting Colin Powell stated that "If you want to solve our drug problem, you won't do it by cutting off the supply and arresting street pushers alone" (Shapiro, 2000c, p. A8). Another reported the possibility that the senate may revise cocaine sentencing and cited Bureau of Prison Statistics revealing that if Congress lowered the mandatory minimum trigger for powder cocaine from the current 500 g to 50 g, it would "add 5,529 inmates to the federal prison system over the next five years and 9, 163 over the next decade" (Cauchon, 1999, p.A4). Most of these new inmates, the article stated, would be racial minorities.

Table 2. Variable Means and Frequencies for Cocaine Powder and Crack Offenders

Variable	Powder cocaine cases (*N* = 5,191)		Crack cocaine cases (*N* = 4,916)	
	N	%	*N*	%
Sentence length in months (mean)	76.5		112.7	
Disposition				
Guilty plea	4,886	94.1	4,543	92.4
Trial	305	5.9	373	7.6
Accepted responsibility				
No	607	11.7	719	14.6
Yes	4,581	88.3	4,195	85.4
Offense type				
Drug trafficking	4,995	96.2	4,762	96.9
Drug possession (reference)	196	3.8	154	3.1
Offender's pretrial status				
Detained	3,576	70	3,761	74.9
Released (reference)	1,532	30	1,191	24.1
Final offense level (mean)	25.4		28.9	
Criminal history category (mean)	1.9		3.1	
Offender sex				
Female	707	13.6	493	10
Male (reference)	4,483	86.4	4,423	90
Number of conviction charges (mean)	1.38		1.52	
Offender age (mean)	33.85		29.86	
Safety valve applicable (% yes)	1807	37.3	692	15.5
Offender education				
No high school degree (reference)	2,375	45.8	2,500	50.9
High school degree	2,769	54.2	2,393	49.1
Departure (% yes)	473	9.3	399	8.4
Substantial assistance departure (% yes)	1,537	30.3	1,527	32.1
Weapon enhancement				
No	5,062	97.5	4,700	95.6
Yes	129	2.5	216	4.4
Offender race/ethnicity				
White (reference)	947	18.4	280	5.8
Black	1,593	31	4,150	85.3
Hispanic	2,600	50.6	434	8.9
Offender is U.S. Citizen	4,999	93.6	3,195	65
Mandatory minimum applied (% yes)	677	13.0	659	13.4

OLS Regression

Quantitative analyses of federal sentencing data reveal several noteworthy findings. Table 2 displays the frequencies and means for federal cocaine offenders sentenced in fiscal year 2000. Frequencies

Table 3. OLS Regression on Number of Months of Imprisonment for Cocaine Powder and Crack Offenders in 2000

Variable	Powder cocaine cases			Crack cocaine cases			Z scores
	b	SE	B	B	SE	B	
Offender went to trial	31.07*	3.19	0.12	27.22*	3.46	0.09	0.82
Offender accepted responsibility	−17.86*	2.65	−0.82	−16.95*	2.80	−0.07	−0.24
Offense = drug trafficking	12.80*	2.70	0.04	19.54*	2.54	0.06	−1.82
Offender was detained pretrial	3.81*	1.35	0.02	6.60*	1.63	0.03	−1.32
Final criminal history category	10.03*	0.46	0.21	12.79*	0.44	0.27	−4.34†
Final offense level	6.76*	0.11	0.65	8.45*	0.14	0.61	−9.49†
Offender is female	−3.65*	1.62	−0.02	−4.36	2.38	−0.02	NS
Number of counts	2.01*	0.53	0.03	4.02*	0.58	0.06	−2.56†
Age	0.92	0.35	0.02	1.16	0.46	0.02	NS
Safety valve applied	−6.9*	1.42	−0.05	−2.94	2.12	−0.01	NS
Offender has high school diploma	−0.85	0.66	−0.01	−.26	0.91	0.01	NS
Downward departure	−24.78*	1.93	−0.11	−40.57*	2.67	−0.12	4.79†
Substantial assistance departure	−42.15*	1.29	−0.29	−58.75*	1.49	−0.34	8.42†
Weapon enhancement applied	52.25*	4.09	0.11	51.98*	3.64	0.12	0.05
Offender is Black	2.22	1.59	0.02	−2.23	2.87	−0.01	NS
Offender is Hispanic	1.5	1.62	−0.01	−8.19*	3.77	−.03	NS
Offender is U.S. citizen	−1.89	1.39	−0.01	−2.94	2.89	−0.01	NS
Defendant sentenced under mandatory minimum	−1.91	1.69	−0.01	5.59*	2.08	.025	NS
Constant	−118.8			−189.1			
Adjusted R²	.736			.746			

Note: "NS" indicates that the coefficients were not significant for both drug types.
*p < .05.
†Z score significant at p < .05.

regarding the type of drug involved reveal that powder cocaine comprised the majority of offenses for both Whites and Hispanics. Blacks represented the majority of offenders in crack cases.

Average ages of crack and powder offenders were similar and males comprised over 85% of offenders for both drug types. Almost half of the offenders for both drug types had less than a high school education and a very small percentage of offenders had a sentence enhancement apply for using a weapon during the offense (2.5% of powder cocaine offenders and 4.4% of crack offenders). Finally, roughly 13% of both crack and powder cocaine offenders had a mandatory drug minimum apply. This suggests that roughly 86% of crack offenders did not meet the minimum trigger threshold of 5 g, yet they are being charged with a federal narcotics offense. One explanation may be that prosecutors are circumventing the minimum statutes to get crack offenders to plead guilty (over 90% of crack offenders plead guilty) and therefore only a small number of them are subject to a drug minimum in 2000.

Table 3 reveals the results of the OLS regression analysis on the length of sentence in months for crack and powder cocaine offenders. For both crack and powder offenses, legally relevant variables were significant predictors of sentence length; each additional point to an offender's final offense level results in 6.7 months more in sentence length on average for powder offenders and 8.5 additional months for crack offenders. Similarly, a higher criminal history score increases sentence length for powder and crack offenders by approximately 10 and 13 months, respectively. For crack offenders, being sentenced under a mandatory drug minimum leads to average sentence lengths almost 6 months longer, but the variable does not reach significance in powder cases. Finally, powder offenders receive an average sentence decrease of 7 months if they receive the safety valve relieve provision for being deemed a low level, first-time offender, but the variable does not reach significance in crack cases. These findings provide some evidence that the minimums adversely affect average sentence lengths for crack but not powder offenders and the safety valve provision decreases the average sentences for first-time powder offenders but not first-time crack offenders.

Regarding departures, it appears that crack offenders receive larger average sentence discounts for both downward (−25 months for powder cocaine and −40 months for crack) and substantial assistance (−42 months for powder cocaine and −59 months for crack) departures. Finally, having a weapon enhancement applied increases average sentence lengths about 50 months for both types of offenders.

The demographic variables examined here were either nonsignificant or had negligible effects. Ethnicity was significant in crack cases; Hispanics received average sentences that were 8 months less than non-Hispanics. Gender was significant in powder cases; females received average sentences that were 3½ months less than males. Generally, however, extralegal variables were nonsignificant. According to these results, one could argue that judges' sentencing decisions in crack and powder cocaine cases in 2000 do not appear to be based solely on attributions of blameworthiness, culpability, and need for protection of the community as they relate to race, ethnicity, gender, or age.

Z tests for equality of regression coefficient (Paternoster, Brame, Mazerolle, & Piquero, 1998) are ordinarily calculated for pairs of coefficients that are significant across models. Although none of the demographic extralegal variables here were significant across both models, these tests were nonetheless performed for the variables in which coefficients were significant in both models. Results of the Z tests are shown in Table 3. These results confirm that final criminal history category, final offense level, and number of counts result in significantly larger sentences for crack as opposed to cocaine offenders. Noteworthy, however, are the differential effects for the two types of downward departures on the sentence length imposed by the judge. Both regular downward and substantial assistance departures had significantly different (i.e., larger) effects on sentence lengths for crack offenders. In other words, the discounts from the guideline sentence that judges granted for crack offenders were significantly larger than those for powder offenders. The regression findings therefore are mixed regarding the treatment of crack and powder offenders; some variables favor powder offenders while others favor crack offenders. The findings from the Z tests seem to suggest that legally relevant factors treat crack offenders more harshly but in instances where judges can inject discretion (departures), crack offenders benefit from judicial attempts to mitigate their sentences perhaps in the belief that they are too punitive.

Conclusions

While the content and regression analyses suggest qualitative and somewhat distinct treatment of cocaine offenders per drug form, we found little support for the idea that crack offenders are portrayed negatively by the media or treated by federal criminal courts more harshly than cocaine offenders. Furthermore, we found no evidence that extralegal factors are linked to attributions of dangerousness and risk in the media that, in turn, might influence judicial sentencing decisions. Most demographic variables observed in the quantitative analysis were not significant; the exceptions being a gender effect for powder cases and an ethnicity effect for crack cases. Likewise, the content analysis of the USA Today found that very few articles reported the gender, age, race, or ethnicity of offenders, instead those articles reporting on extralegal factors used language indicating minorities were more likely to be arrested and prosecuted for cocaine, and specifically crack cocaine, but not more likely the users of these drugs.

Regression analysis found the legally relevant variables to be the most significant positive predictors of sentence length for both drug types. Media portrayals of offenders and offending from the USA Today parallel this result somewhat in focusing on the amount (i.e., weight) of drugs involved, not the characteristics of offenders. In the federal system, sentence lengths for narcotics offenses are proportional to the amount of drugs involved in the offense. To this end, media portrayals from 2000 did not seem to stereotype crack or powder offenders according to racial or ethnic demographics, instead emphasizing the quantity of narcotics or the numbers of arrests made by law enforcement.

A somewhat surprising finding, however, was that a majority of the narcotics articles focused on celebrity or atypical offenders. These articles did not relate the possibility of federal charges, instead downplaying culpability and blameworthiness by focusing on offenders' noncriminal pasts. A small number of USA Today articles did portray narcotics offenders negatively but did so in a general way rather than specifically related to demographic characteristics of offenders.

Direct comparison of offender characteristics across the regression and content analyses is difficult due to the fact that only a few newspaper articles mentioned demographic variables. In official statistics, 31% of powder offenders and 85% of crack offenders were Black, and Hispanics comprised 50.6% of powder and 8.9% of crack cases. This information from official statistics is in line with the USA Today articles that cited racial and ethnic disparities in conviction and imprisonment rates.

The current research provides some support of the possibility of the institutionalization of the crack cocaine epidemic. Out of curiosity, the authors conducted a similar LexusNexus search of the USA Today, this time for the year 1990 and using only the key word cocaine. This search produced 687 articles, the analysis of which is beyond the scope of this article. Nonetheless, this finding seems to suggest rudimentary evidence that the media has substantially decreased reporting of cocaine offending in the last decade. The USSC has published several reports indicating that ideas about cocaine offending, and especially crack cocaine offenders, as dangerous and threatening were unfounded and perhaps media disseminated myths.

The results of the regression analysis found that judges did attempt to re-exert some discretionary power by mitigating sentence lengths for some offenders who received a departure. These sentence decreases were, on average, greater for crack cocaine offenders than for powder cocaine offenders. Recent research has shown that race, ethnicity, and gender are influential predictors in departure decisions (Engen, Gainey, Crutchfield, & Weiss, 2003; Hartley, Maddan, & Spohn, 2007a; Mustard, 2001; Steffensmeier and Demuth, 2000). Further analysis is therefore needed to explore the presence of any extralegal disparities regarding the, possibly systematic, nature of departure decisions.

This study thus provides exploratory information about media characterizations of cocaine offenders and whether these representations condition case outcomes. Although the war on drugs seems to have been deescalated as legislative efforts and media accounts have refocused on the war on terror, insight into media influences of judicial perceptions of crime is theoretically germane to other public policy discussions. Previous research has shown public perceptions to be influential in legislative responses to crime, but less is known about the way media accounts shape perceptions of offender dangerousness, risk, and how the decisions of judges and other actors in the criminal justice system are affected (Surette, 1992).

At the height of the crack epidemic, offenders were portrayed by the media as highly dangerous and the cause for violence on the streets of American cities. The current study suggests that media accounts of crack and powder cocaine offenders in 2000 were not especially negative; the majority of articles in the USA Today did not represent these offenders as dangerous or threatening and therefore could not have influenced public opinion or judicial perceptions of these offenders in a negative way. Nor did the media articles assess blameworthiness or culpability related to race, ethnicity, gender, or age. Some media accounts cited that narcotics legislation was unfair because it targeted minority offenders for increased punishments. It could be argued that the articles reporting on unfair legislation, especially regarding crack cocaine, might have influenced judicial decisions to grant larger departure discounts to crack versus powder cocaine defendants. If judges recognize that the mandatory minimum laws unfairly punish crack cocaine offenders, they may be attempting to mitigate the sentences of some defendants through sentence discounts for departures. Statistical output indicated significant differences between drug types, lending further support for this notion. Whether the judges are sensing this inequality in the law from the media, however, cannot be adequately assessed here, as results generally were not supportive of a focal concerns perspective on judicial decision making.

Although funding for drug war objectives continues to increase, drug war hype, and perhaps media priority, has clearly decreased. Negative media portrayal of cocaine disparities in federal sentencing generally were not found here, at least with respect to attributions concerning extralegal factors. Whether this lack of reporting on cocaine is due to an institutionalization effect or realization by the media that cocaine offending did not reach predicted epidemic proportions cannot be answered here. Accordingly, future research should continue to examine sentencing policy and practices for cocaine offenses.

Cases Cited

Booker v. United States (543 US 220 (1985)).
Kimbrough v. United States (552 US _ (2007)).

Statutes Cited

Pub. L. No. 91-513, 84 Stat. 1236 (1970).
Pub. L. No. 98-473, §503(a), 98 Stat. 2069 (1984).
Pub. L. No. 98-473, §1005(2), 98 Stat. 2138 (1984).
Pub. L. No. 99-308, §104(a) (2) (A-E), 100 Stat. 456 (1986).
Pub. L. No. 99-570, §1102, 100 Stat. 3207-11 (1986).
Pub. L. No. 99-570, §1105(a), 100 Stat. 3207-11 (1986).
Pub. L. No. 99-570, §1402(a), 100 Stat. 3207-39 (1986).
Pub. L. No. 99-570, 100 Stat. 3207 (1986).
Pub. L. No. 100-690, 102 Stat. 4181 (1988).

Notes

1. On Wednesday, April 29, 2009, the Senate Committee on the Judiciary, Subcommittee on Crime and Drugs held a hearing entitled "Restoring Fairness to Federal Sentencing: Addressing the Crack-Powder Disparity," in which testimony was heard on calls for equalizing mandatory penalties for crack and powder cocaine, or at least conflating them, as well as eliminating the mandatory minimum for simple possession of crack cocaine. The Obama administration supports completely eliminating the 100-to-1 mandatory minimum trigger ratio disparity and the USSC has stated

that their 2008 guideline adjustment is only a first step in ameliorating racial disparity and that Congress will need to act to restore fairness to federal cocaine sentencing (USSC, 2008).

2. Twelve articles were randomly drawn (roughly 15%), and an impartial individual coded the information. These newly coded forms were tested against those forms already coded, and 94% of the coded information was in concurrence.

3. The Commission states that the court records received by the commission may suffer from underreporting of guideline cases because the court may (a) fail to submit all documentation for a case; (b) misunderstand the types of cases that are to be submitted; and (c) lose some cases in-transit from the court and to the commission.

4. Those defendants who received a sentence of probation or a life sentence were excluded from the analysis.

5. The variance inflation factors for the variables in both models were in the 1–2 range, indicating no presence of collinearity.

6. A search for the same time period 10 years earlier (October 1, 1989, through September 30, 1990) produced 687 articles using the keyword cocaine alone.

Declaration of Conflicting Interests

The authors declared no conflicts of interest with respect to the authorship and/or publication of this article.

Funding

The authors received no financial support for the research and/or authorship of this article.

References

Abrahamson, M. (1983). *Social research methods.* Englewood Cliffs, NJ: Prentice Hall.

Albonetti, C. A. (1991). An integration of theories to explain judicial discretion. *Social Problems, 38,* 247–266.

Albonetti, C. A. (1997). Sentencing under the Federal Sentencing Guidelines: Effects of defendant characteristics, guilty pleas, and departures on sentence outcomes for drug offenses, 1991–1992. *Law and Society Review, 31,* 789–822.

Angeli, David H. (1997). A "second look" at crack cocaine sentencing policies: One more try for federal equal protection. *American Criminal Law Review, 34,* 1211–1241.

Beckett, K., & Sasson, T. (2000). *The politics of injustice: Crime and punishment in America.* Thousand Oaks, CA: Pine Forge Press.

Berg, B. L. (1986). Arbitrary arbitration: Diverting juveniles into the justice system. *Juvenile and Family Court Journal, 37,* 31–42.

Berg, B. L. (2004). *Qualitative research methods in the social sciences.* Boston, MA: Allyn & Bacon.

Biskupic, J. (2000, September 22). Drug-testing case goes to high court. *USA Today,* p. A3.

Bushway, S., & Piehl, A. (2007). Social science research and the legal threat to presumptive sentencing guidelines. *Criminology and Public Policy, 6,* 461–482.

Cauchon, D. (1999, November 9). Senate might revise cocaine sentencing. *USA Today,* p. A4.

Caulkins, J. P., Rydell, C. P., Schwabe, W. L., & Chiesa, J. (1998). Are mandatory minimum drug sentences cost effective? *Corrections Management Quarterly, 2,* 68–73.

Chiricos, T. (1996). Moral panic as ideology: Drugs, violence, race and punishment in America. In M. Lynch & E. B. Patterson (Eds.), *Justice with prejudice: Race and criminal justice in America* (pp. 19–48). New York: Harrow and Heston.

Chiricos, T. (2004). Media, moral panics and the politics of crime control. In G. Cole, M. G. Gertz, & A. Bunger (Eds.), *The criminal justice system: Politics and policies.* Belmont, CA: Wadsworth.

Chiricos, T., & Bales, B. (1991). Unemployment and punishment: An empirical assessment. *Criminology, 29,* 701–724.

Cohen, S. (1972): *Folk Devils and Moral Panics:* the creation of the mods and rockers. London: MacGibbon and Kee.

Cole, D. (2000, February 3). Denying felons vote hurts them, society. *USA Today,* p. A17.

Creswell, J. (1995). *Research design: Qualitative and quantitative approaches.* Thousand Oaks, CA: Sage.

Dabney, D. A. (1993). Impaired nursing: Nurses attitudes and perceptions about drug use and drug theft. Master's Thesis. Indiana University of Pennsylvania, Indiana, PA.

Daly, K. (1987). Structure and practice of familiar-based justice in a criminal court. *Law and Society Review, 21,* 267–290.

Duffee, D. E. (1990). *Explaining criminal justice: Community theory and criminal justice reform.* Prospect Heights, IL: Waveland Press.

Durham, A. A., Elrod, H. P., & Kinkade, P. T. (1995). Images of crime and justice. *Journal of Criminal Justice, 23,* 143–152.

Eisenstein, J., & Jacob, H. (1977). *Felony justice: An organizational analysis of criminal courts.* Boston, MA: Little & Brown.

Engen, R. L., Gainey, R. R., Crutchfield, R. D., & Weis, J. G. (2003). Discretion and disparity under sentencing guidelines: The role of departures and structured sentencing alternatives. *Criminology, 41,* 99–130.

Fagen, J., & Chin, K. (1990). Violence as regulation and social control in the distribution of crack. In M. de la rosa, B. Gropper, & E. Lambert (Eds.), *Drugs and violence: Causes, correlates and consequences.* U.S. Government Printing Office. Washington, DC: U.S. Government Printing Office.

Farrell, A. (2004). Measuring judicial and prosecutorial discretion: Sex and race disparities in departures from the federal sentencing guidelines. *Justice Research and Policy, 6,* 45–78.

Feeley, M. (1983). *Court reform on trial.* New York: Basic Books.

Feld, B. (2003). The politics of race and juvenile justice: The "due process revolution" and the conservative reaction. *Justice Quarterly, 20,* 765–800.

Fields, G. (1999, November 18). Study: More women imprisoned for drugs. *USA Today,* p. A3.

Fields, G. (2000a, April 26). Campaign tries to reverse rise in drug abuse by girls: It's no longer a young man's problem. *USA Today,* p. A4.

Fields, G. (2000b, June 8). Study: War on drugs is stacked against blacks. *USA Today,* p. A3.

Fields, G. (2000c, March 30). Far-reaching drug busts set DEA records. *USA Today,* p. A3.

Fields, G. (2000d, July 7). Violence of Puerto Rican drug ring made busts a priority. *USA Today,* p. A3.

Fields, G. (2000e, May 5). Mexico arrests alleged No. 3 in violent cocaine cartel: Capture announced as 'major victory' in drug-trafficking fight. *USA Today,* p. A4.

Garcia, G. (1999, December 1). Truly horrid search at border: Dead thought to be victims of drug trade. *USA Today,* p. A3.

Glaser, B., & Strauss, A. (1967). *The discovery of grounded theory: Strategies for qualitative research.* Chicago: Aldine.

Gray, J. P. (2001). *Why our drug laws have failed and what we can do about it: A judicial indictment of the war on drugs.* Philadelphia, PA: Temple University Press.

Greene, E., & Loftus, E. (1984). What's new in the news? The impact of well-publicized news events on psychological research and courtroom trials. *Basic and Applied Social Psychology, 5,* 211–221.

Greene, E., & Wade, R. (1988). Of private talk and public print: General pre-trial publicity and juror decisionmaking. *Applied Social Psychology, 2,* 123–135.

Hartley, R. D., Maddan, S., & Spohn, C. C. (2007a). Prosecutorial discretion: An examination of substantial assistance departures in Federal crack-cocaine and powder-cocaine cases. *Justice Quarterly, 24,* 382–407.

Hartley, R. D., Maddan, S., & Spohn, C. C. (2007b). Concerning conceptualization and operationalization: Sentencing data and the focal concerns perspective—A research note. *The Southwest Journal ofCriminal Justice, 4,* 58-78.

Hatsukami, D. K., & Fischman, M. W. (1996). Crack cocaine and cocaine hydrochloride: Are the differences myth or reality? *Journal of the American Medical Association, 276,* 1580–1588.

Huberman, A. M., & Miles, M. B. (1994). Data management and analysis methods. In N. K. Denzin & Y. S. Lincoln (Eds.), *Handbook of qualitative research* (pp. 428–444). Thousand Oaks, CA: Sage.

Inciardi, J. A. (1987). Beyond cocaine: Basuco, crack, and other coca products. *Contemporary Drug Problems, 14,* 461–492.

Inciardi, J. A., Pottieger, A. E., & Surrat, H. L. (1996). African Americans and the crack-crime connection. In D. D. Chitwood, J. E. Rivers, & J. A. Inciardi (Eds.), *The American pipe dream: Crack cocaine and the inner city.* Fort Worth, TX: Harcourt Brace.

Jensen, E. L., Gerber, J., & Mosher, C. (2004). Social consequences of the War on Drugs: The legacy of failed policy. *Criminal Justice Policy Review, 15,* 100–121.

Jesdanun, A. (2008, October 27). Newspapers see sharp circulation drop. Associated Press Newswire. Retrieved December 18, 2008, from LexisNexis Academic database.

Jones, C. (1999, October 6). N.M. Governor calls for drug legalization. *USA Today,* p. A4.

Kasindorf, M. (2000, March 16). Feud trips LAPD corruption inquiry: Detective told not to share information with prosecutors. *USA Today,* p. A5.

Kautt, P., & Spohn, C. (2002). Crack-ing down on black drug offenders? Testing for interactions among offenders' race, drug type, and sentencing strategy in federal drug sentences. *Justice Quarterly, 19,* 633–705.

Kramer, J. H., & Ulmer, J. T. (1996). Sentencing disparity and departures from guidelines. Justice Quarterly, 13, 401–425.

Leinwand, D. (2000a, September 28). Coast guard cocaine seizure set record: New surveillance and tactics help, but fight still has 'long way' to go. *USA Today,* p. A3.

Leinwand, D. (2000b, February 25). LAPD, neighborhood shaken. *USA Today,* p. A3.

Lockwood, D., Pottieger, A. E., & Inciardi, J. A. (1995). Crack use, crime by crack users, and ethnicity. In D. Hawkins (Ed.), *Ethnicity, race, and crime: Perspectives across time and place.* New York, NY: SUNY Press.

Mauer, M. (1999). *Race to incarcerate.* New York: New Press.

McCain, T. (1992). The interplay of editorial and prosecutorial discretion in the perpetuation of racism in the Criminal Justice System. *Columbia Journal of Law and Social Problems, 25,* 601–643.

Meierhofer, B. S. (1992). *The general effect of mandatory minimum prison terms: A longitudinal study of federal sentences imposed.* Washington, DC: Federal Judicial Center.

Merton, R. K. (1968). *Social theory and social structure.* New York: Free Press.

Miller, J. M., Wright, R. A., & Smith, M. M. (2000). Mostly male and American: The reporting of women and crime scholarship in introductory criminology textbooks. *The Justice Professional, 13,* 233–245.

Mustard, D. B. (2001). Racial, ethnic, and gender disparities in sentencing: Evidence from the U.S. federal courts. *Journal of Law and Economics, 44,* 1–30.

Nardulli, P. (1978). *The courtroom elite: An organizational perspective on criminal justice.* Cambridge, MA: Ballinger.

NHSDA. (2000). National household survey on drug abuse, 2000. Retrieved February 23, 2007, from http:// www. oas.samhsa.gov/NHSDA/2kNHSDA/2knhsda.htm

Ogletree, C. (2004). Discriminatory impact of mandatory minimum sentences in the United States. *Federal Sentencing Reporter, 18*, 273–278.

Paternoster, R., Brame, R. Mazerolle, P., & Piquero, A. (1998). Using the correct statistical test for the equality of regression coefficients. *Criminology, 36*, 859–866.

Pettit, P. N. (2002). Is criminal justice policy feasible? *Buffalo Criminal Law review, 5*, 427–450.

Pritchard, D. (1986). Homicide and bargained justice: The agenda-setting effect of crime news on prosecutors. *Public Opinion Quarterly, 51*, 166–185.

Pritchard, D., Dilts, J., & Berkowitz, D. (1987). Prosecutors' use of external agendas in prosecuting pornography cases. *Journalisn Quarterly, 64*, 392–398.

Reinarman, C., & Levine, H. G. (2004). Crack in the rearview mirror: Deconstructing drug war mythology. *Social Justice, 31*, 182–199.

Reinarman, C., & Levine, H. G. (1997a). Crack in context: America's latest demon drug. In C. Reinarman & H. G. Levine (Eds.), *Crack in America*. Berkeley: University of California Press.

Reinarman, C., & Levine, H. G. (1997b). The crack attack: Politics and media in the crack scare. In C. Reinarman & H. G. Levine (Eds.), *Crack in America*. Berkeley: University of California Press.

Sample, L. L. (2001). *The social construction of the sex offender*. Unpublished dissertation, University of Missouri, St. Louis.

Scalia, J. (2001). Federal drug offenders, 1999 with trends 1984–1999. United States Department of Justice, Bureau of Justice Statistics, Special Report, Washington, DC.

Schulhofer, S. J., & Nagel, I. H. (1997). Plea negotiations under the federal sentencing guidelines: Guideline circumvention and its dynamics in the post-Mistretta period. *Northwestern Law Review, 91*, 1284–1316.

Shapiro, W. (2000a, January 19). Iowa, N.H. white noise drowns out minority issues. *USA Today*, p. A2.

Shapiro, W. (2000b, June 16). Hillary Clinton's crusade of maybes. *USA Today*, p. A10.

Shapiro, W. (2000c, August 2). Powell goes behind bars for free speech. *USA Today*, p. A8.

Smith, E. B. (2000, September 12). Mexico's drug trade taking down its citizens: Abuse problems now touching all walks of life. *USA Today*, p. A22.

Smith, H. W. (1975). *Strategies of social research*. Englewood Cliffs, NJ: Prentice Hall.

Spohn, C. (2000). Thirty years of sentencing reform: The quest for a racially neutral sentencing process. National Institute of Justice: Criminal Justice 2000. Washington, DC: National Institute of Justice.

Spohn, C., & Beichner, D. (2000). Is preferential treatment of female offenders a thing of the past? A multi-site study of gender, race, and imprisonment. *Criminal Justice Policy Review, 11*, 149–184.

Spohn, C., & Holleran, D. (2000). The imprisonment penalty paid by young, unemployed black and Hispanic male offenders. *Criminology, 38*, 281–306.

Spohn, C., & Holleran, D. (2001). Prosecuting sexual assault: A comparison of charging decisions in sexual assault cases involving strangers, acquaintances, and intimate partners. *Justice Quarterly, 18*, 651–685.

Steffensmeier, D., & Demuth, S. (2000). Ethnicity and sentencing outcomes in U.S. federal courts: Who is punished more harshly? *American Sociological Review, 65*, 705–729.

Steffensmeier, D., & Demuth, S. (2001). Ethnicity and judges sentencing decisions: Hispanic-black-white comparisons. *Criminology, 39*, 145–177.

Steffensmeier, D., Kramer, J., & Streifel, C. (1993). Gender and imprisonment decisions. *Criminology, 31*, 411–446.

Steffensmeier, D., & Motivans, M. (2000). Older men and older women in the arms of the criminal law: Offending patterns and sentencing outcomes. *Journals of Gerontology Series B: Psychological Sciences & Social Sciences, 55B*, 141–151.

Steffensmeier, D., Ulmer, J., & Kramer, J. (1998). The interaction of race, gender, and age in criminal sentencing: The punishment cost of being young, black, and male. *Criminology, 36*, 763–797.

Stroman, C., & Seltzer, R. (1985). Media use and perception of crime. Journalism Quarterly, 62, 340–345.

Surette, R. (1990). *The media and criminal justice policy: Recent research and social effects.* Springfield, IL: Charles C. Thomas.

Surette, R. (1992). Methodological problems in determining media effects on criminal justice: A review and suggestions for the future. *Criminal Justice Policy Review, 6,* 291–310.

Surette, R. (1999). Media echoes: Systemic effects of news coverage. *Justice Quarterly, 16,* 601–631.

Surette, R. (2007). *Media, crime and criminal justice: Images, realities and policies* (3rd ed.). Belmont, CA: Wadsworth.

Sutel, S. (2000, May 1). Major newspapers post circulation gains. Associated Press Newswire. Retrieved December 18, 2008, from LexisNexis Academic database.

Tashakkori, A., & Teddlie, C. (1998). *Mixed methodology: Combining qualitative and quantitative approaches.* Thousand Oaks, CA: Sage.

The Sentencing Project. (2002). *Crack cocaine sentencing policy: Unjustified and unreasonable.* Washington, DC: Author.

The Sentencing Project. (2008). *Federal crack cocaine sentencing.* Washington, DC: Author.

Tonry, M. (1995). *Malign neglect: Race, crime, and punishment in America.* New York: Oxford University Press.

United States Department of Justice. Bureau of Justice Statistics. (1992). *Drugs. Crime, and the justice system.* Washington, DC: Author.

United States Department of Justice. Bureau of Justice Statistics. (2001). Key facts at a Glance: Incarceration rates, 1980–2001. Washington, DC: Author.

United States Department of Justice. Bureau of Justice Statistics. (2006). *Prisoners in 2005.* Washington, DC: Author.

United States General Accounting Office. (1993). *Mandatory minimum sentences: Are they being imposed and who is receiving them?* Washington, DC: Author.

United States Sentencing Commission. (1991a). *Mandatory minimum penalties in the Federal Criminal Justice System.* Washington, DC: Author.

United States Sentencing Commission. (1991b). *Special report to Congress: Mandatory minimum penalties in the Federal Criminal Justice System.* Washington, DC: Author.

United States Sentencing Commission. (1995). *Cocaine and federal sentencing policy.* Washington, DC: Author.

United States Sentencing Commission. (1997). *Cocaine and federal sentencing policy.* Washington, DC: Author.

United States Sentencing Commission. (1999). *Federal sentencing guidelines manual.* Washington, DC: Author.

United States Sentencing Commission. (2002). *Cocaine and federal sentencing policy.* Washington, DC: Author.

United States Sentencing Commission. (2007). *Cocaine and federal sentencing policy.* Washington, DC: Author.

United States Sentencing Commission. (2008). *Preliminary crack cocaine retroactivity data report.* Washington, DC: Author.

Vincent, B. S., & Hofer, P. J. (1994). *The consequences of mandatory minimum prison terms: A summary of recent findings.* Washington, DC: Federal Judicial Center.

Weber, R. P. (1990). *Basic content analysis.* Newbury Park, CA: Sage.

Wickham, D. (1999, November 23). Gore view falls short on cocaine disparity. *USA Today,* p. A19.

Willing, R. (2000, February 29). Supreme Court to address hospital's role in drug war. *USA Today,* p. A4.

Wilmot, K., & Spohn, C. (2004). Prosecutorial discretion and real offense sentencing: An analysis of relevant conduct under the Federal Sentencing guidelines. *Criminal Justice policy Review, 15,* 324–343.

Wright, R. A., Miller, J. M., & Britz, M. (2001). Who gets the ink? A page-coverage analysis of the most influential scholars in criminology and criminal justice journals. *Journal of Free Inquiry in Creative Sociology, 28.*

Zimring, F., Hawkins, G., & Kamin, S. (2001). *Punishment and democracy: Three strikes and you're out in California.* New York, NY: Oxford University Press.

Bios

Richard D. Hartley is an assistant professor in the Department of Criminal Justice at the University of Texas at San Antonio. His research interests focus on disparities in sentencing practices, especially regarding narcotics violations, prosecutorial and judicial discretion, and media influences on behavior.

J. Mitchell Miller is a professor in the Department of Criminal Justice at the University of Texas at San Antonio, whose work is oriented around criminological theory development, program evaluation, and criminal subcultures. A former editor of the *Journal of Criminal Justice Education* and the *Journal of Crime and Justice*, Dr. Miller, is the current President of the Southern Criminal Justice Association and was recipient of the 2009 Academy of Criminal Justice Sciences Fellow Award.

MAD MEN, METH MOMS, MORAL PANIC

Gendering Meth Crimes in the Midwest

by Travis Linnemann

Introduction

American social history is marked by the rise and fall of drug panics. From marijuana, heroin, alcohol and crack, varying levels of moral outrage and repression have been cast at those blamed for "demon drugs" (Reinarman and Levine 1997: 5). Regardless of how these panics have played out, the associated blame often betrays broader race, class, and gender based inequalities. Within the last three decades or so, the social apprehensions surrounding drugs and drugs users have been increasingly central to qualitative and quantitative changes in criminal punishments, the salience of crime in governmental discourse, and massive restructuring of the welfare state (Young 2007; Simon 2007; Wacquant 2009). These changes, many argue, have given rise to the largest carceral apparatus in human history (Wacquant 2001). Numerous cultural scapegoats also appeared alongside these changes seemingly to justify the pyrrhic costs of the war on drugs. From Ronald Reagan's yarn of opportunistic welfare queens on the south side of Chicago, Willie Horton's appearance in the 1988 Presidential campaign, to Rudy Giuliani's quality of life attack on squeegee men, latent yet intertwined assertions about race, crime, drugs, and dependency have stirred working class animus, forged public policy, and fed mass incarceration. In the 1990s a group of prominent policy advisors, including former drug czars William Bennett and John Walters and criminologist John DiIulio, produced a body of research heralding coming crime waves rising from inner city ghettos. They argued that inner city poverty and the continued degradation of the urban family would collide with the scourge of crack cocaine and ideal demographic conditions to produce hordes of "morally poor" children or "super-predators". The resultant storm would release unparalleled violence on urban ghettos and spill over onto white America (Bennett et al. 1996: 13). Constructing the "super-predator" crisis, the authors tapped into white America's racial fears, exploiting the caricature of the young black criminal while helping to exclude them both spatially and socially. Though history now disproves the veracity of these claims, fear and irrationality continue to produce real outcomes for those entangled in the machinery of U.S. criminal justice, even as the crack-epidemic and super-predator fade from collective memory (Reinarman and Levine 2004).

Though these particular constructions have faded the public is often eager to learn of the next greatest threat. As if reading from a script describing previous drug panics, policy makers and the media again trumpet the coming of an as-of-yet unrivaled epidemic. New York Senator Chuck Schumer recently warned in an Orwellian manner, "It's 1984 all over again," drawing comparisons between the past crack panic and a new one bubbling under the surface. Schumer warns:

> Twenty years ago, crack was headed east across the United States like a Mack Truck out of control, and it slammed New York hard because we just didn't see the warning signs. Well, the headlights are glaring bright off in the distance again, this time with meth. We are still paying the price of missing the warning signs back then, and if we don't remember our history we will be doomed to repeat it, because crystal meth could become the new crack. (Schumer 2004)

As if it is 1984 again, Schumer warns that like crack, methamphetamine is primed to unleash unpredictable harm. More, because meth is relatively inexpensive and can be produced from common items essentially anywhere it threatens the heart of America— both geographically and metaphorically. Reinforcing the familiar epidemic script, News-week recently dubbed meth "America's Most Dangerous Drug" arguing it's the threat to the "mainstream":

> Once derided as "poor man's cocaine," popular mainly in rural areas and on the West Coast, meth has seeped into the mainstream in its steady march across the United States. Relatively cheap compared with other hard drugs, the highly addictive stimulant is hooking more and more people across the socioeconomic spectrum: soccer moms in Illinois, computer geeks in Silicon Valley, factory workers in Georgia, gay professionals in New York. The drug is making its way into suburbs from San Francisco to Chicago to Philadelphia. (Jefferson 2007)

Perhaps the most striking feature of the growing meth panic is that unlike crack and other drugs allegedly concentrated in poor inner-city neighborhoods, meth is supposedly particularly attractive to rural and suburban America. As Newsweek (2007) warns, meth reaches across the "socioeconomic spectrum" to "computer geeks in Silicon Valley, factory workers in Georgia, gay professionals in New York" (Jefferson 2007). This supposed fact identifies new victims and enemies plucked from middle-class, white America, as opposed to the racialized images of crack babies, welfare queens and urban others of previous decades. In addition, because meth provides the ability to stay awake, permits the user to concentrate and accomplish tasks, is associated with weight loss and sexual pleasure, the drug is particularly attractive to one of the last bastions of white middle-class virtue, the "soccer mom" (Jefferson 2007).

Other descriptions are more racially explicit. As Cobbina's (2008) recent findings show, mediated depictions of crack are most often associated with blacks and violent crime, while methamphetamine is most commonly associated with whites and is framed as a public health problem. Though meth production and use may never be formally declared a white or rural drug, and is increasingly connected to Mexican importers, claims like Newsweek's (2007) and the use of terms like "suburbs", "mainstream", "soccer mom" and "professional" all effectively convey whiteness. As Bonilla-Silva (2003) has shown racial hierarchies are consistently maintained and reinforced in such a way, even while explicit references to race have diminished or disappeared altogether. This sort of symbolic racism replaces the taboo language of overt racism with a language of conceptual slipperiness and equates questions of moral character and deviation from American individualism, with blackness (Bonilla-Silva 2003:6). It is here, in the distinction between the depravity of a ghetto drug like crack, and the creeping of meth into the "mainstream" that the racialized and gendered nature of the so-called meth epidemic becomes most visible.

Though the harmful effects of the drug are undeniable, recent research suggests that its plague-like grip on America is overstated. One report by The Sentencing Project, finds that meth is not only among the least used drugs, but also use rates among the general public are stable since 1999 and are declining among youth (King 2006). This report and others contest the deluge of meth crime blurbs and hyperbolic public service campaigns in states like Montana and Illinois and highlights the contours of a unique drug panic.

The aim of this research is to illustrate socially constructed dimensions of meth crimes. Specifically, this research explores the gendered presentation of meth use by comparing mediated depictions of men and women's involvement with the drug. Emerging from these depictions are culturally constructed notions of the female meth user's hyper-sexuality, immorality, and inability to parent, which stand in stark contrast to concurrent constructions of male meth users as calculating entrepreneurs and criminal mad men. The analysis offers a contextual framework to consider how this sort of mediated dichotomy emerges from and reinforces popular understandings of meth users in rural spaces, gendered notions of criminality, and corresponding social reactions.

Moral Panics, Gender, and Crime

Examining exaggerated constructions of drug crimes provides a glimpse of broader arrangements that structure social life. As Greer (2008: 5) and his colleagues remind us, moral panics or "crises of the present" have much to tell us about salient, yet sometimes unspoken social values. They argue: "within [crises of the present] identities remain mediated accomplishments, circulating from fly posters to websites to video clips, and yet grounded still in gendered, racialized, and class-based notions of ideal parents, ideal victims, and unknown perpetrators" (Greer et al. 2008: 7–8). A powerful example of meth users and victims as mediated accomplishments currently emerges from official state sources as the Montana Meth Project. The project characterizes itself as a large-scale exercise in prevention consisting of, "an ongoing, research-based marketing campaign … that realistically and graphically communicates the risks of methamphetamine to the youth of Montana" (Montana Meth Project 2009). The campaign uses television, print, and radio formats built around graphic depictions of teen meth users as pimps and prostitutes who prey on family, friends, and strangers. Scare tactics aside, the print ads are overtly sexualized, racialized, and gendered representations of meth users. For example, of the fifteen print images available on the organization's website, all of them feature young white users and more than half feature females. In addition to graphic depictions of users picking scabs or "meth bugs" and being raped, each ad contains a warning like "15 bucks for sex isn't normal. But on meth it is" (Montana Meth Project 2009). When examined in context of bygone drug panics, amplified media and governmental attention, and public service campaigns like the Montana Meth Project, it is clear that meth presents a new threat—and one with very clear racialized and gendered elements.

The term moral panic first coined by Young (1971) and elaborated Cohen (2002) has been used extensively to examine the emergence of all manner of social problems. While popular among academics, it is one of the few concepts found in popular culture and invoked on television and in print by government officials and the media (Garland 2008). Moral panic describes the media and authorities' exaggerated reaction or "collective mistake in understanding" to the behavior of a particular group or cultural identity-the folk devil (Ferrell et al. 2008: 48). Often folk devils are young, poor, and powerless emblems of social change and the scapegoats of life in an ontologically uncertain world. In the midst of panic, the public feeds on stylized and exaggerated depictions of a new enemy, as media officials, pundits, and politicians champion traditional morality. Meanwhile, socially accredited experts, such as Bennett and DiIulio, pronounce diagnoses and solutions to calm fears and sway public sentiment. In many cases, reactionary policies that promote inequality remain long after the panic retreats from popular imagination.

Perhaps most central to this discussion is the suggestion that the emergence of a certain folk devil is somehow symptomatic of larger social decay. This element is perhaps more evident when discussing the place of women and racial minorities in drug panics. As I argue, and the literature suggests, the mainstream equate drug use, illicit sex, welfare dependency, and single parenthood to individual level pathologies and indicators broader social decline (Boyd 2004; Daniels 1997; Toscano 2005). In other words, daily newspaper reports, news broadcasts and multi-mediated public service campaigns lead the public to conclude that the phenomenon of the female meth user is a symptom of decay of the core of American social life: motherhood, childhood, and family. Here are women that presumably shirk traditional working-class values of motherhood and service to family for the idleness and debauchery of drug use. While unique in representation, intersecting cultural constructions of race, class, gender, age, appear in both the bygone crack craze that ensnared urban blacks and the growing meth panic pointed at the white countryside. This is interesting considering that moral panics often represent a contradiction, offering the public both a scapegoat and an object of envy able to transgress and subvert the structural traps of everyday life (McRobbie and Thornton 1995). As Young asserts "It cannot be accident that the stereotype of the underclass with its idleness, dependency, hedonism and institutionalized irresponsibility, with its drug use, teenage pregnancies and fecklessness, represents all the traits which the respectable citizen has to suppress in order to maintain his or her lifestyle" (Young 2007: 42). When viewed individually, panics appear episodic, they seem to rise and fall at the whim media and public attention. However, if we pay attention to the cultural script of drug panics and make connections between crises of the present, like crack and meth, a new narrative appears. Here meth is not a new drug epidemic, but a particular face emerging from the monolithic backdrop of crisis, control, and crime-the hegemonic narrative of modern life (Garland 2001; Simon 2007; Feeley and Simon 2007).

Perhaps the greatest problem with the moral panics schema is its misapplication. Often it used as a blanket approach to social problems leaving the identities of folk devils and the contexts which produced them assumed or underdeveloped (Gelsthorpe 2005). For instance, as Miller (2002) argues, though the mandates of masculinity and femininity are pervasive, viewing crime as a predominately masculine endeavor is problematic. In other words, we must expand our conceptions of crime beyond the trap of exclusive masculine and feminine criminal dichotomies (Miller 2002).

Further, feminist scholars argue the importance of recognizing coexisting constructions of race, gender and class as intersectionality (West and Fenstermaker 1995). This suggests that as we cannot fully consider the constructions of gender and race separately, neither can we conceptualize the emergence of a drug panic independent of the intersectional identity of its object. Therefore, moral panics as cultural productions exist at varying intersections of race, class, gender, and sexuality (Gelsthorpe 2005). Moreover while attempting to draw connections between crises of the present, we must do so with the understanding that these axes of oppression do not emerge from a social vacuum, but are rather a product of dynamic and reciprocal social history (Hill-Collins 1995: 504). Therefore analyzing moral panics is most useful "as a means of conceptualizing the lines of power in society" (Jewkes 2006: 85). In this respect, a moral panic rising from threats to the "mainstream" and "soccer mom" offers new insight to dominant notions of morality and processes of criminalization and social control that are ground at specific intersections of race, class, gender, etc. With this in mind, this paper examines the "gendered, racialized, and class-based notions of ideal parents, ideal victims, and unknown perpetrators" for new insights into the exclusionary power of moral panics (Greer et al. 2008: 7–8).

Data and Method

This paper analyzes the construction of meth crimes by examining a sample of Midwestern newspapers. I focus on Midwestern newspapers for a number of reasons. First, when compared with urban areas, the popular conception of the Midwest is that its smaller towns and less dense areas are not prone to the same levels of violence and crime. Therefore, I believe mediated depictions of methamphetamine as an epidemic are more obvious in semi-rural areas of the Midwest. More importantly perhaps, as Newsweek and others assert, methamphetamine production and abuse as portrayed by the media has emerged as a regionally concentrated phenomena. I limit the sample to Midwestern[1] states identified by the HIDTA (High-Intensity Drug Trafficking Areas) program of the Office of National Drug Control Policy (ONDCP 2009). I limit the sample in this manner as I believe the official discussion regarding the importance of meth as a social problem as well as funding to intervene in these areas will influence and reinforce media publication. Queries of the Lexis/Nexis Academic database with general search terms of male and female involvement with meth identify articles for this study. These queries produce two separate samples, one for men and one for women that are mutually exclusive.[2] From the samples I begin with a body of newsprint articles from numerous regional sources for the years 1995–2007.[3]

I restrict the data to articles published in select Midwestern newspapers of study states. I also include Associated Press/Newswire stories that describe events occurring in study states.[4] I eliminate articles that contain the specified search terms but do not pertain to illicit involvement with methamphetamine. Further, to help ensure ease of comparison between men and women I eliminate articles that are unclear who is the main actor or subject of the report (i.e., a married couple arrested

---

1 States included: Iowa, Kansas, Missouri, Nebraska, North Dakota, South Dakota, Oklahoma.

2 General Search Terms: men AND man AND methamphetamine, women AND woman AND methamphetamine.

3 Lexis/Nexis allows retrieved articles to be sorted by relevance. I use this option to ensure that I have examined the most appropriate data and retrieve the first 105 articles in each query.

4 Newspapers selected are: Omaha (NE) World Herald, Lincoln (NE) Journal Star, Topeka (KS) Capitol Journal, St. Louis (MO) Post-Dispatch, Kansas City (MO) Star, Tulsa (OK) World. These papers were the most prominent papers available in the Lexis Nexis database.

together). After theoretically restricting the sample, I analyze 210 articles (105 male, 105 female). To examine the data, I use a combination of quantitative and qualitative strategies. For the quantitative portion of the study, I identify the main depictions of men and women's involvement with the meth trade. For example, one article tells the story of two men arrested while attempting to steal anhydrous ammonia, commonly used in meth production. The article also describes a wild police chase led by the men. In this instance, I identified several important elements of involvement in the meth trade: the men were involved in production—rather than simple distribution or possession, they were involved in obtaining chemical precursors—and when contacted by authorities they went to some lengths to resist apprehension.[5] I analyzed all of the data in both samples in this manner.

After I developed preliminary summary depictions, I reviewed the articles again and categorized them by several emergent themes. While many of the themes cross over between men and women, several themes do not. Presentation of the data in this manner permits comparison between the two samples. After comparing the samples, several points of divergence in the narratives of men and women's meth involvement become apparent. I then focus on these differences, relying on ethnographic content analysis (ECA) to examine differences between the samples. Similar to inductive analysis, ECA, or qualitative document analysis as developed by Altheide (1996), is particularly suited for analysis of these data as it stresses a grounded or reflexive approach to data analysis as opposed to a strictly quantitative approach that fits the data to an instrument or analytic categories. In the attempt to be systematic yet not rigid, "categories and variables initially guide the study, but others are allowed and expected to emerge throughout" (Altheide 1996: 33). After coding, the data fit into four general analytic categories: reasons for involvement, role in the meth market, criminal virility, and outcome of involvement. I include a brief discussion of the analytic categories developed from the quantitative analysis, and then expand upon each of these themes in detail in the qualitative analysis. Table 1 provides a description of the sample, the themes that emerged and the differences between men and women.

Findings

Gendered Reasons

The first and perhaps most striking contrast is reasons for use or involvement with meth. Thirteen percent of the articles suggest that women begin to use meth as a weight loss strategy, for energy to accomplish household tasks, or to enhance sex. Conversely, the articles commonly portray men as rational actors, becoming involved as a business decision connected to economic opportunity, as evidenced by descriptions of large amounts of drugs or money. This dichotomy is possibly the most interesting finding of this research, describing male involvement simply as a business decision while women assume the risks of methamphetamine for banal and vain reasons related to sex, housekeeping, and appearance. Recalling Miller's (2002) work, this is very much a static and gendered portrayal that perpetuates and extends the connection of female criminality to monolithic social structures that shape human behavior (i.e., boys will be boys). As women's reasons for using meth are reflect appropriate feminities, the motivation of men appear to rarely come into question. In this context then, women's experiences as drug users are marginalized and sexualized, if not trivialized. For example, a

---

5 Therefore this article is associated with at least three of the final categories: manufacture, chemicals/ precursors, and attacked or fled police-these categories are not mutually exclusive.

Table 1. Newspaper depictions of Midwestern meth-related crimes 1995–2007

Themes in sample articles	Male (%) N = 105	Female (%) N = 105
Reasons for involvement		
Sex/weight loss/energy	–	12.9
Large amounts of drugs or money	33.3	20.9
Role in the methamphetamine market		
Simple possession	8.6	8.6
Sale-distribute	54.3	26.6
Manufacture	51.4	15.2
Mule/bystander	–	33.7
Securing chemicals or precursors	30.5	7.6
Criminal virility		
Attacked or fled police	18.1	4.8
Weapons involved	16.2	4.8
Abuse-neglect/custody/social services	.9	40.3
Outcome of involvement		
Clean/treatment	–	11.4
Prison sentence	28.6	23.8
Fire/explosion and injury/death	12.4	1.9
Murder	4.8	8.6

consistent suggestion is that women use meth as a weight loss strategy characterized by the term "Jenny Crank Diet", as the following passage from the Topeka Capital Journal asserts:

> One woman said the drug helped her lose weight by taking away her appetite for everything — except meth. (Hrenchir 2000)

Other mediated depictions underscore the collision of drug use, sexuality, and expectations of a physique that fits the racialized, classed beauty norms of modern American life.

> Her life was then a merry-go-round of men and drugs. She eventually settled on meth as her drug of choice, because it helped her stay awake and keep her weight down. (Eiserer 1999)

Here the report suggests that meth use for women is just an accessory or tool to attract men. The article typifies women as those who "eventually settle" on meth to help stay awake in the "merry-go round" of illicit sex with multiple partners. This statement constructs women's meth use as nothing more than a whim, accommodating the moral depravity of promiscuous and lurid sexual habits. Again, this proposes a gendered dichotomy of female offending that Miller (2002) and others have cautioned against.

Although the analyses will later show that women are disproportionately punished for child abuse and neglect resulting from meth use, in this instance oddly, the data purport that women begin using meth to be more effective mothers.

> The young mother felt energized. 'It makes you motivated,' she said. 'You get a lot of stuff done. That's what I like so much about it. I could take care of my kids, get the housework done and not get burned out. (Range 2000)

Here is a strange presentation of meth use encouraged by highly gendered norms. In contrast to men, women start using meth so they can keep up with their housework and children. Hidden within this image, as Bonilla-Silva might agree (2003), are discussions of "housework" and "taking care of my kids" that carry implications diametrically opposed to previous depictions of the welfare queen, who presumably did neither. In this narrative, rural or suburban, and therefore white women, fall prey to a new invader, in part because of the gendered nature of their daily live. Perhaps, as the data seem to suggest, the behavior of meth using women is somehow mitigated because it results from their attempt to satisfy long standing social expectations. The passage below illustrates the disparity between male and female norms that persist even when under the influence of meth:

> [O]ne can often tell where ice is being smoked, because the woman in the house will be a compulsive cleaner and the place with be spick and span. The man, meanwhile, will have become what police officers call a "tweaker," overcome with a manic urge to take things apart, and so car and machine parts will often be scattered on an immaculate lawn. (Goldberg 1997)

As the *Times* describes, male and female meth users follow the typical trajectory of gendered norms; masculine or mechanical chores for men, while women feel compelled to clean their houses. Finally, the following excerpts depict women as not only able to accomplish typical middle-class suburban wifely tasks on meth, but also being able to over-perform such duties on the drug.

> It blew her mind away, she got so much energy from it that she could clean five or six homes a day and still take care of her own home. (Range 2000)
> It's amazing what you can accomplish when you're on meth … it's the superwoman drug. Women use it to be superwife, superemployee, and super thin (Cuniberti 2003)

The excerpts above carry the clear suggestion that women begin using meth to become "superwoman", "superwife", "superemployee", and "super thin". All of these characterizations stand in clear contrast to depictions of men and also starkly oppose the depravity of the inner city other central to the crack panic. Moreover, when the media tells us what it means to be a "superwife" it also imparts very clear racialized meanings that in turn construct notions of ideal criminals and ideal victims, in a new social context.

The final interesting depiction of the female meth user in the Midwest is that she uses the drug to perform sexually. As the Omaha World Herald describes:

> Dubbed by some experts as the "woman's wonder drug," the highly addictive drug can provide a sense of unlimited energy and focus. It suppresses the appetite, causing its users to shed pound after pound without effort. And meth can enhance sexual performance. (Range 2000)

Interviewing a law enforcement official, The New York Times adds that meth helps the user perform as a sex worker: *"There may be piece of it related to weight loss,"* he said, and *"a piece of it related to enabling prostitution, it's a drug that allows you to deal with your feelings of remorse"* (Goldberg 1997). Both quotes give descriptions of how meth can aid women in performing gendered and sexualized tasks expected of them.

This selection of quotes correspond with broad cultural mandates requiring women to remain thin, keep a clean house, keep up with children, and perform sexually. Regardless of the validity of these assertions it leads to the belief that women are so vain that they involve themselves in the drug market to manage their appearance and their households. Meanwhile, tales of men involved with methamphetamine revolve around rational business decisions and the sensual lure of the criminal lifestyle. These depictions diminish the agency of women inside and outside of the meth culture, while also constructing mitigating narratives of the rural or suburban female meth user as victim to "womanly duties" that clash with descriptions of her inner-city counterparts. Moreover, while many believe drug users assume a master status that overrides individual identities, summary depictions of meth users seem to exaggerate taken for granted identities. In this context, the vanity of the feminine form is exaggerated to such a degree that weight loss, sexuality, and household chores sit at the core of meth related crime and deviance.

Meth Jobs and Criminal Virility

The next category, duties in the meth market, reflects' the type of activities individuals have in the meth trade. Though the categories are similar, the data clearly suggest that men are responsible for the production and sale of meth (54.3 and 51.4%, respectively), and women remain accomplices, mules, or bystanders. This finding is similar to Maher's (2000) observations of the Brooklyn crack market that shows while men and women crack users both shared similar risks, female methods to stay afloat in the illicit crack market were consistently subordinate to men.

According to the data, men are primarily responsible for securing chemical precursors, manufacturing, and distributing the drug; women are responsible for delivery or operate as assistant to a man more centrally involved. This finding also complements Collison's (1996) findings that drug dealing activities help construct ideal masculinities for men with little other social resources. The following excerpt details how men secure chemicals necessary for production, a theme that appears in 30.5% of the sampled articles, as opposed to women who appear involved in this behavior in about 7.6% of the articles.

> As Morbach returned to patrolling Nebraska 92, he saw another man filling a 1-gallon gas can from a tank of anhydrous ammonia, a farm fertilizer that can be used to make meth. Morbach said the suspect ran and he tackled him in a nearby farm field. The suspect ... said that the other man was an accomplice and that they planned to make meth in the 1983 Oldsmobile Cutlass Ciera parked by the ammonia tank, Morbach said. Equipment and materials used to make methamphetamine filled the car's trunk and front passenger seat. (Spencer 2000)

Similar to previous binary descriptions of masculine and feminine "tweaking" behaviors (mechanical vs. household tasks), the sample portrays these behaviors as decidedly masculine-men who do the important work of chemical collection and production while women fill in the blanks. Although the dichotomy is clear, it is not clear whether this division of labor is entirely constructed by the media or if the data depict actual differences in duties. Regardless, the mediated depictions illustrate perceived differences in male and female meth use. Whereas men are often portrayed as rational or violent producers or distributors, women are marginalized. The following passages further document this hierarchy, illustrating how the gendered nature of everyday life is present in meth culture as well.

> June Garcia's trial started Monday. She was charged with conspiracy to distribute ... methamphetamine. The crime is a felony punishable by as much as 20 years in prison and a 1 million dollar fine. Garcia was not the main player in the drug ring, but testimony and evidence showed she was clearly involved. (Waltman 2007a, b)

This passage contains an obvious contradiction. Apparently for June Garcia, her role in distribution may result in a prison sentence of 20 years. However, regardless of the severity of her punishment, the media assert that somehow Ms. Garcia was "not the main player" in the conspiracy, leaving the reader to wonder what type of punishment the "main player" might receive—but more centrally this leaves the reader to assume someone more powerful and instrumental was the main player, someone other than June, someone who is in fact likely to have been male. In an even more direct manner, the St. Louis Post Dispatch reports that *Women, [are] traditionally couriers for boyfriends or husbands who sell drugs ...*" (Bryant 1999), again underscoring the hierarchical nature of depictions of Midwest meth culture. Other media reports tell us of a variety of accomplice roles that women occupy, whether mule or maid. One woman describes the extent of the duties necessary to remain in the good graces of her dealers: *"I cooked their food,"* she said. *"I washed their clothes."*(Winter 1997). Facing yet another double stigma, some accounts propose that regardless of their position in the meth industry, women often share an equal or greater burden of criminal punishments.

> At the time, authorities seized a package, which was delivered to the house, that they say contained 32 ounces of methamphetamine, James Johnson III already pleaded guilty in the case. He was the main player in the drug case and testified Tuesday that Taylor (his girlfriend) helped him ship drugs from the Phoenix area to Aberdeen. (Waltman 2007a, b)

The article referencing another case in which the man is the "main player" describes an instance where the man's testimony helps convict his girlfriend, even though he has already been convicted. Ultimately, this theme illustrates that mediated depictions of the meth trade are not substantially different than "mainstream" social life, women's duties and activities remain subordinate to men's.

Mad Men and Meth Moms

Again, clear divisions in the type of interactions individuals had with law enforcement are also evident in the data. The media suggest that men are much more likely to use weapons, or attack or flee from authorities. This reaffirms the depiction of women as passive actors and suggests that men possess more criminal agency then women. However, the clearest division in terms of descriptions of criminality is child abuse. As it relates to meth, women are almost exclusively held responsible for the abuse and neglect of children. Very little discussion of male responsibility for abuse or neglect cases appears in the sample. This finding mirrors broader social norms, placing the bulk of child rearing duties at the feet of women. The finding also suggests that responsibilities in the meth culture are gendered, as are the official responses to child abuse.

The media report that the behavior of men is more erratic and criminally volatile than that of women. For example, I find that the data depict men attacking or fleeing police four times as often as women, as evidenced by the following passages:

> At 9:21 pm, Monday police say they tried to pull over the men's truck for a lane violation near the intersection of Interstate 70 and Highway 47. A chase ensued with speeds reaching 110 mph, and during the pursuit, police saw numerous items being thrown from the passenger window of the truck. (Weich 2005)
>
> Troy police responded to the Dollar General Store … Employees told police that the man had gotten into a truck and driven behind the building. Police drove to the back of the store, saw the truck, and found the man inside a trash bin. (Weich 2003)

These articles support the narrative of male unpredictability and the ongoing distinction between masculine and feminine criminality. When authorities confront male meth users, they confront strong, sometimes violent opposition. This however, appears to not be the case for women or their attempts at alluding authorities are not quite as publicized. In any case, the media provide clear and distinct competing narratives in behavior differences between men and women. Other articles describing sophisticated levels of security and weaponry used by male dealers also help construct the "mad man" identity of men in the meth trade. As the St. Louis Post-Dispatch describes:

> Police searched the home Wednesday morning. Officers found five pipe bombs inside the kitchen, a shotgun, an assault rifle, a .357 Magnum and a crate holding about a thousand rounds of ammunition, authorities said … The level of paranoia is the highest we've ever seen … We've seen surveillance equipment and stuff like that, but it has never gotten to the point where bombs were being manufactured. (Munz 1999)

As the article describes, men are not only sophisticated in their methods, but are dangerous and increasingly paranoid in their activities. Other depictions of men contacted by authorities vacillate between unpredictable and bizarre conduct, as this narrative describes:

> Harr was stopped Jan. 21 for traffic violations … The officer asked the man who is 6-feet-9 inches tall and 200 pounds if had any weapons. The man pulled back his coat to reveal two knives. (Munz 2000)

Though this article successfully conveys male criminal threat, it is impossible to verify the actual context of this arrest. The introduction of physical size and the mention of weapons transform a mundane drug arrest into a strange tale of potential violence. These tales of male criminality are examples of what Reinarman and Levine (1997) call the routinization of caricature or cases in which the media rhetorically construct unusual events as everyday occurrences. In this case, the media tells us that men are either rational actors, or tweaked-out mad men.

Meanwhile, the data present a concurrent, yet altogether different narrative of female meth criminality. For women, their criminality reflects their failures as mothers. Recall this theme that contradicts previous assertions suggesting that women become involved with the drug so they can "keep up with their kids" and "keep a clean house". As Cohen (2002) and others note, this seems to reflect that the media construct "meth moms" as a new folk devil, emblematic of a new threat to traditional morality seeping into Midwestern communities. Additionally, victimhood is an important indicator of the tenor of this panic. Existing media accounts of meth related child abuse portray the children as pure victims of circumstance. However, as we recall this was not the case for children of inner-city crack using welfare queens, constructed as "super-predators" in worst cases and "burdens" to taxpayers at best.

While I do not argue the potential harm that children of drug using parents face, the construction of the "meth mom" provides a clear illustration of the media's portrayal of racialized and gendered differences between men and women in urban and rural contexts. On one hand, meth involved men are exonerated from the task of raising their children, a task which falls squarely upon the shoulders of women. On the other hand, women failing at parenthood are particularly shameful and easily reviled. This theme is associated with women in 40.3% of the articles, while it appears in less than one percent in the male sample. The following quotes provide examples of some of these instances:

> A woman settled her drug debt by 'lending' her 11 year-old daughter to drug dealers who gave the girl drug-laden shoes and used her to mask their crimes (St. Louis Post-Dispatch 1999). Weeping as her 5 year-old daughter watched, a 22 year-old Omaha woman captured in Bolivia pleaded guilty Thursday to a Federal charge of conspiring to deal methamphetamine in Omaha. (Strawbridge 1999)

Despite the fact that no one would excuse these behaviors, the media report them as though mothers are solely responsible. Virtually, no mention of men's failures as parents appears in the sample. Additionally, other instances detail how mothers victimize their children by providing them the drug or encouraging them to traffic meth. Both of the following examples describe such circumstances:

> A Lincoln (Neb) woman has been charged with supplying marijuana and methamphetamine to her two eldest daughters. Cheri L. Ball, 33, was charged Tuesday with two felony drug charges and felony child abuse. A single mother, she was accused of using drugs with her two daughters ages 17 and 13. She also has an 11-year old daughter. (Omaha World Herald 1997)
> A 49-year old mother told police Thursday night that she supplied her son with methamphetamine to help him work long hours at his job as a cook. (Omaha World Herald 1997)

The question persists, what has been the role of men in the lives of children of meth users? Where are media reports of "meth dads" who shirk child support payments, who are inconsistent or altogether absent fathers and leave women to raise families on their own? Yet, in detailing accounts of fatal abuse or neglect cases, little discussion of father's culpability is found. Furthermore, when women fail, not only do they face potent ridicule, they are often deemed incapable of ever being a mother, as the passage below describes:

> It is undeniable that Theresa Hernandez has no business being a mother. The 31-year-old Oklahoma City woman has had five children, all of whom were removed from her custody because of criminal activity and drug use. (Tulsa World 2007)

The assertion that Theresa Hernandez "has no business being a mother" is a powerful one. Statements about her age, number of children, and drug use detail what crimes she has committed against middle-class values. This discussion is quite reminiscent of the cultural calamity surrounding Nadya Suleman, better known as "Octomom". Suleman a single woman was placed at the center of a national spectacle after giving birth to octuplets outside of marriage is equally contemptible for violation of middle-class notions of motherhood and family. Thus, as with welfare queens and crack babies, the media suggest that the meth mom is a cause rather than a correlate of the decline of

Midwestern family life. This theme is punctuated by former drug czar, Barry McCaffery, who asserts that meth "one of few things powerful enough to shatter a mother's love for her child" (Goldberg 1997). Although, the deleterious effects of meth are undeniable, the discussion of meth use and child abuse invariably focuses on the failures of women as mothers. Recalling Cohen (2002), we understand the how vile a creature the meth mom is, because she victimizes the most vulnerable among us all.

Redeeming Good Victims

The final broad category is the outcome of the cases. These themes are most similar between men and women, however, some differences warrant discussion. First, several of the articles discuss the aftermath of a meth lab that exploded, resulting in fire, injuries, and often death. The sample indicates that men are almost exclusively involved in these sorts of situations. This finding is reflective of the type of positions men seem to occupy in the meth trade, such as obtaining chemicals or running labs. It also again indicates that male behavior is perhaps more explosive, and volatile, compared to women's banal, if not pitiful behaviors. More curious though, is the consistent theme of women who seek and obtain some sort of redemption through drug treatment. While prevalent in descriptions of female users, not one account of a man attempting to overcome meth via treatment appears in the sample. The lack of male "success stories" perhaps indicates that women are considered redeemable victims, while men may be too far gone for salvation. This is another interesting dichotomy, illustrating competing constructions of male and female culpability. First, men are typically not portrayed as victims of the drug or the social circumstances that lead many to drug use. The data tell us that men have made a decision to manufacture meth and are deserving of the consequences, whether death or jail. Meanwhile, the articles tell stories of women attempting to recover their lives for themselves and often their children. And although they carry the stigma of meth they also carry elements of a good victim, in that they offer a promise of return to a drug free lifestyle. Often efforts at treatment correspond with the children and family that they have failed as a part of their involvement with meth. As one mother describes:

> I've got two babies in DHS ... I've got a lot to change for. (Sherman 2006)

This statement once again connects women's failures as mothers, and the hope for redemption, to meth use. Other accounts discuss women's efforts to regain the trust of the community once becoming involved with the drug:

> [W]hat we showed the world today is she is going to earn her right back into the community, and she's going to do so quickly, and she's going to do so in a way that says to women all around the world that it's not a crime to stop using drugs. (Evans 2007)
> When her 6-year old son asks her why, she said, she has to explain her addiction. She said the drug she now calls the devil takes your morals and values ... and you don't realize its happening. (Nygren 2006)

These passages describe how women must rationalize their bouts with meth to themselves and their children, and in many cases fault themselves for lack of "morals and values". Further, once confronted by authorities, it appears that these drug using women and mothers must take special efforts to "earn her right back into the community" (Evans 2007). However, I did not encounter a similar assertion regarding men in the sample. It is unclear why these media accounts only portray women users as hopeful for reform. I suspect that this makes good news because the idea of redeemed female abusers suggests that some of the harm constructed around drug use can also be repaired, signaling hope for traditional middle-class, Midwestern values. However, it must be noted that here and elsewhere in the accounts, the media do not encourage neighborhoods, communities, states or the Nation to accept some responsibility for conditions promoting drug use. In the typical American individualistic tradition, the stories document individual pathologies, permitting collective repulsion and social exclusion.

Conclusion

This study is an exploration of popular constructions methamphetamine in the Midwest. The data provide a glimpse of differences in constructions of masculine and feminine criminality and illustrate the unique ways female meth users are demonized, othered, and excluded. The data report that women begin using meth to keep up with children, manage households and their weight. Similar to Miller's (1998) and Maher's (2000) ethnographies, the media insist that women occupy the lowest rung in the meth crime hierarchy, and are often the dupes of men driven by the sensual allure of crime. Meth Moms as folk devils are confronted for their failures as mothers, while men are forgiven of parental obligations. At last, when their stories reach conclusion, men are shuffled off to prison, while some women remain hopeful for redemption. These highly gendered dichotomies represent concentration of disparate relations pervasive to social life. It also shows the media's place in the construction of unique objects of exclusion and inclusion (Greer and Jewkes 2005). Further when juxtaposed against the late-eighties crack panic the racialized construction of meth becomes quite apparent. Meth brings the depravity of urban drug panics to new spaces. As Webster (2008) argues, these mechanisms distinguish between different forms of whiteness, sift through markers and meaning, and identify those acceptable and those not. Meth provides small town authorities and rural claims-makers their own social problem to wage war against and to further legitimize their control efforts. Meth as the crisis of the present illustrates the contours of a drug panic not built upon the tidy stereotypes associated with minority populations and the threat of urban violence. It also illustrates lines of power and the reach of punitive ideologies that make mass incarceration a reality. Understanding this, it is important for scholars to produce and publicize reliable information regarding the nature and extent of methamphetamine use rather than gendered hyperbole (Barak 1988).

As Jenkins (1994) showed fifteen years ago, the fears surrounding methamphetamine are not new. In the end then, the current panic is not a recycling of an old format but its latest stage. It represents the next turn in exclusionary processes separating the social wheat from the chaff. As others show, moral panics and control campaigns manifest in every nook of social life, from the prisonization of public schools (Hirschfield 2008) to the criminalization of "everything" in public space (Ferrell 2002). In this instance control expands beyond the ghetto to new territories and victims, with the ever-present warning—do not stand out, do not transgress; else suffer the fate of those who have gone before.

Acknowledgments   The author would like to thank Don Kurtz, Laura Logan, L. Susan Williams, Dana Britton, Donna Selman, David Kauzlarich, Spencer Wood, the editorial staff and anonymous reviewers for their thoughtful comments on earlier drafts of the manuscript

References

Altheide, D. (1996). *Qualitative media analysis*. New York: Sage.

Barak, G. (1988). Newsmaking criminology: Reflections on the media, intellectuals, and crime. *Justice Quarterly*, 5(4), 565–587.

Bennett, W., Diilulio, J., & Waters, J. (1996). *Body count: Moral poverty and how to win America's war against crime and drugs*. New York: Simon and Schuster.

Bonilla-Silva, B. (2003). *Racism without racists: Color-blind racism and the persistence of racial inequality in the United States*. Oxford, UK: Rowman and Littlefield.

Boyd, S. (2004). *From witches to crack moms: Women, drug law, and policy*. North Carolina: Carolina Academic Press.

Bryant, T. (1999). Women drug dealers gaining prominence. *St. Louis Post-Dispatch*, p. 1b.

Cobbina, J. (2008). Race and class differences in print media portrayals of crack cocaine and methamphetamine. *Journal of Criminal Justice and Popular Culture, 15*(2), 145–167.

Cohen, S. (2002). *Folk devils and moral panics* (3rd ed.). New York, London: Routledge.

Collison, M. (1996). In search of the high life: Drugs, crime, masculinities and consumption. *British Journal of Criminology, 36*, 428–444.

Cuniberti, B. (2003). A recovering addict tells parents, "don't be fooled". *St. Louis Post-Dispatch*, p. E1. Daniels, C. (1997). Between fathers and fetuses: The social construction of male reproduction and the politics of fetal harm. *Signs, 22*, 579–616.

Eiserer, T. (1999). 'I'm sorry for what i'm doing to my kid' mom, daughter shared drug life. *Omaha World Herald*, p. 1.

Evans, M. (2007). *Woman gets 15 years in stillborn case involving meth*. Oklahoma City: The Associated Press & Local Wire.

Feeley, M., & Simon, J. (2007). Folk devils and moral panics: An appreciation from North America. In D. Downes, P. Rock, C. Chinkin, & C. Gearty (Eds.), *Crime, social control and human rights: From moral panics to states of denial, essays in honour of Stanley Cohen* (pp. 39–53). Portland, Orgegon: Willian.

Ferrell, J. (2002). *Tearing down the streets: Adventures in urban anarchy*. New York: Palgrave Macmillan.

Ferrell, J., Hayward, K., & Young, J. (2008). *Cultural criminology and invitation*. Los Angeles: Sage.

Garland, D. (2001). *The culture of control: Crime and social order in contemporary society*. Chicago: The University of Chicago Press.

Garland, D. (2008). On the concept of moral panic. *Crime, Media, Culture, 4*(1), 9–30.

Gelsthorpe, L. (2005). Folk devils and moral panics: A feminist perspective. *Crime, Media, Culture, 1*(1), 112–116.

Goldberg, C. (1997). Ideas and trends; way out west and under the influence. *The New York Times*. Sect. 4, p. 16, Column 1.

Greer, C., Ferrell, J., & Jewkes, Y. (2008). Investigating the crisis of the present. *Crime, Media, Culture, 4*(1), 5–8.

Greer, C., & Jewkes, Y. (2005). Extremes of otherness: Media images of social exclusion. *Social Justice, 32*(1), 20–31.

Hill-Collins, P. (1995). Symposium: On West and Fenstermaker's doing difference. *Gender and Society, 9*(4), 491–506.

Hirschfield, P. (2008). Preparing for prison? The criminalization of school discipline in the USA. *Theoretical Criminology, 12*(1), 79–101.

Hrenchir, T. (2000). Meth gets you high, but fall can be deadly. *Topeka Capital Journal*, p. 3.

Jefferson, D. (2007). Meth: America's most dangerous drug. *Newsweek*, 1–4.

Jenkins, P. (1994). The ice age: The social construction of a drug panic. *Justice Quarterly, 11*(1), 7–31.

Jewkes, Y. (2006). *Media & crime*. London: Sage.

King, R. (2006). *The next big thing? Methamphetamine in the United States*. Washington DC: The Sentencing Project.

Maher, L. (2000). *Sexed work: Gender, race, and resistance in a Brooklyn drug market*. New York: Clarendon.

McRobbie, A., & Thornton, S. (1995). Rethinking 'moral panic' for multi-mediated social worlds. *The British Journal of Sociology, 46*(4), 559–574.

Miller, J. (1998). Up it up: Gender and the accomplishment of street robbery. *Criminology, 36*(1), 37–66.

Miller, J. (2002). The strengths and limits of 'doing gender' for understanding street crime. *Theoretical Criminology, 6*, 433–460.

Mom Accused of Giving Kids Drugs. (1997). *Omaha World Herald*, p. 18.

Montana Meth Project. (2009). http://www.montanameth.org/.

Munz, M. (1999). Meth lab had bombs and guns, police say; couple are arrested at lodge near Cuba, Mo. *St. Louis Post Dispatch*. p. 2.

Munz, M. (2000). Law & order. *St. Louis Post-Dispatch*, p. 13.

Nygren, J. (2006). Ex-teacher, sentenced for meth, vows to do good. *Omaha World Herald*. p. 01b.

ONDCP. (2009). http://www.whitehousedrugpolicy.gov/HIDTA/.

Police Say Woman Gave Meth to Son. (1997). *Omaha World Herald*, p. 18.

Range, S. (2000). 'Woman's wonder drug' Meth entraps more people with its allure of unlimited energy, alertness what meth is and what it does. *Omaha World Herald*, p. 1a.

Reinarman, C., & Levine, H. (1997). *Crack in America: Demon drugs and social justice*. Berkeley, CA: University of California Press.

Reinarman, C., & Levine, H. (2004). Crack in the rearview mirror: Deconstructing drug war mythology, pp. 182–199. *Social Justice, 31*(1), 1–2.

Schumer, C. (2004). http://schumer.senate.gov/new_website/record.cfm?id=265406.

Sherman, B. (2006). Healing waters. *Tulsa World*, p. A1.

Shocking Case. (2007). Opinion. *Tulsa World*, p. A20.

Simon, J. (2007). *Governing through crime: How the war on crime transformed American democracy and created a culture of fear*. New York: Oxford University Press.

Spencer, K. (2000). Butler county arrests two in meth case. *Omaha World Herald*, p. 12.

Strawbridge, P. (1999). Woman, 22, guilty of drug charge. *Omaha World Herald*, p. 12.

Toscano, V. (2005). Misguided retribution: Criminalization of pregnant women who take drugs. *Social & Legal Studies, 14*(3), 359–386.

Wacquant, L. (2001). Deadly symbiosis: When Ghetto and prison meet and mesh. *Punishment Society, 3*, 95–133.

Wacquant, L. (2009). *Punishing the poor: The neoliberal government of social insecurity*. North Carolina: Duke University Press.

Waltman, S. (2007a). Jury convicts Wakpala woman of drug charge. *Aberdeen American News*. State and Regional News.

Waltman, S. (2007b). Drug shipment trial begins in Aberdeen. *Aberdeen American News*. State and Regional News.

Webster, C. (2008). Marginalized white ethnicity, race, and crime. *Theoretical Criminology, 12*(3), 293–312.

Weich, S. (2003). Law & order. *St. Louis Post-Dispatch*, p. 02.

Weich, S. (2005). Law & order. *St. Louis Post-Dispatch*, p. 02.

West, C., & Fenstermaker, S. (1995). Doing difference. *Gender & Society, 9*(1) 1, 8–37.

Winter, D. (1997). Meth the hook into a life of crime. *Bismark Tribune*, p. 01a.

Young, J. (1971). *The drugtakers*. London: Paladin.

Young, J. (2007). *The vertigo of late modernity*. New York: Sage.

THE INFLUENCE OF RAP/HIP-HOP MUSIC

A Mixed-Method Analysis on Audience Perceptions of Misogynistic Lyrics and the Issue of Domestic Violence

by Gretchen Cundiff

Strategic Communications Elon University

I. Introduction

This study examined the culture of rap/hip-hop music and how misogynistic lyrical messages influenced listeners' attitudes toward intimate partner violence. Adams and Fuller (2006) define misogyny as the "hatred or disdain of women" and "an ideology that reduces women to objects for men's ownership, use, or abuse" (p. 939). Popular American hip-hop and rap artists, such as Eminem, Ludacris and Ja Rule, have increasingly depicted women as objects of violence or male domination by communicating that "submission is a desirable trait in a woman" (Stankiewicz & Rosselli, 2008, p. 581). These songs condone male hegemony in which "men find the domination and exploitation of women and other men to be not only expected, but actually demanded" (Prushank, 2007, p. 161). Thus, these messages glorify violence against women, including rape, torture and abuse, and foster an acceptance of sexual objectification and degradation of women (Russo & Pirlott, 2006). These misogynistic themes first emerged in rap/hip-hop songs in the late 1980s and are especially apparent today with women being portrayed as sex objects and victims of sexual violence (Adams & Fuller, 2006; Russo & Pirlott, 2006).

Young adults between the ages of 16 and 30 are the most likely age group to consume rap/hip-hop music, and in turn, may become desensitized to the derogatory lyrics condoning relationship violence and sexual aggression (Smith, 2005). Specifically, the college-aged demographic has been influenced by the prevalence of sexually explicit media and the negative images of women presented in hip-hop culture, which "teach men that aggression and violence are closely linked to cultural views of masculinity" (Wood, 2012, p. 105). Furthermore, the physical abuse of women is celebrated in rap/hip-hop songs promoting "models of masculinity that sustain and encourage misogyny" (Cobb & Boettcher, 2007, p. 3026).

This paper evaluated the impact of cultivation theory and whether exposure to misogynistic rap increases the acceptance of perpetrating violent acts against women (Johnson, Jackson, & Gatto, 1995). Also, this paper incorporated the disinhibition hypothesis in relation to how audiences become desensitized to media violence after repeated exposure (Rosenberry & Vicker, 2009). Analyzing the relationship between rap/ hip-hop lyrical content and song popularity showed how audiences have responded to objectifying messages through their music consumption.

II. Literature Review

Issue of Domestic Violence

Domestic violence is a pressing issue often deemed acceptable by the media, and thus, challenges men and women's perceptions of how they should treat their partners in their relationships. Over the past two decades, the United Nations Commission on the Status of Women "reported a tremendous increase in the representation of violence against women, particularly sexual violence, in the media" (Stankiewicz & Rosselli, 2008, p. 581). Studies suggest that increased exposure to misogynistic messages has desensitized audiences to the issue of intimate partner violence and fosters greater tolerance of male aggression (Barongan & Hall, 1996). The mass media portrays domestic violence both visually and aurally by normalizing the use of force in relationships, which correlates to the fact that "more than one in three women in the United States have been sexually coerced by a partner" (Nettleton, 2011, p. 140). Therefore, it is not surprising that "men commit at least 90% of documented acts of physical intimate partner violence in the U.S." by exerting control over women (Wood, 2012, p. 301).

The ambiguity of what constitutes sexual assault or intimate partner violence contributes to public misperception of domestic violence. The Office of Violence Against Women defines domestic violence as a "pattern of abusive behavior in any relationship that is used by one partner to gain or maintain power and control over another intimate partner" ("What Is Domestic Violence?," 2012). Physical, sexual and psychological actions or threats of abuse toward a partner are the most common forms of domestic violence ("What Is Domestic Violence?," 2012). Domestic violence includes behaviors that "intimidate, manipulate, humiliate, isolate, frighten, terrorize, coerce, threaten, blame, hurt, injure, or wound someone" ("What Is Domestic Violence?" 2012). The National Violence Against Women Survey, conducted by Tjaden and Thoennes (2000), estimates that one in five women in the United States is physically assaulted in her lifetime and one in 13 is raped by an intimate partner (Russo & Pirlott, 2006).

While women of all ages are at risk of experiencing domestic and sexual violence, those between the ages of 20-24 are most susceptible to experiencing nonfatal intimate partner violence ("Get the Facts: The Facts," 2007). According to a 2007 study by Laurel Crown and Linda Roberts, "one-half of college women in their senior year reported one or more unwanted sexual interactions during their college careers" (Wood, 2012, p. 287). The perpetration of violent behavior can be explained using the cognitive learning theory, asserting, "individuals receive messages through society and media that shape relationship ideologies" (Bretthauer, Zimmerman, & Banning, 2006, p. 30). This study specifically analyzed college students' views on the issue of domestic violence and its portrayal in popular rap/ hip-hop music.

Misogyny in Rap/Hip-Hop Music

In a recent content analysis of six types of media, Pardun, L'Engle, and Brown (2005) found that music, in particular, contained substantially more sexual content than any other media outlets. Sexually explicit and derogatory lyrics are especially apparent in rap music, which has been criticized for its graphic derogatory presentation of women using lyrics that objectify, exploit or victimize them (Weitzer & Kubrin, 2009; Cobb & Boettcher, 2007). Adams and Fuller (2006) assert that rap music reduces women to objects "that are only good for sex and abuse," which "perpetuate ideas, values, beliefs, and stereotypes that debase women" (p. 940). This study also noted six themes common in misogynistic rap music, and further examined three of them: derogatory statements about women in relation to sex; statements involving violent actions toward women, particularly in relation to sex; and references of women as usable and discardable beings (Adams & Fuller, 2006).

Armstrong (2001) conducted a content analysis of 490 rap songs from 1987 to 1993, in which 22% contained lyrics featuring violence against women including assault, rape and murder. His study classified rap songs into different categories in which rappers either pride themselves on sex acts appearing to harm women, justify other acts of violence, warn women who challenge male domination that they will be assaulted, and/or seem to invite male violence against women (Armstrong, 2001). Weitzer and Kubrin (2009) conducted a follow-up study analyzing the portrayal of women in 403 rap songs through a content analysis, in which themes of derogatory naming and shaming of women; sexual objectification of women; distrust of women; legitimation of violence against women; and celebration of prostitution and pimping appeared at the greatest frequency. Sexual objectification was found to occur in 67% of the misogynistic lyrics in their songs sampled (Weitzer & Kubrin, 2009). This study further examined the frequency of explicit music content found in the past decade's worth of popular rap/hip-hop music. Furthermore, stereotyped gender roles emerged from lyrics containing sexual imagery that promote the "acceptance of women as sexual objects and men as pursuers of sexual conquest," (Martino, Collins, Elliott, Strachman, Kanouse, & Berry, 2006, p. 438).

Influence on Audience Perceptions

George Gerbner focused on violent television content and how audience exposure to these violent images influences their views and conception of social reality, by cultivating a "common view of the world" (Rosenberry & Vicker, 2009, pg. 165). As a result, Gerbner developed cultivation theory by examining how long-term exposure to violent media messages alters audience perceptions of violence in their everyday lives (Rosenberry & Vicker, 2009). This approach can be applied to all forms of media by interpreting individuals' reactions to violent content; thus, this study will incorporate cultivation theory in an analysis of misogynistic lyrics affecting listeners' attitudes toward domestic violence (Rosenberry & Vicker, 2009).

In reviewing more than five decades worth of research, Potter (1999) extended cultivation theory to determine the following effects of exposure to media violence:

> Exposure to violent portrayals in the media can lead to subsequent viewer aggression through disinhibition. Long-term exposure to media violence is related to aggression in a person's life. Media violence is related to subsequent violence in society. Exposure to violence in the media can lead to desensitization. People exposed to many violent portrayals over time will come to be more accepting of violence. (Rosenberry & Vicker, 2009, p. 169)

In turn, Dr. Edgar Tyson (2006) developed a 26-item instrument, the Rap Music Attitude and Perception (RAP) Scale, the "only tool available to access an individual's attitude toward and perception of rap music lyrics" (p. 212). The RAP Scale contains three constructs: empowerment, artistic aesthetics and violent misogynistic. This study incorporated the empowerment and violent misogynistic constructs to measure "violent, sexist, and misogynistic images conveyed in the lyrics" to examine college students' perceptions of the content through a survey (Gourdine & Lemmons, 2011, p. 65). Using a meta-analysis approach, Timmerman et. al (2008) found that "listening to music generates an effect on listeners consistent with the content of the music," such as when rap/hip-hop artists communicate themes condoning "power over, objectification of and violence against women" (p. 303; Bretthauer et al., 2006, p. 42). This 2008 study applied the term "priming" to determine "whether music serves as a mechanism to 'prime' someone for subsequent actions and behaviors," and in turn, react to, incorporate or reject the media content into the listener's life (Timmerman et. al., 2008, p. 307). While a correlation may exist between exposure to misogynistic music and audience attitudes regarding violent acts against women, a causal link cannot be demonstrated between listening habits and resulting misogynistic behavior (Baran & Davis, 2006, p. 331). Therefore, the consumption of misogynistic music can influence audience perceptions of misogynistic content, but does not directly lead to "subsequent aggressive actions" (Timmerman et. al., 2008, p. 307).

This study expanded upon previous research incorporating the RAP Scale, priming and cultivation theory to determine how college students' perspectives on issues of domestic violence reflect misogynistic themes emphasized in explicit rap/hip-hop music.

Research Questions

This study explored whether consuming rap/hip-hop music containing misogynistic messages affects the attitudes of audiences regarding domestic violence.

RQ. 1: How do college students perceive and respond to the portrayal of women when exposed to misogynistic lyrics?

RQ. 2: Does gender impact how college students interpret misogynistic messages found within popular rap/hip-hop songs?

III. Method

This study used cultivation theory to examine the media effects of misogynistic rap and hip-hop music on shaping audience attitudes toward intimate partner violence. By incorporating a qualitative content analysis and an online survey, this study analyzed the lyrical content of popular rap and hip-hop songs found on Billboard's "Hot 100" chart over the past decade. The sample of 20 songs was drawn from Billboard's Year-End "Hot 100" singles list, which includes the most popular music from various music genres. These were chosen due to the specific violent or objectifying terminology found within the lyrics of top-ranked rap and hip-hop songs during this study's qualitative content analysis. The Billboard "Hot 100," issued weekly by Billboard magazine, is the music industry's standard for measuring song popularity in the United States based on radio airplay, online streaming activity, physical CD sales and digital downloads ("Billboard Hot 100"). Nielsen Soundscan compiles the "Hot 100" chart rankings based on weekly audience impressions starting the first week in December each year ("Billboard Hot 100"). Year-end chart totals are calculated in the final week of November to determine the top 100 songs per year for all music genres combined ("Billboard Hot 100").

Cultivation Theory

The meanings underlying the songs' lyrical messages were analyzed through the lens of cultivation theory, which proposes "when people are exposed to media content or other socialization agents, they gradually come to cultivate or adopt beliefs about the world that coincide with the images they have been viewing or messages they have been hearing" (Gerbner, Gross, Morgan, & Signorielli, 1994, p. 22). Cultivation theory further asserts that the more audiences are exposed to factors such as sexual aggression, submission or violence in intimate relationships, the more they accept the objectification of women over time (Gerbner, et. al, 1994). This study specifically examined gendered audiences' interpretation of misogynistic messages in popular rap/hip-hop songs to see if there were group differences in the effects of media content (Martino, et. al, 2006).

Qualitative Content Analysis

Content analysis is described as "a research technique for objective, systematic and quantitative description of the manifest content of communication" to investigate messages and reduce them into categories (Rosenberry & Vicker, 2009, pg. 42). According to Zhang & Wildemuth (2009), qualitative content analysis "pays attention to unique themes that illustrate the range of meanings of the phenomenon rather than the statistical significance of the occurrence of particular text or concepts" (p. 309). Using a qualitative content analysis guided by cultivation theory, this study examined the presence or absence of violent misogynistic lyrics found in 20 popular rap and hip-hop songs between 2000 and 2010. The song lyrics were obtained from various Internet sources (e.g., azlyrics.com) and coded line by line. Songs were classified into one or more of the following coding categories based on images and messages conveyed in lyrics: demeaning language, rape/ sexual assault, sexual conquest and/ or physical violence. Songs were also labeled according to their level of misogynistic content, based on the number of categories into which the lyrics were coded: high, medium or low levels of misogyny. The coding categories--derogatory naming and shaming of women; sexual objectification of women; and legitimation of violence against women—were adopted from Weitzer and Kubrin's (2009) content analysis study and incorporated into this present study.

Description of coding categories

- Songs referencing acts of physical violence toward women were coded as such if they contained words including: slap, punch, push, beat, hit, bleeding, pain, throw, pin, tie, whippings, murder, etc.
- Songs insinuating rape or sexual assault were coded as such if they contained words/phrases including: fuck, rape, assault, cut up, bust open, etc.
- Songs labeling women in derogatory ways were coded as such for using demeaning language containing the following words: pussy, bitch, pimp, nigga, etc.
- Songs portraying sexual conquest were coded as such if they contained phrases including: love em/ leave em, feel the pain, don't have to fight back, etc.

Frequency/emphasis of misogynistic lyrics

- Songs were first coded for their misogynistic terminology and then evaluated for their amount of misogynistic content and labeled accordingly.
  - One to two misogynistic lyrical references = low level of misogyny
  - Three to four misogynistic lyrical references = medium level of misogyny
  - Five or more misogynistic lyrical references = high level of misogyny

Survey

In conjunction with performing a content analysis, this study administered a survey using Survey Monkey to gauge college students' perceptions of the portrayal of intimate partner violence in the songs examined below. Surveys involve a correlational method by which researchers measure two or more variables and examine relationships between them (Rosenberry & Vicker, 2009). This 12-question survey was disseminated to a convenience, nonprobability sample of 62 Elon University students, 52 women and 10 men, representing sophomores through seniors. These students were asked via email or social media to click a link to a Survey Monkey questionnaire page. The first six questions asked respondents general questions about their viewson rap/hip-hop music and interpretation of musical content. This involved a series of multiple-choice questions evaluating audience listening behavior; the emphasis on lyrics versus melody in this genre; the presence of offensive or degrading lyrical content; and the perception of rap/hip-hop artists overall. The remaining questions, dealing with misogynistic themes apparent in popular rap/hip-hop songs, were prefaced with a disclaimer: for purposes of this study, lyrics are considered misogynistic if they support, glorify, justify, or normalize the objectification, exploitation, or victimization of women. This included an adapted version of the definition of misogyny, as the "promotion, glamorization, support, humorization, justification, or normalization of oppressive ideas about women" to ensure that respondents were familiar with the term (Adams & Fuller, 2006, p. 940). Respondents were presented with multiple choice and Likert scale questions examining offensiveness in misogynistic lyrics; the prevalence of misogynistic lyrics in a sample of rap/hip-hop songs; and attitudes toward the issue of domestic violence.

These questions examined specifically how the college-aged demographic was influenced by the prevalence of derogatory lyrics condoning violent sexual behavior. Students were asked to respond to a list of statements inquiring about their listening habits; opinions on rap and hip-hop songs; knowledge of domestic violence issues; exposure to misogynistic lyrics; and attitudes on sexism. Five of these categories were adapted from Tyson's 2006 RAP scale, measuring interpretations of gender using empowerment and violent misogynistic constructs.

IV. Findings

Part I: Content Analysis

Using a content analysis method, this study analyzed the lyrics of 20 rap/hip-hop songs included in Billboard's Year-End "Hot 100" singles list ranging from 2000-2010. The sample set of music was selected based on the misogynistic themes appearing within the lyrics of these popular hits, all of which were labeled as explicit.

Table 1. Billboard "Hot 100" Singles Year-End (2001–2010)

Song	Artist	Genre	Year	Rank
The Real Slim Shady	Eminem	Hip hop	2000	51
Big Pimpin'	Jay-Z and UGK	East coast hip hop	2000	60
Shake Ya Ass	Mystikal	Hip hop	2000	68
The Next Episode	Dr. Dre and Snoop Dogg	West coast hip hop	2000	76
Danger (Been So Long)	Mystikal and Nivea	Hip hop	2001	58
Livin' It Up	Ja Rule and Case	Hip hop	2001/2002	79/76
Southern Hospitality	Ludacris	Southern rap	2001	77
Lights, Camera, Action	Mr. Cheeks	Hip hop	2002	49
Move Bitch	Ludacris, Mystikal and I-20	Southern hip hop	2002	55
Superman	Eminem	Alternative hip hop	2003	98
Splash Waterfalls	Ludacris	Dirty rap	2004	42
Lovers & Friends	Lil Jon, Usher & Ludacris	Dirty hip hop	2005	25
Some Cut	Trillville & Cutty	Hip hop	2005	49
Lean Wit It, Rock Wit It	Dem Franchize Boyz	Southern hip hop	2006	25
Touch It	Busta Rhymes	East Coast hip hop	2006	73
When I'm Gone	Eminem	Conscious hip hop	2006	90
Crack a Bottle	Eminem, Dr. Dre and 50 Cent	Hardcore hip hop	2009	47
Every Girl	Young Money	Hip hop/dirty rap	2009	67
Love the Way You Lie	Eminem and Rihanna	Hip hop	2010	7
Bottoms Up	Trey Songz	Hip hop/R&B	2010	52

Coding Outcome. As shown in *Figure* 1, eight of the songs (40%) sampled were coded strictly for physical violence; none of the songs were coded for strictly rape/sexual assault; two songs (10%) were coded strictly for sexual conquest; and two songs (10%) were coded strictly for demeaning language. Eight of the songs (40%) contained lyrics coded into more than one category of misogynistic content. Three songs (15%) were coded for the demeaning language and rape/ sexual assault categories. Two songs (10%) were coded for the rape/sexual assault, sexual conquest and demeaning language categories. One song was coded for the physical violence, rape/sexual assault and sexual conquest categories. In addition, one song was coded for the demeaning language and sexual conquest categories, along with one song coded for the rape/ sexual assault and physical violence categories.

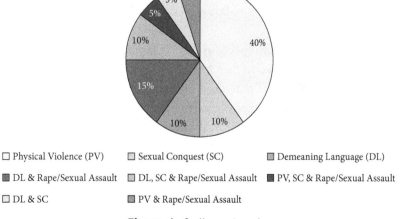

Figure 1. Coding categories

As shown in *Figure* 2, Half of the songs sampled (n = 10) were coded for low levels of misogyny; eight songs (40%) for medium levels of misogyny; and two of the songs (10%) for high levels of misogyny. There were a total of 55 misogynistic references in all the individual song's misogynistic lyrical content.

Five songs by rapper Eminem were included in the coding sample, which represents one-fourth of all songs sampled. Three songs by rap/hip-hop artist Ludacris were included in the coding sample, representing 15% of all songs sampled. Rapper Mystikal was included in the sample for three of his songs, 15% of the study sampling. All of the songs by Eminem and Ludacris featured in the sample included lyrics depicting physical violence against women.

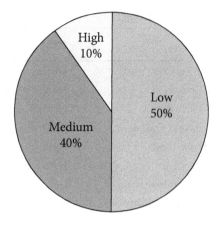

Figure 2. Levels of Misogyny

Three of the songs (15%) fell into the rap genre, with the rest classified as hip-hop music. Eminem was the only Caucasian artist featured in the song sampling, and African American artists performed the remaining 15 sampled songs (75%). Solo artists performed half (n = 10) of the songs in the sample. Two (10%) of the songs sampled included a male/female artist combination, "Danger (Been So Long)" by Mystikal and Nivea and "Love the Way You Lie" by Eminem and Rihanna.

Songs containing misogynistic lyrics appeared in the sample with the greatest frequency during the first half of the decade (2000-2005). Songs featured on the Billboard "Hot 100" chart between 2000 and 2001 (n = 7) contained the greatest concentration of misogynistic lyrics over a two-year period. Four out of seven songs (57.1%) during this timeframe contained two or more references to misogyny in their lyrics. Additionally, all of the songs sampled from 2006, which accounted for 15% of the total sample frame, featured lyrics suggesting physical violence against women. *(For more detail, refer to Appendix 1 to view the coding sheet used in this study.)*

Songs referencing acts of physical violence toward women. The artists whose songs contained lyrics strictly coded under the physical violence category included Eminem; Ludacris, Mystikal and I-20; Dem Franchize Boyz; Busta Rhymes; and Rihanna. There were 17 references to physical violence within this song sample, which are denoted with dotted lines, and the song containing the most references was Eminem and Rihanna's "Love the Way You Lie" (n = 4).

The following are lyrics from Eminem's songs included in the sample that glorify physical violence toward women and included between one to four misogynistic references:

- "The Real Slim Shady"- *Jaws all on the floor, like Pam, like Tommy just burst in the door and started <u>whoopin her ass</u> worse then before.*
- "Superman"- *Don't put out, I'll put you out, won't get out, I'll <u>push you out</u>. There goes another lawsuit, <u>leave handprints all across you</u>. Put anthrax on a tampax, and <u>slap you till you can't stand</u>.*
- "When I'm Gone"- *What happens when you become the <u>main source of her pain</u>? And <u>put hands on her mother</u>, who's a spitting image of her. Daddy it's me, help Mommy, her <u>wrists are bleeding</u>.*
- "Love the Way You Lie"- *Just gonna stand there and watch me burn, But that's alright because I like the way it hurts, Just gonna stand there and hear me cry, You push, pull each other's hair, scratch, claw, hit 'em. Throw 'em down, pin 'em. Im'a tie her to the bed and <u>set this house on fire</u>."*

The following lyrics from individual/group artists also contain one or more references in relation to men's perpetrating violent physical acts toward women:

- Ludacris' "Southern Hospitality"- *Lie through your teeth you could find your mouth, cold and <u>rip out ya tongue</u> cause of what ya mouth, told.*
- Ludacris, Mystikal and I-20's "Move Bitch"- *"I'ma 'bout to <u>punch yo … lights out</u>"*
- Dem Franchize Boyz's "Lean Wit It, Rock Wit It"- *Rock so damn hard, u <u>break your spleen wit it</u>, Perfect example watch me <u>make your face beat up my hands</u>.*
- Busta Rhyme's "Touch It"- <u>*I'ma hit you and your ma. and ima hit you*</u> *where you stand.*

Songs labeling women in derogatory ways using demeaning language. The artists whose songs contained lyrics strictly coded under the demeaning language category were Young Money and Trey Songz. There were five total references in the songs' lyrics labeling women in derogatory ways.

- Young Money's "Every Girl" - *Open up her legs then filet mignon that **pussy**, I'm a get in and on that pussy, If she let me in I'm a own that **pussy**.*
- Trey Songz's "Bottoms Up"- *If a **bitch** try to get cute ima stomp her. Throw alotta money at her then yell **fuck** her.*

Songs portraying sexual conquest. The artists whose songs contained lyrics strictly coded under the sexual conquest category were Ja Rule and Case, and Ludacris. There were two total references in the songs' lyrics that represented men using women only for their sexual value.

- Ja Rule and Case's "Livin It Up"- *I got a stick, I'll ride right next to you. Do a doughnut, and cut, and <u>I'll open it up</u>.*
- Ludacris' "Splash Waterfalls"- *You better not of came, <u>she want to feel the pain</u>.*

Songs coded for two or more categories. The artists whose songs contained lyrics coded for the demeaning language and rape/sexual assault categories included Dr. Dre and Snoop Dogg; Mystikal and Nivea; and Trillville & Cutty. The underlined words were coded under the rape/sexual assault categories, and bolded words were coded under the demeaning language category. There were 10 total instances of referring to women in misogynistic ways in the combined categories above, and the song containing the most references was Mystikal and Nivea's "Danger (Been So Long)" (n = 5).

- Dr. Dre and Snoop Dogg's "The Next Episode"- *And if yo' <u>ass get cracked</u>, **bitch** shut yo' trap.*
- Mystikal and Nivea's "Danger (Been So Long)"- *Leave that **pussy** smoking. If you gonna lose something. Then bend over, <u>and bust that **pussy** open</u>. The **pussy** <u>cutter</u>.*
- Trillville and Cutty's "Some Cut"- *Can a **nigga** get in them guts (them guts)? <u>Cut you up like you ain't been cut (been cut). While I'm beatin and tearin down your walls</u> (oh yeah). It's no limits to what we do, cause tonight we cutting, gut busting. I'm digging in your walls something vicious.*

The artists whose songs contained lyrics coded for the rape/sexual assault, sexual conquest and demeaning language categories were Jay-Z and UGK, and Mystikal. The underlined words were coded under the rape/sexual assault category, bolded words were coded under the demeaning language category and double underlined words were coded under the sexual conquest category. There were 13 total references for the above category, and the song containing the most references was Mystikal's "Shake Ya Ass" (n = 9). This also made it the most misogynistic song overall in the entire coding scheme.

- Jay-Z and UGK's "Big Pimpin'"- *You know I - thug em, **fuck** em, <u>love em, leave em</u>. Cause I don't fuckin need em. <u>In the cut where I keep em til I need a nut,</u> til I need to <u>beat the guts</u>.*
- Mystikal's "Shake Ya Ass"- *Pay ya fare, fix ya hair, throw that **pussy**. <u>I got a job for you</u> - the braided up **pimp** is back. <u>Break them handcuffs, **fuck** you **nigga**</u> move somethin. And I've been <u>beatin that **pussy** up</u> now it's smooth **fuckin**.*

Mr. Cheek's "Lights, Camera, Action" was coded for the demeaning language and sexual conquest categories. The bolded word was coded under the demeaning language category, and the double underlined phrase was coded under the sexual conquest category.

- Booties dancin 'round a **nigga** and I'm killin one. <u>Killin one from the top of the stash</u> and I'm feelin buns.
- Lil Jon, Usher & Ludacris' "Lovers & Friends" was coded into the rape/sexual assault, sexual conquest and physical violence categories. The underlined words were coded under the rape/sexual assault category, double underlined phrases were coded under the sexual conquest category and the dotted-lined phrase was coded under the physical violence category.
- Be a good girl now, turn around, and <u>get these whippings</u>. <u>You know you like it like that</u>, <u>you don't have to fight back</u>, Here's a pillow - bite … that.

Eminem, Dr. Dre and 50 Cent's "Crack a Bottle" was coded into the rape/sexual assault and physical violence categories. The underlined words were coded under the rape/sexual assault category, and the dotted-lined phrase was coded under the physical violence category.

- The moment you've all been waiting for. In this corner: weighing 175 pounds, with a record of <u>17 rapes, 400 assaults</u>, and <u>4 murders</u>, The undisputed, most diabolical villain in the world: Slim Shady.

Part II: Survey

In order to evaluate college students' attitudes toward and perception of misogynistic rap/ hip-hop music, this study conducted a non-probability survey administered via Survey Monkey. Sixty-two Elon University students, 52 women and 10 men, ranging in academic year from sophomores to seniors, responded to the 12-question survey. The survey was designed to gauge how survey respondents perceive and respond to the issue of domestic violence and whether they feel popular rap/hip-hop music has positively or negatively influenced their views. This study specifically examined gendered differences to determine the effect of misogynistic lyrical content on these audiences and their views on the portrayal of women in popular rap/hip-hop songs. The influence of factors including music genre, artist gender and artist race was considered when analyzing relationships between music consumption and gender. *(For more detail, refer to Appendix II to view the survey questions asked in this study.)*

Views on rap/hip-hop music and interpretation of musical content. Six out of ten male respondents rarely listen to rap/hip-hop music in comparison to only 25% of female respondents (n = 13). The majority of female respondents (65.4%) frequently or sometimes listen to rap/hip-hop music. Half of male respondents (n = 5) pay equal amounts of attention to the instrumental aspects and lyrics/messages when listening to rap/hop-hop music, compared to 28.8% of female respondents (n = 15). Over half of female respondents (n = 30) listen to the instrumental aspects of rap/hip-hop music the most. Roughly 20% (n = 11) of female respondents hold positive attitudes toward rap/hip-hop music, while no male respondents held similar views. Sixty percent of male respondents hold negative attitudes toward this music genre, compared to only 23.1% of female respondents (n = 12) with similar views. A majority of both male and female respondents (n = 58) feel rap/hip-hop music is more offensive to women than men.

When evaluating a list of terms this study identified as degrading to women, 71.2% of female respondents (n = 37) considered the word "bitch" degrading compared to all the male respondents (n = 10). Both male and female respondents held similar views by labeling "pussy" and the "N" word as the most degrading terms, 93.5% and 90.3% of the time respectively. Roughly 30% of respondents (n = 20) considered "fuck" and "pimp" as the least degrading words out of the sample. Given a list of 16 popular rap/hip-hop artists, respondents were asked to determine which of the performers they believed perpetrated negative views about women through their songs lyrics. Nearly half of male respondents (n = 4) compared with roughly 70% of female respondents (n = 30) felt Snoop Dogg perpetrates negative attitudes about women in his songs. Three quarters of male respondents (n = 6) indicated that Ja Rule also incorporates misogynistic views in his music compared with 21.4% of female respondents (n = 9). Almost 60% of total respondents (n = 37) consider 50 Cent to be the most misogynistic artist overall.

The prevalence of misogynistic themes in rap/hip-hop music. Both men and women agreed that the legitimation of violence against women is the most offensive aspect of misogynistic lyrics in rap/hip-hop songs, with over half of respondents (n = 34) expressing these views. The sexual objectification of women and the derogatory naming and shaming of women were also considered offensive attributes of misogynistic lyrics. Respondents were then asked to rank the list of 20 songs analyzed in the content analysis portion of this study, based on their misogynistic lyrical content on a scale of 1 (not at all misogynistic) to 5 points (extremely misogynistic). Respondents considered "Every Girl" by Young Money the most misogynistic song, with an average of 4.36 points based on 11 total responses, followed by Ludacris' "Move Bitch," with an average ranking of four based on 34 total responses. Eminem's "When I'm Gone" was considered the least misogynistic song, with an average of 2.22 points based on 18 total responses, followed by his song "The Real Slim Shady," with an average of 2.44 points based on 34 responses. The average number of respondents to rank songs was 9.25, and the average rating for the sample was 3.21 points per song.

Respondents also ranked the degree to which they feel exposure to popular rap/hip-hop songs shape audience attitudes toward the issue of domestic violence on a scale of 1 (not at all) to 5 (significantly). Over half of respondents (n = 35) felt exposure to popular rap/hip-hop songs moderately or significantly shapes audience attitudes toward the issue of domestic violence. In addition, respondents were asked to state their level of agreement/disagreement on a scale of 1 (strongly disagree) to 5 (strongly agree) based on a list of 12 statements involving the depiction of violence toward women in rap/hip-hop music; the portrayal of hip hop culture in society; and the genre's implications on shaping attitudes toward domestic violence in the United States. Responses by men and women were fairly consistent across the board in terms of supplying comparable levels of agreement/disagreement.

The majority of respondents (n = 44) agreed or strongly agreed that rap/hip-hop music encourages disrespectful attitudes toward women, along with a majority of respondents (n = 48) who agreed or strongly agreed that most rap/hip-hop music suggests women are just for male sexual satisfaction. Almost three-quarters of respondents (n = 44) felt rap/hip-hop music does not provide positive messages for its listeners, while 46 respondents stated that rap/hip-hop music does not reflect the realities of intimate partner violence. Over half of respondents (n = 33) felt rap/hip-hop music promotes aggressive and violent behaviors toward women, and exactly half of respondents (n = 31) agreed or strongly agreed that rap/hip-hop music glorifies domestic violence. More than two-thirds of respondents (n = 42) agreed or strongly agreed that explicit rap/hip-hop music is offensive, and a majority of respondents (n = 45) believe that sexism in rap/hip-hop music contributes to sexist behavior. All respondents agreed that misogynistic lyrics are prevalent in rap/hip-hop music to some extent, while almost all respondents (n = 59) consider domestic violence a pressing issue in the United States. Only ten respondents disagreed that rap/hip-hop artists intend to degrade women through their lyrics, while almost half of respondents (n = 29) agreed or strongly agreed that college-aged women are the most susceptible to experiencing gendered violence.

Using crosstabs to analyze relationships. In order to determine subgroup differences regarding how misogynistic rap/hip-hop music affects gendered audiences, this study cross-tabbed listening habits of male and female respondents to other variables. This study interpreted survey results based on the listening habits of respondents and corresponding exposure to misogynistic lyrics in this music. Of those who frequently listen to rap/hip-hop music (n = 14), no respondents claimed to have a negative attitude toward it. This contrasts to those who rarely listen to rap/hip-hop music (n = 19), of which no respondents claimed to have a positive attitude toward this music. Of those who listen to rap/hip-hop music for the lyrical/message aspect of it (n = 8), 37.5% of respondents believe exposure to these songs significantly shapes audiences attitudes toward the issue of domestic violence. In addition, all respondents (n = 8) who listen to rap/hip-hop music for the lyrics agreed or strongly agreed that most rap/hip-hop music suggests women are just for male sexual satisfaction. The study determined the greater the frequency with which audiences listen to rap/hip-hop music, the more they feel exposure shapes audience attitudes regarding domestic violence. The final cross-tab comparing listening habits with views of misogynistic lyrics found all respondents who frequently listen to rap/hip-hop music (n = 14) also agreed or strongly agreed that misogynistic lyrics are prevalent in rap/hop-hop music.

Part III: Comparing Methods

In order to evaluate consistency between the content analysis outcome and survey results, both methods were compared to determine similarities and differences between the content coding results and respondent perceptions of the study's 20-song sample. When analyzing misogynistic lyrical content, half of the songs included in both measures of analysis were considered equally misogynistic. However, there were several discrepancies between survey respondents' views and the content analysis. Survey respondents found the songs "Southern Hospitality," "Lights, Camera, Action," "Move Bitch," "Splash Waterfalls," and "Touch It" more misogynistic than the content analysis coding. In the songs coded for medium levels of misogyny, survey respondents considered "Some Cut" and "When I'm Gone" as not misogynistic, while rating "Every Girl" much more so. Survey respondents rated "Shake Ya Ass," which contained the most misogynistic references of all songs (n = 9) coded in the sample, not as highly for misogynistic content. "Danger (Been So Long)" was also rated much lower by survey respondents for misogynistic levels than its high level of misogynistic content coded in the content analysis. Survey respondents labeled Eminem, Snoop Dogg, Ludacris, 50 Cent, Lil Jon and Young Money as the artists perpetrating the most misogynistic messages in their music. This corresponds with Eminem and Ludacris having the most songs included in the coding sample for misogynistic content.

V. Conclusion

Cultivation theory is supported by this paper's findings, which found continued audience exposure to misogynistic lyrics in popular rap/hip-hop music influences college students' attitudes toward the issue of domestic violence. This study's content analysis approach to examining song lyrics of the most popular rap/hip-hop songs on Billboard's "Hot 100" chart between 2000 and 2010 found messages communicating themes of power over, objectification of and violence against women to be prevalent across the sample selections (Bretthauer et al., 2006). This study's findings are comparable to Bretthauer et al.'s (2006) study, which also uses a qualitative content analysis method to examine all top 20 popular music songs from 1998 through 2003 on the Billboard "Hot 100" chart. Both studies conclude the theme appearing with the greatest frequency throughout the song samples is violence against women; this study's survey results indicate that respondents consider the legitimation of violence against women the most offensive theme in rap/hip-hop songs.

Over half of survey respondents expressed that exposure to popular rap/hip-hop songs moderately or significantly shapes audience attitudes toward the issue of domestic violence. This supports the finding that "misogynistic music also serves as a means to desensitize individuals to sexual harassment, exploitation, abuse, and violence toward women" and "legitimizes the mistreatment and degradation of women" (Adams & Fuller, 2006, p. 953). Exposure to misogynistic messages in rap/hip-hop music has also been shown to "increase hostile and aggressive thoughts," which may correlate to "more permanent hostility toward women" (Russo & Pirlott, 2006, p. 190). More than half of survey respondents believe rap/hip-hop music promotes aggressive and violent behaviors toward women; in addition, a majority of respondents feel this genre's messages encourage disrespectful attitudes toward women.

Listening to misogynistic content may also attribute to listeners' "expression of similar attitudes in their own lives, including accepting the objectification of women" (Dixon, Zhang, & Conrad, 2009, p. 348). Half of survey respondents agree or strongly agree that rap/hip-hop music glorifies domestic violence, and when these messages are conveyed to listeners, it may contribute to the "creation of a social climate in which violence is viewed as acceptable" (Adams & Fuller, 2006, p. 953). Therefore, rap/hip-hop music's portrayal of domestic violence matters because of the significant influence its misogynistic messages have on audiences. This study found male and female college students' listening behaviors greatly affect their perceptions of misogynistic lyrics. Survey results indicate a positive correlation between misogynous thinking and rap/hip-hop consumption, which supports previous study findings in which "greater frequency of listening to rap music was associated with more positive attitudes toward and perceptions of rap music" (Tyson, 2006, p. 215).

Survey respondents agreed that continued audience exposure to misogynistic rap/hip-hop music might reinforce negative attitudes about women because this content is "typically gender specific in its messages" (Martino, et. al, 2006, p. 432). Cobb & Boettcher (2007) determined that males will more likely experience "priming effects of misogynistic rap because they will be less motivated than will women to thoughtfully process the content of the lyrics" (p. 2037). In turn, "because women are often the targets of misogynistic rap lyrics," they will be more inclined to reject these demeaning messages (Cobb & Boettcher, 2007, p. 3029). More than three-fourths of survey respondents agreed that most rap/hip-hop music suggests women are just for male sexual satisfaction, and in turn, nearly all students surveyed found rap/hip-hop songs to be more offensive to women than men. However, most men who took the survey held negative views about rap/hip-hop music compared to most women holding neutral views of the genre.

Limitations

This study used a non-probability, convenience sample of Elon University students, with 62 survey respondents, and as a result, these findings cannot be generalized to the general population of 5,357 undergraduate students ("About Elon University," 2012). Survey results would have been more accurate if every student at Elon had an equal opportunity of participating in the survey. Also, this study's survey received more responses from women than men, which is not an accurate representation of the population. Although race was not a variable measured in this survey, it can be assumed that the majority of student respondents were Caucasian, given Elon's demographic makeup, with non-Caucasians only constituting 14% of undergraduate students ("About Elon University," 2012). In addition, the survey component of this study failed to consider that not all respondents were familiar with the rap/hip-hop songs and corresponding music artists they were supposed to evaluate for misogynistic primes. Therefore, some students may not have been able to offer their correct evaluation, which may skew data if respondents could not directly state they were unfamiliar with an artist or song. A final limitation of this study is that while the researcher coded the songs as objectively as possible, individuals may interpret lyrics differently.

Future Research

Future studies could determine if demographic differences, besides gender, may lead to different views on misogynistic lyrical content. Factors, such as respondent's race, socioeconomic status and age, could alter the study's findings. By comparing gender differences regarding attitudes and perceptions of rap/hip-hop music with ethnic differences, this would determine which variable is more strongly influenced by misogynistic messages in songs (Tyson, 2006). Previous research studies found that the "stereotyping effects of sexually explicit lyrics in rap music might have a greater effect on White audiences," which would create an interesting future comparison in relation to college students' races and their views on rap/hip-hop music (Gan, Zillman, & Miltrook, 1997, p. 392). However, when individuals are exposed to media, "factors such as age, gender, race, or socioeconomic status would not matter," according to Gerbner, because all people who consume similar amounts of misogynistic content would "share the same perceptions" (Rosenberry & Vicker, 2009, pg. 166).

Acknowledgement

This author is thankful to Dr. Scott at Elon University for his guidance and advice, without which the article could not be published. The author also appreciates numerous reviewers who have helped revise this article.

Bibliography

About Elon University. (2012). Retrieved October 30, 2012, from http://www.elon.edu/e-web/about/default. xhtml

Adams, T.M. & Fuller, D.B. (2006). The words have changed but the ideology remains the same: Misogynistic lyrics in rap music. *Journal of Black Studies, 36*, 938–957.

Armstrong, E. G. (2001). Gansta misogyny: A content analysis of the portrayals of violence against women in rap music, 1987–1993. *Journal of Criminal Justice and Popular Culture, 8*(2), 96–126.

Baran, S. J., & Davis, D.K. (2006). *Mass communication theory: Foundation, ferment, and future* (4th ed.). Belmont, CA: Thompson Wadsworth.

Barongan, C. & Hall, G. (1996). The influence of misogynous rap music on sexual aggression against women. *Psychology of Women Quarterly, 19*, 195–207.

Billboard Hot 100. Retrieved October 11, 2012, from Billboard website: http://www.billboard.com

Bretthauer, B., Zimmerman, T. S., & Banning, J. H. (2006). A feminist analysis of popular music: Power over, objectification of, and violence against women. *Journal of Feminist Family Therapy, 18*(4), 29–49.

Cobb, M. D., & Boettcher, W.A. (2007). Ambivalent sexism and misogynistic rap music: Does exposure to Eminem increase sexism? *Journal of Applied Social Psychology, 37*(12), 3025-3039.

Dixon, T. L., Zhang, Y., & Conrad, K. (2009). Self-esteem, misogyny and afrocentricity: An examination of the relationship between rap music consumption and African American perceptions. *Group Processes & Intergroup Relations, 12*(3), 345–360.

Gan, S. L., Zillman, D., & Miltrook, M. (1997). Stereotyping effect of Black women's sexual rap on White audiences. *Basic and Applied Social Psychology, 19*, 381–399.

Gerbner, G., Gross, L., Morgan, M., & Signorielli, N. (1994). Growing up with television: The cultivation perspective. In J. Bryant & D. Zillman (Eds.), *Media effects: Advances in theory and research* (pp. 17–41). Hillsdale, NJ: Erlbaum.

Get the facts: The facts on domestic, dating and sexual violence. (2007). Retrieved September 13, 2012, from Futures Without Violence website: http://www.futureswithoutviolence.org/content/ action_center/detail/754

Gourdine, R. M., & Lemmons, B. P. (2011). Perceptions of misogyny in hip hop and rap: What do the youths think? *Journal of Human Behavior in the Social Environment, 21*, 57–72.

Johnson, J. D., Jackson, L., & Gatto, L. (1995). Violent attitudes and deferred academic aspirations: Deleterious effects of exposure to rap music. *Basic & Applied Social Psychology, 16*, 27–41.

Martino, S. C., Collins, R. L., Elliott, M. N., Strachman, A., Kanouse, D. E., & Berry, S. H. (2006). Exposure to degrading versus nondegrading music lyrics and sexual behavior among youth. *Pediatrics, 118*(2), 430–441.

Nettleton, P. H. (2011). Domestic violence in men's and women's magazines: Women are guilty of choosing the wrong men, men are not guilty of hitting women. *Women's Studies in Communication, 34*, 139–160.

Pardun, C.J., L'Engle, K.I. & Brown, J.D. (2005). Linking exposure to outcomes: Early adolescents' consumption of sexual content in six media. *Mass Communication & Society, 8*, 75–91.

Prushank, D. (2007). Masculinities in teen magazines: The good, the bad, and the ugly. Journal of Men's Studies, 15(2), 160–177.

Rosenberry, J. & Vicker, L. (2009). Applied Mass Communication Theory. A Guide for Media Practitioners.

Russo, N. F., & Pirlott, A. (2006). Gender-based violence: Concepts, methods, and findings. *New York Academy of Sciences*, 178–194.

Smith, S. L. (2005). From Dr. Dre to dismissed: Assessing violence, sex, and substance use on MTV. *Critical Studies in Media Communication, 22*, 89–98.

Stankiewicz, J. M., & Rosselli, F. (2008). Women as sex objects and victims in print advertisements. *Sex Roles, 58,* 579–589.

Timmerman, L. M., Allen, M., Jorgensen, J., Herrett-Skjellum, J., Kramer, M. R., & Ryan, D. J. (2008). A review and meta-analysis examining the relationship of music content with sex, race, priming, and attitudes. *Communication Quarterly, 56*(3), 303–324.

Tjaden, P. & Thoennes, P. (2000). *Full report of the prevalence, incidence, and consequences of violence against women: Findings from the National Violence Against Women Survey.* Washington DC: National Institute of Justice/Centers for Disease Control and Prevention. Available at: http://www.ojp. usdoj.gov/nij

Tyson, E. H. (2006). Rap-music attitude and perception scale: A validation study. *Research on Social Work Practice, 16*(2), 211–223.

Weitzer, R., & Kubrin, C. (2009). Misogyny in rap music : A content analysis of prevalence and meanings. *Men and Masculinities, 12*(1).

What is domestic violence? (2012, August). Retrieved September 29, 2012, from http://www.ovw.usdoj.gov/domviolence.htm

Wood, J.T. (2012). *Gendered Lives* (10th ed.). Cengage Learning.

Zhang, Y. & Wildemuth, B. M. (2009). Qualitative analysis of content. In B. Wildemuth (Ed.), Applications of Social Research Methods to Questions in Information and Library Science (pp.308–319). Westport, CT: Libraries Unlimited.

Appendix I. Coding Sheet

Category Key:
Demeaning Language = DL
Rape/Sexual Assault = RSA
Sexual Conquest = SC
Physical Violence = PV

Race Key:
Caucasian = C
African American = AA

Gender Key:
M = Male
F = Female

Song	Artist	Category	Level of Misogyny	Race
The Real Slim Shady	Eminem	PV	Low	C
Big Pimpin'	Jay-Z and UGK	RSA, SC (2), DL	Medium	AA
Shake Ya Ass	Mystikal	DL (6), RSA, SC (2)	High	AA
The Next Episode	Dr. Dre and Snoop Dogg	DL, RSA	Low	AA
Danger (Been so Long)	Mystikal and Nivea	DL (3), RSA (2)	High	AA
Livin' It Up	Ja Rule and Case	SC	Low	AA
Southern Hospitality	Ludacris	PV	Low	AA
Lights, Camera, Action	Mr. Cheeks	DL, SC	Low	AA
Move Bitch	Ludacris, Mystikal and I-20	PV	Low	AA
Superman	Eminem	PV (3)	Medium	C
Splash Waterfalls	Ludacris	SC	Low	AA
Lovers & Friends	Lil Jon, Usher and Ludacris	RSA, SC, PV	Medium	AA
Some Cut	Trillville & Cutty	DL, RSA (2)	Medium	AA
Lean Wit It, Rock Wit It	Dem Franchize Boyz	PV (2)	Low	AA
Touch It	Busta Rhymes	PV (2)	Low	AA
When I'm Gone	Eminem	PV (3)	Medium	C
Crack a Bottle	Eminem, Dr. Dre and 50 Cent	RSA (2), PV	Medium	C/AA
Every Girl	Young Money	DL (3)	Medium	AA
Love the Way you Lie	Eminem and Rihanna	PV (4)	Medium	C/AA
Bottoms Up	Trey Songz	DL (2)	Low	AA

Appendix II. Survey Monkey Results

1. How often do you listen to rap/hip-hop music?

	Response Percent	Response Count
Very Frequently	4.8%	3
Frequently	22.6%	14
Sometimes	37.1%	23
Rarely	30.6%	19
Never	4.8%	3
answered question		62
skipped question		0

2. What do you pay attention to most when listening to rap/hip-hop music?

	Response Percent	Response Count
The instrumental aspects	54.8%	34
The lyrics/messages	12.9%	8
Both equally	32.3%	20
answered question		62
skipped question		0

3. Overall, I would classify my attitudes toward rap/hip-hop music as:

	Response Percent	Response Count
Positive	17.7%	11
Neutral	53.2%	33
Negative	29.0%	18
answered question		62
skipped question		0

4. Do you feel that explicit rap/hip-hop songs are more offensive to women or men?

	Response Percent	Response Count
Men	0.0%	0
Women	93.5%	58
Equally offensive to both	1.6%	1
Other (please specify)	4.8%	3
answered question		62
skipped question		0

5. Which of the following words, if any, do you consider degrading? (Mark all that apply)

	Response Percent	Response Count
B*tch	75.8%	47
Pussy	93.5%	58
F*ck	32.3%	20
Pimp	32.3%	20
The "N" word	90.3%	56
None	0.0%	0
answered question		62
skipped question		0

6. Which of the following rap/hip-hop music artists, if any, do you feel perpetrate negative attitudes about women through their song lyrics? (Mark all that apply)

	Response Percent	Response Count
Eminem	64.0%	32
Mystikal	22.0%	11
Jay-Z	30.0%	15
Dr. Dre	30.0%	15
Snoop Dogg	68.0%	34
Ja Rule	30.0%	15
Ludacris	64.0%	32
50 Cent	74.0%	37
Lil Jon	64.0%	32
Young Money	64.0%	32
Trillville	18.0%	9
UGK	20.0%	10
Usher	20.0%	10
Dem Franchize Boyz	36.0%	18
Busta Rhymes	32.0%	16
Trey Songz	34.0%	17
answered question		50
skipped question		12

7. Which of the following do you find most offensive in rap/hip-hop songs containing misogynistic lyrics?

		Response Percent	Response Count
Derogatory naming and shaming of women		14.5%	9
Legitimation of violence against women		54.8%	34
Sexual objectification of women		30.6%	19
None of the above		0.0%	0
		answered question	62
		skipped question	0

8. On a scale of 1-5, please rank how misogynic you feel the following songs are if you have listened to them. If you are not familiar with a song, please leave it blank.

	1) Not at all misogynic	2)	3)	4)	5) Extremely misogynic	Rating Average	Response Count
The Real Slim Shady (Eminem)	23.5% (8)	29.4% (10)	29.4% (10)	14.7% (5)	2.9% (1)	2.44	34
Big Pimpin' (Jay-Z)	5.9% (1)	5.9% (1)	41.2% (7)	23.5% (4)	23.5% (4)	3.53	17
Shake Ya Ass (Mystikal)	3.1% (1)	6.3% (2)	15.6% (5)	43.8% (14)	31.3% (10)	3.94	32
The Next Episode (Dr. Dre)	12.5% (1)	0.0% (0)	75.0% (6)	12.5% (1)	0.0% (0)	2.88	8
Danger (Mystikal)	10.0% (1)	20.0% (2)	40.0% (4)	30.0% (3)	0.0% (0)	2.90	10
Livin' it Up (Ja Rule)	15.4% (2)	23.1% (3)	46.2% (6)	15.4% (2)	0.0% (0)	2.62	13
Southern Hospitality (Ludacris)	11.1% (1)	0.0% (0)	22.2% (2)	44.4% (4)	22.2% (2)	3.67	9
Lights, Camera, Action (Mr. Cheeks)	10.0% (1)	0.0% (0)	50.0% (5)	20.0% (2)	20.0% (2)	3.40	10
Move B*tch (Ludacris)	2.9% (1)	11.8% (4)	11.8% (4)	29.4% (10)	44.1% (15)	4.00	34
Superman (Eminem)	0.0% (0)	14.3% (2)	28.6% (4)	35.7% (5)	21.4% (3)	3.64	14
Splash Waterfalls (Ludacris)	0.0% (0)	22.2% (2)	44.4% (4)	33.3% (3)	0.0% (0)	3.11	9
Lovers & Friends (Lil Jon)	0.0% (0)	18.2% (2)	45.5% (5)	36.4% (4)	0.0% (0)	3.18	11
Some Cut (Trillville)	14.3% (1)	28.6% (2)	28.6% (2)	14.3% (1)	14.3% (1)	2.86	7
Lean Wit It, Rock Wit It (Dem Franchize Boyz)	6.9% (2)	44.8% (13)	27.6% (8)	20.7% (6)	0.0% (0)	2.62	29

	1	2	3	4	5	Rating Average	Response Count
Touch It (Busta Rhymes)	7.7% (1)	23.1% (3)	7.7% (1)	38.5% (5)	23.1% (3)	3.46	13
When I'm Gone (Eminem)	38.9% (7)	22.2% (4)	16.7% (3)	22.2% (4)	0.0% (0)	2.22	18
Crack a Bottle (Eminem)	0.0% (0)	31.6% (6)	36.8% (7)	26.3% (5)	5.3% (1)	3.05	19
Every Girl (Young Money)	0.0% (0)	9.1% (1)	9.1% (1)	18.2% (2)	63.6% (7)	4.36	11
Love the Way You Lie (Eminem & Rihanna)	6.7% (3)	17.8% (8)	20.0% (9)	33.3% (15)	22.2% (10)	3.47	45
Bottoms Up (Trey Songz)	18.6% (8)	25.6% (11)	20.9% (9)	30.2% (13)	4.7% (2)	2.77	43
					answered question		52
					skipped question		10

9. To what degree, on a scale of 1-5, do you feel that exposure to popular rap/hip-hop songs shapes audience attitudes toward the issue of domestic violence?

	1) Not at all	2)	3)	4)	5) Significantly	Rating Average	Response Count
	1.6% (1)	9.7% (6)	32.3% (20)	43.5% (27)	12.9% (8)	3.56	62
					answered question		62
					skipped question		0

10. Please state your level of agreement/disagreement with the following:

	1) Strongly disagree	2)	3)	4)	5) Strongly agree	Rating Average	Response Count
Rap/hip-hop music encourages disrespectful attitudes towards women.	1.6% (1)	4.8% (3)	22.6% (14)	53.2% (33)	17.7% (11)	3.81	62
Rap/hip-hop music provides positive messages for its listeners.	25.8% (16)	45.2% (28)	19.4% (12)	8.1% (5)	1.6% (1)	2.15	62
Rap/hip-hop music promotes aggressive and violent behaviors towards women.	1.6% (1)	6.5% (4)	38.7% (24)	41.9% (26)	11.3% (7)	3.55	62
Rap/hip-hop music glorifies domestic violence.	1.6% (1)	16.1% (10)	32.3% (20)	37.1% (23)	12.9% (8)	3.44	62
Explicit rap/hip-hop music is offensive.	0.0% (0)	17.7% (11)	14.5% (9)	41.9% (26)	25.8% (16)	3.76	62
Sexism in rap/hip-hop music contributes to sexist behavior.	0.0% (0)	9.7% (6)	17.7% (11)	38.7% (24)	33.9% (21)	3.97	62
Misogynistic lyrics are prevalent in rap/hip-hop music.	0.0% (0)	0.0% (0)	11.3% (7)	45.2% (28)	43.5% (27)	4.32	62
Rap/hip-hop artists intend to degrade women through their lyrics.	0.0% (0)	16.1% (10)	35.5% (22)	37.1% (23)	11.3% (7)	3.44	62
Domestic violence is a pressing issue in the United States.	0.0% (0)	0.0% (0)	4.8% (3)	35.5% (22)	59.7% (37)	4.55	62
Most rap/hip-hop music suggests that women are just for male sexual satisfaction.	1.6% (1)	4.8% (3)	16.1% (10)	46.8% (29)	30.6% (19)	4.00	62
Rap/hip-hop music reflects the realities of intimate partner relationships.	32.3% (20)	41.9% (26)	17.7% (11)	6.5% (4)	1.6% (1)	2.03	62
College-aged women are the most susceptible to experiencing gendered violence.	3.2% (2)	22.6% (14)	27.4% (17)	32.3% (20)	14.5% (9)	3.32	62
					answered question		62
					skipped question		0

11. What is your gender?

	Response Percent	Response Count
Male	16.1%	10
Female	83.9%	52
answered question		62
skipped question		0

12. What is your academic year?

	Response Percent	Response Count
First year	0.0%	0
Sophomore	9.7%	6
Junior	27.4%	17
Senior	62.9%	39
Fifth year	0.0%	0
answered question		62
skipped question		0

SECTION TWO SUMMARY

Key Discussion Sessions

1. What were the primary findings of Hartley and Miller's study "Crack-ing the Media Myth: Reconsidering Sentencing Severity for Cocaine Offenders by Drug Type" and Linnemann's study "Mad Men, Meth Moms, Moral Panic: Gendering Meth Crimes in the Midwest"? How are drug users depicted in your home region? Have you observed any of the depictions mentioned in the articles in your home region? If so, which depictions, and what impact do you believe they and other depictions have on the attitudes of citizens, police officers, judges, and juries in your home region? If you are from another country, do you see similar depiction patterns of drug users?

2. What were the primary findings of Cundiff's study "The Influence of Rap/Hip-Hop Music: A Mixed-Method Analysis on Audience Perceptions of Misogynistic Lyrics and the Issue of Domestic Violence"? Do you believe that Rap/Hip-Hop is alone in regard to misogynistic lyrics and domestic violence? If they are not alone, what examples can you provide from other genres of music? Could other genres of music support misogyny and domestic violence in other ways? Given that most people listen to music, what impact do such depictions have on policy and lawmakers? If you are from another country, do you see similar portrayals in popular music in your country?

Public Consumption Exercise

Remember, the public consumption exercises in this text build upon each other. You must have completed the exercises in Section 1 to complete the current exercise.

Exercise 3: Just the Facts

Article

Determine which articles in this section provide findings that could help the citizens of your home county the most. Indicate which article you chose and why you believe this to be the best article.

Findings Paragraphs and Writing Level

Identify consecutive paragraphs (no less than three) from the findings or results section of the article that contain the largest portion of key findings, and retype them in a word document; make sure the wording is exact. Follow the instructions in Appendix C to calculate the writing level of the paragraphs. Does the writing level match the average literacy level for your home county? If it is written at a higher level than the average, how many grade levels must the authors of the piece reduce the writing to be easily read by the citizens of your home county?

It is important to note that grade levels are not static. Someone in the 12th grade may read at a 7th grade level while a student in the 7th grade may read at a 12th grade level. Similarly, peer-reviewed research writing levels can vary from publication to publication and from section to section. The key is determining the average literacy level of your target audience and the writing level of the research findings you wish to convey so that you know how many grade levels you need to come down to at least meet the average for the audience. If the material from an article already meets the level, try to reduce it by two more grade levels.

Bulleted Facts

Next, reduce the key findings of the paper into three to four bullets. Utilize no more than two sentences or facts per bullet. Think of the bullets in the context of having to fit key information into a sound bite that will appear on television for only a few seconds or as a quote a newspaper reporter can fit into an article.

Example:
According to a study of the first forty years of the cop film genre by criminologists at Indiana State University:
- Only two films depicted Latino's as city police officers in leading roles.
- Of the two depictions, one was of a female officer who needs saving by a white male, and the other was of an ex-gang member who must choose between protecting his community and becoming a corrupt cop.
- The researchers point to the need for more Latino police officer hires to offset long-held stereotypes by the community.

SECTION THREE
Law Enforcement

BLACK CRIMINALS AND WHITE OFFICERS

The Effects of Racially Misrepresenting Law Breakers and Law Defenders on Television News

by Travis L. Dixon
University of Illinois at Urbana-Champaign

A number of recent investigations have attempted to systematically document the occurrence of crime on television news with an eye towards uncovering the extent to which the crime portrayed in the news is racialized (Dixon, Azocar, & Casas, 2003; Dixon & Linz, 2000a, 2000b; Entman, 1992, 1994; Entman & Rojecki, 2000; Gilliam, Iyengar, Simon, & Wright, 1996; Romer, Jamieson, & de Coteau, 1998). Many of these studies have concluded that news programs tend to misrepresent crime as a rampant problem and people of color as the law breakers responsible for the rise in crime (Gibbons, Taylor, & Phillips, 2005). These same studies have also provided evidence that the Whites featured in crime news often occupy positive roles as police officers (Dixon & Linz, 2000a, 2000b).

For example, Dixon and Linz (2000a) found that Blacks represented 21% of those individuals arrested for crime but were 37% of the perpetrators featured in crime news stories aired on Los Angeles news stations. Simultaneously, Whites were overrepresented as officers (69%) on local television news programs compared to the official employment reports (59%) of the Los Angeles area. Additional studies have found that this overrepre-sentation of Whites as police officers extends to both network news and crime-based reality television (about 91% on network TV vs. 80% in national official records; Dixon et al., 2003; Oliver, 1994). In sum, the prior research indicates that African Americans are associated with negative roles as criminals on television news whereas Whites occupy positive roles as officers. The current study was an experiment designed to determine whether news exposure might contribute to negative stereotypes of African Americans as criminals and positive perceptions of Whites as officers (Dixon, 2006a; Dixon & Maddox, 2005).

Stereotyping, Cultivation, and Chronic Activation

Communication researchers, psychologists, and other scholars have for years contended that exposure to mass media imagery may have an impact on viewers' constructions of social reality (Gerbner, 1990). This general notion has often been termed the cultivation effect or hypothesis (Gerbner, Gross, Morgan, & Signorielli, 1980, 2002). The general notion of cultivation can be applied to issues of stereotyping, crime news, and beliefs about racial groups. However, earlier work on cultivation received criticism for not specifying the underlying mechanisms related to cultivation outcomes (Potter, 1991, 1993). More recently, media effects scholars and psychologists have used theories of stereotyping, specifically chronic activation and accessibility, to assess the underlying mechanisms that may facilitate the cultivation effect (Shrum, 2002).

Prior News Viewing, Stereotypes, and Chronic Activation

Stereotypes are cognitive structures or categories that affect the encoding and processing of information (Hamilton & Trolier, 1986; von Hippel, Sekaquap-tewa, & Vargas, 1995). These structures direct attention to some stimuli and away from others, influence categorization of information, help us "fill-in" missing information, and influence memory (Fiske & Taylor, 1991; Oliver, 1999). Social psychologists and media effects scholars have contended that stereotypes are more likely to be used if they have either recently or frequently been activated (Fiske & Taylor, 1991; Hamilton, Stroessner, & Driscoll, 1994; Higgins, 2000). Much of the prior media effects research addressing racial stereotyping almost exclusively examines recency effects associated with the Black criminality construct (Gilliam & Iyengar, 1998, 2000; John-son, Adams, Hall, & Ashburn, 1997; Oliver, Jackson, Moses, & Dangerfield, 2004; Peffley, Shields, & Williams, 1996). That is, each Black criminal and White officer exemplar featured in the news should activate the stereotypical constructs linking Blacks with lawbreaking and Whites with law defending (Zillmann, 2002).

However, the frequency effects associated with long-term news viewing have received little attention. Frequency effects are important because, in alignment with cultivation processes, news exposure may facilitate the activation of stereotypes. Theoretically, the more these activated stereotypes are used, the more likely they are to be used in the future (Devine, 1989; Fiske & Taylor, 1991; Gilliam & Iyengar, 1998, 2000; Gilliam et al., 1996; Oliver, 1999; Peffley et al., 1996; Power, Murphy, & Coover, 1996). Given the overrepresentation of Black criminals and White officers in crime news, frequent news viewing should increase the accessibility of these constructs when relevant judgments need to be made (Shrum, 1995, 2002).

Stigmatization and Stereotype Valence

The social cognition literature indicates that categorizing individuals as part of stigmatized social groups leads to the activation of constructs that implicitly link group members with various stereotypical traits (Eagly & Chaiken, 1993; Fiske & Taylor, 1991; Hamilton et al., 1994; Higgins, 2000; Livingston, 2001; von Hippel, Sekaquaptewa, & Vargas, 1997). Media scholars have utilized this theoretical concept to investigate whether exposure to African American criminals in the news activates a Black criminal stereotype used in subsequent decision making.

For example, Gilliam and his colleagues exposed participants to either a Black or White suspect in a newscast. Afterwards, they asked participants about their support for punitive crime policy. They found that exposure to Black rather than White suspects in the news led to increased support for the death penalty, three-strikes legislation, and the endorsement of dispositional factors as the cause of criminal behavior (Gilliam & Iyengar, 1998, 2000; Gilliam et al., 1996). They argued that exposure to the Black suspect activated a construct linking Blacks with lawbreaking then used in subsequent decision making. Similar to Gilliam and his colleagues, most of the literature in both social psychology and in media effects has focused on stigmatized groups (e.g., African Americans) and negative stereotypical traits (e.g., criminality) (Dixon, 2006a; Dixon & Maddox, 2005; Oliver, 1999; Oliver & Fonash, 2002; Oliver et al., 2004). Very little research has addressed non-stigmatized groups (e.g., Whites) and positive stereotypical traits (e.g., officers). The current study is designed to overcome this limitation.

Study Innovations: New Tests of Cultivation and Accessibility

Unlike prior research, the frequency effects associated with news viewing are directly assessed in the current study. Two tools are utilized to assess chronic activation. First, unidentified suspects and officers are featured in the manipulation. When presented with unidentified suspects or officers, participants might use multiple exemplars from prior news viewing to "fill-in-the-blank" with stereotypical associations when making relevant judgments (Shrum, 1995, 2002; Zillmann, 2002). The identification of unidentified characters as either Black or White would provide evidence that these stereotypical constructs are highly accessible for news viewers. Such accessibility most likely results from the cultivation of stereotypical constructs through chronic activation while watching the news. Second, prior news viewing is directly measured and comparisons are made between the judgments of heavy and light viewers. If chronic activation influences decision making, heavy news viewers should be more likely than light news viewers to express high likelihoods that officers are White and perpetrators are Black when each is actually unidentified. Unlike most prior research, the current study can investigate how news cultivates and reinforces stereotypical linkages by using role identification (i.e., unidentified officers and perpetrators) to determine whether news viewers invoke the relevant racial stereotype in judgment.

Prior research has also not thoroughly examined whether exposure to media stimuli activates positive stereotypes of non-stigmatized groups. The current study extends prior work by investigating the effects of exposure to White police officers who are arguably representative of a non-stigmatized group and a positive stereotype (Dixon & Linz, 2000a; Oliver, 1994). The current study also seeks to replicate prior work by examining a stigmatized group and a negative stereotype (i.e., Black criminals) (Dixon, 2006a).

STUDY HYPOTHESES

In the current study participants are exposed to Black, White, or Unidentified perpetrators and Black, White or Unidentified officers and then asked to make judgments regarding the likelihood that the suspect and officer were Black or White. In addition, the extent to which participants hold positive perceptions of the officer is assessed. Likelihood judgments, memory assessments and perceptions of depicted characters have all been used to assess the activation and accessibility of stereotypical constructs in prior media effects studies (Dixon & Maddox, 2005; Gilliam & Iyengar, 2000; Oliver, 1999; Oliver & Fonash, 2002; Peffley et al., 1996). Finally, prior news viewing is measured in order to determine whether news viewing increases the accessibility of both negative and positive stereotypical constructs. As described previously, study innovations include: a) the focus on negative and positive stereotypes of stigmatized and non-stigmatized group members, b) the use of unidentified perpetrator and officer conditions to assess chronic activation and cultivation effects, and c) the measurement of prior news viewing to directly assess chronic activation of stereotypical constructs.

Hypotheses

Based on the theories of stereotyping described above, the following hypotheses are proposed:

H1: Unidentified suspects will be perceived as likely being Black, and heavy news viewers will be more likely to hold this perception than light news viewers.

The above hypothesis essentially contends that participants will perceive race unidentified suspects as being likely Black based on prior activation and use of the Black criminal stereotype in previous news viewing contexts. In addition, prior news viewing should contribute to chronic accessibility of this Black criminal stereotype as a result of this chronic activation. As a result, heavy news viewers should be less "correct" when exposed to unidentified suspects, mistaking them for Blacks.

H2: Unidentified officers will be perceived as likely being White, and heavy news viewers will be more likely to hold this perception than light news viewers.

Similar to the process involved with Black suspects, prior association of Whites with law enforcement in the news may form a stereotype of officers as White. As a result, exposure to news presentations featuring unidentified officers should increase the likelihood perceptions that he is White. Furthermore, prior news viewing should increase the accessibility of the construct linking police officers with Whiteness which should accentuate these effects.

H3: Unidentified and White officers will be perceived more positively than Black officers, and heavy news viewers will be more likely than light news viewers to hold this perception.

Given that the news often overrepresents officers as Whites and depicts them as the stabilizing force against crime and criminals, both unidentified and White officers should be perceived more positively compared to Black officers (Dixon & Linz, 2000a; Hall, Critcher, Jefferson, Clarke, & Roberts, 1978). Furthermore, heavy news viewing should increase the accessibility of the construct linking police officers with helpfulness.

Method

Participants

Two hundred and forty undergraduate students enrolled in an introductory Communication Studies course at a large mid-western university took part in this experiment. The sample was 76% White, 7% Black, 4% Latino, 11% Asian, and 2% "Other."

Stimulus Materials

A 20-minute news program was edited such that it contained an embedded crime story about a perpetrator who murders a police officer. Police are said to be on the hunt for the suspect. Both the officer and perpetrator were described as male. The story was manipulated such that the perpetrator and police officer were identified as either Black, White, or were left unidentified. The identification of the perpetrators and officers was created through the insertion of two photos—one for the perpetrator, the other for the officer. In the unidentified condition, no picture was shown. The photos were altered through computer editing so that the featured character would be perceived as authentically White or Black.

Similar methods have been used in prior studies to manipulate race (Gilliam et al., 1996). The approach addresses the criticism that differences seen on the outcome measures are due to other facial features or appearance variables between the Whites and Blacks featured, and not due to race. Such criticism is avoided because the same person with the same clothing and facial features is displayed in all conditions.

Pre-Test of Stimulus Materials

A pre-test was performed on the altered photos in order to insure that the characters portrayed in each picture actually appeared to be White or Black. The pre-test involved 34 undergraduate participants rating the extent to which they believed each model pictured was Black, White, Latino, or another race/ethnic group besides Black, White, or Latino. There were four photos tested. These included the digitally altered Black and White officer photos and the digitally altered Black and White perpetrator photos. Each Black photo was subjected to three t-tests designed to assess whether the photo appeared: 1) more Black than White, 2) more Black than Latino, and 3) more Black than "Other." Similarly, each White photo was subjected to three t-tests designed to assess whether the photo appeared: 1) more White than Black, 2) more White than Latino, and 3) more White than "Other." In total, twelve t-tests were conducted. They revealed that participants did indeed perceive each photo as authentically Black or White (all t-values > 5.50, $p < .001$).

Procedure

Participants were randomly assigned to a 3 (Perpetrator Race—Black, White, or Race Unidentified) $\times$ 3 (Officer Race—Black, White, or Unidentified) video condition. Afterwards they were asked about their news viewing habits. A median split was conducted on the news viewing measure described below, and participants were separated into heavy and light news viewing groups. This yielded a 3 (Perpetrator Race—Black, White, or Race Unidentified) $\times$ 3 (Officer Race—Black, White, or Unidentified) $\times$ 2 (Prior News Viewing—Heavy, Light) between-subjects factorial design. Participants were brought into a laboratory and told that they would be participating in a study designed to assess memory for the news. They would be responsible for watching a news program and then answering a number of questions about what they had seen. After this brief orientation, participants watched a news program in which a crime story was embedded that featured a Black, White, or race unidentified perpetrator and officer. After viewing the news program, participants responded to a number of dependent measures and then to a prior news viewing measure that was embedded within a number of bogus memory items.

Prior News Viewing

In order to take into account prior exposure to television news, weekly television news viewing was measured. Unfortunately, there is no widely accepted validated measure of news viewing (Tewksbury, 2003). Therefore recent articles that assessed news viewing, race, and media effects were reviewed and a news viewing measure was culled from these studies (Dixon, 2006a, 2006b; Dixon & Maddox, 2005). The news viewing measure requires participants to fill out a viewing grid in which they indicate how many hours and minutes they spend watching TV news on each corresponding day of the week (e.g., Sunday, Monday, etc.). These numbers are then converted into minutes and summed across the 7 days for each participant ($M = 160.94$, $SD = 140.40$). The variable was used in order to assess the effects of prior news viewing on race and crime perceptions after exposure to the nine criminal/officer race conditions by dichotomizing it and entering it as a third factor in the design. A median split was performed on the measure (median = 90.00 minutes) that divided participants into heavy and light prior news viewers. It should be noted that 90 minutes is a fairly low number, corresponding to less than 2 to 3 hours a week. However, the current study utilized a student sample, and students tend to watch smaller amounts of television news compared to non-student adults (Dixon, 2006b; Valentino, 1999; Zaller, 1992).

It should also be noted that the television news question was one of many demographic questions asked at the end of the participants' questionnaire. In the definition and examples offered to participants, it was made clear that this question referred to traditional television news imagery that included both local and network news. This question was not an assessment of participant exposure to "fake news" programs or spoof programs such as The Daily Show. It might have been helpful to have created multiple items that independently assessed both local television news and television network news. Local television news has received a substantial amount of scrutiny in the literature regarding its portrayals of race and crime (Dixon & Linz, 2000a, 2000b; Entman, 1992; Gilliam & Iyengar, 1998, 2000; Gilliam et al., 1996). Indeed, most scholars acknowledge that crime news is a staple of local news programming, but this sort of misrepresentation is not as apparent on network news (Dixon et al., 2003; Entman, 1994).

However, network news programming has also been accused of distorted race and crime portrayals (Dixon et al., 2003; Entman, 1994; Entman & Rojecki, 2000; Gilens, 1996; Gilens, 1999; Iyengar, 1987, 1990, 1991). In addition, a few studies have demonstrated a link between exposure to these images and support for conservative public policies (Gilens, 1999). The current measure of television news exposure might be best viewed as a composite measure of one's overall television news diet (Gerbner et al., 1980, 2002). Given prior research in this area, this diet most likely includes distorted race and crime imagery from both local television news and network television news (Dixon et al., 2003; Dixon & Linz, 2000a, 2000b; Entman, 1992, 1994; Entman & Rojecki, 2000).

In order to address the potential problems with dichotomizing news viewing in this fashion, continuous prior news viewing along with other potential confounding variables were entered as controls and assessed simultaneously in complementary analyses to the main ones reported here using modified ANCOVAS. The controls used in the complementary analyses included: a) conservatism on a 1 (liberal) to 7 (conservative) scale, b) family household income on a 1 to 7 scale (less than $30,000; $30,000 to $40,000; $40,000–$60,000; $60,000–$80,000; $80,000–$90,000; $90,000–$100,000; more than $100,000), and c) racism or prejudice using a modified version of the Modern Racism Scale (MRS) (e.g., "Blacks are getting too demanding in their push for equal rights"; 7 items; $\alpha = .82$) (McConahay, 1986). Although the income variable was skewed, it still could serve as a weak proxy for contact with people of color given that society continues to remain segregated by race and class (Delgado, 1994).[1]

Each of the above-mentioned control variables has been used recently by media scholars and psychologists to tap into the constructs under investigation in the current study (Dixon, 2006a, 2006b; Dixon & Maddox, 2005; Eberhardt, Goff, Purdie, & Davies, 2004; Valentino, 1999). However, before news viewing and the control variables could be employed in the complementary analyses, additional tests needed to be performed in order to determine whether the video manipulation influenced these self-reported measures. These tests revealed that the video condition had no effect on any of the controls or on reports of how much television news participants watched, (all F's < 2.05 ns).[2]

Dependent Measures

Three dependent measures were used in this study. Each consisted of several Likert-type scale items ranging from 1 (*not very likely, definitely not, disagree*) to 7 (*very likely, definitely, agree*). Each of these dependent measures were adapted from prior studies of news stories and race judgments (Dixon, 2006b; Dixon & Maddox, 2005). One of the dependent measures asked participants the extent to which they held a positive view or perception of the featured officer (e.g., "How sympathetic do you think the police officer was?"; 7 items, $\alpha = .81$).

Two other measures were designed to assess the extent to which participants expressed a likelihood that the depicted perpetrator or officer was either Black or White. The first variable utilized two items to assess the extent to which participants perceived a high likelihood that the criminal featured in the crime story was Black (i.e., "How likely is it that the perpetrator was Black" & "How likely is it that the perpetrator was White—reverse coded;" $\alpha = .71$). The second variable utilized two items to assess the extent to which participants perceived a high likelihood that the officer featured in the crime story was White (i.e., "How likely is it that the police officer was White" & "How likely is it that the police officer was Black—reverse coded;" $\alpha = .77$). Each of these measures was surrounded by distracter items including perceptions of the anchor and story. In order to ensure that participants did not respond in a leading way, the question ordering for these two measures was counterbalanced. Two orders of the measures were created. In the first order, the "White" questions led. In the second order, the "Black" questions led.

The likelihood measures were used for three reasons. First, they allowed for the use of powerful statistical tests in order to detect differences, and in many cases the effects sizes associated with media effects studies that assess racial stereotypes are relatively small (Dixon, 2006a; Oliver et al.,

---

1   With regard to the Modern Racism Scale (MRS), research has increasingly found that the MRS is correlated more with explicit rather than implicit attitudes and processes. Furthermore, the MRS may be associated more with political conservatism than racism (Fazio, Jackson, Dunton, & Williams, 1995; Phelps et al., 2000). As a result, some participants may offer socially desirable responses to the MRS because of its explicit nature in order to appear less prejudiced (Devine, 1989; Fazio et al., 1995; Givens & Monahan, 2005). In the current sample, most participants did indeed find themselves on the low end of the scale ($M = 2.51$, $SD = 0.93$, $Mdn = 2.43$). However, participants who do not feel this need to control prejudice should be more likely to apply stereotypes to media stimuli, and this variable is designed to tap this explicit stereotype application orientation. As a result, meaningful comparisons can still be made between those individuals who feel free to endorse stereotypes about Blacks and those individuals who are hesitant to endorse these stereotypes for whatever reason (e.g., they genuinely reject them or they feel motivated not to appear to embrace them). Moreover, the correlation between the MRS and conservatism should be attenuated by the inclusion of political ideology as a control variable.

2   It should also be noted that there was no correlation between news viewing and prejudice, $r = -.09$, $p < .18$. These data provide more evidence for a cultivation/chronic activation/accessibility effect in the current study if news viewing interacts with the manipulated conditions to influence subsequent judgments because it rules out the alternative hypothesis that prejudiced people simply watch more news.

2004; Valentino, 1999). Second, the likelihood question represents a perceptual judgment that is more reminiscent of the way in which people watch and think about the news. In other words, people are cognitive misers who do not usually attempt to count or recall the specific race of characters they encounter (Iyengar, 1987; Wicks, 1992). Instead, they usually use shortcuts and think in more generalist or probabilistic terms about what they watch. The likelihood questions are more reflective of this thinking. Third, the likelihood measures were also used to hide the true nature of the study. If participants had been asked for specific recall or memory judgments, it might have raised suspicion about the true nature of the study.

Results

All statistical tests were conducted at the .05 significance level. A separate ANOVA with Perpetrator Race (Black, White, or Race Unidentified), Officer Race (Black, White, or Race Unidentified) and News Viewing (Heavy, Light) was performed on each of the dependent measures—perception of the likelihood that the perpetrator was Black, perception of the likelihood that the officer was White, and positive perceptions of the featured officer. All cells for the tests of the hypothesized two-way interactions contain ns of 17 to 22. The three-way interaction cells contain ns of 6 to 14.

Although not hypothesized, other two-way and three-way interactions might be meaningful if significant. For instance, in cases when a Black perpetrator is depicted, it may facilitate the invocation of the construct linking Whites with officers, and this might vary by news viewing level. The two-way interaction between depicted officer and perpetrator might also influence judgments. For example, when a Black perpetrator is depicted, participants may be more likely to say that the officer is White and have more sympathetic views of the depicted officer because Black perpetrators and White officer are overrepresented on TV news. Similarly, the depiction of White officers might be more likely to invoke the Black criminal construct and increase the confidence that a given suspect is Black. However, low ns in the cells may hamper an investigating of these effects in the current study or may suggest that there is no evidence for such an interaction.[3]

Perceptions of Likelihood that the Perpetrator Was Black

The first hypothesis stated that unidentified suspects would be perceived as Black, and heavy news viewers would be more likely to hold this perception than light news viewers. In order to test this hypothesis, three sets of statistical tests were employed. First, a manipulation and measure check are reported using ANOVA, Scheffe post-hoc tests, and t-tests. Afterwards, these same tests were used to determine whether participants exposed to the unidentified perpetrator condition expressed a likelihood that the perpetrator was Black. Furthermore, ANOVA interactive terms and post-hoc analyses were utilized to determine whether heavy news viewers were more likely than light news viewers to hold these perceptions. Finally, the interactive terms in the ANOVA were used to determine whether there were interactive effects of the race of the officer on likelihood judgments of the perpetrator.

Manipulation and scale check. The ANOVA for perceptions of likelihood that the suspect was Black revealed a significant effect for the race of the featured perpetrator, $F(2, 154) = 36.20$, $p < .001$, $\eta_p^2 = .18$. A Scheffe post-hoc analysis revealed that participants exposed to a Black perpetrator ($M = 4.96$,

---

3   In the one instance in which the main results differed from the complementary results, an explanation is offered.

$SD = 1.45$) reported a higher likelihood that the perpetrator was Black compared to participants exposed to a White perpetrator ($M = 3.39$, $SD = 1.74$), $p < .001$. A one sample t-test was undertaken in order to determine whether the various perpetrator conditions differed from the midpoint (4.00) on the likelihood that the perpetrator was Black scale. A statistically significant difference on either side of the midpoint would allow us to further correlate the likelihood judgment with the perception of the perpetrator as either Black or White rather than undeterminable. Those participants exposed to a Black perpetrator ($M = 4.96$, $SD = 1.45$) significantly differed from the midpoint, $t(58) = 5.09$, $p < .001$. The midpoint test also revealed that White perpetrators ($M = 3.39$, $SD = 1.74$) were more likely to be perceived as White rather than Black or undeterminable, $t(52) = -2.56$, $p < .01$. These analyses suggest that the scale and the perpetrator conditions correctly manipulated and measured perpetrator race and racial perceptions.

Unidentified perpetrator effects. The ANOVA and Scheffe post-hoc anal-yses also revealed that participants exposed to a race unidentified perpetrator ($M = 4.46$, $SD = 1.16$) were more likely to express a likelihood that the perpetrator portrayed in the crime story was Black compared to participants exposed to a White perpetrator ($M = 3.39$, $SD = 1.74$), $p < .001$. There were no statistically significant differences between participants exposed to a Black perpetrator ($M = 4.96$) and participants exposed to an unidentified perpetrator ($M = 4.46$, $SD = 1.16$), $p = .18$. Using the midpoint t-test, the unidentified condition ($M = 4.46$, $SD = 1.16$) did indeed differ from the midpoint of the scale, $t(60) = 3.17$, $p < .01$ further indicating that participants exposed to a race-unidentified criminal tended to perceive him as likely being Black.

Interactive effects of news viewing and suspect exposure. The ANOVA revealed that the interaction between news viewing and the race of the depicted perpetrator was not significant, $F(2, 154) = 0.19$, $p = .82$. This suggests that news viewing did not moderate likelihood judgments after exposure to the featured perpetrator.

Interactive effects of perpetrator race and officer race. Similarly, the ANOVA revealed that the interaction between the race of the depicted officer and the race of the depicted perpetrator was not significant, $F(4, 154) = 1.01$, $p = .41$. This suggests that likelihood perceptions of the race of the perpetrator were not influenced by the race of the officer.

Perceptions of Likelihood that the Officer Was White

The second hypothesis stated that unidentified officers would be perceived as White, and heavy news viewers would be more likely than light news viewers to hold this perception. Similar to the likelihood assessment for perpetrators, the assessment of officers involved several sets of analyses. These are reported below.

Manipulation and scale check. The ANOVA for perceptions of likelihood that the police officer portrayed in the crime story was White revealed a significant main effect for race of featured officer, $F(2, 154) = 38.35$, $p < .001$, $\eta_p^2 = .33$. A Scheffe post-hoc analysis revealed that participants exposed to a White officer ($M = 4.82$, $SD = 1.44$) were more likely than participants exposed to a Black officer ($M = 2.70$, $SD = 1.59$) to perceive that the officer portrayed in the crime story was White, $p < .001$. Similar to the likelihood that the perpetrator was Black analysis, a midpoint (4.00) test was conducted on the likelihood that the officer was White scale using t-tests. The Black officer condition ($M = 2.70$, $SD = 1.59$), $t(56) = 6.15$, $p < .001$ differed from the midpoint indicating that the Black officer was perceived as likely Black. Furthermore, the White officer condition ($M = 4.82$, $SD = 1.44$), $t(56) = 4.40$, $p < .001$ also differed from the midpoint indicating that the White officer was likely perceived as White.

These analyses suggest that the scale and the officer conditions correctly manipulated and measured officer race and racial perceptions.

Unidentified officer effects. Compared to participants exposed to a Black officer ($M = 2.70, SD = 1.59$), Scheffee post-hoc tests revealed that participants exposed to an unidentified officer ($M = 4.02, SD = 0.82$) had higher likelihood ratings that the depicted officer was White, $p < .001$. However, participants exposed to White officers ($M = 4.82, SD = 1.44$) were also significantly more likely to perceive him as White compared to participants exposed to unidentified officers ($M = 4.02, SD = 0.82$), $p < .01$. Moreover, the midpoint t-tests revealed that likelihood ratings for unidentified officers ($M = 4.02, SD = 0.82$) did not significantly deviate from the midpoint (4.00), $t(56) = 0.82, p = .93$. These findings provide evidence that, overall, unidentified officers were rated as undeterminable.

Interactive effects of news viewing and officer exposure. However, the ANOVA also revealed an interaction between prior news viewing and the race of the officer, $F(2, 154) = 4.21, p < .01, \eta_p^2 = .05$. Post-hoc LSD t-tests were used to explore the interaction. They revealed that after exposure to an unidentified officer, heavy news viewers ($M = 4.30, SD = 0.84$) were more likely than light news viewers ($M = 3.76, SD = 0.72$) to express a high likelihood that the officer was white, $t(54) = -1.97, p < .05$. There were no statistically significant differences between heavy and light news viewers exposed to White officers, $t(58) = -0.95, p = .37$, or Black officers $t(54) = 1.51, p = .14$ on likelihood judgments.[4]

Interactive effects of officer race and perpetrator race. The ANOVA revealed that the interaction between the race of the depicted officer and the race of the depicted perpetrator was not significant, $F(4, 154) = 0.92, p = .45$. This suggests that likelihood ratings regarding the officer's race was not dependent upon the race of the perpetrator featured in the video.

Positive Perceptions of the Featured Officer

The final hypothesis stated that exposure to unidentified and White officers would lead to more positive perceptions of the featured officer, and that heavy news viewers hold more positive perceptions than light news viewers. This hypothesis was tested with ANOVA and post-hoc tests. The ANOVA revealed that there were no main effects for the race of the depicted officer or perpetrator on positive perceptions of the featured officer, (Fs $< 1, ns$).

However, the ANOVA for positive perceptions regarding the featured officer did reveal a significant interaction between the race of the officer featured and prior news viewing, $F(2, 149) = 3.16, p < .05, \eta_p^2 = .04$. Exploratory post-hoc LSD t-tests indicated that heavy news viewers ($M = 4.20, SD = 0.59$)

---

4   The main effect of the featured officer on likelihood judgments that the officer was White was also revealed when news viewing was measured continuously and the income, ideology, and prejudice controls were entered simultaneously, $F(2, 143) = 11.64, p < .001, \eta_p^2 = .14$. None of the covariates were statistically significant, (all Fs < 1 ns). However, the interaction between news viewing and the depicted officer dropped to marginal significance once news viewing was measured continuously and the controls were entered into the analysis, $F(2, 143) = 2.23, p = .11$. In order to determine why this situation may have occurred, several statistical tests were conducted. First, the ANCOVA was re-run by including the continuously measured TV news viewing variable and excluding the controls. The ANCOVA again yielded an insignificant interaction, $F(2, 154) = 2.18$, $p < .11$. Next, the distribution of scores was reexamined in order to determine if there was some skew in the data that may have rendered the interaction insignificant. The TV news variable was slightly positively skewed, (Skew = 1.41, SE = .19). Therefore a square root transformation was undertaken to address the skew (Tabachnick & Fidell, 2001). The transformation and subsequent transformations were not successful in rendering the distribution normal. In these circumstances, it is usually recommended to examine the variable dichotomously, something already undertaken in the main analysis (Tabachnick & Fidell, 2001). In one final test, participants who saw an unidentified officer were selected and a correlation was run between the likelihood measure that the officer was white and television news viewing measured continuously. If news viewing leads to an increase in the perception that unidentified officers are most likely white officers, then the correlation should be positive. The analysis provided evidence for this conclusion ($r = .35, p < .01$).

were more likely than light news viewers ($M = 3.86$, $SD = 0.70$) to view the officer positively when he was unidentified, $t(53) = -1.95$, $p < .05$. Conversely, heavy news viewers were less likely ($M = 3.88$, $SD = 0.73$) than light news viewers ($M = 4.24$, $SD = 0.84$) to perceive the featured officer in a positive manner when he was depicted as Black, $t(31) = -2.78$, $p < .01$. There were no statistically significant differences between heavy ($M = 5.10$, $SD = 1.40$) and light ($M = 4.72$, $SD = 1.62$) news viewers exposed to White officers on positive perceptions of the officer, $t(55) = 1.66$, $p = .10$, though both groups appear to have a fairly positive view of White officers. This suggests that the news viewing helps facilitate the view of officers in a positive manner, except for when the officer is depicted as Black. Finally, there was no interaction between the race of the featured officer and perpetrator on positive perceptions of the officer, $F(4, 154) = 0.74$, $p = .56$, suggesting that perceptions of the officer were not dependent on the interaction between the depicted officer and perpetrator.

Discussion

The current experiment was designed to test whether varying the race of perpetrators and officers in a newscast would have an impact on judgments regarding the officers and perpetrators portrayed in a crime story. The current study was also designed to uncover whether news viewing increased the accessibility of stereotypical constructs. The experiment revealed that participants perceived a strong likelihood that a suspect was African American even though he was unidentified. In addition, heavy news viewers were more likely than light news viewers to perceive a high likelihood of an officer being White when he was unidentified. Furthermore, heavy news viewers were more likely than light news viewers to have positive perceptions of the featured officer when he was unidentified. However, the converse was true when the officer was depicted as Black. Below the theoretical implications of this study are discussed.

Unidentified Suspects as Black Suspects

In general, participants exposed to a race-unidentified suspect expressed a high likelihood that he was African American. The implication is that unidentified criminal suspects are assumed to be Black (Devine, 1989; Johnson et al., 1997). This finding provides some evidence for the chronic activation of the stereotype linking Blacks with lawbreaking in news programs that cultivates a perception of Blacks as lawbreakers (Gerbner et al., 2002; Shrum, 2002). Alternative explanations for the results, such as the notion that prejudiced people simply tend to watch more news, appear to be less likely given the complementary findings indicating that prejudice was not related to news viewing or to the manipulations in the current study.

It is well documented that television news consistently overrepresents African American criminality (Dixon & Linz, 2000a, 2000b; Entman & Rojecki, 2000). Perhaps the news overrepresents African American criminals to such a large degree that the cognitive association between Blacks and lawbreaking is perpetually reinforced. According to social psychologists and media effects scholars, certain constructs become chronically accessible if they have been frequently activated in previous contexts (Devine, 1989; Fiske, 1989; Fiske & Taylor, 1991; Price & Tewksbury, 1997). Moreover, recent work has established that in certain cases, cognitive associations are so strong that simple exposure to a particular trait (e.g., criminality) may nonetheless elicit thoughts about a particular racial group (e.g., African Americans) (Eberhardt et al., 2004). Hence, the cognitive link between African Americans and crime may maintain high activation potential at all times as a result of prior activation via news exposure (Price & Tewksbury, 1997).

However, it should be noted that a direct measure of prior news viewing did not appear to moderate this particular effect. One explanation may be that news viewing's influence could not be observed in the current study because television news successfully cultivates a perception of perpetrators as Black for all viewers.[5] In summary, even though prior news viewing was not found to directly moderate the perpetrator findings, the results still theoretically appear to be related to chronic activation. The implication of the current study is that viewers exposed to crime news devoid of explicit racial identification will associate the lawbreaking they see with African Americans (Dixon, 2006a).

White Officers, Chronic Activation and Prior News Viewing

The most significant results of the current study may be that the process of news viewing contributes to a stereotype of officers as being both White and benevolent. Heavy news viewers were more likely than light news viewers to misremember an unidentified officer as a White officer and to view unidentified officers positively. There are at least three potential reasons for this effect.

First, most citizens have little direct contact with police officers outside of the occasional traffic infraction (Delgado, 1994; Romer, Jamieson, & Aday, 2003). Therefore, contact with the police is largely an experience shaped by media exposure. As a result, media depictions have the possibility of having a significant impact on viewers' perceptions of officers (Harris, 1999).

Second, content analyses of news programs have consistently found that Whites are significantly overrepresented as police officers (Dixon et al., 2003; Dixon & Linz, 2000a; Oliver, 1994). In addition, the news tends to focus on stories that portray society as chaotic and full of crime, usually perpetuated by African Americans (Dixon & Linz, 2000a; Kaniss, 1991; Klite, Bardwell, & Salzman, 1997; Pritchard & Hughes, 1997; Romer et al., 2003; Van Dijk, 1993). The heroes in most of these news stories tend to be the police officers who act as a stabilizing force against the anarchy created by African American perpetrators (Campbell, 1995; Hall et al., 1978). Positive hero imagery more than likely perpetuates a positive perception of the officers (Harris, 1999).

It should also be noted that this effect is most likely to occur in news imagery and not in entertainment programs. The news depicts police officers as reasonable and effective White interveners in society's chaos. Entertainment programs, meanwhile, tend to portray many officers as African Americans who are short tempered, domineering, and in positions of authority (Deroche & Deroche, 1991; Harris, 1999). Future research should continue to investigate whether the current set of findings extends to perceptions of Black officers in other television genres outside of the news.

Finally, the news may facilitate an impression of positive officers who are White due to chronic activation and multiple exemplars of White officers featured in news contexts. Stereotypical constructs are more likely to be used in the future the more they have been activated in the past (Fiske & Taylor, 1991; Higgins, 2000; Shrum, 2002). Apparently, news viewing contributes to the frequent activation of the White officer stereotype, and over time, viewing news programming makes this stereotype more likely to be used in perceptual judgments. As a result, use of the stereotype begins to affect how heavy prior news viewers feel about the White and unidentified officers they encounter in news programs. Diverse role portrayals may be the key to counteracting this effect over time (Dixon, 2006a; Hamilton et al., 1994; Hamilton & Trolier, 1986).

---

5 In fact, both heavy ($M = 4.56$, $SD = 1.15$) and light viewers ($M = 4.38$, $SD = 1.18$) exposed to unidentified suspects had likelihood estimations that unidentified perpetrators are Black.

In addition, the kinds of tasks used in the experiment encouraged the use of the stereotypical constructs via an availability heuristic (Shrum, 1996; Shrum, 2002). When forced to make a difficult judgment (e.g., "remembering" someone not shown or making a judgment about someone not met), it was probably easiest for heavy news viewers to rely on these stereotypical constructs that seemed most familiar. The news typically airs unusual phenomena that portray the world as a threatening place with unfamiliar (e.g., Black) menacing characters and familiar (e.g., White) helpful characters, especially from the perspective of White viewers (Dixon & Linz, 2000a, 2000b; Hall et al., 1978). As a result, heavy news viewers have a number of exemplars featuring White officers from which to chose when making their judgments (Pritchard & Hughes, 1997; Shrum, 2002; Zillmann, 2002).

It should be noted that there are two other plausible alternatives besides chronic activation for the moderating effects of news viewing on perceptions of officers. One of them is that heavy news viewers are simply racists before they watch the news. In other words, a kind of selective perception may be at work (Vidmar & Rokeach, 1974). However, it is notable that the complementary results yielded these same interactions even after controlling for racism. In addition, though implicit stereotyping might play a role in the effects observed, explicit stereotyping and motivation to apply stereotypes to news stimuli do not appear to be explanatory factors in the current study. Most of the participants in the experiment scored at the lower end of the Modern Racism Scale that was utilized as a covariate in the complimentary analysis. This suggests that the participants were not explicitly prejudiced or predisposed to apply stereotypes to media stimuli. In fact, the opposite would be more likely. However, future research should attempt to employ implicit stereotype measures in order to investigate whether implicit stereotyping influences responses to crime news stimuli.

The second alternative explanation is that heavy news viewers are simply more attentive than light news viewers to news content, and they simply used the base-rate information derived from their prior news exposure to make their judgments. However, the reality is that people often ignore base rate information in lieu of stereotypes (Fiske & Taylor, 1991; Higgins, 2000). In addition, the attentiveness argument might apply to the likelihood judgments, but it cannot account for why heavy news viewers were less likely than light news viewers to view an African American officer positively. The explanation that appears to fit best with the data is chronic activation. However, future studies should be dedicated to further investigating chronic activation and ruling out these alternative hypotheses. An overview of a few of these studies is offered below.

Limitations and Future Studies

The one-story manipulation is useful for understanding the extent to which specific elements of a news story might influence judgments. However, studies that mimic the actual television environment where White officers and Black suspects are overrepresented might reveal additional information about the effects of such content on viewers. Some scholars have begun to undertake studies that more specifically resemble the home viewing environment (Dixon, 2006a, 2006b; Gilliam & Iyengar, 2000; Gilliam et al., 1996; Gilliam, Valentino, & Beckmann, 2002). Future studies might attempt to employ survey methodology to deal with this issue. These surveys might also assist in attempting to understand the influence of news from a multivariate perspective.

Another area for future work includes an examination how Blacks react to racialized intergroup portrayals. Because so few people of color were able to be recruited for this study, this inter-racial comparison was not performed. Are people of color more or less likely to use a Black criminal stereotype moderated by news viewing while making social judgments?

In addition, future research should be undertaken to further study the extent to which prior news viewing might shape race and crime perceptions. The current study demonstrates that prior news viewing may influence race and crime judgments. The most likely theoretical explanation for this moderating power is tied to cognitive accessibility. One of the ways to continue to investigate this would be to attempt to replicate the current study with a non-exposure group in order to understand whether exposure to the news sets an occasion and primes participants to react in a biased way. If the current pattern of findings holds up, chronic news watching would remain the best explanation for the observed effects.

A complementary area that could be explored more in the future includes the interactive effects of the race of perpetrators and officers featured in a newscast. Although the current study attempted to explore these potential interactive effects, none of them was statistically significant. Most likely these null findings resulted from a lack of sample size. In addition, local news viewing and network news viewing were not assessed separately. This measurement problem might have also influenced the results. Future research should fully investigate this issue by utilizing multiple measures of news viewing and accessibility and testing them in the same study with larger samples.

Finally, process measures need to be further explored in future studies. The underlying mechanisms responsible for the moderating effects of prior news viewing need to be explored in future research. One approach might be to investigate accessibility using a speed of responding or recognition task. In addition, it might be possible that the perception that officers were White might actually moderate perceptions about the officer. Various analytical strategies such as mediational analyses could not be undertaken in the current study due to sample size and other issues. However, it should be undertaken in future research in order to answer these questions.

Conclusion

The current study provides three insights. First, it provides evidence that news viewers exposed to unidentified criminality will associate what they see with African Americans. Second, unidentified officers will be perceived as being both White and positive figures among heavy news viewers. Third, chronic activation via news exposure can maintain and reinforce stereotypes.

References

Campbell, C. (1995). *Race, myth and the news*. Thousand Oaks, CA: Sage Publications.

Delgado, R. (1994). Rodrigo's eighth chronicle: Black crime, white fears-on the social construction of threat. *Virginia Law Review, 80*, 503–548.

Deroche, C., & Deroche, J. (1991). Black and white: Racial construction in television police dramas. *Canadian Ethnic Studies, 23*(3), 69–91.

Devine, P. G. (1989). Stereotypes and prejudice: Their automatic and controlled components. *Journal of Personality & Social Psychology, 56*, 5–18.

Dixon, T. L. (2006a). Psychological reactions to crime news portrayals of Black criminals: Understanding the moderating roles of prior news viewing and stereotype endorsement. *Communication Monographs, 73*, 162–187.

Dixon, T. L. (2006b). Schemas as average conceptions: Skin tone, television news exposure, and culpability judgments. *Journalism and Mass Communication Quarterly, 83*, 131–149.

Dixon, T. L., Azocar, C., & Casas, M. (2003). The portrayal of race and crime on television network news. *Journal of Broadcasting & Electronic Media, 47,* 495– 520.

Dixon, T. L., & Linz, D. G. (2000a). Overrepresentation and underrepresentation of African Americans and Latinos as lawbreakers on television news. *Journal of Communication, 50*(2), 131–154.

Dixon, T. L., & Linz, D. G. (2000b). Race and the misrepresentation of victimization on local television news. *Communication Research, 27,* 547–573.

Dixon, T. L., & Maddox, K. B. (2005). Skin tone, crime news, and social reality judgments: Priming the stereotype of the dark and dangerous black criminal. *Journal of Applied Social Psychology, 38,* 1555–1570.

Eagly, A., & Chaiken, S. (1993). *The psychology of attitudes.* Fort Worth, TX: Harcourt Brace.

Eberhardt, J. L., Goff, P. A., Purdie, V. J., & Davies, P. G. (2004). Seeing black: Race, crime and visual processing. *Journal of Personality and Social Psychology, 87,* 876–893.

Entman, R. (1992). Blacks in the news: Television, modern racism, and cultural change. *Journalism Quarterly, 69,* 341–361.

Entman, R. (1994). Representation and reality in the portrayal of Blacks on network television news. *Journalism Quarterly, 71,* 509–520.

Entman, R., & Rojecki, A. (2000). *The Black image in the White mind: Media and race in America.* Chicago: University of Chicago Press.

Fazio, R. H., Jackson, J. R., Dunton, B. C., & Williams, C. J. (1995). Variability in automatic activation as an unobtrusive measure of racial attitudes: A bona fide pipeline? *Journal of Personality and Social Psychology, 69,* 1013–1027.

Fiske, S. T. (1989). Examining the role of intent: Toward understanding its role in stereotyping and prejudice. In J. S. Uleman & J. A. Bargh (Eds.), *Unintended thought* (pp. 253–283). New York: Guilford Press.

Fiske, S. T., & Taylor, S. E. (1991). *Social cognition* (2nd ed.). New York: McGraw-Hill.

Gerbner, G. (1990). Epilogue: Advancing the path of righteousness (maybe). In N. Signorielli & M. Morgan (Eds.), *Cultivation analysis: New directions in media effects research* (pp. 242–262). Newbury Park, CA: Sage.

Gerbner, G., Gross, L., Morgan, M., & Signorielli, N. (1980). The "mainstreaming" of America: Violence profile no. 11. *Journal of Communication, 30*(3), 10–29.

Gerbner, G., Gross, L., Morgan, M., & Signorielli, N. (2002). Growing up with television: Cultivation processes. In J. Bryant & D. Zillmann (Eds.), *Media effects: Advances in theory and research* (pp. 43–67). Hillsdale, NJ: Lawrence Erlbaum Associates, Inc.

Gibbons, J. A., Taylor, C., & Phillips, J. (2005). Minorities as marginalized heroes and prominent villains in the mass media: Music, news sports, television, and movies. In R. W. Walker & D. J. Herrmann (Eds.), *Cognitive technology: Essays on the transformation of thought and society* (pp. 149–171). Jefferson, NC: McFarland & Company, Inc.

Gilens, M. (1996). "Race coding" and white opposition to welfare. *The American Political Science Review, 90,* 593–604.

Gilens, M. (1999). *Why Americans hate welfare: Race, media and the politics of antipoverty policy.* Chicago: University of Chicago Press.

Gilliam, F. D., & Iyengar, S. (1998). The superpredator script. *Nieman Reports, 52*(4), 45–46.

Gilliam, F. D., & Iyengar, S. (2000). Prime suspects: The influence of local television news on the viewing public. *American Journal of Political Science, 44,* 560– 573.

Gilliam, F. D., Iyengar, S., Simon, A., & Wright, O. (1996). Crime in Black and White: The violent, scary world of local news. *Harvard International Journal of Press/Politics, 1,* 6–23.

Gilliam, J. F. D., Valentino, N. A., & Beckmann, M. N. (2002). Where you live and what you watch: The impact of racial proximity and local television news on attitudes about race and crime. *Political Research Quarterly, 55,* 755–780.

Givens, S. M. B., & Monahan, J. L. (2005). Priming mammies, jezebels, and other controlling images: An examination of the influence of mediated stereotypes on perceptions of an African American woman. *Media Psychology, 7,* 87–106.

Hall, S., Critcher, C., Jefferson, T., Clarke, J., & Roberts, B. (1978). *Policing the crisis: Mugging, the state, and law and order.* New York: Holmes & Meier.

Hamilton, D. L., Stroessner, S. J., & Driscoll, D. M. (1994). Social cognition and the study of stereotyping. In P. G. Devine, D. L. Hamilton & T. M. Ostrom (Eds.), *Social cognition: Impact on social psychology* (pp. 292–323). San Diego, CA: Academic Press.

Hamilton, D. L., & Trolier, T. K. (1986). Stereotypes and stereotyping: An overview of the cognitive approach. In J. Dovidio & S. Gaertner (Eds.), *Prejudice, discrimination, and racism* (pp. 127–163). Orlando, FL: Academic Press.

Harris, R. J. (1999). *A cognitive psychology of mass communication* (3rd ed.). Mahwah: NJ: Lawrence Erlbaum Associates.

Higgins, E. T. (2000). Social cognition: Learning about what matters in the social world. *European Journal of Social Psychology, 30,* 3–39.

Iyengar, S. (1987). Television news and citizens' explanations of national affairs. *American Political Science Review, 81,* 815–831.

Iyengar, S. (1990). Framing responsibility for political issues: The case of poverty. *Political Behavior, 12,* 19–40.

Iyengar, S. (1991). *Is anyone responsible?: How television frames political issues.* Chicago: University of Chicago Press.

Johnson, J. D., Adams, M. S., Hall, W., & Ashburn, L. (1997). Race, media and violence: Differential racial effects of exposure to violent news stories. *Basic & Applied Social Psychology, 19,* 81–90.

Kaniss, P. (1991). *Making local news.* Chicago: University of Chicago Press.

Klite, P. K., Bardwell, R. A., & Salzman, J. (1997). Local TV news: Getting away with murder. *Harvard International Journal of Press/Politics, 2,* 102–112.

Livingston, R. W. (2001). What you see is what you get: Systematic variability in perceptual-based social judgement. *Personality and Social Psychology Bulletin, 27,* 1086–1096.

McConahay, J. B. (1986). Modern racism, ambivalence, and the modern racism scale. In J. Dovidio & S. Gaertner (Eds.), *Prejudice, discrimination, and racism* (pp. 91–125). Orlando, FL: Academic Press.

Oliver, M. B. (1994). Portrayals of crime, race, and aggression in "reality-based" police shows: A content analysis. *Journal of Broadcasting & Electronic Media, 38,* 179–192.

Oliver, M. B. (1999). Caucasian viewers' memory of Black and White criminal suspects in the news. *Journal of Communication, 49*(3), 46–60.

Oliver, M. B., & Fonash, D. (2002). Race and crime in the news: Whites' identification and misidentification of violent and nonviolent criminal suspects. *Media Psychology, 4,* 137–156.

Oliver, M. B., Jackson, R. L., Moses, N. N., & Dangerfield, C. L. (2004). The face of crime: Viewers' memory of race-related facial features of individuals pictured in the news. *Journal of Communication, 54,* 88–104.

Peffley, M., Shields, T., & Williams, B. (1996). The intersection of race and crime in television news stories: An experimental study. *Political Communication, 13,* 309–327.

Phelps, E. A., O'Connor, K. J., Cunningham, W. A., Funayama, E. S., Gatenby, J. C., Gore, J. C., et al. (2000). Performance on Indirect Measures of Race Evaluation Predicts Amygdala Activation. *Journal of Cognitive Neuroscience, 12*(5), 729–738.

Potter, W. J. (1991). Examining cultivation from a psychological perspective: Component subprocesses. *Communication Research, 18,* 77–102.

Potter, W. J. (1993). Cultivation theory and research: A conceptual critique. *Human Communication Research, 19,* 564–601.

Power, J. G., Murphy, S. T., & Coover, G. (1996). Priming prejudice: How stereotypes and counter-stereotypes influence attribution of responsibility and credibility among ingroups and outgroups. *Human Communication Research, 23,* 36–58.

Price, V., & Tewksbury, D. (1997). News values and public opinion: A theoretical account of media priming and framing. In G. A. Barnett & F. J. Boster (Eds.), *Progress in the communication sciences* (pp. 173–212). New York: Ablex.

Pritchard, D. P., & Hughes, K. D. (1997). Patterns of deviance in crime news. *Journal of Communication, 47*(3), 49–67.

Romer, D., Jamieson, K. H., & Aday, S. (2003). Television news and the cultivation of fear of crime. *Journal of Communication, 53,* 88–104.

Romer, D., Jamieson, K. H., & de Coteau, N. J. (1998). The treatment of persons of color in local television news: Ethnic blame discourse or realistic group conflict? *Communication Research, 25,* 268–305.

Shrum, L. J. (1995). Assessing the social influence of television: A social cognition perspective on cultivation effects. *Communication Research, 22,* 402–429.

Shrum, L. J. (1996). Psychological processes underlying cultivation effects: Further tests of construct accessibility. *Human Communication Research, 22,* 482–509.

Shrum, L. J. (2002). Media consumption and perceptions of social reality: Effects and underlying processes. In J. Bryant & D. Zillmann (Eds.), *Media effects: Advances in theory and research* (2nd ed.). Mahway, New Jersey: Lawrence Erlbaum Associates.

Tabachnick, B. G., & Fidell, L. S. (2001). *Using multivariate statistics (Fourth Edition).* Needham Heights, MA: Allyn and Bacon.

Tewksbury, D. (2003). What do Americans really want to know? Tracking the behavior of news readers on the Internet. *Journal of Communication, 53,* 694–710.

Valentino, N. (1999). Crime news and the priming of racial attitudes during evaluations of the president. *Public Opinion Quarterly, 63,* 293–320.

Van Dijk, T. A. (1993). *Elite discourse and racism.* Newbury Park, CA: Sage.

Vidmar, N., & Rokeach, M. (1974). Archie Bunker's bigotry: A study in selective perception and exposure. *Journal of Communication, 24,* 36–47.

von Hippel, W., Sekaquaptewa, D., & Vargas, P. (1995). On the role of encoding processes in stereotype maintenance. *Advances in Experimental Social Psychology, 27,* 177–254.

von Hippel, W., Sekaquaptewa, D., & Vargas, P. (1997). The linguistic intergroup bias as an implicit indicator of prejudice. *Journal of Experimental Social Psychology, 33,* 490–509.

Wicks, R. H. (1992). Schema theory and measurement in mass communication research: Theoretical and methodological issues in news information processing. In S. A. Deetz (Ed.), *Communication yearbook* (Vol. 15, pp. 115–145). Newbury Park: Sage.

Zaller, J. (1992). *The nature and origins of mass opinion.* New York: Cambridge University Press.

Zillmann, D. (2002). Exemplification theory of media influence. In J. Bryant & D. Zillmann (Eds.), *Media Effects: Advances in Theory and Research* (pp. 19–41). Mahwah, NJ: Lawrence Erlbaum Associates.

THE CRIMINOLOGICAL CULTIVATION OF AFRICAN AMERICAN MUNICIPAL POLICE OFFICERS

Sambo or Sellout

by Franklin T. Wilson[1] and Howard Henderson[2]

Since the days of their systematic exclusion, African American police officers have made huge strides in increasing their representation at all levels of law enforcement (Gabbidon & Greene, 2013). In fact, the presence of minority police officers has been shown to increase the likelihood of perceived departmental legitimacy while also incrementally dismantling the sociopolitical hurdles within the previously excluded field of American policing (Jollevet, 2008). Despite these advances, the African American community remains the (1) most likely to view police negatively, (2) least likely to support and/or call on law enforcement in times of crisis, and (3) least likely to view law enforcement as a career choice (Rocque, 2011). As a result, recruiting minorities into the ranks of American policing remains a sociopolitical and psychological challenge, ultimately impacting the degree and extent to which African Americans seek careers in law enforcement. Consequently, given this supposed "postracial" America, coupled with the consistent negative perceptions of police by the African American community, it is ever more critical that these barriers between the police and the hiring of African Americans remain at the forefront.

Given the increase in popular media outlets (Surette, 2007) and the controversial nature of many of the minority–police interactions, it is of no surprise that the media serve as a conduit of these often negative encounters. Research has demonstrated that these media outlets are reflectors and reinforcers of the sociopolitical law enforcement experience (Graziano, Schuck, & Martin, 2010). To date, examinations of media depictions of minority police officers are virtually

1   Department of Criminology and Criminal Justice, Indiana State University, Terre Haute, IN, USA
2   College of Criminal Justice, Sam Houston State University, Huntsville, TX, USA

nonexistent. We maintain this is due to the traditional approaches to academic media studies and the disconnect between media examinations and criminological research regarding law enforcement. Wimmer and Dominick (2003) point out that academic media studies are primarily centered around the antisocial and prosocial effects of specific media content, uses and gratifications, agenda setting by the media, and the cultivation of perceptions of social reality. It is this cultivation of perceptions of social reality to which this article lends its focus. More specifically this article points to the need for criminologists to explore what we are entitling criminological cultivation. Cultivation theory, one of the most widely used theories in mass media studies, hypothesizes that long-term exposure to a repetitive and stable system of messages delivered through media programming can have cumulative consequences leading to the gradual adoption of beliefs about the nature of the social world. Cultivation researchers maintain that these messages represent consistent patterns in the portrayal of specific issues, policies, and topics, many of which are in conflict with their occurrence in real life (Wimmer & Dominick, 2003). Similarly, criminological cultivation consists of the development of specific perceptions of any aspect of crime, deviance, and/or the criminal justice system due to long-term exposure to a repetitive system of messages delivered through media outlets. Criminological cultivation studies are differentiated from traditional cultivation studies in that the studies focus primarily on the disjuncture between media depictions and real-life occurrences regarding crime and the criminal justice system. More specifically criminological cultivation studies primarily utilize the criminology and criminal justice peer-reviewed literature to determine the baseline of what real-world occurrences entail. Further, specific emphasis is given to how cultivated perceptions impact various aspects of the real-world criminal justice system.

First step of cultivation analyses consist of examinations of large blocks of media content to determine what overarching messages are being conveyed through the medium in question (Wimmer & Dominick, 2003). Second-step cultivation studies utilize these findings to determine if there is an actual cultivation effect. Therefore, the findings presented here represent the first step of the cultivation analysis process and do not seek to identify a cultivation effect. As Mastro and Behm-Morawitz (2005) state "Although effects cannot be determined from content, such data provide insights into the potential influence of consumption on consumers when viewed from the perspectives of cultivation theory" (p. 110). Therefore, we assert that our findings identify a potentially underexamined variable (i.e., depictions of African American municipal police officers) in the recruitment, acceptance, and retention of African American police officers. The findings of this study point to the need to expand the application of cultivation analysis to the field of criminology and criminal justice research. While this article has potential implications for those individuals employed by or seeking employment within law enforcement, the concept of criminological cultivation should be expanded to all players in the criminal justice system as well as the public's perception of these individuals.

African American Law Enforcement Experience

Historical Context

Given the history of race relations in the United States it is not surprising that the experience of African American police officers differ considerably from White officers. In examining the history of law enforcement in the United States, there have been two distinct periods during which African Americans participated in law enforcement: post–Civil War and post–World War II (Dulaney, 1996). These reference points were separated by more than half a century, during which Blacks were systematically excluded from employment as police officers, consistent with other outlets of socio-economic advancement at this time. Therefore, before exploring the quantity and quality of African American police officer portrayals in film, one must first understand the progress made by African Americans in law enforcement, in spite of the documented employment challenges.

The first African American police officers in the United States were known to be "free men of color," who served as members of the New Orleans city guard in 1803 (Dulaney, 1996; Moskos & Jay, 2008). These men held their positions as a result of their status in the city's unique multiracial society. They sought to establish their connection to the city's White citizenry and distance themselves from the subservient reality of being Black in the South. It is estimated that at the turn of the 20th century Blacks comprised 2.7% of all law enforcement and firemen (Kuykendall & Burns, 1980). Given the race relations in the country, Black officers experienced differential treatment by their fellow White officers and supervisors. This racist treatment was echoed in Rudwick's (1962) classic research in which he surveyed 130 police departments and found that 53% of the departments required Black officers to request assistance from White officers before they arrested other Whites. In other locales, Black officers were subjected to riding in police cars marked "Colored Police" and were only allowed to police other Blacks (Dulaney, 1996; Sullivan, 1989). It was not until the 1960s that there began to be major advances toward the hiring of Black officers, primarily in the major urban communities across the country.

Despite the signing of the Civil Rights Act of 1964, there were as many as 28 law enforcement agencies that continued to limit the arrest powers of Black officers in the mid- to late 1960s, the majority of which were located in the segregated South (Ebony, 1996). In the 1960s, as a result of race riots, it was theorized that the hiring of minority officers would decrease the tensions between the African American community and law enforcement personnel. An example of this was the Kerner Commission's recommendation to hire minority officers as a way to halt the serious race riots of the day. The Commission cited that the lack of diversity was a major impetus behind the heated racial tensions. The 1970s ushered in a significant increase in African American officers as a result of Supreme Court decisions, governmental reports, Congressional legislation, and the formation of Black police unions. In the following decade, there was a continued increase in the number of African Americans into the ranks of law enforcement; and by the 1990s, African American officers accounted for 10.5% of local police departments (Reaves, 1996).

More recently it has been reported that African American's comprise approximately 20% of metropolitan police agencies with representation dwindling in smaller departments (Gabbidon & Greene, 2013). In spite of numerous challenges, the percentage of African American police officers today approximates their proportion in the general population (Gaines & Kappeler, 2005). However, despite increased representation, African American police officers continue to encounter various community and organizational challenges. African Americans face many challenges that deter them from entering a career in law enforcement or from achieving success once they choose this career path. Some of these barriers include racist attitudes, and various forms of racial discrimination and harassment, often expressed as a lack of recognition, rewards, support from superiors, and favoritism (Leinen, 1984).

Proportional Representation and Dual Marginalization

The barriers to increasing the number of African American law enforcement officers have typically been in the form of institutional and cultural challenges (Gaines, Kappeler, & Vaughn, 1997). These institutional challenges have typically come in the form of a host of complicated application processes, a lack of diversity, and discriminatory assignments. Many of these issues reportedly remain today, all across the country (for a detailed discussion, see Brunson & Gau, 2011).

However, the most difficult barrier, according to Peak (2005), has to deal with the image that minority communities have of police officers. It has been well documented that traditionally police officers have been seen as symbols of oppression that use excessive brutality and are often perceived as an army of occupation (see Alexander, 2010; Shelden, 2008 for examples). Perceptions of African American officers impact not only the way in which Blacks working in law enforcement are treated but also the possibility that they will choose law enforcement over other career paths. For many of those African Americans in uniform, a double marginality has existed, whereby they feel accepted neither by their own minority group nor by the White officers. This observation was supported by Kaminski (1993) who examined whether attitudes toward the police affected the likelihood of high school seniors responding positively to a hypothetical offer of a job as a police officer. The Black respondents expressed less favorable attitudes toward the police than the White respondents. However, Whites were somewhat less likely to accept the job offer when they believed that police treated minorities unfairly. The Black respondents were significantly more likely than the White respondents to report that people who live in their neighborhood did not respect the police and therefore expressed less interest in police work. These findings are not surprising, given the apparent view by many in the African American community that the police serve as, or an extension of, an oppressive regime. Therefore, joining the police force would be viewed by some in the African American community as "Uncle Tom-ing," or selling out. Such views could impact the recruitment and retention of African American police officers and, to a lesser degree, any who see the position as discriminatory.

This double marginality among African American officers results from feelings of social isolation and social distancing (Buzawa, 1981). As a result of this social isolation and distancing one often finds a sense of racial pride and solidarity among African American policemen (Strokes & Scott, 1996). This has arguably contributed to a more aggressive, assertive posture than has been seen in the past. Dowler (2005) found that African American police officers were more likely to feel criticized and believed they were perceived as militant. Therefore, African American police officers are often encumbered with the choice between social isolationism and being perceived as a militant. The impact of social isolationism and public perceptions of African American police officers is not restricted to law enforcement organizations and the police culture. This same affect has been observed within the African American community (see Wilson, 1990). Therefore, this article seeks to determine the quantity of African American municipal police officer depictions as well as the quality of the depictions in order to determine the overarching messages conveyed through the core cop film genre. We go on to explore the potential role of film depictions in the cultivation of social reality perceptions that may amplify the aforementioned double marginalization between African American officers and the communities they serve. Before doing this however we briefly discuss the primary tenets of cultivation theory and the cop film genre.

Cultivation Theory

Cultivation theory, as it was originally developed and tested by George Gerbner in the 1970s, hypothesizes that long-term exposure to a repetitive and stable system of messages delivered through television programming can have cumulative consequences. More specifically, it is believed by cultivation theorists that the viewing of television leads to the gradual adoption of beliefs about the nature of the social world. Beliefs that conform to the selective representation of reality were portrayed in a systematic way on television (Wimmer & Dominick, 2003).

Cultivation studies consist of two separate steps. In the first step, large segments of media content are analyzed to identify the overarching messages delivered by the media source. It is believed by cultivation theorists that these messages represent consistent patterns in the portrayal of specific issues, policies, and topics, many of which are in conflict with their occurrence in real life (Wimmer & Dominick, 2003). The findings acquired in Step 1 studies are utilized in Step 2 studies to develop a set of questions that are designed to detect a cultivation effect (see Wimmer & Dominick, 2003 for more details).

Several examinations of cultivation studies (see Hawkins & Pingree, 1981; Morgan & Shanahan, 1997; Morgan & Shanahan, 2010; Shrum & O'Guinn, 1993) have established that the research as a whole has demonstrated a consistent television-viewing effect on a variety of subject's perceptions of social reality (Wimmer & Dominick, 2003). Due to Gerbner developing the theory in the late 1960s and early 1970s, television was for a longtime the primary medium cultivation researchers would examine. But over time the number of television channels, media outlets, and viewer types has also expanded. Due to this perpetual expansion, the types of mediums examined by cultivation researchers have also expanded (Wilson, 2009). One now sees cultivation researchers examining mediums such as newspapers (Vergeer, Lubbers, & Scheepers, 2000) and video games (Williams, 2006), among others. However, with this expansion of visual media sources comes the ability of viewers to watch increasingly more narrow or specialized genres (Prior, 2005). In fact, some studies have shown that the power of the cultivation effect increases the narrower the genre viewed (Hawkins & Pingree, 1981). This study expands cultivation research not only to the field of criminology and criminal justice but continues the expansion of mediums by examining film. It also focuses on a narrow or specialized genre, core cop film genre, to determine both the quantity and the quality of African American municipal police officers portrayals in the first 40 years of the genre.

Cultivation research has long appeared on the periphery of criminological studies through examinations of the mediated depictions of various variables such as race, gender, sexuality, and crime, among others. Second-step cultivation studies have examined the subsequent impact of such mediated depictions on the perceptions of social reality. However, with the possible exception of Escholz, Sims Blackwell, Gertz, and Chirico's (2002) examination of the impact of watching reality police programs on attitudes toward the police, the research on the depiction of homosexual police officers by Wilson, Longmire, and Swymeler (2009) and female police officers by Wilson and Blackburn (in press), virtually no one has utilized cultivation theory in the direct context of criminological and criminal justice research. In this study, we seek to bring cultivation theory out of the periphery and into the center of criminological and criminal justice studies. This study represents the first step toward future cultivation analyses concerning the cultivation of African American police recruits, police officers in general, and the general public's perceptions of African American municipal police officers. However, before discussing the methodology and findings of this study, it is necessary to be clear as to what films constitute the core cop film genre.

Core Cop Film Genre

The law enforcement figure was portrayed primarily in Westerns and noirs up until the 1970s. They were portrayed as lone sheriffs or detectives. Depictions of foolish patrolmen (keystone cops), tough federal agents, or cool private investigators were how police officers were portrayed (Rafter, 2000). While the lampooned police officer continues today (Surette, 2007) the Western and noir era gradually lost its appeal throughout the 1950s and 1960s, opening the door for the cop film era to arise (Rafter, 2000; Surette, 2007). In the 1960s and 1970s public opinion began moving toward the law-and-order perspective, arguably due to the unrest of the 1960s, allowing filmmakers to transform the lone gunslinger of westerns to a modern municipal police officer (Rafter, 2000). Compelled by the underlying belief that liberal laws had tied the cops' hands, thus keeping them from catching criminals, the 1971 release of the vigilante-like justice film *Dirty Harry* would serve as the archetype for the modern cop film genre.

Rafter (2000) reveals the cop film genre as not so much a new genre but rather a new strategy for investigating the nature of heroism and the hero's relationship to society:

> Like the Westerner, Harry Callahan patrols a border between barbarity and society, abandon and self-control, what John Cawelti in another context calls the 'frontier between savagery and civilization. That frontier is both geographical and psychological, a line that must be drawn within the city and within the hero himself. (Rafter, 2000, p. 76)

In the 1980s and 1990s, the genre would develop subgenres of the traditional cop film genre. These splinter or subgenres include, but are not limited to, the "rogue cop films," "corrupt cop films," "buddy cop films," and "cop comedy films," among others; arguably moving further and further away from the initial characteristics of the cop film. However, these researchers argue that despite the splintering of the cop film genre, the core characteristics that originally defined the cop film have endured and it is those films that make up the core cop film genre.

The intent of this study is to examine the quantity and quality of African American police officer portrayals in the core cop film genre to determine the overarching messages conveyed over the first 40 years of the core cop film genre. The unique contributions of this analysis are fourfold. First, we address the gap in the literature regarding the mediated depiction of African American municipal police officers in theatrically released films. More specifically we identify a disturbing 40-year trend of African American municipal police officers being depicted as either comedic fodder or sellouts to the African American community. Second, the article addresses the potential impact of said images on the recruitment, retention, and perceptions of African American municipal police officers. Third, this study seeks to introduce as well as promote the utilization of cultivation theory, what we establish as criminological cultivation, in the field of criminal justice and criminology. Finally, we introduce the reader to the unified film population identification methodology (UFPIM), a relatively new methodology that many may not yet be familiar. The UFPIM provides future researchers with a mechanism for establishing entire film populations that have clearly defined parameters as opposed to the utilization of traditional convenience sampling techniques that are open to criticisms of representativeness and replicability.

Methods

Identifying the Study Population

In an effort to address the issue of population replicability in studies of social science issues in theatrically released films, Wilson (2006) developed a methodology for systematically identifying large replicable film populations. Wilson (2009) later refined the parameters of the said methodology and named it the UFPIM. The UFPIM is specifically designed to help film researchers systematically identify replicable film populations (Wilson, 2009).

The UFPIM utilizes the Internet Movie Database Power Search (IMDbPS) as part of its three-phase process of identifying specific film populations (for further details see Wilson, 2006, 2009). However, it is designed so that any searchable database of films could be substituted for the IMDbPS depending on the researchers' desired parameters. In Phase I of the UFPIM, the relevant literature associated with the film population in question is used to develop a definition of the film population to be analyzed. In Phase II, the IMDbPS is utilized to identify a base film list. This list is developed by utilizing at a minimum the IMDbPS search criterion of "key words in the movie plot summaries," "movie genre" (the primary genre to which the IMDbPS associates a film), "year" (the year or series of years in which films were released), and "key words" (for further details see Wilson, 2006 or Wilson, 2009). Phase III constitutes a two-stage process, the first of which involves the development of an identification-coding sheet designed to further isolate those films that meet the definition established in Phase I. Stage II involves the examination of plot summaries for all the films identified in Phase II utilizing the aforementioned coding sheet. In Stage II of Phase III, plot summaries from at least two independent sources, in this study IMDb and Amazon.com, are to be examined to help ensure the accuracy of the final population. In this study, the UFPIM was used to identify the core cop film population to be examined.

Analysis

In this study, Phase I resulted in the first four decades of the core cop film genre being defined as (a) theatrically released films between 1971 and 2011, (b) that take place in the United States, (c) where one or more actors play the hero who is an active urban (municipal) police officer of traditional ranks, (d) either acting alone or with a partner in a street cop/detective role, (e) in the past or present, that appear to be reality based. Given this definition, films that depict police officers who are outside their jurisdictional boundaries (i.e., the *Beverley Hills Cop* series), in specialized units that do not traditionally fall into the day-to-day crime fighting units in police department organizational structures (i.e., internal affairs, forensic units) or scenarios that do not appear to be reality based (i.e., supernatural phenomenon, alien encounters, and/or futuristic depictions) are excluded from the genre.

When this research was conducted, films could be categorized into 19 genres in the IMDb (action, adventure, animation, comedy, crime, documentary, drama, family, fantasy, film noir, horror, music, musical, mystery, romance, sci-fi, thriller, war, and western). In order to further isolate those films that met the core cop film definitional criteria of "occurring in the past or present and appearing to be reality based" each of the IMDb genre definitions was examined to determine which would be searched and which would be excluded. Of the 19 potential genre classifications, 8 of the film genres were chosen to search for films (crime, drama, action, adventure, mystery, family, romance, and thriller). Based on the genre definitions provided by the IMDb (see Wilson, 2009), the remaining genres were excluded. A total of four searches were conducted on the eight chosen genre categories using the IMDb Power Search for a total of 28 searches. The IMDb Power Search categories used included "plot summary words," "country of origin," "genre," "language," "year," "must have," "TV movies," "direct to video," and "TV series." Each of these categories assisted in the isolation of strictly theatrically released films between 1971 and 2011. In each of the four searches under each of the eight genres, the search criteria constituted films (a) that occurred in the United States (country of origin), (b) in which the dominant language was English (language), (c) released in theaters between 1971 and 2011 (year), and (d) that had to contain a plot summary (must have) and excluded films (e) that went direct to video or were TV movies and series. The only categories that were adjusted were the genres searched and the key terms searched for in the plot summary. Based on common language utilized both in film research literature and in law enforcement research literature, the key terms searched for under each genre in the plot summaries were "cop," "police," "detective," and "law enforcement" (Wilson, 2009).

At the end of Phase II, a base film list of over 500 films was produced. In Stage I of Phase III, the core cop film identification-coding sheet was developed. In Stage II of Phase III, over 1,000 plot summaries from both the IMDb and Amazon.com were evaluated using the core cop film identification-coding sheet resulting in a final population of 130 films. However, throughout the examination process, several films were excluded for a variety of reasons. Eight films could not be located and were determined to be out of production. The three films, *Electra Glide in Blue* (1973), *The Indian Runner* (1991), and *Partners in Crime* (2000), were excluded because the films involved officers who were not municipal police officers. Additionally, two films were excluded due to not fitting into one of the required genre categories. Upon viewing, it was determined that the film *The Black Marble* (1980) was a comedy and the film *God Told Me To* (1976) fell more appropriately into the horror film genre. The film *The Onion Field* (1979), although dealing with the shooting of police officers, primarily focused on the justice system rather than law enforcement. The films *Wild Things* (1998) and *Cement* (1998) both were excluded due to the fact the police were not portrayed as heroes in any way. Finally, two films were excluded due to the leading heroic characters were not law enforcement officers. In *Unstoppable* (2004) Wesley Snipes' character is a military retiree and in *Gone Baby Gone* (2007) Casey Affleck's character is a private investigator. Therefore, due to the fact that 8 films could not be located and an additional 10 films were excluded for the reasons noted previously, the final population for the first four decades of the core cop film genre totaled 112 films. Each of the 112 films represented units of analysis and was examined to determine both the quantity and quality of African American municipal police officer depictions. Specifically, films were viewed and film jackets were referenced in order to determine if a film portrayed an African American municipal police officer in the leading or joint leading role. Further, detailed notes were taken in regard to how the African American municipal police officers were portrayed informed both by the literature associated with real-world police officers and by independent observational notes.

Findings

Dynamics of Representation

Before discussing the following findings, it is important to reiterate that this is a first-step criminological cultivation study to determine what overarching messages are being conveyed regarding African American municipal police officers. We are not seeking to determine an actual cultivation effect but rather provide the basis for future second-step cultivation analyses. It is also important to emphasis that the definitional parameters of the core cop film genre were designed to allow for the isolation of those cop films that portray leading hero characters in the most serious and realistic municipal police officer depictions. That said, in the first four decades of the core cop film genre, White municipal police officer depictions dominated the genre. Of the 112 films analyzed, White officers were depicted as the sole leading character 64% ($n = 72$) of the time. Whites were also joint leading character with another White officer in 15% ($n = 17$), with an African American officer in 9% ($n = 10$) and an Asian American officer in 1% ($n = 1$) of the films analyzed. Therefore, White officers were depicted as leading or joint leading municipal police officer characters in 89% ($n = 100$) of the 112 films produced between 1971 and 2011. Comparatively, African American municipal police officers represented the second highest depiction rate at 19% ($n = 21$) followed by Hispanic Americans at 2% ($n = 2$) and Asian Americans at 1% ($n = 1$). Given that African Amer-ican police officers have exceeded their national proportion in the

Table 1. Core Cop Films Depicting African American Municipal Police Officers in Lead or Joint Lead Role by Year of Release.

Core cop films	Year	Lead role	Joint lead role
The Organization	1971	X	
Fatal Beauty	1987	X	
Lethal Weapon I	1987		X
The Kill Reflex	1989	X	
Lethal Weapon 2	1989		X
Downtown	1990		X
Lethal Weapon 3	1992		X
Rising Sun	1993	X	
Seven	1995		X
The Glimmer Man	1997		X
Murder at 1600	1997	X	
Lethal Weapon 4	1998		X
Rush Hour	1998	X	
In Too Deep	1999	X	
The Bone Collector	1999		X
Shaft	2000	X	
Training Day	2001		X
Kept	2001	X	
Dirty	2005		X
Miami Vice	2006		X
Inside Man	2006	X	

general population, comprising 20% of the nation's metropolitan police force, the percentage of African American municipal police officer depictions appears, at face, to be representative (Gabbidon & Greene, 2013). These aggregate numbers are, however, deceiving, given the temporal placement and quality of the said depictions; in short, the depictions are not distributed evenly across the four decades.

Of the 21 films that depicted African American municipal police officers, 95% ($n = 20$) did not occur until after 1987 (see Table 1). Additionally, 52% ($n = 11$) portrayed the officer in a joint leading role and 48% ($n = 10$) as the leading municipal police officer character. These statistics reflect that despite the steadily increasing number of African Americans becoming police officers in the United States, the core cop film genre has traditionally not portrayed them in leading roles. This is demonstrated by the fact not only that the majority of films that present African Americans as primary or joint leading characters came into being after 1987 but that of those African American municipal police officer characters who share the lead character role, all but one shared that role with a White officer. In fact, throughout the first four decades of the core cop film genre, only the film *Dirty* (2005) depicted minority municipal police officer partners (Hispanic and African American) in a joint leading role. Therefore, based on the definitional parameters of what constitutes a core cop film and the IMDbPS primary genre categorizations at the time of this study, there were no films in the first four decades of the core cop film genre that depicted two African American municipal police officers in joint leading roles.

Due to the strict parameters for inclusion of films, it could be argued that we should have included such films as *Running Scared* (1986), *Bad Boys I* (1995), and *Bad Boys II* (2003). Each of these films depicted African American municipal police officers and in the case of the *Bad Boys* series the depiction of two African American municipal police officers in joint leading roles. However, these films were excluded in the initial analysis due to being classified by the IMDb as part of the comedy genre; a genre excluded due to the definitional parameters of what constitutes a core cop film. Additionally, as was stated earlier the *Beverly Hills Cop* series (1984, 1987, and 1994) was excluded due to taking place outside the officer's jurisdictional boundaries as well as being classified as comedies. Similarly, the films *Rush Hour 2* (2001) and *Rush Hour 3* (2007) were excluded due to taking place outside the United States and being classified as comedies. We mention these excluded films at this point because we believe that the inclusion of the aforementioned excluded films, given their comedic nature, would have only served to amplify the findings that follow. Additionally, given this study was designed to isolate those films that depict officers in a serious and realistic light, we posit that the restrictive standards and subsequent exclusions only serve to solidify the importance of our findings.

The aforementioned aggregate findings arguably portray a dependency upon White counterparts. This perspective is only strengthened when the quality of African American municipal police officer depictions is examined. Analysis of these depictions reveals two stark findings. First, a trend of Stepin Fetchit caricatures in depictions of African American municipal police officers was revealed. Second, the few depictions of double marginalization that did occur were portrayed as the officer either having to be a sellout to their community and/or becoming a corrupt police officer if they are going to continue to be a police officer. We will first address the issue of Stepin Fetchit characterizations.

Remnants of Sambo and Stepin Fetchit in Policing Portrayals

Our findings highlight a continued portrayal of stereotypically derogatory comedic depictions of African Americans within the film industry. In fact, the storied history of African Americans as comedic outlets extends back to the slavery experience (Hall, 1993). During this period, African Americans were often utilized as comedy for the dominant majority. As a response to the cultural and personal degradation, Blacks began using this role to diffuse the often physical and emotional abuse received. It is this experience that arguably serves as the embryonic stage of the comedic experience that soon manifests as an often-portrayed African American stereotype. Ultimately, it was this socially accepted and culturally internalized misperception that served as the motivating catalyst behind the minstrel shows of the mid-1830s and the concept of a Sambo.

The minstrel shows parodied African Americans as buffoons among other derogatory characterizations (Kentrick, 2003; Pilgrim, 2012). The blackface characters generally appeared as servants who served as comedic relief in the shows (Cockrell, 1997). According to Cockrell (1997), *The Boston Post* reported in the 1830s that Queen Victoria and Jim Crow were the most popular characters in the world at the time; Jim Crow being in reference to a famous blackface song and dance number entitled "Jump Jim Crow." These early 17th-century Sambo characters were first portrayed by White actors in blackface. It was not until the 1840s and 1950s that one saw African Americans performing in the minstrel shows (Toll, 1974). And while the minstrel show represented one of the first opportunities for African Americans to gain access to the American entertainment industry, the stereotypes popularized through the minstrel shows resulted in members of the African American community facing White retaliation if they did not fulfill the stereotypical expectations (Watkins, 1994). The derogatory characterizations would continue until the demise of the minstrel show in the early 1900s, but the derogatory depictions would continue to be perpetuated in film.

While the derogatory minstrel characterizations in film began with White actors appearing in black-face, Black actors would soon follow suit. Perhaps the most popular, of these Black actors was Stepin Fetchit, the stage name of Lincoln Perry. It was in the 1920s and 1930s that Perry helped popularize the stereotype of the lazy and simpleminded Black man through film; still providing the comedic relief. His portrayals became so synonymous with the stereotype that in the African American community Stepin Fetchit, not unlike the term Sambo used in the 1800s, is often used to denote any African American whose job can be seen as a form of entertainment for Whites (Baraka, 1987). As Dirks and Mueller (2007) point out modern popular culture depictions of African Americans have changed very little since the time of the minstrel show Sambo but potentially have a large impact on the African American community than earlier depictions.

> Under critical historical examination, images of "blackness" found in popular culture today have shifted very little from their historical counterparts. Yet, as Patricia Hill Collins (2004) explains, "In modern America, where community institutions of all sorts have eroded, popular culture has increased in importance as a source of information and ideas" (p. 121). This is particularly problematic for black American youth, as popular culture has come to authoritatively fill the void where other institutions that could "help them navigate the challenges of social inequality" are beginning to disappear (p. 121). (Dirks & Mueller, 2007 p. 124)

Given our predominant findings of Black police officer depictions as comedic caricatures, it appears that African American police officer portrayals are not immune to falling into the scope of the Sambo and Stepin Fetchit lineage; in fact, they appear to personify it.

The analysis of the quality of African American municipal police officer depictions revealed that 52% ($n = 11$) of the 21 films that portrayed an African American municipal police officer in a sole or joint leading role portrayed the officers in a comedic light. While these are qualitative observations, we define comedic light as the character serving as the primary source of comedy in the film; either by being the specific target of jokes, subject of comedic situations, or their comedic banter with other characters. This does not mean the character is void of serious moments but rather that the comedic depictions were prominent in the film and often a key element to the character's personality. Arguably the most prevalent example of such portrayals occurs in the *Lethal Weapon* series (1987, 1989, 1992, 1998). Roger Murtaugh (Danny Glover) consistently finds himself either the subject of his White partner's jokes and/or facing embarrassing situations (i.e., stranded on his toilet due to a bomb being placed under it, being made fun of due to his daughter's condom commercial, having his boat destroyed, or being asked to strip down to his heart-covered boxers and cluck like a chicken to distract a criminal so that the White officer can save the day). No matter what the situation, Murtaugh finds himself most often the focus of the humor and quite often the officer in need of rescue by his White partner. Similarly, to varying degrees, Whoopi Goldberg in *Fatal Beauty* (1987); Keenen Ivory Wayans in *The Glimmer Man* (1997); Wesley Snipes in *Rising Sun* (1993); Chris Tucker in *Rush Hour* (1998); Ice-T in *Kept* (2001); and Cuba Gooding, Jr. in *Dirty* (2005) all find themselves the object of humor from both their White colleagues and/or members of society.

The Stepin Fetchit role of entertaining Whites is arguably still present if one considers that of the 11 films that portray the African American officer in a comedic light, 82% ($n = 9$) have the officers partnered with either a White officer or a White civilian. The remaining 18% ($n = 2$) team the African American officer with another minority. However, the two films in which African American officers are teamed with another minority, *Rush Hour* (1998) and *Dirty* (2005), the African American officer is still portrayed as a source of comedy for their White superiors. As for the 10 films that portray the African American officer in a serious light, 40% ($n = 4$) have the officer partnered with a White Officer. The remaining 60% ($n = 6$) depict the African American officer in a sole leading role. Therefore, of the 112 films that comprise the first 40 years of the core cop film genre African American municipal police officers were only depicted in a noncomedic light while teamed with a White officer or civilian in 4% ($n = 4$) and in a noncomedic light sole leading character role in 5% ($n = 5$) of the films.

The potential significance of this finding is only amplified when one considers that of the 100 films that depict a White municipal police officer in a joint or sole leading character role, 17% ($n = 17$) depict a White officer in a comedic light and 83% ($n = 83$) in a serious light. A stark contrast to the 52% ($n = 11$) of African American depictions in a comedic light. Additionally, of the 89 films that depict a White municipal police officer in the sole or joint leading role with a character that is not a minority police officer, 92% ($n = 82$) depict the White officer or officers in a serious light, while only 8% ($n = 7$) portray that officer in a comedic light. Further, if the films that team the White municipal police officer with a nonpolice officer minority character are excluded, only 3% ($n = 3$) of the 89 films portray White officers in a comedic light.

It should be made clear that while these African American police officer portrayals are the subject of jokes, they often make others the object of humor as well. Therefore, these researchers are not trying to portray the African American officers as defenseless victims. Instead, it is simply being noted that based on these findings there is a clear pattern of African American municipal police officers being portrayed in a comedic light at a much higher rate than White officers. Based on cultivation theory's basic premise that long-term exposure to a repetitive and stable system of messages delivered through various mediums can have cumulative consequences, these findings at a minimum raises the question as to what impact such depictions might have on the expected role of African American municipal police officers by both fellow officers and the community.

A majority of research in this area has centered on the news and entertainment outlets and has primarily relayed a stereotypical perception (Ramasubramanian, 2011). Within criminal justice studies examining the portrayal of African Americans in film is virtually nonexistent. In fact, few studies on media representations have sought to determine the degree and extent to which the depictions influence actualized realities, stereotypes, and the perceived legitimacy of various criminal justice institutions and positions. This lack of criminal justice research is all the more troubling, given the impact of media portrayals on the social judgments of others, self, worldviews, emotions, and expressed bias toward others (Shrum, 2008).

Our findings demonstrate the continued misrepresentation of African Americans in the media. Scholars in various other disciplines have long noted the relationship between stereotype portrayals and a host of negative outcomes. More to the point of our findings, Akbar (1996) held that, "Mockery is one the more sophisticated forms of humiliation." Therefore, we suggest that along with additional first- and second-step cultivation studies, researchers also examine the impact of such depictions on various behavioral and emotional outcomes.

Community or Department? Depictions of Double Marginalization

It is more than feasible that the domination of White police officer portrayals contributes to the development of societal perceptions of police officers. Perhaps the best real-world indicator in the literature at this time, of these perceptions, concerns the fears African Americans have in regard to becoming a police officer. Recruiting minority police officers has proven a difficult task for police departments. This is primarily associated with the image the minority community has of police officers as an army of occupation. Police officers are associated with the use of excessive force and oppression on minorities; therefore, when an African American becomes a police officer, they are often viewed as a sellout by their community. "For many of the African-Americans in uniforms, a so-called double marginality has existed, whereby the African-American officers feel accepted neither by their own minority group nor by the White officers" (Peak, 2005, p. 364). Therefore, this double marginalization is rooted in perceptions, which we believe are created by and/or perpetuated, at least in part, through media depictions.

While a few films hint at the dual marginalization of African American officers, only a few portray it in detail. The films *In Too Deep* (1999), *Shaft* (2000), *Training Day* (2001), and *Dirty* (2005) specifically portray African American municipal police officers that have or are struggling with being accepted by both their department and their community. These four films present two competing natures of double marginalization. The films *In Too Deep* (1999) and *Shaft* (2000) serve as examples of good officers dealing with the struggle of not being fully accepted by their community or the police force. In *Shaft*, the officer is forced to leave the force to protect the community properly; while in the film *In Too Deep*, the officer had to watch his community suffer in order to be a good cop. In short, *Shaft* makes the statement that he is "too Black for the uniform, too blue for the brothers." In this one sentence, *Shaft* summarizes the double marginalization that Black police officers often experience. The films *Training Day* (2001) and *Dirty* (2005) arguably serve as examples of why African American officers are often ostracized by the African American community. Both films depict officers that abuse their powers in an effort to gain status within the police force and power over the community rather than serving the community. So in sum when the double marginalization of African American municipal police officers is depicted the depictions are of selling out one's community or giving up the force to rejoin the community.

Conclusion

While this study focused on theatrically released films, we do not purport to downplay the influence of other media outlets. In fact, we contend that media outlets can no longer be considered mutually exclusive of one another and that the focus should turn toward preferred content by the viewer. As was stated earlier, cultivation theorists have traditionally focused on the impact of repeated messages conveyed through television. This is due to the fact that the theory was developed in the 1960s and 1970s when television programming was relayed across just three major networks and concerns of television influence first began to arise. Still today these concerns are arguably well founded if one considers that until the "1990's television viewing ranked as the third most time-consuming activity (after sleep, work, or school) for Americans" (Surette, 2007 p. 13). Further, for the average American, for every 10 years of life a person spends one solid year (8,760 hours) watching television (Surette, 2007). Nielsen (2011) noted that the amount of television viewing has only increased. The average American now spends over 34 hours per week watching live television. This means the average American will now spend over 2 years (17,680 hours) for every 10 years of their life watching television. This does not include the additional 3–6 hours watching programs that have been recorded. The report also reveals that approximately 36 million Americans are watching video on smartphones now. Additionally, it points out that as Americans grow older, they watch more television programming. These numbers in conjunction with the fact that through various sources, be it normal network programming, movies on demand, and so on, collectively this new and recycled content makes crime and violence the most common content found on television (Surette, 2007). In short, we currently live in the most mediated society.

However, despite the continued prevalence of television programming in recent years with the proliferation of various media outlets, the mediums examined in cultivation studies have expanded (newspapers, video games, film, etc.; Wilson, 2009). It has also been shown that with the expansion of media choices it is now easier for people to view their preferred content (Prior, 2005). In his study of 2,358 U.S. residence, Prior (2005) found that content preference became a better predictor of political knowledge as media choices increased compared to the number of options available. Additionally, cultivation studies have also shown that the cultivation effect increases when narrow genres of programming are watched (Hawkins & Pingree, 1981). Therefore, in this study, we expanded cultivation analysis to theatrically released films and narrowed our examination to the specific genre of core cop films. We contend that the influence of theatrically released films can no longer be viewed as stopping at the theater. Films released theatrically are quickly being absorbed by other media outlets and thereby arguably having their overall influence amplified. For example, *The Economist* (2011) reported:

> Films open on big screens but make money on small ones. After a four-month exclusive run in cinemas (a "window", in Hollywood jargon) they become available as DVDs and Blu-ray discs—and, often, as on-demand videos and digital downloads. In 2010 Americans spent $18.5 billion on such things. Just $10.6 billion was spent on cinema tickets in North America. Another window opens about six months later, when films are sold to cable- and satellite-television companies. Perhaps two years after that they will be sold to free broadcast channels. Like cars, films become cheaper as they age.

Therefore, theatrically released films quickly become integrated into television programming, arguably still the most influential source of cultivation today.

Given that this study did not propose to determine the level of a cultivation effect but rather to identify the dominant messages conveyed through the core cop film genre, the extent to which recruitment, retention, and the acceptance of African American police officers are influenced by media imagery and representation is not clear. The role such representations might play in the double marginalization of African American police officers often face is unexplored. However, the findings presented here, when considered in a cultivation context, at a minimum points to some stark possibilities as to what socially constructed perceptions are being cultivated. First, if the mere portrayal of a particular race of police officer does cultivate public perceptions, then the dominant accepted image would be that of a White officer; given that White officers were the leading or joint leading character in 89% ($n = 100$) of the 112 films examined. Second, if the quality of depiction plays a role in the cultivation process then social realities would be tainted to expect African American police officers to serve as comedic relief, sellouts to their communities, and/or become corrupt officers. In short, African American municipal police officers would not be viewed as serious or deserving of the respect afforded to honest law enforcement officers.

Indications of a cultivation affect in which viewers of specific forms of media expect offenders and police officer to be of a certain race may have already been identified. For example, in his study of light and heavy television news viewer's, Dixon (2007) explores their perceptions of lawbreakers and law defenders. In Dixon's study, subjects were exposed to embedded crime stories in newscasts. If the race of the perpetrator was not revealed, subjects rated a high likelihood that the perpetrator was Black. Further, heavy news viewers were more likely than light news viewers to express a high likelihood that an unidentified officer would be White. Additionally, heavy viewers were more likely than light viewers to not have positive perceptions of Black police officers featured in newscasts.

Supported by the existent literature such as Dixon's (2007) study coupled with the exponential growth of visual media viewership and our findings, we suggest future researchers examine the impact that mediated messages and images play in the cultivation of perceptions of African American municipal police officers. Additionally, given that law enforcement research makes specific distinctions between types of law enforcement (municipal, county, state, federal, etc.) future criminological cultivation researchers should also make these distinctions in an effort to (a) better understand any differences that may exist and (b) more readily compare findings to the policing literature. However, given the widespread depiction of various aspects of the U.S. Criminal Justice System in the media (Surette, 2007), the scope of such research should not be limited to just law enforcement officers or theatrically released films. First-step criminological cultivation analysis, which consists of examinations of large blocks of media content, can be applied to the depiction of all players in the criminal justice system (i.e., judges, lawyers, prison guards, criminals, victims, etc.). Additionally, first-step criminological cultivation analysis should not just be applied to the players in the criminal justice system but also the depictions of criminal justice issues (e.g., policies, laws, deviant acts, crimes, etc.). Upon completion of first-step criminological cultivation research, second-phase projects that explore the actual impact on criminal justice employees and citizens should be pursued. Finally, while this study focused on theatrically released films, future research should examine television programming and continue to expand into other mediums (e.g., print media, video games, YouTube, social media, music, etc.).

Declaration of Conflicting Interests

The author(s) declared no conflicts of interest with respect to the research, authorship, and/or publication of this article.

Funding

The author(s) received no financial support for the research, authorship, and/or publication of this article.

References

Aaron, P. (Producer/Writer), Brown, M. (Producer/Writer), & Rymer, M. (Director). (1999). *In too deep* [Motion Picture]. USA: Dimension Films.

Akbar, N. (1996). *Breaking the chains of psychological slavery.* Tallahassee, FL: Mind Production.

Alexander, M. (2010). *The new Jim crow: Mass incarceration in the age colorblindness.* New York, NY: The New Press.

Baraka, I. (1987). Black art. *The Black Scholar, 18*, 23–30.

Bergman, P. (Producer), Lusting, D. (Producer), Harris, T. (Producer), & Warren, J. (Director). (2000). *Partners in crime* [Motion Picture]. USA: Artisan Home Entertainment.

Birnbaum, R. (Producer), Davis, A. Z. (Producer), Glickman, J. (Producer), Sarkissian, A. (Producer), Stern, J. (Producer) & Ratner, B. (Director). (2007). *Rush hour 3* [Motion Picture]. USA: New Line Cinema.

Birnbaum, R. (Producer), Glickman, J. (Producer), Sarkissian, A. (Producer), Stern, J. (Producer) & Ratner, B. (Director). (2001). *Rush hour 2* [Motion Picture]. USA: New Line Cinema.

Birnbaum, R. (Producer), Sarkissian, A. (Producer), Glickman, J. (Producer), & Ratner, B. (Director). (1998). *Rush hour* [Motion Picture]. USA: New Line Cinema.

Bregman, M. (Producer), Stroller, L.A. (Producer), Bregman, M. (Producer), & Noyce, P. (Director). (1999). *The bone collector* [Motion Picture]. USA: Universal Pictures.

Bruckheimer, J. (Producer) & Bay, M. (Director). (2003). *Bad boys II* [Motion Picture]. USA: Columbia Pictures.

Bruckheimer, J. (Producer), Simpson, D. (Producer), & Bay, M. (Director). (1995). *Bad boys* [Motion Picture]. USA: Don Simpson/Jerry Bruckheimer Films.

Bruckheimer, J. (Producer), Simpson, D. (Producer), & Brest, M. (Director). (1984). *Beverly Hills cop* [Motion Picture]. USA: Paramount Pictures.

Bruckheimer, J. (Producer), Simpson, D. (Producer), & Scott, T. (Director). (1987). *Beverly Hills cop II* [Motion Picture]. USA: Paramount Pictures.

Brunson, R., & Gau, J. (2011). Officer race versus macro-level context: A text of competing hypotheses about Black citizens' experiences with and perceptions of Black police officers. *Crime & Delinquency, 59,* 1–30.

Buzawa, E. S. (1981). The role of race in predicting job attitudes of patrol officers. *Journal of Criminal Justice, 9,* 63–77.

Capra, F. (Producer), Wambaugh, J. (Writer), & Becker, H. (Director). (1980). *The Black Marble* [Motion Picture]. USA: Anchor Bay Entertainment.

Coblenz, W. (Producer), Wambaugh, J. (Writer), & Becker, H. (Director). (1979). *The onion field* [Motion Picture]. USA: Black Marble Productions.

Cockrell, D. (1997). *Demons of disorder: Early blackface minstrels and their world.* Cambridge, England: Cambridge University Press.

Cohen, L. (Producer/Writer/Director). (1976). *God told me to* [Motion Picture]. USA: Miracle Pictures.

Collins, P. H. (2004). *Black sexual politics: African Americans, gender, and the new racism.* New York, NY: Routledge.

Dirks, D., & Mueller, J. C. (2007). "Racism and popular culture." In H. Vera & J. Feagin (Eds.), *Handbook of the sociology of racial and ethnic relations* (pp. 115–129). New York, NY: Springer.

Dixon, T. L. (2007). Black criminals and White officers: The effects of racially misrepresenting law breakers and law defenders on television new. *Media Psychology, 10,* 270–291.

Donner, R. (Producer/Director), & Silver, J. (Producer). (1987). *Lethal weapon* [Motion Picture]. USA: Warner Bros. Pictures.

Donner, R. (Producer/Director), & Silver, J. (Producer). (1989). *Lethal weapon 2* [Motion Picture]. USA: Warner Bros. Pictures.

Dowler, K. (2005). Job satisfaction, burnout, and perception of unfair treatment: The relationship between race and police work. *Police Quarterly, 8,* 476–489.

Dulaney, W. M. (1996). *Black Police in America.* Bloomington: Indiana University Press.

Dunner, R. (Producer), Silver, J. (Producer), & Donner, R. (Director). (1992). *Lethal weapon 3* [Motion Picture]. USA: Warner Bros. Pictures.

Ebony Magazine. (1996). *The negro handbook.* Chicago, IL: Johnson Publishing.

Escholz, S., Sims Blackwell, B., Gertz, M., & Chiricos, T. (2002). Race and attitudes toward the police: Assessing the effects of watching "reality" police programs. *Journal of Criminal Justice, 20,* 327–341.

Foster, D. (Producer), Turman, L. (Producer), & Hyams, P. (Director). (1986). *Running scared* [Motion Picture]. USA: Metro-Goldwyn-Mayer (MGM).

Gabbidon, S., & Greene, H. (2013). *Race and crime*. Thousan Oaks, CA: Sage.

Gaines, L., & Kappeler, V. (2005). *Policing in America*. Cincinnati, OH: Anderson Publishing.

Gaines, L., Kappeler, V., & Vaughn, J. (1997). *Policing in America* (2nd ed.). Cincinnati, OH: Anderson Publishing.

Grazer, B. (Producer), Lee, S. (Director), & Gewirtz, R. (Writer). (2006). *Inside man* [Motion Picture]. USA: Universal Pictures and Imagine Entertainment.

Graziano, L., Schuck, A., & Martin, C. (2010). Police misconduct, media coverage, and perceptions of racial profiling? An experiment. *Justice Quarterly, 27*, 52–76.

Guercio, J. (Producer/Director). (1973). *Electra glide in blue* [Motion Picture]. USA: MGM Home Entertainment.

Hall, R. (1993). Clowns, buffoons, and gladiators: Media portrayals of African American men. *The Journal of Men's Studies, 1*, 239–251.

Hawkins, R., & Pingree, S. (1981). Using television to construct social reality. *Journal of Broadcasting, 25*, 347–364.

Jacobson, T. (Producer), Wedaa, J. (Producer), & Carson, D. (Director). (2004). *Unstoppable* [Motion Picture]. USA: Millennium Films.

Jollevet, II, F. (2008, March). African American police executive careers: Influences of human capital, social capital, and racial discrimination. *Police Practice and Research, 9*, 17–30.

Kaminski, R. J. (1993). Police minority recruitment: Predicting who will say yes to an offer for a job as a cop. *Journal of Criminal Justice, 21*, 395–409.

Kaufman, P. (Producer/Director). (1993). *Rising sun*. USA: Twentieth Century Fox.

Kentrick, J. (2003). History of the musical minstrel shows. Retrieved from http://www.musicals101.com/minstrel.htm

Kopelson, A. (Producer), Carlyle, P. (Producer), & Fincher, D. (Director). (1995). *Seven* [Motion Picture]. USA: New Line Cinema.

Kopelson, A. (Producer), Milchan, A. (Producer), & Little, D. (Director). (1997). *Murder at 1600* [Motion Picture]. USA: Warner Bros. Pictures.

Kroll, L. (Producer), & Holland, T. (Director). (1987). *Fatal beauty* [Motion Picture]. USA: Metro Goldwyn Mayer.

Kuykendall, J., & Burns, D. (1980). The Black police officer: An historical perspective. *Journal of Contemporary Criminal Justice, 1*, 103–113.

Ladd, A. Jr. (Producer), Rissner, D. (Producer), Bailey, S. (Producer), & Affleck, B. (Director). (2007). *Gone baby gone* [Motion Picture]. USA: Miramax Films.

Leinen, S. (1984). *Black police, white society*. New York: New York University Press.

Liber, R. (Producer), Jones, S. (Producer), Peters, S. (Writer), & McNaughton, J. (Director). (1998). *Wild things* [Motion Picture]. USA: Columbia Pictures.

Maguire, C. (Producer), & Benjamin, R. (Director). (1990). *Downtown* [Motion Picture]. USA: Twentieth Century Fox.

Mastro, D. E., & Behm-Morawitz, E. (2005). Latino representation on primetime television. *Journalism & Mass Communication Quarterly, 82*, 110–130.

Mirisch, W. (Producer), & Medford, D. (Director). (1971). *The organization* [Motion Picture]. USA: Mirisch Production.

Morgan, M., & Shanahan, J. (1997). Two decades of cultivation research. In B. R. Burleson (Ed.), *Communication yearbook 20* (pp. 1–47). Thousand Oaks, CA: Sage.

Morgan, M., & Shanahan, J. (2010). The state of cultivation. *Journal of Broadcasting & Electronic Media, 54*, 337–355.

Moskos, P. C., & Jay, J. (2008). Two shades of blue: Black and white in the blue brotherhood. *Law Enforcement Executive Forum, 8*, 57–87.

Neufeld, L. (Producer), Rehme, R. (Producer), & Landis, J. (Director). (1994). *Beverly Hills cop III* [Motion Picture]. USA: Paramount Pictures.

Nielsen. (2011). State of the media: Trends in TV viewing—2011 TV Upfronts. Retrieved May 19, 2013, from http://www.nielsen.com/content/dam/corporate/us/en/newswire/uploads/ 2011/04/State-of-the-Media-2011-TV-Upfronts.pdf

Paul, D. J. (Producer), Pasdar, A. (Director), & Monjo, J. (Writer). (1998). *Cement* [Motion Picture]. USA: Lion's Gate Home Entertainment.

Peak, K. J. (2005). *Policing America: Methods, issues, challenges* (5th ed.). Upper Saddle River, NJ: Pearson Education.

Philips, D. (Producer), & Penn, S. (Writer/Director). (1991). *The Indian runner* [Motion Picture]. USA: MGM Home Entertainment.

Pilgrim, D. (2012). The coon caricature. Retrieved from http://www.ferris.edu/jimcrow/coon/

Prior, M. (2005). News vs. entertainment: How increasing media choice widens gaps in political knowledge and turnout. *American Journal of Political Science, 49,* 577– 592.

Rafter, N. (2000). *Shots in the mirror: Crime films and society.* New York, NY: Oxford University Press.

Ramasubramanian, S. (2011). The impact of stereotypical versus counter stereotypical media Exemplars on racial attitudes, causal attributions, and support for affirmative action. *Communication Research, 38,* 497–516.

Reaves, B. (1996). *Local police departments 1993.* Washington, DC: Government Printing Office, U.S. Department of Justice, Bureau of Justice Statistics.

Rocque, M. (2011). Racial disparities in the criminal justice system and perceptions of legitimacy: A theoretical linkage. *Race and Justice, 1,* 292–315.

Rudin, S. (Producer), & Singleton, J. (Producer/Writer). (2000). *Shaft* [Motion Picture]. USA: Paramount Pictures.

Rudwick, E. (1962). *The unequal badge: Negro policemen in the south, report of the Southern Regional Council.* Atlanta, GA: Southern Regional Council.

Seagal, S. (Producer), Nasso, J. (Producer), & Gray, J. (Director). (1997). *The glimmer man* [Motion Picture]. USA: Warner Bros. Pictures.

Semenza, A. (Producer), Henry, N. (Producer), Raymond, E. R. (Producer), & Pietro, G. S. (Director). (2001). *Kept* [Motion Picture]. USA: Phoenician Entertainment.

Shah, S. (Producer), Brooker, B. (Producer), & Fisher, C. (Directed/Written). (2005). *Dirty* [Motion Picture]. USA: Silver Nitrate Pictures and Destination Films.

Shelden, R. (2008). *Controlling the dangerous classes: A history of criminal justice in America.* Boston, MA: Pearson Education.

Shrum, L. J. (2008). *The psychology of entertainment media: Blurring the lines between entertainment and persuasion.* New Jersey, NJ: Taylor & Francis.

Shrum, L., & O'Guinn, T. (1993). Process and effects in the construction of social reality. *Communication Research, 20,* 436–471.

Silver, J. (Producer), Donner, R. (Producer), & Donner, R. (Director). (1998). *Lethal weapon 4* [Motion Picture]. United States: Warner Bros. Pictures.

Silver, J. (Producer), Newmyer, B. (Producer), & Fuguia, A. (Director). (2001). *Training day* [Motion Picture]. USA: Warner Bros. Pictures.

Strokes, L. D., & Scott, J. F. (1996). Affirmative action and selected minority groups in law enforcement. *Journal of Criminal Justice, 24,* 29–38.

Sullivan, P. (1989). Minority officers: Current issues. In R. G. Dunham & G. P. Alpert (Eds.), *Critical issues in policing: Contemporary readings* (pp. 331–345). Prospect heights, IL: Waveland Press.

Surette, R. (2007). *Media, crime, and criminal justice: Images, realities, and policies.* Belmont, CA: Thomson/ Wadsworth.

Toll, R. C. (1974). *Blacking up: The minstrel show in nineteenth-century America*. New York, NY: Oxford University Press.

Unkind unwind: The film industry tries to revive the ailing home-entertainment business. (2011). *The Economist*. Retrieved from http://www.economist.com/node/18386456

Vergeer, M., Lubbers, M., & Scheepers, P. (2000). Exposure to newspapers and attitudes toward ethnic minorities: A longitudinal analysis. *The Howard Journal of Communications, 11*, 127–143.

Watkins, M. (1994). *On the real side: Laughing, lying, and signifying—The underground tradition of African-American humor that transformed American culture, from slavery to Richard Pryor*. New York, NY: Simon & Schuster.

Williams, D. (2006). Virtual cultivation: Online worlds, offline perceptions. *Journal of Communication, 56*, 69–87.

Williamson, F. (Producer). (1989). *The kill reflex* [Motion Picture]. USA: RCA Columbia Pictures.

Wilson, A. N. (1990). *Black-on-Black violence: The psychodynamics of Black self-annihilation in service of White domination*. New York, NY: Afrikan World Infosystems.

Wilson, F. T. (2006). *A qualitative examination of the Core Cop film genre: Thirty years of instrumental and expressive police violence* (Doctoral dissertation, Sam Houston State University, 2006). *Dissertation Abstracts International, 68*, 740.

Wilson, F. T., (2009). Identifying large replicable film populations in social science film research: A unified film population identification methodology. *Criminal Justice and Law Review Journal, 1*, 19–40.

Wilson, F.T., & Blackburn, A. G. (in press). The depiction of female municipal police officers in the first four decades of the core cop film genre: It's a man's world. *Women & Criminal Justice*.

Wilson, F.T., Longmire, D., & Swymeler, W. (2009). The absence of gay and lesbian police officer depictions in the first three decades of the core cop film genre: Moving towards a cultivation theory perspective. *Journal of Criminal Justice and Popular Culture, 16*, 27–39.

Wimmer, R. D., & Dominick, J. R. (2003). *Mass media research: An introduction*. Belmont, CA: Wadsworth/Thomson Learning.

Yerkovich, A. (Producer), & Mann, M. (Producer, Director, Writer). (2006). *Miami vice* [Motion Picture]. USA: Universal Pictures.

Author Biographies

Franklin T. Wilson is an assistant professor at Indiana State University in the Department of Criminology and Criminal Justice. His primary area of research is the analysis of law enforcement depictions in the media and the sociohistorical analysis of prison cemeteries. His research has been featured in numerous news outlets including the *New York Times*, *Pittsburg Gazette*, *Houston Chronicle*, and *U.S. Catholic*.

Howard Henderson is an associate professor at Sam Houston State University in the College of Criminal Justice. His research interests are centered on predictive bias as well as correctional and cultural matters within criminal justice.

THE DEPICTION OF FEMALE MUNICIPAL POLICE OFFICERS IN THE FIRST FOUR DECADES OF THE CORE COP FILM GENRE

"It's a Man's World"

by Franklin T. Wilson
Department of Criminology and Criminal Justice, Indiana State University,
Terre Haute, Indiana, USA

Ashley G. Blackburn
Department of Criminal Justice, University of Houston–Downtown,
Houston, Texas, USA

Introduction

The extent to which media influences the acceptance of female municipal police officers by fellow law enforcement personnel and the general public has been virtually unexplored. In addition, the extent to which media influences females to choose a career in law enforcement is also unclear. This may be because of a number of factors, not the least of which is the laborious nature of conducting analyses of large blocks of media content. Furthermore, even if one did conduct such an analysis in the past, the findings would most likely have faced scrutiny based on the speculative accuracy of the samples and/or populations analyzed. Moreover, what significance could such findings have in the real world? After all, the units of analysis are simply caricatures of police officers. In this study the issue of speculative samples and/or populations is addressed through the utilization of the unified film population identification methodology (UFPIM), a methodology specifically designed to isolate large film populations. Furthermore, the role mediated caricatures of female municipal police officers may play is addressed by exploring the applicability of cultivation theory, which postulates that a diet of repeated imagery or messages through the media impacts perceptions of social reality.

Media studies by academics address issues such as antisocial and pro-social effects of specific media content, uses and gratifications, agenda setting by the media, and the cultivation of perceptions of social reality (Wimmer & Dominick, 2003). It is the cultivation of perceptions of social reality that is addressed in this article. The findings of the present study of female municipal police officer depictions represent the first step of the cultivation analysis process, which involves the analysis of large blocks of media content (Wimmer & Dominick, 2003). Based on their examination of depictions of Latinos in prime-time television, Mastro and Behm-Morawitz (2005) stated, "Although effects cannot be determined from content, such data provide insights into the potential influence of consumption on consumers when viewed from the perspectives of cultivation theory" (p. 110). Similarly, in this study the findings point to what may prove to be a significant variable in future studies of recruitment, fellow officer acceptance, and consequent retention of female municipal police officers. Given the findings of this study, we point to a need to extend the application of cultivation analysis to criminal justice majors and criminal justice professionals, with particular emphasis on those individuals seeking employment with, or actively employed by, law enforcement agencies.

Female Law Enforcement Officers

A Brief History

The first known female presence to work on behalf of the U.S. criminal justice system was the Quaker "prison matron" volunteers of the 1820s, who provided secular training and care for females incarcerated at that time (Alpert, Dunham, & Stroshine, 2006). It was not until 1905 that the first female, Lola Baldwin, was hired onto the Portland, Oregon, Police Bureau (Harrington, 2006) and 1910 that Los Angeles hired the first woman given the power to arrest, Alice Stebbins Wells (Schulz, 1993). Following these advancements, it was nearly 60 years before two female officers working in the Indianapolis Police Department were "assigned to patrol on an equal status with their male counterparts" (Woolsey, 2010, p. 1). These women were pioneers in the field, as it was not until the early 1970s that women and other racial minority officers were represented in substantial numbers on police forces across the nation (Alpert et al., 2006). This growth in racial minority and female officers was due in large part to the civil rights movement of the 1960s and was in direct relation to the 1972 addition of Title VII to the 1964 Civil Rights Act. Title VII, which prohibited employment discrimination based on race, gender, color, religion, and national origin in almost every aspect of employment, including but not limited to recruitment, hiring, wages, assignments, promotions, and benefits, opened the doors of law enforcement to all minority groups, including women (U.S. Equal Employment Opportunity Commission, 2007).

Although Title VII prohibited overt discrimination in hiring practices and affirmative action regulations required the recruitment of minority officers, including women, like other minority groups women have had a difficult time becoming an accepted part of the law enforcement community. Whereas racial minorities continue to face problems of covert racial discrimination when attempting to assimilate into an occupation of predominantly White males, it is covert gender discrimination and gender ideology that continues to impede women from attaining prosperous law enforcement careers. The most recent statistics indicate that women account for only about 12% of all law enforcement officers in the United States (Archbold, Hassell, & Stichman, 2010) while composing slightly more than half of the general population (U.S. Census Bureau, 2012). Furthermore, women of racial minority groups who aspire to become law enforcement officers have had to overcome a double disadvantage: covert racial and gender discrimination. In fact, in 2002 it was found that women of color accounted for only 4.8% of the 12.7% of female officers employed by large municipal, county, and state law enforcement agencies (Lonsway et al., 2002). Lonsway and colleagues (2002) further found that women of color are almost nonexistent in small and rural agencies, accounting for only 1.2% of officers. Although female law enforcement officers have made great strides over the past century, they remain vastly underrepresented. In this article we suggest that many of the historical barriers faced by female police officers have often been rooted in misconceptions, many of which are arguably perpetuated and/or maintained because of mediated depictions of female police officers still today. This overall lack of female representation, even today, across law enforcement agencies nationwide is thought to be due to a number of barriers female officers continue to face.

Barriers to Female Law Enforcement Officers

Women seeking to join the law enforcement community face many barriers that oftentimes encumber them from achieving successful law enforcement careers (Felkenes & Schroedel, 1993; Lonsway, 2007; Lonsway et al., 2002; Pogrebin, Dodge, & Chatman, 2000; Schroedel, Frisch, Hallamore, Peterson, & Vanderhorst, 1996; Seklecki & Paynich, 2007; Zhao, Herbst, & Lovrich, 2001). Based on a national survey of female police officers ($N = 531$), Seklecki and Paynich (2007) found that although respondents generally felt equally as capable as their male counterparts, a significant percentage indicated a work environment that remains hostile to females employed in law enforcement. Theoretical explanations used to explain the hostility toward and the oppression of female police officers include the male peer support model (Franklin, 2007) and the generally masculine organizational culture found within law enforcement agencies (Kingshott, 2009). Research based on these explanations shows that a more feminist orientation, particularly related to leadership, would benefit law enforcement agencies and the female officers employed within.

Specific barriers faced by female police officers include sexual harassment, gender harassment, and gender discrimination, including pregnancy discrimination, which all lead to hostile work environments for women. Sexual harassment may include unwanted sexual advances by coworkers or comments of a sexual nature, whereas gender harassment and discrimination may include negative remarks made about females in general, perhaps referring to weakness or an inability to perform certain tasks, specifically physical tasks, like a man. Gossett and Williams (1998) found that although the female officers in their study felt like progress had been made in lessening negative reactions to females in law enforcement, they still perceived gender discrimination from fellow officers, including superiors, and the communities that they served. More recently, Lonsway (2007) found that such attitudes remain the most common barrier female officers have to overcome. These obstacles begin at the recruitment and hiring phase and may impact a hired female officer throughout her career.

Hiring and Training

Although agencies are increasing the recruitment of female applicants, especially on college campuses, it is oftentimes difficult for women to overcome the pre-employment physical testing required for most law enforcement agencies. Physical agility and strength testing are used as a way to screen out weak candidates, and historically it has been women applicants who have been disproportionately screened out through the hiring process (Peak, 2006). In their study of municipal policing hiring practices throughout the 1980s and early 1990s, Sass and Troyer (1999) found that the hiring of female applicants was inversely related to the percentage of males already employed by the department and that the higher the proportion of male officers, the more likely the agency was to employ physical fitness testing, known to be a possible impediment for women recruits. Lonsway (2001) indicated that policing is dominated by a "warrior image" of a muscular and strong male officer who uses physical traits to solve crimes and handle dangerous situations. Because they do not fit this stereotype, women are thought to be less capable than their male counterparts. However, as we discuss later, women officers are valued for their ability to use empathy, intelligence, and conversation instead of physical strength and violence to diffuse dangerous situations.

Once through the hiring process, women continue to face discriminatory practices during academy and field training operations. It is important that agencies integrate this training and provide strong female mentors and role models for newly hired women so as to lessen the effects of possible discrimination and harassment. As for assignments, women officers are oftentimes tasked with social service, or traditionally female, roles or are assigned to special investigation units, including child abuse, sex crimes, and school programs, but precluded from traditionally male roles such as SWAT team member, undercover officer, and homicide detective (Peak, 2006).

Merit and Promotion

Women are also often overlooked for promotions and raises. This could be because of the perception that females cannot perform as well as male officers. This is especially true when it comes to women who have children, as they may be thought of as preoccupied or otherwise distracted by family life and may be perceived as somehow less devoted to their career than male officers.

Lonsway and colleagues (2002) found that, of the agencies they surveyed, 55.9% of the large agencies and 97.4% of the small agencies had no women in top command positions and that a majority (87.9%) of the large agencies had no women of color among their highest ranks. Studies have examined the plight of specifically Black and Hispanic female officers in policing, finding patterns of both racial and gender discrimination perpetrated by fellow officers and supervisors at all phases of their careers, including hiring and promotion (Felkenes & Schroedel, 1993; Martin, 1994; Pogrebin et al., 2000; Schroedel et al., 1996; Zhao et al., 2001). This goes to show that although women may be hired more often than before, they very seldom get promoted to policymaking and supervisory positions.

Although these barriers remain, findings from more recent research have been positive for female law enforcement officers. For example, using Hall's Professionalism Scale, Carlan and McMullan (2009) compared male police officer respondents to female police officer respondents ($N = 1,085$; females, $n = 89$) in relation to professionalism, stress, and job satisfaction. Based on their findings, Carlan and McMullan contended that there are not significant differences between male and female officers. Furthermore, the authors discussed the resiliency and psychological fortitude shown by the female officers in their sample. In addition, following her earlier research, Lonsway (2007) posed the question, Are we there yet? This was in reference to the progress that had been made breaking down the barriers for females in law enforcement. Her findings suggested that despite the fact that women continue to constitute a small percentage of officers and that barriers do remain, there has in fact been progress made in bettering the working environment for females employed in law enforcement.

The studies discussed in this section suggest that although strengths of women in law enforcement are recognized, female officers continue to face the same barriers they did decades ago. Whether it is perceptions of physical strength, sexual harassment, or covert discrimination based on pregnancy or other gendered experiences, barriers remain to the recruitment, hiring, promotion, and retention of female officers. Overcoming these barriers is essential for an increased presence of women among the ranks of law enforcement which, as we discuss in the following section, is advantageous for law enforcement agencies.

Advantages to Hiring Female Law Enforcement

Over time, it has come to be recognized that there are many advantages to hiring female law enforcement officers (Lonsway, Moore, Harrington, Smeal, & Spillar, 2003). For one thing, women have been proven to be just as competent, if not better at some roles, than their male counterparts (Carlan & McMullan, 2009; Lonsway et al., 2003). Next, female officers have been found to be less likely than male officers to use excessive force when handling suspects (Schuck & Rabe-Hemp, 2007). This is a positive attribute for agencies looking to lessen their liability and litigation concerns. Although this is the case, female officers are not meek when it comes to confrontation. For example, Paoline and Terrill (2004) found that women in law enforcement are not reluctant to utilize verbal and physical coercion with suspects when necessary.

Lonsway and colleagues (2003) further pointed out that women officers often use a community-oriented style of policing. Community-oriented policing has been praised for improving relationships, lessening tension that may exist between the police and the community that they serve (Correia, 2000; Peak & Glensor, 2002). It has been estimated that more than 40% of violent crime calls to the police involve family and domestic disputes (Strandberg, 1998). Lonsway and colleagues (2003) noted that another advantage to hiring female officers is that they have been found to be better able to respond to and diffuse domestic and family violence incidents as well as better able to assist victims, as the majority of domestic violence victims are also female. Finally, increasing the number of women in a department will serve to decrease sexual harassment and gender discrimination and bring about valuable changes in policy that impact all officers, male and female. These advantages impact not only law enforcement agencies but the community as well and should be recognized by law enforcement administrators.

In order to not only recruit but also retain female officers, agencies must acknowledge the importance of having female mentors and role models at all levels of the agency. Peak (2006) noted that law enforcement administrators need to be aware of gender integration, the use of female mentors, objectivity in hiring and promotion practices, and other issues related to women officers, such as pregnancy and child care. If these issues are given increased attention, it is likely that the percentage of women at all levels of law enforcement will increase and be retained over time.

Perceptions of Female Officers

Perceptions of female officers impact not only the way in which females working in law enforcement are treated but also the possibility that a woman will choose law enforcement over other career paths. Overall, studies have shown that the general public feels positively about females involved in law enforcement. Bloch and Anderson (1974) found that both male and female Washington, DC residents surveyed generally supported female involvement in law enforcement and felt that females performed law enforcement duties just as well as male officers. Leger (1997) found that respondents were accepting of women in law enforcement positions and felt that females are effective in performing law enforcement duties, including those involving violent encounters and physical ability. Furthermore, Leger found that her sample gave favorable responses with regard to females in administrative and supervisory positions.

Research on perceptions of females in law enforcement has also focused on student communities. Koenig (1978) found that although female students were more supportive, most students had favorable opinions of females in law enforcement. In their study of undergraduate students, however, Austin and Hummer (1999) found that female students, regardless of major, were more accepting of females in law enforcement than male students, including males majoring in criminal justice. What is interesting is that they also found that if the respondent had a relative who worked in law enforcement, he or she was less supportive of females working in the field. Using a sample of 178 undergraduate students, Haba, Sarver, Dobbs, and Sarver (2009) found that criminal justice majors and those students with a stronger feminist orientation were significantly more likely to express support for females working in law enforcement.

Even with these findings, studies such as Kurtz, Linnemann, and Williams (2012) found that law enforcement officers in three midwestern police departments still expected female officers, despite the female officers' preference and skill sets, to tend to children, delinquents, and female victims, much like the police matrons of old. Arguably such results are not surprising if one considers the findings of Rabe-Hemp and Beichner's (2011) study of U.S. print advertisements of police officers in *Police Chief* magazine between 1996 and 2006. Rabe-Hemp and Beichner stated that women were "underrepresented and socially excluded from the imagery of crime-fighting; rather, they are portrayed as being in lower ranks, stereotypically as caretakers and nurturers" (p. 63). Although generally research suggests that there exists support for females in law enforcement among undergraduate students, female students may be impacted by the lack of portrayals of women police officers in addition to the hostility facing women interested in a law enforcement career. For example, based on a survey of 256 undergraduate criminal justice students, Yim (2009) found that female criminal justice undergraduates in her sample were significantly less likely to want a career in law enforcement than male criminal justice undergraduates. Although admittedly not a comprehensive explanation for this lack of interest, Yim's findings did indicate that females felt significantly less competent in their ability to be a police officer compared to their male counterparts.

It is well documented that men have traditionally been disproportionately represented in many career fields and that in the past three to four decades female representation has increased greatly. However, as Shelley, Morabito, and Tobin-Gurley (2011) pointed out, there have not been equal strides when it comes to policing. They also pointed out that the current literature does not thoroughly address advancement barriers or retention issues faced by female police officers. The present article seeks to address these issues and others through the implementation of a first-step cultivation theory analysis, a method relatively unexplored by the field of criminology and criminal justice studies to date. In order to better understand the applicability of cultivation theory to the field of criminology and criminal justice, as well as the unique contribution of the current study, the next section provides a brief review of cultivation theory history, traditional mediums, and topics of analysis.

Cultivation Theory

Cultivation theorists maintain that "viewing television gradually leads to adoption of beliefs about the nature of the social world that conform to the stereotyped and selective view of reality portrayed in a systematic way on television" (Woo & Dominick, 2003, p. 110). More specifically, they theorize that there is a cumulative consequence of being exposed to long-term repetitive messages delivered through television or other media outlets. Developed by George Gerbner in the 1970s, cultivation analysis consists of two discrete steps. In Step 1, large blocks of media content are analyzed to identify the messages delivered by the media source. Cultivation theorists maintain that these messages denote steady patterns in the depiction of specific issues, policies, and topics, many of which are at odds with real-world manifestations (Wimmer & Dominick, 2003). Utilizing the findings from Step 1, Step 2 entails the development of questions designed to detect a cultivation effect (see Wimmer & Dominick, 2003, for more details). The current study signifies the first step toward future cultivation analyses of female recruits', police officers', and the general public's perceptions of female municipal police officers.

A number of analyses of cultivation studies (see Hawkins & Pingree, 1981; Morgan & Shanahan, 1997; Shrum & O'Guinn, 1993) have determined that the research, as a whole, reveals consistent television viewing effects on perceptions of social reality (Wimmer & Dominick, 2003). Furthermore, a large number of diverse issues have been examined utilizing cultivation analyses, including topics such as authoritarianism, cultural values, fear of crime, juvenile crime, representations of Blacks and Latinos, violence, and White police officers, among others (F. T. Wilson, Longmire, & Swymeler, 2009). Cultivation theory has also been used to examine an array of television viewing subjects, such as international college students, Israeli students, Chinese college students, and elderly viewers, among others (F. T. Wilson et al., 2009).

Although still debated today, a large portion of recent studies have produced findings that continue to support cultivation theory to varying degrees (see J. Cohen & Weimann, 2000; Diefenbach & West, 2001; Dixon, 2007; Gentles & Harrison, 2006; Goidel, Freeman, & Procopio, 2006; Gutschoven & Van den Bulck, 2005; Hammermeister, Brock, Winterstein, & Page, 2005; Hetsroni & Tukachinsky, 2006; Nabi & Sullivan, 2001; Reeber & Chang, 2000; Vergeer, Lubbers, & Scheepers, 2000; B. J. Wilson, Martins, & Marske, 2005; Woo & Dominick, 2003; Zhang & Harwood, 2002). Furthermore, early criticisms of cultivation theory have been dispelled by being proven faulty (see Gutschoven & Van den Bulck, 2005) or disproved in more recent studies that have addressed and/or controlled for the issues in question (F. T. Wilson et al., 2009).

Although television has served as the principal medium, cultivation theorists have examined mediums such as newspapers (Vergeer et al., 2000) and video games (Williams, 2006) in recent years. This demonstrates not only that the issues and type of viewers examined have expanded since Gerbner's first inception of the theory but that the mediums explored have moved beyond just television programming (F. T. Wilson et al., 2009; F. T. Wilson & Henderson, 2014). Hendriks (2002) notes, "Gerbner formulated his theory in the late 1960s when three major networks and a public broadcast service dominated television. The invasion of cable and satellite has likely altered the accuracy of the assumption that all television content is equal" (p. 112). Studies have shown that the effects of cultivation increase in strength when narrow genres of programming are watched (Hawkins & Pingree, 1981). Therefore, the findings presented here continue the aforementioned expansion of mediums and analyses of specific genre content. Given that cultivation theory hypothesizes a cumulative impact on a viewer's perceptions due to long-term exposure to repetitive messages, the present study sought to understand what, if any, repeated messages are conveyed regarding female municipal police officers. Particular attention was given to how often key issues such as sexual harassment, gender harassment, and gender discrimination faced by real-world female police officers are portrayed in the core cop film genre.

Core Cop Film Genre

Rafter (2000) pointed out that, prior to the late 1960s, police officers were depicted as foolish patrolmen (keystone cops), tough federal agents, or private investigators. It was during the 1950s and 1960s that film audiences became increasingly attracted to urban police officer depictions while Westerns and noir films lost their appeal. This was in part the result of the public's call for the police officer to be better educated (Rafter, 2000). One saw a rise in urban disorder and street crime during the 1970s that led to the public supporting the law-and-order perspective (Rafter, 2000). The increasing belief that liberal laws were handicapping police officers from catching criminals created an atmosphere that was amenable to the transition of the traditional western gunslinger to an urban police setting (Rafter, 2000). This transition point is readily marked by the release of *Dirty Harry* (Daley & Siegel, 1971) in 1971, thereby establishing the beginning of what is now known as the cop film genre (Rafter, 2000). The traditional cop film genre would begin to fragment into subgenres in the 1980s and 1990s with the development of buddy cop films, cop comedy films, corrupt cop films, and rogue cop films, among others (Rafter, 2000). However, as F. T. Wilson (2009) pointed out, many of the original defining characteristics of cop films endured, and it is this group of films that this study refers to as the *core cop film genre*.

Methodology

Identifying the Study Population

The study of social science issues in film has been bound, for the most part, to qualitative observation techniques and/or nonprobability sampling techniques. In an examination of 94 peer-reviewed journal articles published between 1996 and 2006 and focusing on social science issues in theatrically released films, F. T. Wilson (2009) found only one study that attempted to utilize probability sampling. F. T. Wilson (2009) suggested that the lack of probability sampling has been due to the difficult task of identifying clear film populations from which samples can be drawn. Therefore, F. T. Wilson (2009) developed the UFPIM in an effort to alleviate this problem. The UFPIM was designed to help film researchers who wish to utilize probability sampling techniques to make a statistical inference regarding their findings or simply to establish a replicable film population (F. T. Wilson, 2009).

The UFPIM utilizes the Internet Movie Database Power Search (IMDbPS) as part of its three-phase process of identifying specific film populations (for further details, see F. T. Wilson, 2006, 2009). In Phase I of the UFPIM, a definition is developed for the film population to be analyzed based on the relevant literature surrounding the film population in question. In Phase II, the IMDbPS is utilized to identify a base film list. This list is developed by utilizing, at minimum, the IMDbPS search criteria of key words in the movie plot summaries, movie genre (the primary genre with which the IMDbPS associates a film), year (the year or series of years in which a film was released), and key words (for further details, see F. T. Wilson, 2006, 2009). Phase III constitutes a two-stage process, the first of which involves the development of an identification coding sheet designed to further isolate those films that meet the definitional parameters established in Phase I. The second stage involves the examination of plot summaries for all of the films identified in Phase II utilizing the aforementioned coding sheet. In the second stage of Phase III, plot summaries from at least two independent sources, one being the IMDb, are examined to help safeguard the accuracy of the final population. In this study, the UFPIM was used to identify the core cop film population to be examined.

In Phase I of the UFPIM, the first four decades of the core cop film genre were conceptualized as films (a) released in theaters between 1971 and 2011; (b) that take place in the United States; (c) in which one or more actor(s) play the hero, who is an active urban police officer of traditional ranks; (d) in which the hero is either acting alone or acting with a partner in a street cop/detective role; (e) set in the past or present that appears to be reality based. At the end of Phase II, a base film list of more than 500 films was produced. In the first stage of Phase III, the core cop film identification coding sheet was developed. In the second stage of Phase III, more than 1,000 plot summaries from both the IMDb and Amazon.com were evaluated using the core cop film identification coding sheet, resulting in a final population of 130 films.

During the examination process, several of the films were subsequently excluded for a variety of reasons. Eight films could not be located and were determined to be out of production. The three films *Electra Glide in Blue* (Guercio, 1973), *The Indian Runner* (Philips & Penn, 1991), and *Partners in Crime* (Bergman, Lusting, Harris, & Warren, 2000) were excluded because the films involved police officers who were not working in a municipal capacity. In addition, two films were excluded because they did not fit into one of the required genre categories. Upon viewing, it was determined that the film *The Black Marble* (Capra, Wambaugh, & Becker, 1980) was a comedy and the film *God Told Me To* (Cohen, 1976) fell more appropriately into the horror film genre. The film *The Onion Field* (Coblenz, Wambaugh, & Becker, 1979), although dealing with the shooting of police officers, primarily focused on the justice system rather than law enforcement. The films *Unstoppable* (Jacobson, Wedaa, & Carson, 2004) and *Gone Baby Gone* (Ladd, Rissner, Bailey, & Affleck, 2007) were excluded because the leading heroic characters were not law enforcement officers. Lastly, the films *Wild Things* (Liber, Jones, Peters, & McNaughton, 1998) and *Cement* (Paul, Pasdar, & Monjo, 1998) both were excluded due to the fact that the police were not portrayed as heroes in any way. Therefore, due to the fact that eight films could not be located and an additional ten films were excluded for various reasons, the final population for the first four decades of the core cop film genre totaled 112 films. Although F. T. Wilson (2009) presented the UFPIM as a tool by which researchers can now identify an entire population of films and subsequently draw samples, in this study the entire core cop film genre population was examined.

Analysis

In this study, content analysis was used as a collection device for descriptor variables (i.e., race and gender of police officers), and qualitative analysis was used to examine scenes in which female municipal police officers were presented. Content analysis can be defined in numerous ways. As Wimmer and Dominick (2003) described it,

> Walizer and Wiener (1978) define it as any systematic procedure devised to examine the context of recorded information; Krippendorf (1980) defines it as a research technique for making replicable and valid references from data to their context. Kerlinger's (2000) definition is fairly typical: Content analysis communication in a systematic, objective, and quantitative manner for the purpose of measuring variables. (pp. 140–141)

Schutt (2004) defined *content analysis* as a research method for systematically analyzing and making inferences from text.

For this study, we adhered to Berg's (2001) argument that "content analysis can be effective in a qualitative analysis—that "counts" of textual elements merely provide a means of identifying, organizing, indexing, and retrieving data" (p. 242). Rather than using content analysis as a reductionis-tic positivistic tool, we used it as a tool to help understand the patterns of police depictions in core cop films. Therefore, the 112 films represented the units of analysis in the present exploratory descriptive analysis of female police officer depictions.

Each of the 112 films was examined to determine both the quantity and quality of female police officer depictions. Specifically, films were viewed and film jackets were referenced in order to determine whether a film portrayed a city/municipal female police officer in the leading or joint leading role. Specifically, *leading role* was defined as top billing both in the list of credits on the film jacket and in the context of the film when viewed. *Joint leading roles* included those instances in which the actress portraying the female police officer received secondary billing but was portrayed or even described as a costar in the film.

Detailed notes were taken in regard to how the female police officers were portrayed based on both the literature associated with real-world police officers and independent observational notes. Specifically, using the literature as a base, we attempted to identify which of the aforementioned barriers, including sexual harassment, gender harassment, and gender discrimination, all of which are known to lead to hostile work environments for women, were depicted in the films. *Sexual harassment* was loosely defined as including unwanted sexual advances by coworkers or comments of a sexual nature. *Gender harassment* and *discrimination* were defined to include negative remarks made about females in general, including referring to weakness or an inability to perform certain tasks, specifically physical tasks, like a man. In addition, although it was not initially identified or defined as an issue to be observed upon viewing the films, a pattern of portraying female police officers with what can best be described as a variety of mental health or emotional issues became apparent. So although it was not an anticipated issue for observation before beginning this study, we felt that the issue deserved to be noted. Therefore, this study is different from prominent studies of female police officer portrayals in the past (i.e., Hale, 1998) in that this study focused directly on portrayals of city/municipal female police officers in lead roles.

Findings

In the first four decades of the core cop film genre, 15 of the 112 films examined were identified as portraying a woman in either a sole or a joint leading police officer character role (see Table 1). The first two decades (1970s and 1980s) produced only three of these films: *The Enforcer* in 1976 (Daley & Fargo, 1976) followed 11 years later by the films *Under Cover* (Golan, Globus, & Stockwell, 1987) and *Fatal Beauty* (Kroll & Holland, 1987) in 1987. The film *The Enforcer*, the third of five *Dirty Harry* films, represents the only film that addresses directly the aforementioned barriers (physical abilities and sexual/gender harassment) facing female police officers from both fellow officers and promotion boards. This differentiates *The Enforcer* from the remaining 14 films, which portray female officers who have apparently already overcome some of these barriers. *The Enforcer* is the only film that directly addresses concerns or beliefs as to whether or not female police officers can handle police work, both physically and/or emotionally. Inspector Kate Moore, played by Tyne Daly, ultimately proves herself to the male chauvinist Inspector Harry Callahan (Clint Eastwood) by saving Callahan's life on two separate occasions: once by shooting a suspect who is about to shoot Callahan and again by getting shot and dying while saving Callahan.

Table 1. Core Cop Films Depicting Female Police Officers in Lead or Joint Lead Roles by Year of Release.

Core cop films	Year of release	Lead role	Joint lead
The Enforcer	1976		X
Fatal Beauty	1987	X	
Under Cover	1987		X
Blue Steel	1990	X	
A Stranger Among Us	1992	X	
Lethal Weapon 3	1992		X
Striking Distance	1993		X
Copycat	1995	X	
Bodily Harm	1995	X	
Lethal Weapon 4	1998		X
Oxygen	1999		
The Bone Collector	1999		X
Angel Eyes	2001	X	
Dragon and the Hawk	2001	X	
Suitable for Murder	2008		X

In only one of these films, *Fatal Beauty* (1987), is the female police officer portrayed as the sole police officer leading character. *Fatal Beauty* also represents the only film in the first four decades of the core cop film genre in which the sole or joint police officer leading character is an African American female. Whoopi Goldberg, who plays undercover police detective Rita Rizzoli, portrays a female whom the male police officers fear, given her hypermasculine nature and willingness to place herself and others in harm's way. Despite her demeanor, she still faces sexually harassing comments from fellow officers, which are quickly shot down through her immediate responses. Rizzoli is portrayed as becoming a drug detective and having a special place in her heart for drug addicts. It is revealed in the film that, growing up, she came from what she describes as a family of beautiful people who always reminded her she was ugly. This situation led to her dating someone, becoming pregnant, and having a child at the age of 14. After discovering that the father only went out with her on a dare, she becomes further traumatized and turns to drugs. Ultimately, when she returns from making a drug run one day, she finds that her daughter has found her stash and died as a result. As we demonstrate later, this film arguably starts a trend of leading female police officer characters with damaged pasts or other personal issues that, in many cases, lead them to police work. The remaining 80% (*n* = 12) of those films in which a female police officer is portrayed as either the sole or joint lead character were released after the year 1990. Therefore, there are few portrayals of female police officers as leading characters during the first 19 years of the core cop film genre.

Even after 1990, only 58% (*n* = 7) of the remaining 12 films portray a female as the sole leading police officer character. These films include *Blue Steel* (Pressman, Stone, & Bigelow, 1990), *A Stranger Among Us* (Golin, Sighvatsson, Rosenman, & Lumet, 1992), *Bodily Harm* (Curtis & Lemmo, 1995), *Copycat* (Milcan, Tarlov, & Amiel, 1995), *Oxygen* (Stern & Shepard, 1999), *Dragon and the Hawk* (Cypser & Grove, 2001), and *Angel Eyes* (Canton, Samaha, & Mankoki, 2001). In five out of the seven films (*Blue Steel, A Stranger Among Us, Bodily Harm, Copycat,* and *Oxygen*), the female lead character is portrayed as having had a romantic relationship. Romantic relationships constituted having dated or married a fellow police officer, most of whom were portrayed as being or having been the female's senior officer. This is a distinct change from the three films produced prior to 1990, in which no romantic relationships are portrayed. Sexual harassment is only clearly portrayed in two of the seven films, *A Stranger Among Us* and *Angel Eyes,* and in both films the harassment is in the form of verbal comments from both fellow officers and the general public. Both Jennifer Lopez as Officer Sharron Pogue in *Angel Eyes* and Melanie Griffith as Detective Emily Eden in *A Stranger Among Us* portray female officers who seemingly accept the harassment as part of the job and oftentimes respond with derogatory comments themselves. It is interesting that not one of the seven portrayals depict the female officer as lacking in physical agility or strength. Lastly, at least five of the films depict the leading female character as having varying degrees of personal issues. In *A Stranger Among Us,* Melanie Griffith's character is portrayed as taking unnecessary risks in the field, ultimately connected to her desire to earn her retired police officer father's love and support. Similarly, Jennifer Lopez (*Angel Eyes*) portrays a character who became a police officer to protect people, a feeling that is revealed to be rooted in her childhood when she watched her father beat her mother. A similar scenario is depicted in the film *Blue Steel,* in which Jamie Lee Curtis portrays rookie police officer Megan Turner. During the film, Turner states that she has always wanted to be a police officer, but the storyline arguably could lead one to believe that her career path may have been strongly influenced by watching her father verbally and physically abuse her mother. In addition, Maura Tierney (*Oxygen*) portrays a female police officer who is addicted to being abused by strangers in her private life. She is portrayed as begging for permission to see and subsequently going to an unidentified individual who provides her with alcohol and who burns her with cigarettes.

Of the remaining 42% (*n* = 5) of the 12 films released after 1990, each portrays a female in a joint leading role with a White male police officer. These five films are *Striking Distance* (Milchan, Thomopoulos, Lowry, & Herrington, 1993), *Lethal Weapon 3* (Donner, Silver, & Donner, 1992), *Lethal Weapon 4* (Silver, Donner, & Donner, 1998), *The Bone Collector* (Bregman, Stroller, Bregman, & Noyce, 1999), and *Suitable for Murder* (Nagy, Watkins, & Watkins, 2008). In both *Lethal Weapon 3* and *Lethal Weapon 4* Rene Russo plays Internal Affairs Detective Lorna Cole, sharing lead status with Mel Gibson (Martin Riggs) and Danny Glover (Roger Murtaugh). Cole is portrayed as a female equivalent of the highly volatile Riggs character, both of whom are thrill-seeking police officers who oftentimes place themselves in situations of mortal danger that most police officers would never consider. Ultimately, Cole and Riggs become romantically involved and get married. In the three remaining films, *Striking Distance, The Bone Collector,* and *Suitable for Murder,* Sarah Jessica Parker (*Striking Distance*), Angelina Jolie (*The Bone Collector*), and Ali Faulkner (*Suitable for Murder*) portray rookie female police officers under the tutelage of senior male police officers, and in all three films the female officers become romantically involved with their male counterparts. However, at least one of these characters is not without some sort of commitment issue. In *The Bone Collector,* Jolie's character is portrayed initially as having commitment issues with a male partner whom, it is insinuated, she uses for sex only. In addition, in the five films, the only distinct portrayal of harassment of any sort, also verbal in nature, occurs in *The Bone Collector* when Officer Amelia Donaghy, portrayed by Angelina Jolie, is demeaned and dismissed by senior White police detectives for doing her job correctly.

Conclusion

Despite the sheer scarcity of core cop films that portray female municipal police officers in lead or joint leading roles, the 15 portrayals described here reveal three distinct trends. First, there is an apparent reliance or past reliance on older and/or senior male police officers, given that 7 out of the 12 films produced after 1990 involve female officers having intimate relationships with such officers. This number increases to 9 of 12 films if one includes *Lethal Weapon 3* (1992) and *Lethal Weapon 4*

(1998), in which intimate relations exist but are between officers of nearly the same age and rank. Second, one sees 8 of the 12 films produced after 1990 portraying female police officers as being emotionally or mentally scarred, insinuating that females who become police officers have something wrong with them. Third, many of the known barriers that female police officers face in the real world either are not addressed (e.g., physical agility/strength, denial of promotions, female police officers who are mothers, among others) or are downplayed (i.e., sexual harassment) and depicted as something that should just be accepted as part of the job.

This study is not without its limitations. One of the limitations of this study, and of most studies of film, is that some films were missed. Upon completion of this study we realized that we had missed at least one film that met the parameters of the core cop film genre definition and contained a female municipal police officer in the leading character role: *Murder by Numbers* (Crystal, Hoffman, & Schroeder, 2002). If this film had been included, it would have only served to further substantiate the findings. In this film, Cassie Mayweather, played by Sandra Bullock, has a reputation of sleeping with her partners and then pushing them away because of apparent commitment issues. Her nicknames among her male counterparts are "Hyena" (because the female has a pseudo-penis) and "Scorpion" (because of her stinging comments). Similar to the other female municipal police officers depicted, she too became a police officer because traumatic events in her past left her scarred emotionally. Specifically, she was beaten by an abusive spouse and, when she attempted to leave, her husband stabbed her 17 times and dumped her body on a country road. She points out that she is scarred in the sense that she sees him in every case and every guy she dates. When asked by her partner if she ever received help for the trauma she states, "Yeah, I became a cop." So here again is a female municipal police officer being depicted as regularly sleeping with colleagues and becoming a police officer because of being emotionally scarred from past traumatic events.

Another limitation of this study is that, by focusing only on films in which the leading or joint leading character is a municipal police officer, we may have excluded some notable depictions. An example of this would be the film *Fargo* (Coen & Coen, 1996), which contains the depiction of a female municipal police officer character. This film was excluded due to the fact that the character of Officer Marge Gunderson (Francis McDormand) is technically considered a supporting role. The leading role in this film is actually Jerry Lundegaard (William H. Macy), who is arguably overlooked because of the strong and/or more relatable performance by Francis McDormand. The character of Officer Marge Gunderson does not appear in the film for the first 33 minutes and only appears for a total of 34 minutes of the 98-minute film. This said, future researchers may want to expand the scope of roles examined beyond that of lead or joint lead character in order to capture significant supporting character depictions such this one.

So although it is possible that some films escaped our analysis, it is our belief that we have examined a large enough portion of core cop films released between 1971 and 2011 that we can state that there are specific trends in the characterization of female municipal police officers. According to cultivation theory, such depictions would cultivate a perceived social reality in which females only become police officers if they are scarred and intimacy with male colleagues is the norm. Therefore, given the findings of this study in conjunction with the issues faced by female police officers in today's society, additional analysis is justified, in regard to both further content analyses of large media blocks to determine whether the findings of this study are consistent and the progression to the second step of cultivation analysis.

As was noted earlier, cultivation analyses have examined a wide variety of issues, television viewer types, and genres while at the same time increasing their specificity in these categories. Such studies have also expanded to other media formats. Given the ever-expanding mediums through which films can be accessed (e.g., movie rentals, television programming, on-demand rentals, the Internet, cell phones), it is our contention that the impact of theatrically released films is no longer relegated to the movie theater. In fact, we argue that, upon leaving theaters, theatrically released films quickly become integrated into television programming and are arguably becoming more influential. It is therefore time for specific analysis of films to occur. This said, future researchers should not ignore the potential impact of standard television programming (DeTardo-Bora, 2009) and its role in the cultivation of female municipal police officers. Many current primetime portrayals of female police officers, such as Detective Kate Becket from the television show *Castle* (Marlowe, 2009–2013), who became a police officer because her mother was murdered, and Detective Olivia Benson of *Law & Order: Special Victims Unit* (Wolf, 1999–present), who became a police officer because she was the child of a rape, suggest that many of the findings identified in this study will most likely be found in examinations of regular television programming.

Furthermore, there has been little, if any, examination of the applicability of cultivation theory among criminology/criminal justice majors and criminal justice professionals, such as police officers. We argue that the examination of such portrayals could prove to be a key variable in better understanding public perceptions as well as trends in choice of major, law enforcement recruitment, job expectations, and subsequent retention issues in regard to females and other minority groups.

This study is only the first step in understanding the overall implication of female police officer depictions in theatrically released films and media in general. We emphasize that, in order to properly explore this area of research, the first steps of cultivation analysis must be broken up by municipal, county, state, and federal law enforcement officer portrayals. It is understandable that the general public may not make the technical distinction between different levels of law enforcement like those who study law enforcement do. However, we would argue that it is imperative that the distinction be made when conducting analyses of law enforcement portrayals in order establish hard foundational data that can be compared to real-world law enforcement research that does make the distinction. Future research should therefore endeavor to utilize cultivation theory to examine films and other media formats, such as television, that portray female law enforcement officers at the municipal, county, state, and federal levels. Subsequent second-step cultivation analysis studies should focus on how portrayals of females impact the perceptions of female police officers, their fellow officers, and the general citizenry of the communities in which they serve.

References

Alpert, G., Dunham, R., & Stroshine, M. (2006). *Policing: Continuity and change.* Long Grove, IL: Waveland Press.

Archbold, C. A., Hassell, K. D., & Stichman, A. J. (2010). Comparing promotion aspirations among female and male police officers. *International Journal of Police Science and Management, 12*(2), 287–303.

Austin, T., & Hummer, D. (1999). What do college students think of policewomen? An attitudinal assessment of future law enforcement personnel. *Women & Criminal Justice, 10*(4), 1–24.

Berg, B. L. (2001). *Qualitative research methods for the social sciences* (4th ed.). Boston, MA: Allyn and Bacon.

Bergman, P. (Producer), Lusting, D. (Producer), Harris, T. (Producer), & Warren, J. (Director). (2000). *Partners in crime* [Motion Picture]. United States: Artisan Home Entertainment.

Bloch, P., & Anderson, D. (1974). *Policewomen on patrol: Final report.* Washington, DC: The Police Foundation.

Bregman, M. (Producer), Stroller, L.A. (Producer), Bregman, M. (Producer), & Noyce, P. (Director). (1999). *The bone collector* [Motion picture]. United States: Universal Pictures.

Canton, M. (Producer), Samaha, E. (Producer), & Mankoki, L. (Director). (2001). *Angel eyes* [Motion picture]. United States: Warner Bros. Pictures.

Capra, F. (Producer), Wambaugh, J. (Writer), & Becker, H. (Director). (1980). *The black marble* [Motion picture]. United States: Anchor Bay Entertainment.

Carlan, P. E., & McMullan, E. C. (2009). A contemporary snapshot of policewomen attitudes. *Women & Criminal Justice, 19*, 60–79.

Coblenz, W. (Producer), Wambaugh, J. (Writer), & Becker, H. (1979). *The onion field* [Motion picture]. United States: Black Marble Productions.

Coen, E. (Producer), & Coen, J. (Director). (1996). *Fargo* [Motion picture]. United States: PolyGram Filmed Entertainment.

Cohen, J., & Weimann, G. (2000). Cultivation revisited: Some genres have some effects on some viewers. *Communication Reports, 13*(2), 99–114.

Cohen, L. (Producer/Writer/Director). (1976). *God told me to* [Motion picture]. United States: Miracle Pictures.

Correia, M. (2000). The conceptual ambiguity of community in community policing: Filtering the muddy waters. *Policing, 23*(2), 218–220.

Crystal, R. (Producer), Hoffman, S. (Producer), & Schroeder, B. (Director). (2002). *Murder by numbers* [Motion picture]. United States: Film Unit Productions.

Curtis, B. C. (Producer), & Lemmo, J. (Writer). (1995). *Bodily harm* [Motion picture]. United States: Rysher Entertainment.

Cypser, D. (Producer), & Grove, M. S. (Director). (2001). *Dragon and the hawk* [Motion picture]. United States: Inferno Film Productions.

Daley, R. (Producer), & Fargo, J. (Director). (1976). *The enforcer* [Motion picture]. United States: Warner Bros. Pictures.

Daley, R. (Producer), & Siegel, D. (Director). (1971). *Dirty Harry* [Motion picture]. United States: Warner Bros. Pictures.

DeTardo-Bora, K. A. (2009). Criminal justice "Hollywood style": How women in criminal justice professions are depicted in prime-time crime dramas. *Women & Criminal Justice, 19*(2), 153–168.

Diefenbach, D. L., & West, M. D. (2001). Violent crime and Poisson regression: A measure and a method for cultivation analysis. *Journal of Broadcasting and Electronic Media, 45*, 432–445.

Dixon, T. L. (2007). Black criminals and White officers: The effects of racially misrepresenting law breakers and law defenders on television news. *Media Psychology, 10*(2), 270–291.

Donner, R. (Producer), Silver, J. (Producer), & Donner, R. (Director) (1992). *Lethal weapon 3* [Motion picture]. United States: Warner Bros. Pictures.

Felkenes, G. T., & Schroedel, J. R. (1993). A case study of minority women in policing. *Women & Criminal Justice, 4*(2), 65–89.

Franklin, C. A. (2007). Male peer support and the police culture. *Women & Criminal Justice, 16*(3), 1–25.

Gentles, K. A., & Harrison, K. (2006). Television and perceived peer expectations of body size among African American adolescent girls. *Howard Journal of Communication, 17*, 39–55.

Goidel, R. K., Freeman, C. M., & Procopio, S. T. (2006). The impact of television viewing on perceptions of juvenile crime. *Journal of Broadcasting and Electronic Media, 50*(1), 119–139.

Golan, M. (Producer), Globus, Y. (Producer), & Stockwell, J. (Director). (1987). *Under cover* [Motion picture]. United States: Cannon Releasing Corporation.

Golin, S. (Producer), Sighvatsson, S. (Producer), Rosenman, H. (Producer), & Lumet, S. (Director). (1992). *A stranger among us* [Motion picture]. United States: Paramount Pictures.

Gossett, J. L., & Williams, J. E. (1998). Perceived discrimination among women in law enforcement. *Women & Criminal Justice, 10*(1), 53–73.

Guercio, J. (Producer/Director). (1973). *Electra glide in blue* [Motion picture]. United States: MGM Home Entertainment.

Gutschoven, K., & Van den Bulck, J. (2005). Television viewing and age at smoking initiation: Does a relationship exist between higher levels of television viewing and earlier onset of smoking? *Nicotine and Tobacco Research, 7*(3), 381–385.

Haba, C. W., Sarver, R. A., III, Dobbs, R. R., & Sarver, M. B. (2009). Attitudes of college students toward women in policing. *Women & Criminal Justice, 19*, 235–250.

Hale, D. (1998). Keeping women in their place: An analysis of policewomen in videos, 1972–1996. In F. Bailey & D. Hale (Eds.), *Popular culture, crime and justice* (pp. 159–179). Belmont, CA: Thompson and Wadsworth.

Hammermeister, J., Brock, B., Winterstein, D., & Page, R. (2005). Life without TV? Cultivation theory and psychosocial health characteristics of television-free individuals and their television-viewing counterparts. *Health Communication, 17*(3), 253–264.

Harrington, P. (2006). Women in policing: Past, present, and future. In K. Peak (Ed.), *Policing America: Methods, issues, challenges* (5th ed. pp. 358–360). Upper Saddle River, NJ: Pearson Education.

Hawkins, R., & Pingree, S. (1981). Using television to construct social reality. *Journal of Broadcasting, 25*(4), 347–364.

Hendriks, A. (2002). Examining the effects of hegemonic depictions of female bodies on television: A call for theory and programmatic research. *National Communication Association, 19*(1), 105–123.

Hetsroni, A., & Tukachinsky, R. H. (2006). Television-world estimates, real-world estimates, and television viewing: A new scheme for cultivation. *Journal of Communication, 56*(1), 133–156.

Jacobson, T. (Producer), Wedaa, J. (Producer), & Carson, D. (Director). (2004). *Unstoppable* [Motion picture]. United States: Millennium Films.

Kingshott, B. F. (2009). Women in policing: Changing the organization culture by adopting a feminist perspective on leadership. *Criminal Justice Studies, 22*(1), 49–72.

Koenig, E. (1978). An overview of attitudes toward women in law enforcement. *Public Administration Review, 38*, 267–275.

Kroll, L. (Producer), & Holland, T. (Director). (1987). *Fatal beauty* [Motion picture]. United States: Metro Goldwyn Mayer.

Kurtz, D. L., Linnemann, T., & Williams, L. S. (2012). Reinventing the matron: The continued importance of gendered images and division of labor in modern policing. *Women & Criminal Justice, 22*(3), 239–263.

Ladd, A. Jr. (Producer), Rissner, D. (Producer), Bailey, S. (Producer), & Affleck, B. (Director). (2007). *Gone baby gone* [Motion picture]. United States: Miramax Films.

Leger, K. (1997). Public perceptions of female police officers on patrol. *American Journal of Criminal Justice, 21*(2), 231–249.

Liber, R. (Producer), Jones, S. (Producer), Peters, S. (Writer), & McNaughton, J. (Director). (1998). *Wild things* [Motion picture]. United States: Columbia Pictures.

Lonsway, K. (2001). *Dismantling the warrior image: The role of women in community policing*. Retrieved from http://www.pennyharrington.com/ diswarriorimage.htm Lonsway, K. A. (2007). Are we there yet? The progress of women in one large law enforcement agency. *Women & Criminal Justice, 18*(1–2), 1–48.

Lonsway, K., Carrington, S., Aguirre, P., Wood, M., Moore, M., Harrington, P., ... Spillar, K. (2002). *Equality denied: The status of women in policing, 2001*. Los Angeles, CA: National Center for Women & Policing.

Lonsway, K., Moore, M., Harrington, P., Smeal, E., & Spillar, K. (2003). *Hiring and retaining more women: The advantages to law enforcement agencies.* Los Angeles, CA: National Center for Women & Policing.

Marlowe, A. W. (Producer). (2009–2013). *Castle* [Television Series]. Los Angeles, CA: Beacon Pictures.

Martin, S. (1994). "Outsider within" the station house: The impact of race and gender on Black women police. *Social Problems, 41,* 383–400.

Mastro, D. E., & Behm-Morawitz, E. (2005). Latino representation on primetime television. *Journalism & Mass Communication Quarterly, 82*(1), 110–130.

Milchan, A. (Producer), Tarlov, M. (Producer), & Amiel, J. (Director). (1995). *Copycat* [Motion picture]. United States: Warner Bros. Pictures.

Milchan, A. (Producer), Thomopoulos, T. (Producer), Lowry, H. (Producer), & Herrington, R. (Director). (1993). *Striking distance* [Motion picture]. United States: Columbia Pictures.

Morgan, M., & Shanahan, J. (1997). Two decades of cultivation research. In B. R. Burleson (Ed.), *Communication yearbook 20* (pp. 1–47). Thousand Oaks, CA: Sage.

Nabi, R. L., & Sullivan, J. L. (2001). Does television relate to engagement in protective action against crime? A cultivation analysis from a theory of reasoned action perspective. *Communication Research, 28,* 802–825.

Nagy, R. (Producer), Watkins, F. P. (Producer), & Watkins, F. P. (Director). (2008). *Suitable for murder* [Motion picture]. United States: Film Unit Productions.

Paoline, E. A., & Terrill, W. (2004). Women police officers and the use of coercion. *Women & Criminal Justice, 15*(3/4), 97–119.

Paul, D. J. (Producer), Pasdar, A. (Director), & Monjo, J. (Writer). (1998). *Cement* [Motion picture]. United States: Lion's Gate Home Entertainment.

Peak, K. (2006). *Policing America: Methods, issues, challenges* (5th ed.). Upper Saddle River, NJ: Pearson Education.

Peak, K., & Glensor, R. (2002). *Community policing and problem solving: Strategies and practices.* Upper Saddle River, NJ: Pearson Education.

Philips, D. (Producer), & Penn, S. (Writer/Director). (1991). *The Indian runner* [Motion picture]. United States: MGM Home Entertainment.

Pogrebin, M., Dodge, M., & Chatman, H. (2000). Reflections of African-American women on their careers in urban policing: Their experiences of racial and sexual discrimination. *International Journal of the Sociology of Law, 28,* 311–326.

Pressman, E. R. (Producer), Stone, O. (Producer), & Bigelow, K. (Director). (1990). *Blue steel* [Motion picture]. United States: Lightning Pictures.

Rabe-Hemp, C., & Beichner, D. (2011). An analysis of advertisements: A lens for viewing the social exclusion of women in police imagery. *Women & Criminal Justice, 21,* 63–81.

Rafter, N. (2000). *Shots in the mirror: Crime films and society.* New York, NY: Oxford University Press.

Reeber, H. R., & Chang, Y. (2000). Assessing cultivation theory and public health model for crime reporting. *Newspaper Research Journal, 21*(4), 99–112.

Sass, T., & Troyer, J. (1999). Affirmative action, political representation, unions, and female police employment. *Journal of Labor Research, 20,* 571–587.

Schroedel, J. R., Frisch, S., Hallamore, N., Peterson, J., & Vanderhorst, N. (1996). The joint impact of race and gender on police department employment practices. *Women & Criminal Justice, 8*(2), 59–77.

Schuck, A. M., & Rabe-Hemp, C. (2007). Women police: The use of force by and against female officers. *Women & Criminal Justice, 16*(4), 91–117.

Schulz, D. (1993). From policewoman to police officer: An unfinished revolution. *Police Studies, 16,* 90–99.

Schutt, R. (2004). *Investigating social world: The process and practice of research—Textbook only* (4th ed.). Newbury Park, CA: Pine Forge Press.

Seklecki, R., & Paynich, R. (2007). A national survey of female police officers: An overview of findings. *Police Practice and Research, 8*(1), 17–30.

Shelley, T. O., Morabito, M. S., & Tobin-Gurley, J. (2011). Gendered institutions and gender roles: Understanding the experiences of women in policing. *Criminal Justice Studies, 24*(4), 351–367.

Shrum, L., & O'Guinn, T. (1993). Process and effects in the construction of social reality. *Communication Research, 20*, 436–471.

Silver, J. (Producer), Donner, R. (Producer), & Donner, R. (Director). (1998). *Lethal weapon 4* [Motion picture]. United States: Warner Bros. Pictures.

Stern, J. (Producer), & Shepard, R. (Writer/Director). (1999). *Oxygen* [Motion picture]. United States: Ardustry Home Entertainment.

Strandberg, K. (1998). Reducing family violence. *Law Enforcement Technology, 25*(1), 32–36.

U.S. Census Bureau. (2012, December 10). *State and county quickfacts: USA.* Retrieved from http://quickfacts. census.gov/qfd/states/00000.html

U.S. Equal Employment Opportunity Commission. (2007). *The law: Civil Rights Act of 1964.* Retrieved from http:// www.eeoc.gov/abouteeoc/35th/thelaw/index. html

Vergeer, M., Lubbers, M., & Scheepers, P. (2000). Exposure to newspapers and attitudes toward ethnic minorities: A longitudinal analysis. *Howard Journal of Communications, 11*, 127–143.

Williams, D. (2006). Virtual cultivation: Online worlds, offline perceptions. *Journal of Communication, 56*, 69–87.

Wilson, B. J., Martins, N., & Marske, A. L. (2005). Children's and parents' fright reactions to kidnapping stories in the news. *Communication Monographs, 72*(1), 46–70.

Wilson, F. T. (2006). A qualitative examination of the core cop film genre: Thirty years of instrumental and expressive police violence. *Dissertation Abstracts International, 68*, 740.

Wilson, F. T. (2009). Identifying large replicable film populations in social science film research: A unifying film population identification methodology. *Criminal Justice and Law Review Journal, 1*(1), 19–40.

Wilson, F. T., & Henderson, H. (2014). The criminological cultivation of African American municipal police officers: Sambo or sellout. *Race and Justice, 4*(1), 45–67.

Wilson, F. T., Longmire, D., & Swymeler, W. (2009). The absence of gay and lesbian police officer depictions in the first three decades of the core cop film genre: Moving toward a cultivation theory perspective. *Journal of Criminal Justice and Popular Culture, 16*(1), 27–39.

Wimmer, R. D., & Dominick, J. R. (2003). *Mass media research: An introduction.* Belmont, CA: Wadsworth/Thomson Learning.

Wolf, D. (Producer). (1999–present). *Law & order: Special victims unit* [Television series]. New York, NY: Wolf Films.

Woo, H., & Dominick, J. R. (2003). Acculturation, cultivation, and daytime TV talk shows. *Journalism & Mass Communication Quarterly, 80*(1), 109–127.

Woolsey, S. (2010, October). Challenges for women in policing. *Law and Order.* Retrieved March 6, 2014 from http://www.hendonpub.com/resources/article_ archive/results/details?id=1614

Yim, Y. (2009). Girls, why do you want to become police officers? Career goals/choices among criminal justice undergraduates. *Women & Criminal Justice, 19*, 120–136.

Zhang, Y. B., & Harwood, J. (2002). Television viewing and perceptions of traditional Chinese values among Chinese college students. *Journal of Broadcasting and Electronic Media, 46*(2), 245–264.

Zhao, J., Herbst, L., & Lovrich, N. (2001). Race, ethnicity and the female cop: Differential patterns of representation. *Journal of Urban Affairs, 23*(3–4), 243–257.

SECTION THREE SUMMARY

Key Discussion Sessions

1. What were Dixon's primary findings in "Black Criminals and White Officers: The Effects of Racially Misrepresenting Law Breakers and Law Defenders on Television News"? Do you believe that Dixon's findings would hold true for any of the communities you profiled in Section 1? If so, which communities and why? What were the major findings of the Wilson and Henderson piece "The Criminological Cultivation of African American Municipal Police Officers: Sambo or Sellout"? Can you think of any television shows that are not comedic, science fiction, or animated in nature where an African American plays the leading city police officer character and is portrayed as a hero? If so, how many and what are they? What do you believe the impact of Wilson and Henderson's findings might have on society's perceptions of African American police officers? What impact could these findings have on the citizens in the community where you grew up? If you are from another country, what impact do you believe such depictions might have on international perceptions of police officers in the United States and in other countries?

2. Considering the history of female police officers covered by, and the findings of, Wilson and Blackburn in "The Depiction of Female Municipal Police Officers in the First Four Decades of the Core Cop Film Genre: 'It's a Man's World,'" can you think of any leading female city police officer characters in television shows who are portrayed as having had sex with their senior officers? Can you think of any leading female city police officer characters in television shows who are depicted as becoming officers because they were damaged somehow (raped, beaten, drug addicted, etc.)? If so, how many and what are the shows? What do you believe the impact of Wilson and Blackburn's findings might have on the perception of women who become police officers? How might the findings impact recruitment of female police officers and their expectations of how they will be treated? If you are from another country, what impact do you believe such depictions might have on international perceptions of female police officers in the United States and in other countries?

Public Consumption Exercise

Remember, the public consumption exercises in this text build upon each other. You must have completed the exercises in Sections 1 and 2 to complete the current exercises.

Exercise 4: Paraphrasing Findings

Article

Determine which articles in this section provide findings that could help the citizens of the county from another region given the demographic data you gathered on this group in Section 1. Indicate which article you chose and why you believe this to be the best article.

Findings Paragraphs and Writing Level

Identify consecutive paragraphs (no less than three) from the findings or results section of the article that contain the largest portion of key findings and retype them in a word document; make sure the wording is exact. Follow the instructions in Appendix C to calculate the writing level of the paragraphs. Does the writing level match the average literacy level for the county from another region? If it is written at a higher level than the average, how many grade levels must the authors of the piece reduce the writing to be easily read by the citizens of that county?

Bulleted Facts

Utilize the bulleted facts exercise from Section 2 to create a set of bulleted facts from the entire results or findings section for this article.

Paraphrased Findings

Next, write a two to three paragraph (not more than four sentences per paragraph) summary of the findings. Write the piece at the average reading level of the citizens of the county from another region. Do not worry about citations; you are practicing your paraphrasing skills at this point. (For help with paraphrasing, see the following website or other similar sites: https://owl.english.purdue.edu/owl/resource/563/1/.)

SECTION FOUR

Courts

CSI AND FORENSIC REALISM

by Sarah Keturah Deutsch
University of Wisconsin Law School

Gray Cavender
Arizona State University
School of Justice & Social Inquiry

Introduction

C *SI: Crime Scene Investigation* (*CSI*) has enjoyed an enviable status in television. Having completed its eighth season, a longevity that is rare in prime time television, this crime drama consistently has been the top rated program in its time slot both in its first run and rerun incarnations (see Nielsen Ratings, June 20–26, 2005; Toff, 7 April 2007: A16). Not only has *CSI* generated two successful spin-off series (*CSI: Miami* and *CSI: NY*), it has pushed forensic science terms and concepts into the popular discourse. Accompanying this diffusion has been the sense that science and the police are virtually infallible.

Crime genre programs have been a staple since television's inception. The success of programs from *Dragnet* to *NYPD Blue* has evidenced the audience's fascination with crime dramas. In one sense, *CSI* has been another program in a long line of television crime dramas, and it has exhibited features common to the genre, for example, plots that were driven by violent crimes and the search for the criminal. At the same time, *CSI*'s forensic science theme, which was unique when the program began in 2000, has initiated a trend in television crime dramas toward more realistic portrayals of technology and science in policing. In this paper, we focus on how *CSI* has combined the traditions of the crime genre with a sense of forensic realism through what we call a strategic web of forensic facticity. This web has included the sense of realism that is characteristic of the crime genre, but also its portrayal of science, for example, in the use of scientific equipment and jargon. Through this web, *CSI* has circulated and validated cultural meanings about crime as a threat to the social order.

CSI is an interesting analytic site, first because of its phenomenal popularity, and second, because of its amalgam of crime genre traditions with the additional dimension of forensic science. Accordingly, in this paper we analyze the content and tactics of *CSI*'s very successful first season.

Television Crime Drama and the Police Procedural

CSI is a part of a long tradition in popular culture: crime has been an enduring genre across media, including television. Genres, which are categories of cultural production, are characterized by stability, i.e., predictable elements that define them, but also by elements that change with the times. Defining features of the crime genre include an emphasis on violent crime, usually murder (Perlmutter, 2000), and protagonists who search for and apprehend the criminal, and with that solution, restore order (Cavender, 2004). Of course, these fictional depictions enjoy a degree of poetic license because they differ from actual crime data. Television crime dramas over-emphasize crimes like murder and under-emphasize more commonplace property crimes. This is understandable from a narrative sense because violent crimes are sensational and visually interesting (Soulliere, 2003). Similarly, presenting crime as a morality play complete with notions of good (heroes) and evil (villains) is an effective storytelling technique (Mawby, 2003). However, this morality play is ideological in nature: it circulates and reinforces cultural meanings about social disorder and criminality (Wilson, 2000:6). As a social institution, the police have the power to classify crime and criminals, and that definitional power becomes even more taken-for-granted when combined with television's storytelling capabilities (Loader, 1997).

Notwithstanding these ideological messages, television crime drama depictions diverge from crime data in many significant ways. Television crime drama tends to over-represent white criminals and victims (Perlmutter, 2000; Eschholz, Mallard and Flynn, 2004). Men are more likely than women to be victims, but crime dramas often feature women victims (see Eschholz, Mallard and Flynn, 2004). Women are more likely to be victimized by acquaintances or intimates, but television often reinforces the belief that women are victimized by strangers (Soulliere, 2003). Although these depictions have persisted for years, the crime genre does change with the times. For example, although the heroes are still usually men, heroism today is more a matter of expertise than the physical strength that defined heroism in television's early days. The quest for justice has changed, too. Today, police detectives like *NYPD: Blue's* Andy Sippowitz are television's preferred agents of justice. Police drama now dominates television's crime genre. Indeed, police officers may be television's most over-represented profession (Wilson, 2000:2).

To varying degrees, these dramas resemble the police procedural, a crime subgenre which emerged in film after World War II. Early procedurals were based on actual (or seemingly real) crimes which gave them a "realistic aesthetic" (Krutnik, 1991:202). They focused on the inner workings of the police organization, revealing backstage routines and procedures.

Contemporary television procedurals differ somewhat from their predecessors. Compared to *Dragnet's* "just the facts, ma'am" approach, they feature more melodramatic narratives. This is occasioned, in part, through the use of ensemble casts that also allow programs to include women and racial/ethnic minorities as police officers (Wilson, 2005:48). The increasingly melodramatic aspect of police drama is consistent with other trends in prime time television programming (Wilson, 2000; Wittebols, 2004). In crime and other prime time programs, these melodramatic aspects are thought to produce a sense of audience loyalty to programs and characters, and, ironically, a sense of believability in them (Wittebols, 2004: 215).

Despite its use of melodrama, the crime genre is known for its surface realism (Wilson, 2000). The police procedural makes this realism a defining characteristic. Early procedurals incorporated actual crimes into stories that focused on police detectives who pursued the truth through "systematized technological investigative procedures" (Krutnik, 1991:203). Contemporary police dramas like *CSI* affect a forensic realism that owes much to those early procedurals. In an era when the police employ sophisticated science and technology in their work, it is not surprising that police dramas on television also utilize science and technology. The dramatic usage of science and technology maintains the genre's tradition of realism and authenticity.

Perhaps it is ironic to use words like realism and authenticity when discussing a program like *CSI*; it is, after all, a television drama. However, we suggest that *CSI*'s success can be attributed to what we call its "strategic web of forensic facticity," a term that we borrow from Gaye Tuchman (1978). Tuchman coined the term "strategic web of facticity" in her analysis of the news, not as a product of objective journalism, but rather as a social construction. For Tuchman, a web of facticity is a strategic, ritualistic practice which ensures that a group of presented facts is seen as credible and objective (1978:86), and that, "when taken together, present themselves as both individually and collectively self-validating" (1978:106). Tuchman also was interested in how the news shapes cultural meanings about such matters as conformity, deviance, and threats to social stability (1978:184). Indeed, she sees not only the news but the entire consciousness industry, including entertainment programming, as supportive of existing social hierarchies (1978:156).

We posit that *CSI* uses a web of facticity to bolster the seeming authenticity and accuracy of its forensic realism even as it disseminates meanings about criminals, their threat to society, and the police who are aligned against them. Through the usage of narrative, gear, and other production techniques, *CSI* advances the perception that something scientific is indeed taking place. The program's construction of science is combined with those conventions that produce the crime genre's sense of realism.

With its emphasis on teamwork, police labs, and police routines, *CSI* resembles earlier television procedurals like *Dragnet* (Mittell, 2004:151). It uses more melodramatic narratives, but also fosters the seeming authenticity of the procedural, in this case, in terms of forensic realism. As a result, *CSI* is a very popular television program, but it also has affected the public consciousness about policing and science.

CSI Synopsis

CSI opens with what its transcripts call a "cold shot," i.e., a shot of the Las Vegas strip, usually at night. This establishing shot depicts a city with which many in the audience are familiar, both in terms of its past, i.e., images of gambling and organized crime, and its current status as a destination for family vacations. These establishing shots function in much the same manner as location shooting in the early police procedural films or in *Dragnet*. The camera then cuts to a crime or a crime scene which acts as a teaser for the week's episode. A series of shots follow which present the regular cast members: Gil Grissom, the head of the CSI unit, and investigators Catherine Willows, Sara Sidle, Warrick Brown, and Nick Stokes. These also are establishing shots, but in terms of the competency of the *CSI* cast.

As the episode unfolds, the *CSI* team is confronted with crimes. Often, they have no information about motive, the criminal, or even the victim's identity. They discover these "unknowns" and solve crimes through a combination of police work, laboratory re-constructions and experiments, and cop/scientific knowledge. All of this occurs amid a careful balance of crime genre staples, melodrama, and forensic science.

Methodology

Several research questions informed our analysis. We were interested in how *CSI* compared with other television crime dramas. In part, this was a numerical question: what crimes, criminals, and victims were depicted on *CSI*? We also were interested in a more qualitative dimension: were *CSI*'s representations similar to or did they diverge from the conventions of television police dramas? Finally, we were especially interested in the question of how *CSI* created its representations of science and technology.

We conducted a content analysis of *CSI*'s 2000–2001 season. We were interested in the debut season because it established *CSI* as a dominant force in television crime drama. Arguably, the success of the first season as measured by viewer ratings started a trend in television wherein the police increasingly use science and technology in their investigations. We analyzed the episodes from that first season in close detail.

CSI's 2000–2001 season was available through a DVD compilation that included all 23 episodes. The 23 episodes contained a total of 74 cases; the case served as the unit of analysis in our crime statistics section. Our referencing system began with the number 100, the pilot episode, and continued consecutively through the episodes as they appeared in the DVD compilation.

We watched four episodes and used these observations to formulate a code sheet (see Appendix). Because of our research questions, our code sheet was attentive to dimensions of police drama discussed in the literature on television crime programs, e.g., standard elements of police procedurals, and to our interest in understanding how *CSI* employed a web of forensic facticity and created a believable sense that the characters used science to solve crimes. This was not a large data set so we used one coder, the first author, who has a background both in justice-related research and in chemistry. Accordingly, we did not employ measures of inter-coder reliability that are common with large data sets and multiple coders (Bertrand and Hughes, 2005:200). However, as a methodological safeguard, the second author reviewed a small sample (four episodes) of the first author's coding observations. There was unanimous agreement, which is not surprising given the straightforward nature of the coding, e.g., information about types of crime or dialogue with scientific jargon. The code sheet was organized into three aspects of the programming: (1) crime statistics: types of crimes and demographic details about criminals and victims; (2) crime genre: tactical methods typical of the crime genre such as police procedural concepts; and (3) markers of forensic realism such as scientific equipment and jargon.

The use of code sheets promoted a more systematic analysis (Bertrand and Hughes, 2005:201) and also permitted more efficient coding: many dimensions of interest were quickly checked or circled. The use of a DVD compilation facilitated observations by allowing the coder to pause or rewind the action if longer notes were desired, for example, to capture a piece of dialogue. When coding was completed, we simply tallied numerical data such as the number of murders or the usage of knives as weapons. However, on the more qualitative dimensions of our observations, such as the presence of police procedural elements or of scientific language, we repeatedly read our code sheets, looked for patterns, refined categories, and considered dialogue quotes that we could incorporate into our analysis.

Our analysis has three sections. The first section presents information about the crimes, criminals and victims depicted in *CSI*'s first season. Such a compilation is a standard feature in criminological research about crime genre presentations; it provides a bench mark for comparisons with other programs and across time. In the second and third sections, we present more qualitative data. In the second section, we considered how *CSI* used the conventions of the television crime genre to entertain and to set the stage for forensic realism. In the third section, we considered how *CSI* established and emphasized a web of forensic facticity which strategically validated the show's forensic realism. We follow our analysis with a section wherein we discuss the implications of our findings.

Analysis

Crime Statistics

Interestingly, television crime drama and television news offer similar presentations about crime: both exaggerate violent, personal crimes (Eschholz, Mallard, and Flynn, 2004). As we see in Table 1, during its first season, 72% of *CSI*'s crimes (53 of 74 crimes) were violent (e.g., murder, rape). Although these were the sort of crimes that a *CSI*-type unit would investigate, the depictions paralleled other television crime drama. A miscellaneous category (24% or 18 of 74) included the disposal of a corpse by a funeral director to cut burial costs and the poaching of a gorilla. These crimes added an exotic element to *CSI*'s cases. But, murder was *CSI*'s crime of choice. The network even marketed reruns of *CSI*'s first season with an ad promising: "This weekend's gonna be MURDER." Thus, the remaining statistics pertain to the offenders, victims, and weapons involved in *CSI*'s murder cases.

Table 1. Number and Percentage of Types of Offenses[1]

Offense	CSI[2] (N=74)	
	%	N
Violent Crime	**72**	**(53)**
Murder[3]	64	(47)
Forcible Rape	3	(2)
Robbery	3	(2)
Aggravated Assault	3	(2)
Property Crime	**4**	**(3)**
Burglary	3	(2)
Larceny-Theft	1	(1)
Motor Vehicle Theft	0	(0)
Arson	0	(0)
Miscellaneous	**24**	**(18)**
Suicide	3	(2)
Sexual Molestation	1	(1)
Kidnapping	3	(2)
Bombing	4	(3)
Extortion	3	(2)
Accident[4]	5	(4)
Other[5]	5	(4)

[1]Percentages are based upon the total number of crimes committed during the entire first season.
[2]Percentages may not add to 100% due to rounding.
[3]Vehicular manslaughter (Episode 103) and justifiable homicide (Episode 122) were included in the murder category for CSI
[4]The accident category includes a boating accident, two inadvertent fires, and a building collapse
[5]The other category includes corpse disposal by a funeral director, drunk driving, spitting, and poaching

Tables 2 and 3 represent the depiction of criminals and victims by gender and race/ethnicity. Seventy-seven percent of *CSI*'s murders were committed by males, 19% by females, and 4% by unknown offenders. In terms of race, 87% (41 of 47) of *CSI*'s murderers were Caucasian, 6% (3 of 47) were African-American, and 6% (3 of 47) were unknown; no Hispanic murderers appeared in the first season. *CSI*'s over-representation of Caucasian murders paralleled the depictions in other television crime programs (Perlmutter, 2000).

Table 2. Number and Percentage of Murder Offenders by Race and Sex

Characteristics	CSI (N = 47)	
Sex of Offender	%	N
Male	77	(36)
Female	19	(9)
Unknown	4	(2)
Race of Offender	%	N
Caucasian	87	(41)
African-American	6	(3)
Other	0	(0)
Unknown	6	(3)

Although more than twice as many male (n=31 or 66%) than female victims (n=15 or 32%) were murdered during the first season, *CSI* still over-represented female victims. Such a depiction reproduced television's titillating gender stereotypes. *CSI*'s murder victims were overwhelmingly Caucasian (91%). This skew toward Caucasian murder victims was consistent with television crime drama generally (Perlmutter, 2000).

Table 3. Number and Percentage of Murder Victims by Race and Sex

Characteristics	CSI (N = 47)	
Sex of Offender	%	N
Male	66	(31)
Female	32	(15)
Unknown	2	(1)
Race of Offender	%	N
Caucasian	91	(43)
African-American	4	(2)
Other	0	(0)
Unknown	4	(2)

Sixty-two percent (n=29 of 47) of *CSI*'s murderers knew their victims. However, in 36% (n=17 of 47) of the murders, offenders and victims were strangers. This over-representation of situations in which victims did not know their assailants reflected television's penchant for "stranger danger."

Table 4. Number and Percentage of Weapons Used to Commit Murder

Weapon	CSI (N = 47)	
	%	N
Firearms	36	(17)
Knives or cutting instruments	17	(8)
Personal Weapons (hands, fists, feet, etc.)	15	(7)
Unknown or other dangerous weapons (see breakdown below)	32	(15)
	Unknown or other dangerous weapons (N=15)	
Type	%	N
Vehicle	4	(2)
Bomb	6	(3)
Other[6]	19	(9)
Unknown	2	(1)

[6]The other category includes a golf club, club, dingle-dangle, rock, ice pick, curtain sash, ceramic figurine, potholder, and dog

As we see in Table 4, firearms were the most common murder weapons during the first season (36%, n=17); knives were the second most used weapon (17%, n=8). A variety of weapons comprised an "other" category (32%, n=15), e.g., a golf club, a curtain sash. Personal weapons such as fists and feet were utilized in 15% (n=7) of CSI's murders. These personal weapons often were a part of the narrative; they provided incriminating forensic evidence, e.g., a heel impression.

These sensational images were consistent with news depictions and with the conventions of the television crime genre. They were a part of the dramatic narrative that CSI employed to lure an audience. In the next section, we offer a qualitative assessment of how CSI employed genre conventions to entertain but also to generate loyalty to the program, its cast of characters, and to create a sense that they are smart, competent people who use science to catch criminals.

CSI and the Television Crime Genre

As measured by ratings and longevity, CSI has been one of contemporary television's most successful programs. Its success has been attributable, in part, to the long-standing popularity of the crime genre. To tap into the genre's popularity, CSI had to meet its audience's genre-specific expectations. For example, as noted in the previous section, it offered its audience a heavy dose of murder, a crime drama staple. CSI dealt in other genre conventions. It is expected that protagonists will chase criminals, but increasingly in television crime drama they do so as members of a police organization. Another genre convention is that crime dramas employ melodrama in their narratives. These melodramatic features entertained but they also enhanced the sense of being backstage with the police, and thus contributed to the program's authenticity.

The Police Organizations

CSI was consistent with the trend toward crime dramas that feature the police organization. It was the police as an organization, not merely individual protagonists, who apprehended criminals. Of course, the various duties that comprise an actual police investigation are divided among many individuals and specializations. On CSI, however, the team handled most of the procedures: they processed the crime scene, questioned witnesses and interrogated suspects, collected and analyzed evidence, and ultimately solved the crime.

Television crime dramas have featured the police as an organization for several decades, but there have been narrative shifts in the genre, for example, they increasingly feature melodrama. One standard melodramatic plot device depicts a sense of tension between the protagonist and others. CSI employed tension as a plot device during its first season. In some cases, the narrative tension was between Gil Grissom, who headed the unit, and the heads of other police units (Episodes 106 and 111). In Episode 122, Gil was removed from a case for disagreeing with the FBI, but he defied orders, investigated the case, and proved that the FBI had arrested the wrong man. Often tension established the uniqueness of the team. In the first scene of the first episode, a police detective referred to the CSI team as "the nerd squad" (Episode 100). Sometimes team members asserted their superiority to other police when it came to solving crime. CSI investigator Catherine Willows stressed this superiority to Holly Gribbs, a new recruit. Catherine: "The cops? Forget it. They wouldn't know fingerprints from paw prints and the detectives chase the lie. We solve" (Episode 100). Perhaps the program's writers employed the "tension as uniqueness" device because CSI, with its forensic science focus, was a different type of crime drama and they wanted to establish the legitimacy of the investigators.

As noted, contemporary police procedurals feature ensemble casts who include women and members of various racial/ethnic groups. CSI followed this trend. Gil Grissom played something of a gruff father figure. His advice to younger subordinates played as a kind of forensic philosophy. In Episode 115, Gil quoted Locard's Exchange Principle (criminals leave a trace of themselves at the scene of the crime, and the crime scene leaves a trace on the criminals; see Ramsland, 2001:3). Gil's masculinity was less a matter of physical strength and more a matter of scientific knowledge (Connell, 1993; Messerschmidt, 1993). CSI's depiction of its continuing women characters was perhaps more ambiguous. Two series regulars, Catherine Willows and Sara Sidle, were portrayed as competent crime scene investigators. At the same time, they were still feminized for television. Catherine was a mother and this frequently figured into story lines. In Episode 110, when Catherine's ex-husband reported her to child protective services because she failed to pick up her daughter from dance practice, a colleague attested to the agency that she was a good mom. Catherine and Sara may be forensic scientists, but they were depicted in a manner that was consistent with gender stereotypes.

In terms of race/ethnicity, CSI resembled other police programs because, as noted, its criminals and victims were primarily Caucasian. However, one continuing character, Warrick Brown, was an African-American investigator. In Episode 103, his racial status was relevant: he befriended another African-American character.

These melodramatic dimensions are now common in the crime genre, and they were prevalent during CSI's first season. Such scenarios humanized the characters and made them more attractive to the audience. They served to 'de-science' (our term) CSI, which made the show more accessible. However, forensic realism was the core of CSI's premise. Accordingly, although it is a television crime drama, CSI had to make its presentation of forensic realism seem to be authentic. To accomplish this task, CSI adhered to the conventions of realism in the police procedural and also steeped virtually every aspect of the program within the aura of science.

Strategic Web of Forensic Facticity

We adapted Tuchman's idea of a strategic web of facticity (1978:86) and employed it to understand how CSI constructed its own strategic web of forensic facticity. Throughout its first season, CSI spun an intrinsic web of forensic facticity which (1) bolstered its backstage police realism, (2) validated its science claims, and (3) made scientific crime detection both accessible and fun even as it disseminated and reinforced cultural meanings about criminals and the police.

Police Procedural Realism

Realism, a characteristic of the crime genre, is a defining feature of the police procedural. *CSI* stressed the systematic procedures of the police as an organization--the Las Vegas Crime Lab—and gave the audience a backstage glimpse of these routines.

Following the procedural tradition, *CSI* used establishing shots of Las Vegas and positioned its protagonists in these scenes which suggested a geographic realism. In such locales, the regular cast members were portrayed as scientists and cops. Indeed, they had a wealth of detective-type knowledge about crime and criminals. Their expertise was depicted at the crime scene when they spotted innocuous clues (cop knowledge) and in the lab (scientific knowledge). In both locations, the audience was privy to backstage behavior and conversations. We saw a smoothly running police organization in which experts, acting as a team, were on the case. In the contemporary world, employers want workers to work as a team.

Consistent with the procedural tradition, *CSI* drew upon real cases. Some, like early procedurals, were drawn from news presentations of sensational crimes, e.g., to cut burial costs, a funeral director trashed a corpse (Episode 105). Others were supplied by *CSI*'s technical consultant, Elizabeth Devine, a former criminalist for the L.A. County Sheriff's Department (LaTempa, 2002). One of her cases appeared in Episode 117. A hit man took money from the client and the target, and then murdered both of them. When he was stranded at the scene of the second murder, he claimed that he was trying to save the victim with CPR. The explanation failed because the victim's bloody handprint was on the hit man's shirt. This bizarre case resembled a double homicide that Devine investigated; in that case, a bloody handprint also was the killer's undoing.

In the hands of professional writers, these cases increased *CSI*'s entertainment value. At the same time, these backstage glimpses at solving "real cases" promoted a sense of realism that was characteristic of the police procedural. Plots based on "real cases" supported Tuchman's (1978:3) observation that news and entertainment media work in tandem to produce a web of facticity, in this case, a web that portrayed the police as legitimate crime solvers. On *CSI*, these cops also were forensic scientists.

Scientific Realism

CSI gave its characters the gear and the knowledge of science. Characters and sets exuded the look of science. First, they dressed the part. Especially in the crime lab, lab coats and other aspects of wardrobe offered a visual display of scientific affiliation. Second, the characters used specialized equipment which suggested science in action. At the crime scene, their gear was more police-oriented, although even here they used specialized chemicals and equipment. When the action shifted to the crime laboratory, the set was equally convincing. The lab housed scientific apparatus, e.g., beakers filled with mysterious liquids and high-tech microscopes. The characters were depicted as knowing how to use this equipment to solve crimes. By using a gas chromatography mass spectrometer, Sara determined that a substance which melted on the timing device of a bomb was polyethylene terephtalete (polyester), which she traced to an orange, polyester Thrift-Right Car Rental coat (Episode 112).

The characters augmented their scientific knowledge by their usage of scientific jargon which further established *CSI*'s forensic facticity. Their language covered a vast array of scientific specializations. Gil was proficient in entomology. At a crime scene, he examined insects feeding on a corpse. Gil: "Pupa, stage 3." Jim: "English, I'm not an entomologist." Gil: "It's the third stage of larva metamorphosis. This guy's been dead 7 days" (Episode 100). In another case (Episode 116), Gil identified a woman who was missing for 21 years from a fingerprint taken when she was only four years old. Gil explained: "Since fingerprints are set for life during the fourth month of fetal development, I look beyond the size differential." Gil's usage of terminology such as ulnar loops, recurve, and ridge endings established his expertise. In both the entomology and the fingerprint cases, scientific knowledge linked directly to cop knowledge. Both swatches of dialogue were laced with scientific terms.

In order to enhance this web of forensic facticity, the actors were coached on their articulation of scientific language and the use of specialized equipment by Elizabeth Devine, CSI's technical consultant (LaTempa, 2002). They explained the lab equipment as they used it. If the facticity of this forensic equipment was challenged, they reasserted it. When Detective O'Riley called the tool that Gil was using "a toy," Gil retorted, "It is not a toy, O'Riley, it's an electrostatic dust print lifter ... it is like a super charged lint remover, only it lifts foot prints" (Episode 107).

Tuchman's (1978) web of facticity offered insights for an understanding of CSI's forensic realism. It was predictable that a television program, especially a police drama that tries to evoke a sense of realism, would use appropriate wardrobe, sets, and dialogue. However, Tuchman's web of facticity, which we adapted for our analysis, suggested that the news consists of ritualistic practices that produce facts that seem to be credible and objective (1978:86). She made an important point about objectivity. For Tuchman, the production of news was a part of the construction of knowledge; although a social construction, when produced by appropriate news gathering procedures, the news claims to be objective fact (1978:178–179). Similarly, one of the most interesting aspects of CSI's web of facticity was that the program privileged the facticity of physical evidence. Like the news, CSI presented scientifically gathered evidence as objective fact. Throughout the first season, the dialogue consistently referred to the superiority of physical evidence; it was portrayed as accurate and infallible. A team member put this way: "We are not detectives. We are crime scene analysts. We are trained to ignore verbal accounts and rely instead on the evidence a scene sets before us" (Episode 101). Gil's classic formulation of this position was that they "chase the lie 'til it leads to the truth" (Episode 111). Recall the scene noted earlier wherein Catherine told new recruit Holly Gribbs that, in contrast to the police who chased the lie, the crime scene investigators got to the truth through scientific investigations (Episode 100). They conducted lab experiments and re-enactments which scientifically confirmed their theory of the crime.

These scientific techniques were so successful, the evidence so compelling, that during the first season the investigators solved all but four crimes. And in only two of these were they truly stumped. In Episode 114, a local gambler was found shot to death in a casino elevator. There were too many fingerprints in the elevator to identify the killer, but it seemed to have been a professional hit because a quarter covered the bullet wound to the victim's forehead (cop knowledge). In a case that involved a dismembered gorilla, they could not discover the culprits although they assumed it was poachers because the gorilla was skinned and was missing its head, hands and feet (Episode 121).

Scientific Policing as Accessible and Fun

CSI offered a sense of forensic realism, both the realism of a police procedural and of scientific investigations. However, to maintain its high ratings, its web of forensic facticity also had to be both accessible and entertaining to the audience. It had to be television-friendly.

CSI's narratives placed the audience at the crime scene, interviewing witnesses and suspects or looking for clues. Camera work drew our attention to a witness or to a possible clue. The camera lingered on a suspicious witness or on an investigator's reaction to the witness. At the crime scene, the camera zoomed in with a close-up shot as an investigator saw something of interest, say a quarter on a dead man's head (Episode 114). These techniques called our attention to clues and made it appear as if we also spotted them.

CSI employed similar techniques with the scientific aspects of crime scene detective work. Explanatory dialogue instructed the audience seemingly as it instructed a younger investigator. The investigators sprayed luminol on a suspicious surface and applied a blue light, which caused invisible blood traces to glow. If the luminol did not work, they employed an alternate light source (ALS). In Episode 106, when investigating a crime scene, Gil, the veteran, and Nick, a younger investigator, used luminol and the blue light, but no blood was revealed on a floor. Gil: "Let's try the ALS." Nick: "Why use the alternate light source if luminol didn't pick up anything?" Gil: "Luminol works on the surface. ALS chases the protein molecules in blood. It actually penetrates the wood." As Gil predicted, the ALS penetrated the layers of lacquer and wood, and a blood stain was found on the floor.

Most viewers lack a science background so, in addition to such dialogue, CSI used cinematographic effects and visually supplemented its scientific jargon. Executive producer Carol Mendelsohn referred to the practice as "visual storytelling" (LaTempa, 2002). This included close-ups of microscopic evidence and graphic journeys into the human body. As a medical examiner explained a victim's death, viewers took the bullet's perspective as it entered and exited the body; this provided an inner visual of the wounds and damage that the medical examiner described (Episodes 108, 110, and 115). As series creator Anthony Zuiker explained, "the visual image will sell it on CSI" (LaTempa, 2002).

CSI's web of forensic facticity was established by its narratives, its dialogue, and the accoutrement of science. Some devices were consistent with the traditions of the police procedural but others were unique to a program which foregrounded science. Together, they produced a sense of forensic realism which suggested that science and police scientists solved crimes, and that the audience was a part of the solution. Just as the news shapes attitudes about politics and economics, a program like CSI circulated meanings about crime, the police, and the social order.

Discussion

At the outset, we posed a series of research questions about CSI. We hope that through our analysis we reveal how CSI maintains its popularity as it foregrounds the use of science and technology in police investigations. We think that our analysis goes beyond understanding a television program, and now turn to these larger implications.

Durkheim (1964) argues that the criminal sanction expresses society's condemnation of criminals and reaffirms the moral boundaries that crime threatens. However, since punishments are no longer public spectacles, in contemporary society it is often the media, including entertainment media that socially condemn fictional criminals (Schattenberg, 1981). The crime genre is like morality plays that reinforce cultural meanings about crime (Cavender and Jurik, 1998).

In this paper, we adapt Tuchman's (1978) web of facticity to understand how CSI creates a web of forensic facticity in the portrayal of scientific police investigations. As we note, however, Tuchman's observations do more than explain news as a social construction. For us, the deeper significance of her insights is the understanding that, as the news and entertainment media shape public attitudes, they are doing ideological work: they reinforce social hierarchies; they use procedures that make social constructions appear to be not only objective but taken-for-granted; they preclude alternative viewpoints. Loader (1997) makes a similar point about police in contemporary society. Drawing on

Tuchman and Loader, we focus on how *CSI* parallels other police dramas in its representations of crime and the police. *CSI* goes a step further in its representations of science as an investigative tool of the police.

Our analysis provides insights about *CSI*, but there is a need for more research about this very popular television program. One line of inquiry might address the affect of watching *CSI* on various audiences. This could include focus groups with viewers to discover why they watch and how the program influences their views of the police and of science. It might be the case, for example, that watching *CSI* affects how viewers evaluate the performance of the police (see Iyengar and Kinder, 1987). Some research (Hallett and Powell, 1995) suggests that reality crime programs are popular with and affect police officers. Accordingly, focus groups might include criminal justice personnel who watch *CSI*.

Another interesting line of research pertains to the "CSI Effect" in which jurors acquit criminal defendants if prosecutors lack the definitive scientific evidence that is *CSI*'s trademark (Cole and Dioso, 2005). For now, the "CSI Effect" remains largely anecdotal. Indeed, Mopas (2007) is critical because the "CSI Effect" frames the issue as what is real rather than to "concentrate on the interactions between what is presented on TV and what we often describe as the 'real world' of forensics and criminal justice" (2007:110). For Mopas, the interesting research point is the claim, oft-cited on *CSI*, that the evidence speaks for itself. Obviously, whether on *CSI* or in that "real world," scientific evidence does not simply appear; rather, it is developed and used by the police. Mopas' final observation and another worthy line of inquiry pertains to how prosecutors and defense attorneys, knowing *CSI*'s popularity, modify their theory of the case during trial preparation (2007:114–115). That is, regardless of any "CSI Effect," does this popular program have some sort of legal reality for prosecutors and defense attorneys? There are, of course, limitations in the research that we present in this paper. We think the first season is important, but it is only one season. There may have been changes in the program in subsequent seasons or in the spin-off series. Moreover, our analysis focuses in detail on the program; we have no data on its impact on audiences.

In any case, *CSI* is an extremely popular program. Its ratings and its impact on television police dramas make it a worthy site for analysis.

Conclusion

CSI resembles a traditional television police drama. Story lines center around violent crime, usually murder, criminals and victims tend to be white, victims are disproportionately women, and elements of melodrama appear in its narratives. While *CSI* does not adopt *Dragnet's* documentary style, its reliance on actual cases and its focus on the routines of policing lend an air of authenticity and mark it as a contemporary television police procedural.

But what makes *CSI* unique, especially in its debut season, is its emphasis on forensic science. Its focus on forensic science combines with the authenticity of the procedural to generate the program's forensic realism. *CSI* generates this sense of realism by engaging in what we call a web of forensic facticity. Adapting a concept borrowed from media scholar Gaye Tuchman (1978), we demonstrate that *CSI* imbues every aspect of the program--set, dress, language, the method for solving crimes—with a sense of science, and with the validity of scientific evidence and of science itself. An aspect of this facticity is that sense of realism that is a characteristic of the police procedural. We are privy to the backstage world of the police, a technique that enhances a sense of reality and audience identification; we, too, seem to have cop and science knowledge. We see the *CSI* unit as a highly functioning organization. As Catherine tells that new recruit, "We solve. We restore piece of mind, and when you're a victim, that's everything" (Episode 100).

The reality, of course, is that, notwithstanding its forensic realism, *CSI* is a television crime drama. Its investigators exhibit almost super human levels of expertise—both cop and scientific knowledge. And while they almost always solve the crime, real criminals do not always confess, the police do not always solve crimes, and when they do, as often as not solutions are based not only on brilliant scientific investigatory work but on citizens' tips (Ericson, Baranek, and Chan, 1991). Indeed, as we know from the daily newspaper, neither the police nor science are infallible. There are breaches in the chain of evidence, delays in laboratory results, and interpretations of laboratory reports that are equivocal and occasionally dishonest.

And yet, *CSI* is consistently the top rated program in its time slot. Perhaps it provides the closure that is always a part of the crime genre. Crimes are solved, victims are avenged, and order is restored. But, *CSI* is fiction; its web of forensic facticity is a social construction. Of course, so is the news (Tuchman, 1978). Crime fact and crime fiction are similar in their depictions of crime (Eschholz, Mallard, and Flynn, 2004). The problem with this, as criminologists have long noted, is that, taken together, news and crime drama have the potential to generate a misunderstanding about issues of crime. These media presentations provide a kind of ideological closure that cloaks the infallibility of the police with the mantle of science. Such closure tends to forestall critical questions about policing in the United States.

References

Bertrand, I., Hughes, P. (2005). *Media Research Methods: Audiences, Institutions, Texts.* London: Palgrave/Macmillan.

Cavender, G. (2004). Media and Crime Policy: A Reconsideration of David Garland's The Culture of Control. *Punishment & Society, 6*(3) 335–348.

Cavender, G., Jurik, N. (1998). Jane Tennison and the Feminist Police Procedural. *Violence Against Women* 4.10–29.

Cole, S., and Dioso, R. (2005). Law and the Lab. *Wall Street Journal*, 13 May.

Connell, R. (1993). The Big Picture: Masculinities In Recent World History. *Theory and Society*, 22 597–623.

Durkheim, E. (1964). *The Division of Labor in Society.* New York: The Free Press.

Ericson, R., Baranek, P., Chan, J. (1991). *Representing Order: Crime, Law and Justice in the News Media.* Toronto: University of Toronto Press.

Eschholz, S., Mallard, M., Flynn, S. (2004). Images of Prime Time Justice: A Content Analysis of *NYPD Blue* and *Law and Order.*" *Journal of Criminal Justice and Popular Culture, 10*(3) 161–180.

Hallett, M., Powell, D. (1995). Backstage With Cops? The Dramaturgical Reification of Police Subculture in American Crime Info-tainment. *American Journal of Police 14*, 101–129.

Iyengar, S., Kinder, D. (1987). *News That Matters: Television and American Opinion.* Chicago: University of Chicago Press.

Krutnik, F. (1991). *In a Lonely Street: Film Noir, Genre, and Masculinity.* London: Routledge.

LaTempa, S. Oct. 2002. The Women of *CSI*: Tough Girls Do Dance. Retrieved February 17, 2005. http://www.wga.org/WrittenBy/1002/csi.html.

Loader, I. (1997) Policing and the Social: Questions of Symbolic Power. *British Journal of Sociology* 48. 1–18.

Mawby, R. (2003). Completing the 'Half-Formed Picture'? Media Images of Policing, in Paul Mason (ed.), *Criminal Visions: Media Representations of Crime and Justice*, 214–237. Cullompton: Willan Publishing.

Messerschmidt, J. (1993). *Masculinities and Crime: Critique and Reconceptualization of Theory*. Lanham: Rowman & Littlefield.

Mittell, J. (2004). *Genre and Television: From Cop Shows to Cartoons in American Culture*. London: Routledge.

Mopas, M. (2007) Examining the 'CSI Effect' though an ANT Lens. *Crime Media Culture 3*. 110–117.

Nielsen Ratings. 26 June 2005. Top Ten Primetime Broadcast TV Programs. *Nielsen Media Research, Inc.* http//:www. nielsenmedia.com/ratings/broadcast_programs.html.

Perlmutter, D. (2000). *Policing the Media: Street Cops and Public Perceptions of Law Enforcement*. Thousand Oaks: Sage.

Ramsland, K. (2001). *The Forensic Science of C.S.I.* New York: Berkley Boulevard Books.

Rapping, E. (2003). *Law and Justice as Seen on TV*. New York: New York University Press.

Schattenberg, G. (1981). Social Control Functions of Mass Media Depictions of Crime. *Sociological Inquiry* 71–77.

Soulliere, D. (2003). Prime-Time Murder: Presentations of Murder on Popular Television Justice Programs. *Journal of Criminal Justice and Popular Culture, 10*(1). 12–38.

Toff, B. (2007). Crime Pays. *New York Times*. April 7, p. A16.

Tuchman, G. (1978). *Making News: A Study in the Construction of Reality*. New York: Free Press.

Wilson, C. (2000). *Cop Knowledge: Police Power and Cultural Narrative in Twentieth-Century America*. Chicago: University of Chicago Press.

Wilson, C. (2005). Let's Work out the Details: Interrogation and Deception in Prime Time. *Journal of Criminal Justice and Popular Culture, 12*(1) 47–64.

Wittebols, J. (2004). *The Soap Opera Paradigm: Television Programming and Corporate Priorities*. Lanham: Rowman & Littlefield Publishers.

Endnote

1. Sarah Deutsch graduated summa cum laude from Arizona State University and the School of Justice & Social Inquiry in 2004 and graduated from the Barrett Honors College in 2005. Ms. Deutsch is studying law at the University of Wisconsin Law School where she is interested in public interest law.

2. Gray Cavender is a Professor in Justice & Social Inquiry at Arizona State University. He teaches courses on Media, Law & Society, and Punishment. His primary research interest is in the media, and includes topics ranging from reality television to how the media depict crime. Recent publications include several articles about the British made-for-TV *Prime Suspect* films.

Appendix

Main Characters Present

_____Gil Grissom   _____Nick Stokes   _____Warrick Brown
_____Catherine Willows   _____Sara Sidle   _____ Jim Brass
_____Greg Sanders   _____Al Robbins

Emotional Connection

Forensic Facticity
Clothing/Appearance:
Lab coat/Apron   Goggles   Gloves   ID Badges   Briefcase   Masks

Other_____

Tools/Equipment:
Tweezers   Luminol   Fluorescence/Lights   Adhesives   Flashlight

Vial/Test Tube   Camera   Dusting Brush   Dusting Powder   Plasters

Chromatography   Spectrophotometer   Spectrograph   Centrifuge   Microscope

Other_____

Language/Scientific Jargon:

Special Graphical Features

Reinforcement of Evidence

CSI/Law Enforcement Tension
Crime 1:_____
Team:

Type of Investigation/Crime
Homicide   Suicide   Rape   Molestation   Kidnapping   Robbery   Bombing   Accident

Other_____

Perpetrator
Sex: M   F   Unknown
Race: White   Black   Hispanic   Asian   Native   American   Other_____
Relationship to Victim: Stranger   Acquaintance

Victim

Sex: M   F   Unknown

Race: White   Black   Hispanic   Asian   Native   American   Other_____

Weapon

Gun   Knife   Hands   Rope   Vehicle   None   Other_____

Details/Observations

Crime 2: _____

Team:

Type of Investigation/Crime

Homicide   Suicide   Rape   Molestation   Kidnapping   Robbery   Bombing   Accident

Other_____

Perpetrator

Sex: M   F   Unknown

Race: White   Black   Hispanic   Asian   Native American   Other_____

Relationship to Victim: Stranger Acquaintance

Victim

Sex: M   F   Unknown

Race: White   Black   Hispanic   Asian   Native American   Other_____

Weapon

Gun   Knife   Hands   Rope   Vehicle   None   Other_____

Details/Observations:

MEDIA ECHOES

Systemic Effects Of News Coverage

by Ray Surette*
University of Central Florida

T he trial of O.J. Simpson and the Polly Klass murder are recent examples of intensive news media attention and of their influence on the operation of criminal justice in the United States. In high-profile trials, media attention affects the actions of attorneys, witnesses, judges, jurors, and the audience involved with the publicized case. High-profile trials also influence the everyday practices of law enforcement and adjudication, and affect the outcomes of numerous low-profile cases (Barak 1996). Empirical research on this extended effect is lacking, and is needed in the present media environment that surrounds the U.S. criminal justice system. Barak (1995) offers the following description of this media effect: "When the media or public makes noise about certain problems such as prostitution and gambling, the police and prosecution respond, at least for a while, but sooner or later the patterns of law enforcement return to normal" (p.1).

This effect, herein termed a news media echo effect, therefore occurs when a highly publicized criminal case results in a shift in processing for similarly charged but nonpublicized cases (Surette 1989, 1995). It was first described by Lofton:

> But while the impact of the press is most direct on specific cases covered, there is good reason to believe that [their] sway extends considerably beyond [these] cases ... From the cases that are covered,

* Ray Surette is a Professor of Criminal Justice at the University of Central Florida. His research interests include the interactions between the mass media and crime and justice. He has also published on the application of communications technology in criminal justice and copy cat crime. His most recent book is Media, Crime, and Criminal Justice: Images and Realities.

officials become conditioned to expect demands for stern treatment from the press, and in the unpublicized cases they probably act accordingly. (1966:138)

Kaplan and Skolnick later comment:

> This unwillingness [to plea bargain] appears to occur relatively infrequently. It is most likely to occur when there is strong pressure upon the prosecution to obtain maximum sentences for a particular class of crime: for example, after a notorious case of child rape, the prosecutor may refuse to bargain, for a time, with those charged with sex offenses involving children; after a series of highly publicized drug arrests allegedly involving dealers or pushers, the prosecution may be unwilling, for a time, to engage in reduction of charges from sales to possession. (1982:467–68)

As conceptualized, the echo effect portends a spillover from the coverage of publicized criminal cases onto nonpublicized ones. To date, the courts and social science researchers have focused almost exclusively on news media effects on the cases that directly receive the coverage. The result is an extensive body of research on pretrial publicity and on its direct effects on cases receiving coverage. [1] Specific echo effects on systemwide case processing remains poorly researched, however. Despite the common acceptance of pervasive and systemic media effects and anecdotal descriptions of their operation, no one had conducted an empirical analysis of the nature, duration, or magnitude of an echo effect.

Addressing this deficiency, I explore an echo effect through the empirical examination of systemwide effects related to a pair of highly publicized criminal cases. My thesis is that following the publicized cases, the "echo" of the publicity sensitizes the local criminal justice system so that a greater number of similarly charged cases will enter the system at higher rates and will be processed differently, whether or not these new cases receive media attention. I use the term *echo* to distinguish this effect from a "history" effect—a purely methodological concern wherein the media or some other external event confounds ongoing research.[2] In this study, the media effect is the focus of the research; no extant research exists to be biased.

Literature Review

An echo effect can be regarded as specialized agenda setting within the criminal justice system, in which one type of case is elevated through media attention on the agenda of criminal justice personnel. Thereby it influences the importance of an issue or (as in this instance) a type of case by the way it is portrayed (Entman 1989:355; McCombs 1994:9).[3] Fishman (1978) has noted effects for elderly victimization cases, Hall and his colleagues (1981) for muggings, and Snow (1984) for insanity pleas. In

---

[1] See Pember (1987) and Surette (1998) for overviews. Another area of serious interest has been the relationship between policy makers, the public, the media, and the formation of public policy. A long-standing relationship between the press and policy makers in general has been reported, as well as benefits to both groups resulting from mutual cooperation (Protess et al. 1994; Schlesinger, Tumber, and Murdock 1991). The media and criminal justice system decision makers have a particularly close relationship, with frequent contact (Doppelt 1992; Surette 1990). Furthermore, decisions sometimes are made in reaction to, or anticipation of, coverage (Doppelt 1992:115).

[2] A history effect is due to an unplanned event outside the system (Cook and Campbell 1979:51). A common source of history effects is the mass media, especially the news media (Dye and Zeigler 1986; Surette 1995).

[3] In local environments, the media are seen as helping to shape criminal justice policy by establishing ongoing relationships with local criminal justice policy makers. (See Doppelt and Manikas 1990; Protess et al. 1985.) This body of research has taken shape under a local political/social environmental approach that has been termed "ecological."

a study that examines the extent of media's influence, Doppelt (1992:125) surveys agency officials and estimates the extent of media coverage influence thus: "[O]f the 152 government officials surveyed, 46 (or 30 percent) said news coverage had led to recent changes in their agency's operations." Greene and Loftus (1984) and Greene and Wade (1988) report experimental evidence of an echo effect from general pretrial publicity on jurors. They found that exposure to publicity which questions eyewitnesses' accuracy influences jurors' decisions in later, nonpublicized cases. In their research, the effect was a reduction in guilty pleas, or a lenient echo effect.[4]

Specifically in regard to prosecutors and echoes, Pritchard, Dilts, and Berkowitz (1987) report that for Indiana prosecutors the press was an important factor in deciding whether to prosecute pornography charges. They concluded that among criminal justice system personnel, at least prosecutors, respond to what they perceive to be media opinion in determining their policy course (Pritchard et al. 1987:396). A media influence on prosecutors is further supported in research by Cook et al. (1983) and by Pritchard (1986).

More general and more pervasive echo-type effects that extend throughout a criminal justice system have been observed by McCain (1992), who charges that pretrial publicity and sensational news coverage contribute to racism in the criminal justice system. McCain reports that such publicity can affect all segments of the court system for a defendant, such as charging, bail decisions, and sentencing. McCain states that a "generic prejudice" is created, whereby future African-American defendants will receive similar unfair treatment regardless of media attention.

Similarly, Roberts and Edwards (1989) conceptualize an echo effect on the general public as anchoring. Anchoring works through media emphasis on violent or sensational crimes, which cause public feelings of anger toward the criminal justice system. The anger at perceived leniency carries over into many offenses and criminals, both violent and nonviolent. In the Roberts and Edwards study when the initial story was particularly dramatic and serious the public reacted more harshly to the next reported crime. Thus, for the public, anchoring works similarly to an echo, sensitizing the public to respond differently to crimes other than the crimes initially covered.

In addition, a third-person effect has been reported in the public opinion literature, whereby the media did not affect those receiving the coverage, but influence another group (Lasorsa 1992:165). In a third-person effect, coverage of child victims should influence criminal justice system decision makers, the third persons. Insofar as the media have been found more likely to influence an agency's policy decisions when the agency believes that it is responsible for solving the specific problem covered by the media (Pritchard 1992:111), it is reasonable to expect that prosecutors will respond to coverage depicting rampant child victimization. In sum, as key case-processing decision makers, prosecutors who do not wish to appear unresponsive to public concerns frequently respond to media coverage (Davis 1986).

Finally, a significant body of research relates media coverage to general public policy and agenda setting. As stated earlier, an echo effect can be regarded as a media policy effect directed at a specific type of case. This effect is believed to be particularly likely for prosecutors because of their discretion and the political nature of their positions. In the jurisdiction examined in this study, the chief prosecutor is elected by direct popular vote. Prior research indicates that an echo effect is likely to result from prosecutors' ability to choose to invoke or not invoke their usual discretion, and to prosecute or not prosecute particular types of cases during sensitized times to influence media coverage and criticism. Frequently as a result, more criminal defendants should be tried than was typical before the news coverage of a high-profile criminal case (Barak 1996:109).

---

[4] For discussions, see Kaplan and Skolnick (1982); Lofton (1966); Radin (1964); Surette (1989).

Methodology

To examine an echo, I analyze the processing of 3,453 criminal cases over a 10-year period including five years before and five years after heavily covered cases involving the sexual abuse of toddlers at a private suburban day-care center. I use two sets of criminal cases spanning these 10 years in an extended empirical case study.

Hypothetically, an echo effect should follow the publicized high-profile cases as alterations in the processing of cases with charges similar to those in the highly publicized cases. I examine a second set of cases with dissimilar charges as a control group. The controls are felonious property damage charges; they include various arson charges as well as trespass with property damage without injury. Insofar as the control cases involve property damage and the publicized cases involved direct sexual assaults on children, the control cases represent charges diametrically opposite to those found in the publicized cases. Therefore the controls (unlike rape or other assault cases) should not be influenced by any confounding systemic processing dynamics caused by the media coverage. No media echo should be perceived in these cases.

In the analysis I will examine changes over time in the two sets of cases. A media-generated echo effect will be indicated by significant changes in the processing of the series of child sexual abuse cases following the publicized case, which are not observed in the control case series.

The Fuster Child Abuse Cases

The cases of Frank Fuster and his wife Ileana Fuster came to light in summer 1984, when charges of sexual abuse were brought against the Fusters by parents who had placed their children under the Fusters' care in a Miami day-care center. At least 15 children, age 3 to 10, told of "games" at the Country Walk neighborhood daycare center, which included oral sex, fondling, digital penetration, urination, and defecation. One Child contracted gonorrhea. Fuster and his wife were arrested on August 23, 1984; their cases were filed on August 24. They were subsequently charged with 10 counts of capital sexual battery and three counts of lewd and lascivious assault. Frank Fuster's case was closed 411 days later, on October 9, 1985; his wife's 459 days later, on November 26.

The two cases, in combination, came to be known in the local press as the Country Walk case. They were the subject of hundreds of news articles and television segments, from the filing of Frank Fuster's case to the closing of Ileana's case. They were one of a set of prominent cases across the nation during the mid-1980s, which dealt with sexual abuse of children in day-care facilities (Waterman et al. 1993).

Data

The data for this study were obtained from the Office of Data Management for the Eleventh Circuit Court of Florida. At my request, the office downloaded from its case management files a data set containing all cases involving the same charges as in the Fuster case. Simultaneously, a set of control cases involving arson and trespass was downloaded. Cases for the five years preceding the filing date of the Frank Fuster case and for the five years following were provided. The first case was filed on January 5, 1979; the last was filed on March 18, 1990.

This information provides a set of cases with two divisions: (1) all cases (excluding the two Fuster cases) that involved the same charges as brought in the Fuster case: either lewd and lascivious assault on a child or sexual battery on a minor, hereafter termed echo cases, and (2) all cases that involved a set of control charges concerning felonious property damage (arson, arson first degree, arson second degree, and trespass with property damage), hereafter termed control cases.

For every case in the data set the following variables were provided: case number, booking date, filing date, closing date, charge number, charge descriptions, disposition, sentence, and plea at arraignment. I transformed specific case variable information into monthly time-series data sets. Each time series is composed of the monthly averages based on the specific case variables.

The original 3,453 cases are distributed as follows:

	Echo Cases	Control Cases
Pre-Fuster trials: January 1979 to August 23, 1984 (67 months)	670	448
During Fuster trials: August 24, 1984 to November 26, 1985 (16 months)	352	171
After Fuster trials: November 27, 1985 to March 18, 1990 (52 months)	1,283	529
Totals	2,305	1,148

Variable Time Series and Dependent Variables

The independent variable for this study is a case's temporal relationship to the Fuster case. This relationship is based on Fuster's filing date, August, 29, 1984, and on his wife's closing date, November 26, 1985. The conceptualization of a case's temporal position in relation to the Fuster cases is somewhat confounded by the fact that a few cases were filed before the Fuster case filing date but were closed after that date. Similarly, a number of cases were filed before the Fuster cases ended but were closed after the closing of the Fuster cases. Thus, for a few cases, the relationship to the Fuster cases is determined by whether one looks at filing dates or closing dates.

As a resolution to this dilemma, it is theoretically more plausible that variables associated with the beginnings of cases (number of cases filed, number of charges brought, and proportion of not guilty pleas) should be related more closely to filing dates. Therefore, in cases filed after Frank Fusters case was filed, the initial processing factors should be influenced. According to similar logic, variables related to the final disposition (proportions of cases sentenced to jail, proportions of cases dismissed, total processing time, and length of jail sentences) should be related more closely to closing dates. Employing this argument and using the aggregate procedure in SPSS, I generated a set of seven time series based on the cases occurring in each particular month.[5] Each of the seven time series contains 270 time units for analysis. The seven dependent time-series variables thus include a set of system-processing and disposition variables based on monthly aggregate values.

The processing variables include the following:

---

[5] I created the monthly time series by first assigning a month number based on the year and month when a case was filed. In the aggregate procedure I then calculated the number of cases filed each month, the average time from filing to final disposition, the proportion of cases entering not guilty pleas, and so on for the seven variable time series, for both echo and control cases. I also calculated and examined weekly series; no substantial differences in analysis emerged. A number of weeks contained no cases, however, and thus generated zero values, which are problematic for time-series analysis. Use of the monthly values avoids this problem.

Number of cases filed: Based on monthly totals, these range from 1 to 43 cases per month; 2,305 echo cases and 1,148 control cases were filed over the period of the study.

Proportion of cases pleading not guilty at arraignment: Based on monthly totals, this proportion ranges from 0 percent (31 of 270 months) to 100 percent (12 of 270 months). The mean and the median both equal 42 percent.

Average processing time: This is the number of days occupied by cases from their filing date to their closing date, based on monthly averages. Average processing time ranges from 11.5 to more than 700 days. The average monthly processing time is 214 days; the median is 189 days.

Total number of charges per case: Based on monthly averages, the number of charges ranges from 1 to 35, with a median of two charges per case for the individual cases. Forty-nine percent of the cases involve only one charge; 3 percent involve six or more. The average number of charges per month ranges from 1 to 4.25, with a mean and a median of 2.0.

Disposition variables include the following:

Proportion of cases sentenced to jail: Based on monthly totals, this series ranges from 0 percent (proportion for 83 months) to 100 percent (proportion for one month), with a mean value of 18.4 and a median of 16.7.

Proportion of cases dismissed: (dismissal, nolle prosequi, no action, or other end to prosecution): Based on monthly totals, the proportion of cases dismissed ranges from 0 percent (value for six months) to 100 percent (value for 21 months). The mean and the median proportions are 58 percent.

Average jail sentence: Based on monthly averages, this is the number of sentenced jail time days for cases that received jail sentences. Monthly average jail terms range widely from four days to 10 years, with a mean of 7.8 years and a median of five years.

Hypotheses

The expectations of this study are as follows. As the system is sensitized, discretion in the prosecutor's office should be reduced regarding the echo cases, and law enforcement should be more active in bringing similar cases into the system. The available research and literature suggest that the echo of the Fuster cases should result in a more punitive system, in which plea bargains are offered less often, are less appealing, and are rejected more often. For the echo cases, it is expected that changes in the dependent variables will occur during the Fuster cases' processing, and that these changes will diminish after the Fuster cases close and as the hypothesized echo fades. Control cases should display no echo effects. On the basis of these theoretical expectations, the following hypotheses result:

Hypothesis 1: Cases with charges similar to those in the Fuster cases should be processed significantly differently after the beginning of the Fuster trials.

Hypothesis 1a: The number of cases entering the system with charges similar to those in the Fuster cases should increase significantly after the beginning of the Fuster trial. Sensitized to this set of offenses, law enforcers should be more willing to charge defendants with similar charges; the prosecutor's office should be more active in promoting similarly charged cases.

Hypothesis 1b: Not guilty pleas should increase for echo charged cases during the Fuster trials. In reaction to the hypothesized increase in the system's punitiveness and the less attractive plea bargain offers, more echo case defendants should plead not guilty.

Hypothesis 1c: Processing time should increase for echo cases during the Fuster trials and should decrease after their completion, in comparison with control cases. The system should become more sensitive and more punitive toward these cases; as a result, fewer and less attractive plea bargains should be offered and system discretion in handling these cases should be reduced. Loss of discretion and restrictions on plea bargaining should result in longer processing time.

Hypothesis 1d: The total number of charges per case should increase for echo cases during the Fuster trials and should decline after their completion, in comparison with control cases. In addition the criminal justice system can become more punitive by including additional charges and dropping fewer charges for echo cases.

Hypothesis 2: As an ultimate result of the echo effect, the final dispositions of similarly charged cases will be altered significantly. Influenced the by potential for negative media scrutiny, the system should dispose of the echo cases more harshly wherever possible.

Hypothesis 2a: The proportion of similarly charged cases dismissed should decrease significantly after the beginning of the Fuster trials. Prosecutors should be more aggressive in pursuing these types of cases, and judges should be less willing to dismiss cases.

Hypothesis 2b: The proportion of similarly charged cases sentenced to jail should increase significantly after the beginning of the Fuster trials. Similarly charged defendants found guilty should receive harsher sentences, and more of these defendants should be sentenced to jail time.

Hypothesis 2c: Jail time should increase significantly for similarly charged cases after the beginning of the Fuster trials. As the system becomes more punitive toward these offenses, jail sentences should be more common and be for longer terms.

Results: Processing Variables

Number of Cases Filed, by Month

The first and most direct echo effect from a highly publicized case should be the effect on the quantity of similar cases entering a judicial system. Figure 1 depicts the number of filings per month for echo cases and for control cases. Table 1 presents the analysis results for the two case series. As expected, growth in the system is reflected in the increase in the numbers of both types of cases over time. The increase is larger and more dramatic for the echo cases, however, after the Fuster case opens.[6]

---

6 A similar dramatic pattern is observed when the closing date is used to generate the time series.

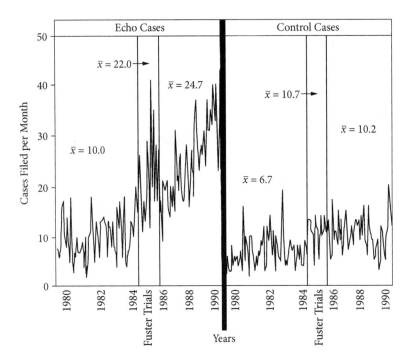

Figure 1. Cases Filed

The pattern of case filings reveals that echo cases are more common than control cases over the study's entire time span. Like the control cases, echo cases increase in frequency over the study period. Growth is not surprising for an expanding metropolitan area, and echo cases with Fuster-type charges are prevalent in the system. An analysis of variance on the monthly averages reveals that the increase observed in both the echo and the control cases at the time of the Fuster trial is significant for both types.[7] The echo cases, however, which initially are only slightly more common than the control cases, become more than twice as common after the Fuster cases formally enter the system.

Table 1. Regression Analysis: Cases Filed per Month, Echo and Control Cases

	B	Beta	Tolerance
Echo Cases[a]			
Full time span (1/79–3/90)	.076*	.316	.248
Fuster trials (8/84–11/85)	8.650**	.295	.727
After Fuster trials (12/85–3/90)	.320**	.540	.235
Control Cases[b]			
Full time span (1/79–3/90)	.030	.304	.139
Fuster trials (8/84–11/85)	.006	.133	.128
After Fuster trials (12/85–3/90)	2.68*	.223	.509

[a] $R^2 = .698$; adjusted $R^2 = .691$; $F = 101.1, p = .001$; Durbin-Watson = 2.08
[b] $R^2 = .222$; adjusted $R^2 = .205$; $F = 12.53, p = .001$; Durbin-Watson = 1.72
* $p = .05$; ** $p = .001$

---

[7] ANOVA results on average number of cases filed per month before, during, and after Fuster trials: echo cases, $F = 83.83$, $p = .000$); control cases, $F = 18.28, p = .000$.

With the beginning of the Fuster trials, this preference for Fuster-type echo cases increases. The gap between echo cases and control cases, in raw numbers of cases entering the system, widens rapidly. Echo cases begin to appear at a much greater rate and continue, into the 1990s, to enter the system at substantially higher rates than control cases.

What level of explanatory power can be attributed to the influence of the Fuster cases on the distribution of echo cases? I explore this question using a time series-based regression analysis. (A similar analysis is applied to the other six dependent variables.)

With the regression analysis results reported in Table 1, I aim to empirically assess the impact of the Fuster cases' introduction into the Eleventh Circuit judicial system. In this analysis, the Fuster cases are considered as a treatment effect introduced in August 1984 and removed in November 1985. Using a research methodology suggested by Meier and Brundnay (1993), I examine this effect with a model in which I regress the monthly file counts on three time variables.[8] The first variable is the month number, which runs consecutively from 1 to 270, includes the entire period of the analysis, and covers any trend effect present in the series. The second variable denotes the period of the Fuster cases as a dichotomous variable: Months preceding and following the cases receive a value of 0, and the months which the cases occurred receive a value of 1. In the examination for a systemic trend effect following the publicized cases, the third time variable is a trend variable beginning with 1 at the end of the Fuster cases and increasing by 1 each month through the end of the series.

The primary concern in using regression analysis with time-series data is serial correlation. Diagnostic statistics, however, indicate that serial correlation is not a problem in this analysis.[9] Mutticollinearity is also a potential hazard because the three independent variables are sequential; I consider it in the context of each analysis.

The regression model analysis shows that the periods during and following the Fuster trials are related significantly to an increase in echo case filings but not in filings of control cases. The three time variables account for 69 percent of the variance in the filings of echo cases. Tolerance values show that multicollinearity between the variables is not problematic in this instance and that all three time variables are significantly predictive of the number of cases filed (Norusis 1995:485).

Over the course of the series, filings for echo-type cases increase .08 for each month in the series. During the Fuster trials, echo cases increase dramatically by 8.65 filings for every month in which the trials continued. After the trials, echo cases continue to be filed more frequently, increasing by a factor of .32 times the number of months from the end of the trials.[10]

For case filings, the echo appears as theoretically expected during the trials but does not fade as expected: it persists through the end of the data series. As theoretically expected, the control cases are related less substantially to the three periods, which collectively explain 21 percent of the variance in control case filings. The B associated with the period of the Fuster trials displays a marginally significant relationship with the control case filings; it reflects a slight upward trend for control case filings during

---

[8] I also explored variations of this model (for example, using a trend variable from the start of the trial), but I believe that this model is the best theoretical fit to the expectations of the hypothesized echo effect. None of the alternate models emerges as a more accurate empirical predictor of the data series (also see Swaminathan and Algina 1977).

[9] I ran a standard set of diagnostic statistics on all of the regressions reported, including an examination of residuals and residual-based histograms, plots, scatter-plots, and partial plots. For this design ($n = 135, k = 3$) the Durbin-Watson statistic indicates the absence of autocorrelation with no uncertainty in a range from 1.67 to 2.33.

[10] Thus, in the twelfth month after the trials end, echo cases increase by .32 × 12. The full equation for predicting the number of echo case filings for this month would be as follows: number of filings = 7.56 + [.08 × 95 (series month number)] + [8.65 × 0 (non-Fuster trial period)] + [.32 × 12 (number of months after Fuster trials end)] = 19.00. The actual number of echo cases filed that month = 20.

the same period in which the echo case filings increase dramatically.[11] The slopes (*B* values) of the two series remain significantly different, however, even though both increase significantly. Hence, during the Fuster trials, echo case filings increase at nearly three times the rate of control case filings (8.65 per month compared with 2.68 per month). Overall the regression analysis strongly supports a significant, substantial, and surprisingly persistent effect: an effect that appears, with the beginning of the Fuster trials, among the echo cases but not among the control cases.

Not Guilty Pleas at Arraignment

The second series to be examined is the proportion of not guilty pleas entered at arraignment. Having established that significantly more echo cases are entering the system, the proportion of not guilty pleas provides a measure of case treatment at the beginning stages of case processing. Not guilty pleas reflect plea bargains offered by the prosecutor's office; changes in the proportion of these pleas should be related to any punitive stance taken by the state. Figure 2 and Table 2 report the trend and analysis for the echo and control cases.

Figure 2 reveals a large amount of variance from one month to the next for both the echo and the control cases in the proportion of cases pleading guilty in the five years preceeding the Fuster cases. During the Fuster trials, the variance decreases for the echo cases and remains tess turbulent thereafter.[12] An analysis of variance (ANOVA) shows that the three time reference periods do not differ significantly within either type of case.[13] When the types are compared with each other, however, the proportion of guilty pleas changes in the expected direction with a punitive echo. In the period preceeding the Fuster trials, defendants in the echo cases are as likely to plead not guilty as are defendants in the control cases. Echo case defendants become slightly but not significantly more likely to plead not guilty during and after the trials (increasing from 42% to 48%), while control case defendants become less likely to plead not guilty during and after the trials (declining from 42% to 34%). After the end of the Fuster trials, echo and control defendants differ significantly in their likelihood of pleading not guilty (48% vs. 34%).

For some undetermined reason, the variance in the proportion of defendants pleading guilty for both echo and control cases decreased during the Fuster trials. At the beginning of the 10-year period, defendants in echo and control cases plead not guilty at equivalent levels. They begin to diverge during the Fuster trials, and they differ significantly by the end of the period. This finding, however, is compromised to a degree by the presence of heteros-kedasticity. Not surprisingly, then, the regression analysis in Table 2 reveals that these shifts are not very important. The three variables in the regression model explain only 4 percent of the variance in guilty pleas in the echo cases; the trend following the Fuster trials emerges as the only significant time variable. For the control cases, as shown, none of the three trend variables are related significantly to the percentage of not guilty pleas per month.

---

[11] Multicollinearity between the full series and posttrial variables creates difficulty in estimating their *B*-values for the control cases. In this and subsequent analyses, to allow the long-term process to be examined and considered, I reran the regression with the full-series variable included and without the posttrial trend variable. For the control case filing numbers, the second regression reveals that both the full series and the trial period are significant: Adjusted R^2 = .208; *F* = 18.68, p = .000; full series *B* = .024, p = .000; trial period *B* = 2.11, p = .0238.

[12] A Levene test for differences in variance revealed significant shifts.

[13] ANOVA results on percentage of not guilty pleas per month before during, and after Fuster trials, echo cases, *F* = 1.219, p = .298); control cases, *F* = 1.319, p = .271.

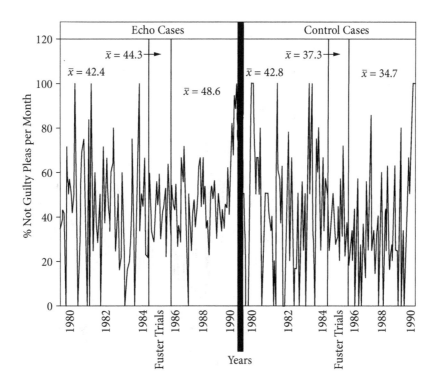

Figure 2. Percentage of Not Guilty Pleas

Table 2. Regression Analysis: Percentage of Not Guilty Pleas per Month, Echo and Control Cases

	B	Beta	Tolerance
Echo Cases[a]			
Full time span (1/79–3/90)	.128	−.230	.251
Fuster trials (8/84–11/85)	7.24	.108	.725
After Fuster trials (12/85–3/90)	.613*	.441	.239
Control Cases[b]			
Full time span (1/79–3/90)	.085	.121	.142
Fuster trials (8/84–11/85)	−8.46	−.101	.509
After Fuster trials (12/85–3/90)	−.082	−.238	.131

[a] $R^2 = .066$; adjusted $R^2 = .045$; $F = 3.09$; Durbin-Watson = 1.80
[b] $R^2 = .016$; adjusted $R^2 = .006$; $F = .713$; Durbin-Watson = 1.70
* $p = .05$

Processing Time in Days

Another set of comparisons is afforded by the comparisons of the mean number of days required to process cases. Because cases must be closed if we are to calculate their processing time, it is necessary to compare cases on the basis of their closing dates rather than their filing dates for this series. Figure 3 provides the monthly average processing time in days for echo and control cases.

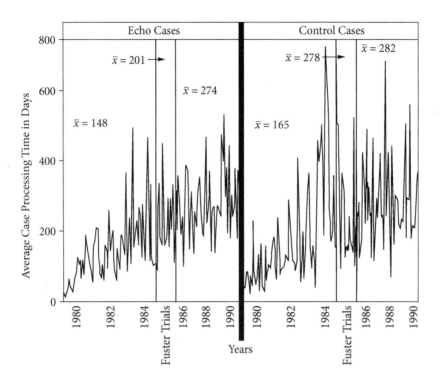

Figure 3. Average Processing Time

Figure 3 shows a pattern of increasing processing time for both echo and control cases across the entire period of the study. According to an ANOVA, processing time increases significantly for both types of cases at the beginning of the Fuster trials.[14] The regression analysis displayed in Table 3 suggests that both the full series and the post-Fuster trials have a relationship to processing time for the echo cases. Additional analysis, however, reveals that the full-series variable alone is as effective in predicting processing times as are the three time variables collectively.[15] The regression of control cases' reflects similar results with smaller predictive ability.[16] The sole difference is that the echo cases are processed in a significantly shorter time during the Fuster trials than are the control cases, opposite what a punitive echo would predict. In general, average processing time in the echo cases does not differ substantively from that in the control cases, and no echo effect from the Fuster trials is substantiated empirically.

---

[14] ANOVA results on average case processing time in days before, during, and after Fuster trials: echo cases, $F = 24.15$ $p = .000$; control cases, $F = 11.61$, $p = .000$.

[15] Regression of processing time on full-series variable alone: $R = .63$, $R^2 = .40$, $B = 1.87$, $p = .000$.

[16] Multicollinearity between the full-series variable and the post-Fuster trials variable generates instability in value estimations in the regression for the control cases, as reflected in the beta value of 1.04.

Table 3. Regression Analysis: Average Processing Time, Echo and Control Cases

	B	Beta	Tolerance
Echo Cases[a]			
Full time span (1/79–3/90)	2.56**	.878	.237
Fuster trials (8/84–11/85)	−46.82	−.132	.714
After Fuster trials (12/85–3/90)	−1.94*	−.278	.225
Control Cases[b]			
Full time span (1/79–3/90)	3.99**	1.04	.133
Fuster trials (8/84–11/85)	−51.28	−.111	.503
After Fuster trials (12/85–3/90)	−1.16*	−.626	.122

[a] $R^2 = .427$; adjusted $R^2 = .414$; $F = 32.60$, $p = .001$; Durbin-Watson = 2.15
[b] $R^2 = .297$; adjusted $R^2 = .281$; $F = 18.37$, $p = .001$; Durbin-Watson = 1.76
* $p = .05$; ** $p = .001$

Number of Charges per Case

The number of charges leveled against a defendant reflects both the seriousness of the case and a discretionary decision by the state prosecutor. A punitive echo predicts that more charges on average will be brought against echo case defendants after the beginning of the Fuster trials. Figure 4 displays the trends for both echo and control cases.

Figure 4 and the accompanying analysis in Table 4 show a temporal trend in the direction that a punitive echo would predict. Both types of cases change significantly in the monthly average number of charges: Echo cases increase and control cases decrease.[17] The difference is not significant, however, until the post-Fuster trials period. On average significantly more charges are leveled in the echo cases than in the control cases only after the Fuster trials end. The regression analysis reported in Table 4 bears out the weakness of the temporal relationship. The echo case series has a barely significant relation to the three time variables, and the explained variance is only 3 percent.[18] The control cases are related slightly more closely to the time variables, with an explained variance of 6 percent; the posttrial trend variable shows a significant B-value.

---

[17] ANOVA results on average number of charges per case before, during, and after Fuster trials: echo cases, $F = 4.24$, $p = .0164$; control cases, $F = 4.46$, $p = .0133$.
[18] When the full-series variable is run alone, a slight positive trend is revealed for the echo cases: adjusted $R^2 = .04$, $B = .002$, $p = .019$. For the control cases, a slight negative full-series trend is revealed: adjusted $R^2 = .016$, $B = −.002$, $p = .044$.

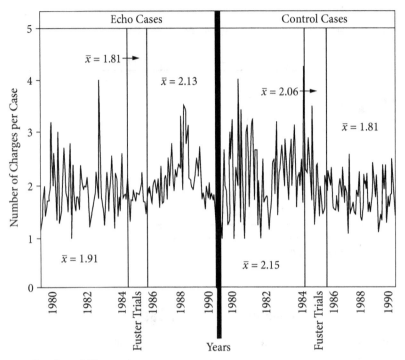

Figure 4. Average Number of Charges

Table 4. Regression Analysis: Average Number of Charges per Case, Echo and Control Cases

	B	Beta	Tolerance
Echo Cases[a]			
Full time span (1/79–3/90)	.003	.247	.248
Fuster trials (8/84–11/85)	−.247	−.163	.727
After Fuster trials (12/85–3/90)	−.001	−.056	.235
Control Cases[b]			
Full time span (1/79–3/90)	.006	.407	.139
Fuster trials (8/84–11/85)	−.362	−.184	.509
After Fuster trials (12/85–3/90)	−.005*	−.653	.128

[a] $R^2 = .058$; adjusted $R^2 = .036$; $F = 2.68$, $p = .05$; Durbin-Watson = 1.73
[b] $R^2 = .086$; adjusted $R^2 = .065$; $F = 4.12$, $p = .05$; Durbin-Watson = 2.10
* $p = .05$

Results: Disposition Variables

Figures 5 through 7 show the results for the three disposition variables. The first two variables examine the proportion of cases each month that are dismissed and that end in jail sentences; the final series looks at the monthly average jail sentence for cases involving such sentences.

Monthly Percentage of Cases Dismissed, Resolved by Nolle Prosequi, or Otherwise Removed from the System

In Figure 5 and Table 5, the pattern for the proportion of cases dismissed is similar for echo and for control cases, and shows a significant decline in both types. As the study period proceeded, the judicial system became generally more punitive and less likely to dismiss cases. This downward trend in case dismissals is less for the echo cases than for the control cases: The echo cases begin the period as slightly less likely to be dismissed, and end as significantly more likely.

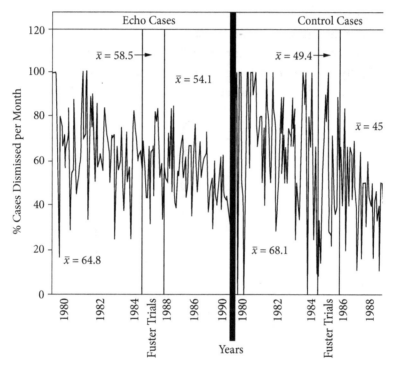

Figure 5. Percentage of Cases Dismissed

Table 5. Regression Analysis: Percentage of Cases Dismissed per Month, Echo and Control Cases

	B	Beta	Tolerance
Echo Cases[a]			
Full time span (1/79–3/90)	−.100	−.236	.240
Fuster trials (8/84–11/85)	−2.66	−.051	.715
After Fuster trials (12/85–3/90)	−.160	−.156	.228
Control Cases[b]			
Full time span (1/79–3/90)	−.089	−.128	.135
Fuster trials (8/84–11/85)	−15.04	−.179	.506
After Fuster trials (12/85–3/90)	−.100	−.295	.124

[a] $R^2 = .142$; adjusted $R^2 = .122$; $F = 7.29$, $p = .001$; Durbin-Watson = 1.96
[b] $R^2 = .173$; adjusted $R^2 = .154$; $F = 9.17$, $p = .001$; Durbin-Watson = 1.89

After the end of the Fuster trials, the proportion of echo cases dismissed is significantly greater than the proportion of control cases dismissed (54% to 45%), contrary to the prediction of a punitive echo would predict. The regression analysis on dismissal percentages also reflects a weak long-term decline. For both echo and control cases, a full time-series decline in the percentage of cases dismissed emerges as the sole significant predictor.[19] In sum, the analysis does not evince a punitive echo; instead it shows a shift in the opposite direction.

Percentage of Cases Sentenced to Jail

Figure 6 displays the trends for the proportion of cases in which defendants are adjudicated guilty and receive jail time. Without the cases dismissed or found not guilty, this time series represents a smaller set of cases: those which actually were at risk of a jail sentence. Before the Fuster trials, although defendants were found guilty, in some months no defendants were sentenced to jail time in either type of case. An ANOVA reveals an increased punitive tendency after guilty adjudications for both case types.[20]

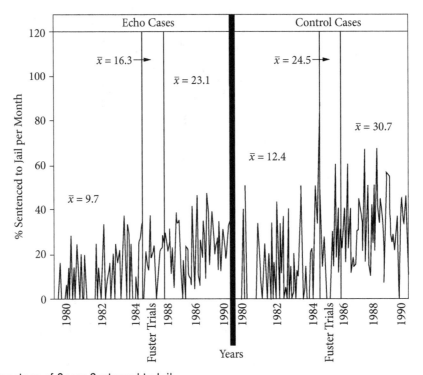

Figure 6. Percentage of Cases Sentenced to Jail

Both the echo and the control cases adjudicated guilty become progressively more at risk for jail time over the course of the study period. Also, although the echo cases are consistently less at risk of jail sentences, the echo cases and the control cases show no significant difference in risk during any period.[21]

---

[19] Regressions for both the echo and the control cases on only the full-series variable reveal similar long-term negative trends as explanatory for both case sets. Echo regression on full-series trend: adjusted $R^2 = .13, B = -.157, p = .000$. Control regression on full-series trend: adjusted $R^2 = .15, B = -.275, p = .000$. ANOVA results on percentage of cases dismissed before, during, and after Fuster trials: echo cases, $F = 6.57, p = .002$; control cases, $F = 13.30, p = .000$.

[20] ANOVA results on percentage of cases sentenced to jail before, during, and after Fuster trials: echo cases $F = 18.74, p = .000$); control cases, $F = 15.83, p = .000$.

[21] The after-Fuster trial peried (echo proportion 23.13, control proportion 30–7) just fails to reach the .05 level of significance.

Indeed, the risk of jail for the echo cases increases more slowly than for the control cases, although a punitive, media-driven echo effect would predict that their risk should increase faster. The analysis reported in Table 6 shows that the full-series time variable **emerges** as the most significant variable for both echo and control cases.[22] In total, we find no evidence of an echo effect.

Table 6. Regression Analysis: Percentage of Cases Sentenced to Jail per Month, Echo and Control Cases

	B	Beta	Tolerance
Echo Cases[a]			
Full time span (1/79–3/90)	.201**	.595	.240
Fuster trials (8/84–11/85)	−1.80	−.043	.715
After Fuster trials (12/85–3/90)	−.058	−.071	.228
Control Cases[b]			
Full time span (1/79–3/90)	.164	−.327	.135
Fuster trials (8/84–11/85)	−4.90	−.080	.506
After Fuster trials (12/85–3/90)	−.031	−.126	.124

[a] $R^2 = .285$; adjusted $R^2 = .269$; $F = 17.59$, $p = .001$; Durbin-Watson = 1.97
[b] $R^2 = .199$; adjusted $R^2 = .180$; $F = 10.85$, $p = .001$; Durbin-Watson = 1.71
** $p = .001$

Monthly Average Jail Sentence

Finally, we examine the monthly average jail sentence given to echo and control cases. Figure 7 and Table 7 report the trends. Because these trends are based only on cases that receive jail sentences, analogous to percentage of cases sentenced to jail, the numbers of cases on which the series are based are less than for the other series.[23]

The first observation is that defendants in echo cases are consistently sentenced to longer jail terms than those in control cases. Second, ANOVA shows that jail sentences for the control cases do not change significantly over the study, but that sentences for the echo cases do change.[24] The pattern for the echo cases is not straightforward, however. The longest average jail sentences were imposed in the period preceding the Fuster trials; the shortest sentences were imposed during the trials period.[25] Insofar as sentences in the control cases are relatively stable over the entire decade, the instability in the echo case sentences is curious. A purely punitive echo would predict that the length of jail sentences would increase significantly after the beginning of the Fuster trials, but the average sentence in fact is shorter. Figure 7 shows that the half-year preceeding the Fuster trials reflects a period of shorter jail sentences, and that in comparison the length of sentences increases during the Fuster trials period. Sentences increase throughout the Fuster trials period, decline about a half-year after

---

[22] A regression run on the echo cases with the full-series time variable prow duced an adjusted R^2 of .27, $B = .18$, $p = .000$. For the control cases, adjusted $R^2 = .18$, $B = .22$, $p = .000$.

[23] Therefore, for this series only, the number of months in the series = 90, compared with 135 for the other dependent variables.

[24] ANOVA results on average length of jail sentence before, during, and after Fuster trials: echo cases, $F = 3.21$ $p = .04$; control cases, $F = .236$, $p = .789$.

[25] Examination of the median jail sentences reveals the same relationship. Echo cases, median jail terms in days: before Fuster trials = 2,691, during Fuster trials = 2,188, after Fuster trials = 3,121. Control cases, median jail terms in days: before Fuster trials = 1,338, during Fuster trials = 1,288, after Fuster trials = 1,245.

the trials' end, and then resumes a long-term increase. The control and the echo cases are statistically similar only during the Fuster trials period; both before and after the trials, defendants in echo cases are sentenced to significantly longer jail terms. Furthermore, the initial regression analysis (see Table 7) shows no significant relationship between the control cases' jail sentences and any of the three time variables.[26]

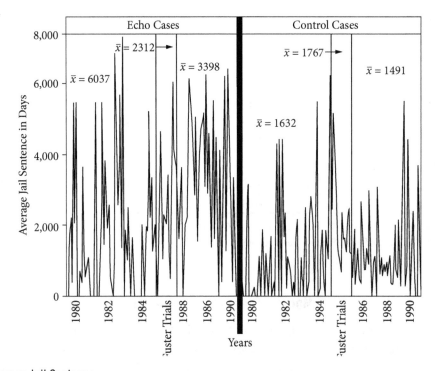

Figure 7. Average Jail Sentence

Table 7. Regression Analysis: Average Jail Sentence Length per Month, Echo and Control Cases

	B	Beta	Tolerance
Echo Cases[a]			
Full time span (1/79–3/90)	−14.58	−.264	.220
Fuster trials (8/84–11/85)	−99.47	−.019	.706
After Fuster trials (12/85–3/90)	45.12	.428	.193
Control Cases[b]			
Full time span (1/79–3/90)	−14.93	−.371	.111
Fuster trials (8/84–11/85)	646.79	.160	.430
After Fuster trials (12/85–3/90)	5.35	.319	.093

[a] $R^2 = .065$; adjusted $R^2 = .032$; $F = 2.00$; Durbin-Watson = 2.10
[b] $R^2 = .021$; adjusted $R^2 = .011$; $F = .660$; Durbin-Watson = 2.00

The regression for echo cases is also insignificant: The three time variables explain only 3 percent of the variation in jail sentences. In an extended period that includes the four months just before and

---

26   Noting the low tolerance values, I conducted regression runs on the separate variables but did not obtain different results

just after the Fuster trials, however, we find a significant positive relationship. Jail sentences for the echo cases increase by one-third of a year for every month during this period.[27] Empirically this means that although echo case sentences were significantly shorter during the Fuster trials than in the rest of the study period, they also experienced a significant increase that began just before the trials and continued for a brief time after they ended.

Summary of Results

In the initial processing of echo and control cases, we observe a significant increase in the number of echo cases filed and strong evidence of a punitive echo. For not guilty pleas, we find reduced variance during the Fuster trials and weak evidence of a punitive echo. Although an echo is suggested, the results do not show a strong effect, as we found for case filings. Idiosyncratic case factors probably explain the high variance in the series and dominate any echo effect that may be operating. For case processing time we see no evidence of an echo. Average processing time is not different in the echo cases, and no echo effect from the Fuster trials is demonstrated empirically. Lastly, the number of charges per case increases slightly, but not until after the Fuster trials.

In general we find weak results concerning an echo effect on the final disposition variables. Thus, for the percentage of cases dismissed from the system, the echo cases begin the ten-year period as less likely than the control cases to be dismissed, and end as significantly more likely to be dismissed. The analysis does not evince a punitive echo; instead it shows a shift in the opposite direction. Similarly, in regard to the percentage of defendants sentenced to jail, the regression analysis does not support a punitive echo. We find evidence of a dispositional punitive echo, only in the realm of the average jail sentence imposed on defendants sentenced to jail, and even in this variable it is marginal and mixed. No dramatic change occurs during the Fuster trials, but a 10-year downward trend in the length of echo case jail sentences is neutralized and reversed during the period that begins just before Frank Fuster's indictment and ends soon after his wife's sentencing.

Insofar as the direction of sentences shifts toward a punitive echo and the shift is significant over this extended span, the findings suggest that an echo effect is operating at least partially. In the absence of any change in control case sentences, no alternative explanation readily presents itself. This is also the only instance in which we find any evidence of a fading echo effect after the Fuster trials.

In sum, evidence of an echo effect on case processing and dispositional decisions is not found across the board. The effect appears to concentrate in case filings and to be merely suggested in not guilty pleas and sentence length. We find no evidence of an effect extending to processing time or number of charges, percentage of cases dismissed, or percentage of defendants sentenced to jail.

Discussion

Implications for Original Hypotheses

In regard to the original sets of hypotheses, I offer the following conclusions.

For Hypothesis 1a, "The number of cases entering the system with charges similar to those in the Fuster case should increase significantly after the beginning of the Fuster trials," is strongly supported.

---

[27] A regression on this 24-month period alone produces an adjusted R^2 of .225, $F = 7.66$, $p = .011$, $B = 101.5$ (95% confidence intervals, range is 25 to 188 days).

Hypothesis 1b, "Not guilty pleas should increase for echo charged cases during the Fuster trials," is partially supported. A speculative but plausible explanation of these results is that defendants in the Fuster-charge cases were not offered attractive plea bargains after the Fuster trial began; the result was the slight observed increase in not guilty pleas. Perhaps at least partially in compensation for more punitive treatment of the echo cases and for their increasing numbers, defendants in the control cases were simultaneously offered more attractive plea bargains, which resulted in a decrease in their not guilty pleas. After the period of the trials, reflecting the continued punitive position regarding echo cases, the proportion of not guilty pleas became significantly higher for the echo cases than for the controls.

Although an echo is weakly suggested, these results do not clearly show a strong effect, as was found for case filings. Idiosyncratic case factors could explain the high variance in the series and could dominate any echo effect that may be operating. Despite some suggestive empirical evidence of a relationship between the Fuster trials and not guilty pleas for echo cases, the evidence is neither consistent nor strong enough to confirm a punitive echo effect.

Hypothesis 1c, "Processing time should increase for echo cases during the Fuster trials and should decrease after their completion, in comparison with control cases," is not supported.

For Hypothesis 1d, "The total number of charges per case should increase for echo cases during the Fuster trials and should decline after their completion, in comparison with control cases," the results cannot be interpreted as supporting an echo effect. They could be supportive only if the explanation of a lagged effect from the trials were accepted. Although lagged media effects have been reported elsewhere,[28] there is no strong theoretical reason why one would appear here. It is more plausible that changes in the number of charges are influenced by other factors and are not due to the systemic sensitizing publicity of the Fuster cases. Therefore this hypothesis is not supported.

Regarding Hypothesis 2a, "The proportion of similarly charged cases dismissed should decrease significantly after the beginning of the Fuster trials," the weak effect found is opposite that of a punitive echo: The echo cases become more likely than the control cases to be dismissed. This finding could reflect an adjustment or correction on the part of the system to the increased number of echo cases entering the system. A possible explanation is that the state, reacting to increased sensitivity to echo-type cases, files on weaker and more marginal echo cases. Thus, although the system became more punitive and dismissed a smaller percentage of echo cases over the decade, it became even more punitive toward control cases, at least in regard to the case dismissal decision. Like the results for number of charges, however, this difference becomes statistically significant only after the Fuster trials end; this lag weakens support for the difference as evidence of an echo effect.[29] Hence there is no evidence of a punitive echo effect.

For Hypothesis 2b, "The proportion of similarly charged cases sentenced to jail should increase significantly after the beginning of the Fuster trials," the finding that the jail risk for echo cases increases more slowly than for control cases suggests two competing explanations. Either an echo effect does not extend to jail sentence decisions, or the increased but still smaller risk of jail for the echo cases than for the control cases reflects a systemic correction for the increased number of echo cases entering the judicial system. The results of the analysis support the former explanation more strongly than the latter: We see no evidence of an echo effect on the percentage of defendants sentenced to jail time.

---

[28]   See Phillips and Carstensen (1986); Phillips and Hensley (1984); Phillips and Paight (1987).

[29]   I also examined the monthly percentage of cases adjudicated guilty. The pattern displayed for the proportion of cases found guilty shows similar trends for both the echo and the control cases: Both types of cases are more likely to be adjudicated guilty over the period of the study. Contrary to the theorized echo effect, however, although the increase is in the direction that a punitive echo would predict, it is smaller for the echo cases than for the control cases. This finding agrees with the trend observed for cases dismissed.

Concerning Hypothesis 2c, "Jail time should increase significantly for similarly charged cases after the beginning of the Fuster trials," we find partial evidence of a punitive echo: Echo cases begin to show an increase in the length of jail sentences over an extended period that brackets the Fuster trials. As a punitive echo would predict, the length of echo case sentences was at its nadir just before the Fuster trials, increased significantly during the trials, and declined shortly thereafter. This increase, however, is empirically only a return to sentence lengths that existed in the years before the Fuster trials. After the brief decline following the trials, sentences returned to their previous lengths.

This pattern is not observed in the control cases, which show no significant downward or upward trends at any point in the 10-year period. A likely explanation is that the system reacted rapidly to the Fuster cases, responding to pre-arrest publicity and launching an immediate punitive response against similarly charged defendants who had been found guilty and judged as deserving jail time. Because the influx of new filings could not have worked their way through to sentencing at this point, these pre-Fuster cases represent a group of defendants arrested and filed upon under the pre-Fuster trial standards. These standards are indicated, in the analysis of not guilty pleas, as more stringent.[30] As these and the new echo filings worked their way through the system, the length of sentences increased. It decreased again after the Fuster trials ended, as theoretically expected. Whether this interpretation is justified is unknown. The findings suggest a punitive echo but certainly are not conclusive; evidence for a punitive echo is therefore muddled.

This analysis reveals that the period of the Fuster trials was a time of general turbulence in the Eleventh Circuit Court system, but that the turbulence was reflected to a greater degree in echo charged cases. These cases were treated differently than the control cases, but only along some dimensions; sometimes the outcome was opposite the hypothesized direction. On some measures, such as processing time, echo cases were caught up in the general trends in the system. On others, such as number of charges and percent jailed, they showed some significant divergence but not in the direction predicted by a punitive echo.

The clearest effect is found in the raw number of cases entering the system; the local criminal justice system strongly shifted its attention to echo cases after the Fuster trials began. In this study, almost 140 more echo cases were introduced into the system during the Fuster trials alone than would have been expected on the basis of past trends. At that time, echo cases became, and long remained, a focus of the system. Aside from the quantity of cases entering, however, the echo effects are muted, and we find suggestions of system corrections to increased punitiveness. Processing time, jail sentences, and the other variables move in various directions. Along some dimensions, echo cases appear to be treated more leniently.

After the Fuster trials begin, for example, the odds of case dismissal for an echo defendant remained better than 50-50. For defendants in the control cases, the odds of case dismissal declined to no better than 1 in of 3. If found guilty, however, echo defendants were more likely to be sent to jail than were control case defendants. After the Fuster trials, if a defendant was charged with a crime similar to those for which Fuster and his wife were convicted, that defendant's case was much more likely to be dismissed than if he or she faced a control case charge. This finding suggests that the police were more likely to make an arrest and that the state's attorney was more likely to file on marginal echo charge cases, and to "let the courts sort it out." This does not appear to be true before the Fuster trials. Thus, although proportionally more Fuster-type cases entered the system after the Fuster case, they were also more likely to exit the system, probably because of weaknesses in the cases.

The most surprising finding is that the echo did not fade after the end of the Fuster trials. This may have occurred because a local echo was confounded by the echoes of national coverage of child care

---

[30] Before the Fuster trials, a similar increase in filings is also present in Figure 1.

abuse cases. The McMartin Day Care abuse trial in California, for example, became a national news item in the late 1980s (Waterman et al. 1993). An examination of a treatment effect from the beginning of the McMartin case or from sentencing in that case revealed no significant systemic changes in the Eleventh Circuit judicial system. It is more likely that once the Fuster case had sensitized the system in the mid-1980s, the continued coverage of similar cases across the country kept the pressure high in the Eleventh Circuit. In effect, a national echo may have confounded a local echo to prolong and amplify the echo of the Fuster trials in the Dade County judicial system.

This study offers an empirically supported example of an echo effect in criminal justice generated by the news media. The analysis showed marked increases in filings of cases involving child victimization following the publicized case, a short-term increase in the length of sentences in cases adjudicated guilty, and a possible increase in the number of not guilty pleas. As expected because of the nature of the publicized cases, the echo effect as found in this study is largely punitive but contains suggestions of system corrections in the adjudication process. The sentencing literature contains references to a homeostasis process, whereby a judicial system has a set level of punishment: When punishment is increased for one set of cases, it adjusts its actions by changing the processing of another set (Blumstein, Cohen, and Nagin 1976, Walker 1994:51-52).

Accordingly the results of the analysis suggest the following dynamics regarding media echoes. Significant echo effects exist but are bounded by wider trends in the criminal justice system. The echoes are most evident in the filings of cases. The judicial system appears to make some adjustments to the increased flow of cases related to echo effects, modifying the impact of the echo by instituting changes in other case types. It may be that the criminal justice system, having arrived at its own notions of serious and nonserious offenses, responds to high-profile cases by prosecuting them for the public benefit, but still processes them as usual. In such a scenario, total punitiveness is still increased for the class of echo offenders because more such offenders are prosecuted. Thus the system is quantitatively more punitive by being equally or even slightly less punitive to an expanded pool of defendants. In regard to the societal picture and the criminal justice system as a collective entity, greater punitiveness requires no increase in the punishment of individuals when the number of individuals being punished has increased.

Conclusion

Media echo effects can be understood more fully from a "social construction of reality" perspective. The construction of reality in the criminal justice system and in judicial work groups is a matter of primary interest (Adoni and Mane 1984; Barak 1994; Barrile 1984; Best 1989; Carlson 1985; Cohen, Adoni, and Bentz 1990; Cohen and Young 1981; Eisenstein and Jacobs 1977; Ericson, Baranek, and Chan 1991; Hawkins and Pingree 1982; Schneider 1985; Surette 1998). From this perspective, echo effects are a media-induced reconstruction of reality concerning the importance of a set of cases. Prior research shows that prosecutors are the key work group actors, are the most sensitive to echo effects, and therefore are most likely to reconstruct the importance of a class of cases into a new reality as a result of media activities (Pritchard 1986; Pritchard et al. 1987).

Although this research documents the existence and magnitude of one such effect, we still do not clearly understand the general manner and conditions in which this reconstruction occurs. The findings reported here, concerning a study of a single type of case in a single jurisdiction, may be idiosyncratic. The significant results, however, underscore the need to conduct this kind of empirical work on echo effects throughout the criminal justice system, particularly with prosecutors. The findings reported here agree with earlier research on the media and the setting of the prosecutor's agenda (McCain 1992; Pritchard 1986, 1992; Pritchard et al. 1987). But beyond their influence on specific prosecutorial steps and decisions, the impact of the media is not clear. It is probably related to specifics of cases and to local systems' idiosyncrasies.

Detailed knowledge of the operation of the echo, and of its implications for sentencing, would be useful for echo case defendants, their attorneys, and their prosecutors. Such detailed knowledge would serve all parties better than a vague sense that the times are changing. At least the attorneys of the nonpublicized but publicity affected defendants would become aware that their clients may be anonymous to the media but that their cases are still undergoing systemic media influences.

Further research is also needed to specify the relationships and roles of other work group actors in determining echo effects. Also interesting would be the response, to media coverage and echoes, of public defenders, defendants, and elected versus nonelected judges.

Finally, it would be important to know whether in certain circumstances an echo effect can be suppressed by actions of judicial work group members, and when and how corrective responses by the criminal justice system are activated. By empirically demonstrating a significant echo effect in one jurisdiction hopefully this study wilt spur research into these and other questions. In the contemporary infotainment, hypermedia atmosphere, echo effects are likely to be ever-present.

References

Adoni, H. and S. Mane. 1984. "Media and the Social Construction of Reality." *Communication Research* 11:323–40.

Barak, G. 1994. *Media, Process, and the Social Construction of Crime: Studies in Newsmaking Criminology.* New York: Garland.

_____. 1995. Comments American Society of Criminal Justice Panel Discussant. Unpublished manuscript: Boston, Mass.

_____. 1996. "Media, Discourse, and the O.J. Simpson Trial: An Ethnographic Portrait." Pp. 104–22 in *Representing O.J.: Murder, Criminal Justice and Mass Culture,* edited by G. Barak. Albany: Harrow and Hestor.

Barrile, L. 1984. "Television and Attitudes about Crime: Do Heavy Viewers Distort Criminality and Support Retributive Justice?" Pp. 141–58 in *Justice and the Media,* edited by R. Surette. Springfield, IL: Thomas.

Best, J. 1989. *Images of Issues: Typifying Contemporary Social Problems.* New York: Aldine.

Blumstein, A., J. Cohen, and D. Nagin. 1976. "The Dynamics of a Homeostatic Punishment Process." *Journal of Criminal Law and Criminology* 67:20–26.

Carlson, J. 1985. *Prime Time Law Enforcement.* New York: Praeger.

Cohen, A., T. Adoni, and C. Bantz. 1990. *Social Conflict and Television News.* Newbury Park, CA: Sage.

Cohen, S. and J. Young. 1981. *The Manufacture of News: Social Problems, Deviance, and the Mass Media.* London: Constable.

Cook, T. and D. Campbell. 1979. *Quasi-Experimentation.* Boston: Houghton Mifflin.

Cook, T., T. Tyler, E. Goetz, M. Gordon, D. Protess, D. Left, and H. Molotch. 1983. "Media and Agenda Setting: Effects on the Public, Interest Group Leaders, Policy Makers, and Policy." *Public Opinion Quarterly* 47:16–35.

Davis, R. 1986. "Pretrial Publicity, the Timing of the Trial, and Mock Jurors' Decision Processes." Journal of Applied Social Psychology 16:590–607.

Doppelt, J. 1992. Mlarching to the Police and Court Beats." Pp. 113–30 in *Public Opinion and the Press,* edited by J.D. Kennamer. Westport, CT: Praeger.

Doppelt, J. and P. Manikas. 1990. "Mass Media and Criminal Justice Decision Making" Pp. 129–42 in *The Media and Criminal Justice Policy Making,* edited by R. Surette. Springfield, IL: Thomas.

Dye, T. and H. Zeigler. 1986. *American Politics in the Media Age.* Pacific Grove, CA: Brooks/Cole.

Eisenstein, J. and H. Jacobs. 1977. *Felony Justice: An Organizational Analysis of Criminal Courts.* Boston: Little, Brown.

Entman, Robert M. 1989. "How the Media Affect What People Think: An Information Processing Approach." *Journal of Politics* 51:347–70.

Ericson, R., P. Baranek, and J. Chan. 1991. *Representing Order: Crime, Law, and Justice in the News Media.* Toronto: University of Toronto Press.

Fishman, M. 1978. Crime Waves as Idealogy. *Social Problems* 25:531–43.

Greene, E. and E. Loftus. 1984. "What's New in the News? The Impact of Well-Publicized News Events on Psychological Research and Courtroom Trials." *Basic and Applied Social Psychology.* 5:211–21.

Greene, E. and R. Wade. 1988. "Of Private Talk and Public Print: General Pre-Trial Publicity and Juror Decision-Making." *Applied Cognitive Psychology.* 2:123–35.

Hall, S., C. Chritcher, T. Jefferson, J. Clarke, and B. Roberts. 1981. "The Social Production of News: Muggings in the Media," Pp. 335–67 in the Manufacture of News, edited by S. Colen and J. Young. Thousand Oaks, CA: Sage.

Hawkins, R. and S. Pingree. 1982. "Television's Influence on Social Reality." Pp. 224–47 in *Television and Behavior: Ten Years of Scientific Progress and Implications for the Eighties,* vol. 2, edited by D. Pearl, L. Bouthilet, and J. Lazar. Washington, DC: U.S. Government Printing Office.

Kaplan, J. and J. Skolnick. 1982. *Criminal Justice.* Mineola, NY: Foundation Press.

Lasorsa, D. 1992. "Policymakers and the Third-Person Effect." Pp. 163–75 in *Public Opinion and the Press,* edited by J.D. Kennamer. Westport, CT: Praeger.

Lofton, J. 1966. *Justice and the Press.* Boston: Beacon.

McCain, T. 1992. "The Interplay of Editorial and Prosecutorial Discretion in the Perpetuation of Racism in the Criminal Justice System." *Columbia Journal of Law and Social Problems* 25:601–43.

McCombs, M. 1994. "News Influence on Our Pictures of the World." Pp. 1–16 in *Media Effects: Advances in Theory and Research,* edited by J. Bryant and D. Zillman. Hillsdale, NJ: Erlbaum.

Meier, K. and J. Brundnay. 1993. *Applied Statistics for Public Administration.* Belmont, CA: Wadsworth.

Norusis, M. 1995. *SPSS: Guide to Data Analysis.* Englewood Cliffs, NJ: Prentice-Hall.

Pember, D. 1987. *Mass Media Law.* Dubuque: Brown.

Phillips, D. and L. Carstensen. 1986. "Clustering of Teenage Suicides after Television News Stories about Suicide." *New England Journal of Medicine* 315:685–89.

Phillips, D. and J. Hensley. 1984. "When Violence Is Rewarded or Punished: The Impact of Mass Media Stories on Homicide." *Journal of Communication* 34(3):101–16.

Phillips, D. and D. Paight. 1987, "The Impact of Televised Movies about Suicide." *New England Journal of Medicine* 315:809–11.

Pritchard, D. 1986. "Homicide and Bargained Justice: The Agenda-Setting Effect of Crime News on Prosecutors." *Public Opinion Quarterly* 50:143–59.

_____. 1992. "The News Media and Public Policy Agendas." Pp. 103–12 in *Public Opinion and the Press,* edited by J.D. Kennamer. Westport, CT: Praeger.

Pritchard D., J. Dilts, and D. Berkowitz. 1987. "Prosecutors' Use ef External Agendas in Prosecuting Pornography Cases." *Journalism Quarterly* 64:392–98.

Protess, D., F. Cook, T. Curtin, M. Gordon, D. Left, L. McCombs, E. Maxwell, and P. Miller. 1985. "Uncovering Rape: The Watchdog Press and the Limits of Agenda Setting." *Public Opinion Quarterly* 49:19–37.

Protess, D., F. Cook, J. Doppelt, J. Ettema, M. Gordon, D. Left, and P. Miller. 1994. "Building Policy Agenda." Pp. 83–101 in *Politics and the Media,* edited by R. Davis. Englewood Cliffs, NJ: Prentice-Hall.

Radin, E. 1964. *The Innocents*. Fairfield, NJ: Morrow.

Roberts, J. and D. Edwards. 1989. "Contextual Effects in Judgments of Crimes, Criminals, and the Purposes of Sentencing." *Journal of Applied Social Psychology* 19:902–17.

Schlesinger, P., H. Tumber, and G. Murdock. 1991. "The Media Politics of Crime and Criminal Justice." *British Journal of Sociology* 42:397–419.

Schneider, J. 1985. "Social Problems Theory: The Constructionist View." *Annual Review of Sociology* 11:209–29.

Snow, R. 1984. "Crime and Justice in Prime-Time News." Pp. 212–32 in *Justice and the Media,* edited by R. Surette. Springfield, IL: Thomas.

Surette, R. 1989. "Media Trials." *Journal of Criminal Justice* 17:293–308.

_____. 1990. *The Media and Criminal Justice Policy*. Springfield, IL: Thomas.

_____. 1995. "A Serendipitous Finding of a News Media History Effect: A Research Note." *Justice Quarterly* 12:355–64.

_____. 1998. *Media Crime and Criminal Justice: Images and Realities*. Belmont, CA: West/Wadsworth.

Swaminathan, H. and J. Algina. 1977. "Analysis of Quasi-Experimental Time-Series Designs." *Journal of Multivariate Behavioral Research* 12:111–31.

Walker, S. 1994. *Sense and Nonsense about Crime*. Pacific Grove, CA: Wadsworth.

Waterman, J., R. Kelly, M. Otiveri, and J. McCord. 1993. *Behind the Playground Walls: Sexual Abuse in Preschool*. New York: Guilford Press.

SHOULD WE BLAME JUDGE JUDY?

The messages TV courtrooms send viewers

by Kimberlianne Podlas

A recent study suggests that while syndicated television court-rooms do, indeed, teach the public about the justice system, the content of this curriculum leaves much to be desired.

In the last decade, syndicated television courtrooms have crowded the television "docket." Despite their popularity, however, their impact on the viewing public's perceptions of the justice system and judges is unclear: Do these television representations educate citizens about simple legal rules and encourage jury service, or, in light of their trademark verbally aggressive, sarcastic judges, do they misrepresent the proper role of 'judge" and reduce respect for the justice system?

KIMBERLIANNE PODLAS is an assistant professor in the Department of History and Social Sciences at Bryant College.

To answer this question, a study of 241 individuals reporting for jury duty was conducted. It investigated the correlation between frequent syndi-court viewing and attitudes about the bench. Findings suggest that syndi-court does, indeed, teach the public about the justice system, but that the content of this curriculum leaves much to be desired.

For instance, frequent viewers tend to believe that judges should be active, ask questions during the proceedings, hold opinions regarding the outcome, and make these opinions known. Furthermore, unlike non-viewers, frequent viewers expressed a desire to uncover clues to a judge's opinion and interpreted judicial silence as indicating belief in one of the litigants.

Although the justice system rests on the creation of and adherence to legal rules and principles, its efficacy depends on collective respect generated from public opinion.[1] Positive opinions reinforce the validity of the justice system, its actors and outcomes, while negative ones undermine its credibility. Such opinions are formed in many ways. Sometimes citizens are influenced by personal experiences as litigants or employees of the court system. Other times information is gained through such means as academic coursework. In most instances, however, citizens do not have intimate contacts with the justice system; thus, media portrayals of courts fill the void.[2]

Both legal scholars and behavioral scientists have asserted that televising trials educates the public by providing a frame of reference for what the court system is, its fairness, and who its arbiters of justice are.[3] Similarly, the Supreme Court,[4] the American Bar Association,[5] and New York's chief judge[6] have all presumed an educative effect on behalf of televised law.

Though televised law has traditionally been confined to news coverage of noteworthy trials and obvious dramatizations, the last decade has marked the era of the syndicated courtroom (syndi-court). "Reality" law programs like 'Judge Judy" and "The People's Court"[7] now populate the dial. Although individuals within the legal profession may disregard these "syndi-courts" as aberrational or embarrassing, for many citizens they provide the most accessible court information available.

Indeed, syndi-court is accessible to the average person in a way and to a degree that other televised legal proceedings are not. On any weekday anyone with a television can find at least one syndi-court; cable is not a prerequisite. They are also intellectually accessible: The stories are easily digestible, the conflicts clear, and the resolutions swift. And they follow a remarkably similar format: What one sees on Judge Judy is confirmed by what is seen on Judge Mathis, thus creating a unified body of information.

Ratings demonstrate that syndi-courts are actually seen by a significant portion of the public. One year after her 1996 debut, 'Judge Judy" boasted the nation's top syndicated ratings,[8] and continues to

---

[1] Selya, *The Confidence Games: Public Perceptions of the Judiciary*, 30 New Eng. L. Rev. 909, 909–10 (1996). Opinions about the fairness of the justice system reflect its legitimacy: "[A] decision contrary to the public sense of justice ... diminish[es] respect for the courts and for law itself. *Flood v. Kuhn*, 407 U.S. 258, 293 n.4 (1972) (Marshall dissenting).

[2] Selya, *supra* n. 1, at 913; Harris, *The Appearance of Justice: Court TV, Conventional Television, and Public Understanding of the Criminal Justice System*, 35 Ariz. L. Rev. 785, 786, 798 (1993); Slotnik, *Television news and the Supreme Court: a case study*, 77 Judicature 21, 22 (1993) (majority of public obtains only information about law from television).

[3] Selya, *supra* n. 1, at 913–14 (education of public should include media); *cf* Roberts, *An Empirical And Normative Analysis of The Impact of Televised Courtroom Proceedings*, 51 SMU L. Rev. 621, 627 (1998) (prohibiting public from viewing trials eliminates educational opportunity).

[4] *See e.g.*, Estes v. Texas, 381 U.S. 532 (1965) (State asserting First Amendment right to view trial); Richmond Newspapers, Inc. v. Virginia, 448 U.S. 555, 575 (1980) (Burger noting "educative effect" of televised proceedings on the public and right of press and public to attend trial implicit in First Amendment); Chandler v. Florida, 449 U.S. 560, 571 (1981) (State has interest, independent of wishes of defendant, to view and televise trial).

[5] A recent American Bar Association report suggested "that the media can and does impact some people's knowledge" of the law. As reprinted in, *Symposium: American Bar Association Report on Perceptions of the US Justice System*, 62 Alb. L. Rev. 1307, 1315 (1999), reprinted report, "Perceptions of the US Justice System," sponsored by the American Bar Association.

[6] Kaye, Symposium, *Rethinking Traditional Approaches*, 62 Alb. L. Rev. 1491, 1493 (1999).

[7] There are approximately 10 syndicated courtroom shows presently airing. Belcher, *New Court Shows, Dab Of Talk, Games Fill TV Docket*, Tampa Tribune, Sept. 11, 2000, at 1.

[8] Gunther, *The Little Judge Who Kicked Oprah's Butt; Daytime Television's Hottest Property*, Fortune, May 1999, at 32; Schlosser, *Another Benchmark for Judge Judy*, 'Broadcasting & Cable, Mar. 29, 1999, at 15.

enjoy significant popularity.[9] As a result, these shows possess a tremendous potential for impacting public opinion about the justice system.

These attributes make syndi-courts strong vehicles for cultivation and social learning. Cultivation theory considers the relationship between watching television and holding particular beliefs about the world.[10] According to this paradigm, watching a great deal of television will be associated with a tendency to hold beliefs consistent with the primary images and values depicted on screen. The closely related concept of social learning theory posits that viewers will look to the symbols and stories on television, and use these as schemata for their own behavior. In other words, media messages will teach and influence by providing explicit, concrete "models" for behavior, attitudes, and feelings.[11]

With regard to syndi-court, what viewers see on syndi-court will teach them how judges act. The intertwining of social learning and cultivation speaks to the effects that the stable, repetitive, and pervasive images and ideologies presented via televised syndi-court have on the non-litigious majority of the viewing public: Televised courtrooms become a primer through which the viewing public will come to know (or believe they know) how the law and judges operate.

One of the most visible symbols of law is the judge. Not only are judges vested with authority to orchestrate legal proceedings, but empirical evidence suggests that a judge can direct a jury to a verdict, even one the jury feels is unjust.[12] The primary focus in syndi-court is also the judge. Most shows are named after the judge, and the judge monopolizes much of the airtime. Even when litigants speak, the camera pans to the judge to capture his or her reaction.

Yet, many viewers do not understand that syndi-court is not a real court and that television brethren are not acting as (or may not even be) real judges. In fact, "the public regularly submits complaints about Judge Judy and other TV judges" to the California Commission on Judicial Performance. Apparently, many viewers do not "understand that Judge Judy and most of her cohorts are not present members of any judiciary.[13] This confusion is not surprising, as the tag-line of many of these shows reminds viewers that they are watching "real people," "real judges," and "real cases." Thus, the line between law and pop-culture blurs.

The study

Despite the intuitive logic that television images of law have some educative effect, neither the overall nor educational impact of televised trials (real or syndicated) on the public's perception of the legal system is known. Thus, this study sought to discover whether those who did and did not regularly watch syndi-court held different opinions regarding judges and their expected behavior.

The study also considered whether prior court-related experience stymied any influence of syndi-court. Prior research suggests that people who lack direct experience with the court system are most influenced by television portrayals,[14] and, therefore likely to use them as substitutions. This

[9]   "Judge Judy" presently garners 7,061,000 viewers and remains among the top 10 syndicated shows. Keveny, *Syndicated Goldies Are Oldies: New Shows Are No Match,* USA Today, Nov. 26, 2001, at 4D.

[10]   Shanahan and Morgan, Television and Its Viewers, Cultivation Theory and Research, 172 (1999). Cultivation speaks to the implications of stable, repetitive, and pervasive images and ideologies that TV, here, syndi-court, provides.

[11]   Bandura. Social Learning Theory (1977).

[12]   Olson and Olson, *Judges' Influence On Trial Outcomes and Jurors' Experiences of Justice. Reinscribing Existing Hierarchies Through The Sanctuary Trial,* 22 J. Applied Comm. Res. 16 (1994).

[13]   Farrel, *If Judge Judy Could Only Be Judged …,* Broward Daily Business Rev., July 7, 2000, at B4.

[14]   Eschholz, *The Media And Fear Of Crime: A Survey of The Research,* 9 U. Fla. J.L. & Pub. Pol'y 37, 43 (1997) (viewers with no prior criminal justice experiences were more likely than viewers with previous experience to believe that police show

might apply to syndi-court viewers: Experienced individuals who have seen a real judge in action and been instructed regarding the role of the judge, burdens of proof, and appropriate behavior of trial participants might be less inclined to exhibit the characteristics of the frequent viewers.

One criticism of many jury studies is that their findings lack practical value and cannot be generalized to actual jurors. Consequently, this study surveyed individuals reporting for jury duty, i.e., 241 juror-respondents from courthouses in Manhattan, the District of Columbia, and Hackensack, New Jersey.

While queuing up to enter the courthouse (and, in some instances, during breaks), individuals called for jury duty were approached, identified as being on jury duty, and asked to complete a questionnaire. Questionnaires were immediately retrieved as jurors completed them, and, in exchange for their participation, jurors were given elite pens and candy bars. All jurors approached returned question-naires. Questionnaires that were substantially incomplete, and those collected from individuals unable to communicate with the researcher in English, were excluded from analysis.

To discern whether viewing was associated with certain factors contemplated by the questionnaire, the 225 respondents ultimately analyzed were divided into two groups: frequent viewers [FV] or non-viewers [NV]. A "frequent viewer" watched syndi-court between two to three times and more than five times per week. Non-viewers did not watch syndi-courts or did so, at most, once per week. Of the 225 juror responses analyzed, 149 (66 percent) were FV and 76 (34 percent) NV.

Findings

The questions highlighted in this article focused on negative characteristics that may be associated with syndi-court judges and their potential ramifications. Among the questions posed were:

- Should a judge have an opinion about the outcome/verdict in the case?
- Should a judge make her/his opinion about a case clear or obvious to the jury?
- Will you look for clues or try to figure out what the judge's opinion about the case is?
- Should a judge frequently ask questions?
- Should a judge be aggressive with the litigants OR express her/his displeasure with their testimony or behavior?

As reported in Table 1, though it appeared that some respondents of both groups envisioned an "active" bench, frequent viewers anticipated this to a much greater degree. Indeed, frequent viewing was associated with beliefs that judges should have an opinion regarding the verdict (FV = 75 percent, NV = 49 percent) and make it "clear or obvious" (FV = 77 percent, NV = 32 percent). The import of this intensifies as frequent viewers also stated they would "look for clues" or "try to figure out" the judge's opinion (FV = 75 percent, NV = 32 percent).

Frequent viewers also treated judicial silence differently. One question asked whether the judge's silence meant that she favored the plaintiff, favored the defendant, had no opinion, or it would depend on the evidence. Whereas few (13 percent) of non-viewers attributed any significance to silence, a majority of frequent viewers (74 percent) concluded (incorrectly so) that it meant that the judge strongly favored *either* the plaintiff or defendant.

---

portrayals were accurate).

Table 1. Summary of findings

	FV	NV
Judicial opinions, activity		
judges should have opinion regarding verdict	75%	48.6%
judge should make opinion "clear"	76.5%	31.58%
jurors will "look for clues" to judge's opinion	74.5%	31.58%
Aggressive, investigatory behaviors		
judges should ask questions during trial	82.5%	38.16%
judge should "be aggressive with litigants or express displeasure with treir testimony"	63.76%	26.32%
Interpretation of judicial silence		
judge's silence indicates belief in litigant	73.8%	13%

Table 2. Express negative view of beach

Experience level	FV	NV
Prior court service or experience	23%	19%
No prior court service or experience	77%	80%

Differences also emerged regarding the expectation of aggressive and investigatory judicial behavior. Eighty-three percent of frequent viewers (NV=38 percent) believed that judges should ask questions during proceedings and 64 percent (NV=26 percent) believed that a judge should "be aggressive with the litigants or express his/her displeasure with their testimony or behavior."

Finally, there was no evidence that prior court service either mediated the effects of frequent viewing or otherwise explained the differential responses of the frequent and non-viewers. Instead, prior court service was not shown to be positively or negatively associated with any of the variables assessed, such as opinions regarding judicial activity or its meaning. Additionally, as shown in Table 2, prior court experience was also not predictive of whether jurors held a negative or positive view of the bench.

Implications

The study suggests that the TV experiences provided by syndi-court are either substituted for accurate, firsthand court experience or integrated with existing knowledge of the court system. Moreover, there is little check on this stream of information as few competing models (such as regular transmission of complete trials) to syndi-court's representation exist. Rather, five days a week, episodes reinforce the model of the syndi-court judge: a not-so-neutral arbiter who is aggressive, inquisitive, and often sarcastic; someone who will indicate his or her opinion about the evidence or witnesses obviously and often; and will do so even when silent.

Reducing respect for the bench. The American legal system sets a high bar for the behavior of judges. It envisions a bench that is metered and thoughtful and the pinnacle of propriety. Indeed, this philosophy is reflected in The Model Code of Judicial Conduct. Canon 1 of The Code requires judges, at all times, to conform with the highest behavioral standards "so that the integrity and independence of the judiciary will be preserved." With regard to the appearance of impropriety, it is applied to judges both on and off the bench, in their professional activities as well as their personal lives.

Canon 2 is concerned with the appearance of justice, and recognizes the connection between the public's observation of judges and their perception of the integrity of the judicial system. It requiresjudges, at all times, to act in a manner that promotes public confidence in the integrity and impartiality of the judiciary:"Public confidence in the judiciary is eroded by irresponsible or improper conduct by judges." Canon 3 provides that a judge shall be patient, dignified, and courteous to litigants, and shall perform duties without bias or prejudice.

Yet, the syndi-court bench seems to operate in opposition to these standards. Syndi-court judges are typically sarcastic, accusatory, and opinionated. When the public is fed the judicial model of syndi-court to the exclusion of accurate judicial representations, it is likely to conclude that these traits are common to real judges. Hence, the syndi-court personality may eclipse or infect the true behavior of judges, reducing respect for the bench and the decisions it must enforce. This diminishes the "brand" of judge—what a judge is supposed to be, supposed to represent—and breeds contempt for the judicial system as a whole.[15]

Moreover, that shows feature judges who continue to or have recently sat on the bench furthers this effect. For example, during the first years of his nationally syndicated television show 'Judge Joe Brown" continued to sit in Shelby County, Ten-nessee. Judge Judy and The People's Court Presiding Justice Gerry Sheindlin both left the bench to pursue television opportunities.

Misinterpreting judicial behaviors and temperament. The law assumes that jurors enter the courtroom as blank slates free of bias. Yet people tend to interpret new information in the light of past experience.[16] The lesson of syndi-court is such a past experience that jurors may bring into the courtroom and apply during trial. Indeed, it sends messages about judge behavior that viewers may later use as interpretive guides in jury service.

Although caselaw establishes that a judge should neither be the focal nor vocal center of attention at trial,[17] syndi-court does not endorse this model of judicial restraint. To the contrary, viewers see precisely the opposite, and, therefore, are taught (as demonstrated by the responses of frequent viewers) that judges should, do, and will disclose opinions regarding the case. This may cause them as jurors to unduly focus on the judge and imbue banal action with profound, yet unintended, meaning. When confronted with uncertainty of whether a doubt qualifies as reasonable or whether evidence quantifies as preponderant, jurors may look for other clues, particularly from a legal expert who has also heard the evidence.

Indeed, the U.S. Supreme Court has recognized that the judge possesses a tremendous potential to influence the jury.[18] Where a jury is given clues to a judge's belief regarding the case or the parties, even a suggestion of opinion might be seized upon by the jury, "throw the scales [of justice] out of balance," and influence the eventual out-come.[19] Seeking to limit this effect, the

---

[15] The 1999 ABA "Perceptions of the US Justice System" study, *supra* n. 5, reported that only one-third of respondents felt very strong or strong confidence in judges. This did not apply to the Supreme Court, in which 50 percent of respondents reported strong confidence.

[16] This is consistent with research demonstrating that non-evidentiary information can sensitize jurors to evidence or testimony elicited at trial. *See* Kovera, Gresham, Borgida, Gray, and Regan, *Does Expert Psychological Testimony Inform or Influence Juror Decision Making? A Social Cognitive Analysis,* 82 J. APPLIED PSYCH. 178–80 (1997).

[17] People v. Jamieson, 47 N.Y.2d 882, 883–84 (1979).

[18] Turner v. Louisiana, 379 U.S. 466, 472 (1965) (juries are "extremely likely to be impregnated by the environing atmosphere").

[19] People v. Bell, 38 N.Y.2d 116, 120 (1975).

law cautions that the power of the judge must "be exercised sparingly, without partiality, bias, or hostility … ."[20]

Courts have reversed criminal convictions where the running commentary of one judge mimicked that of syndi-court[21] or where the judge engaged in prolonged questioning.[22] Such questioning, even without an inappropriate or obviously disparaging tone, suggests to the jury that the court doubts the credibility of that particular witness, and deprives the accused of her constitutional right to a fair trial.

Furthermore, frequent viewers even believe that silence is meaningful, indicating the court's belief in one of the litigants. This is not surprising for, in syndi-court, activity and commentary is the norm. It appears that the only time the judge is silent (and not mugging disdain) is when the testimony or evidence is beyond reproach. Thus, silence is significant, equaling belief in one of the parties. Unfortunately, this inverts and misinterprets the accurate judicial standard of silence and neutrality.

Altering expectations of the legal system. Syndi-court also becomes an Emanuel for the procedure of trials and litigation of disputes. It creates in viewers expectations regarding legal rules and becomes a barometer against which all other judicial action is evaluated. When real courts fail to conform to these television expectations, the public, or at least frequent viewers, may become disillusioned with the justice system or lose respect for it.

For example, in syndi-court, the stories are easily digestible, the conflicts clear, and the resolutions swift. They promise instant legal gratification that real courts cannot. There are never breaks for in limine motions or hearings on admissibility. Thus, "the public is mystified when they see actual court cases taking so long to be decided. [It] wonders why judges and lawyers seem to encumber the process with so many unnecessary technicalities and criticizes them for it."[23] As judges fail to live up to their television personae, disputes drag on for more than 22 minutes, and decisions are not contemporaneous, confidence in the justice system is eroded.[24]

Syndi-court viewers may also reconceive how the law is supposed to function and what it is supposed to do. Syndi-court's themes of humiliation and moral reproach seep in and distort the public's context for personal and social judgments regarding the law. For instance, the president of the California Judges Association stated that sitting judges are reported to the commission or that some litigants are disappointed when they win the case but the judge has not humiliated their opponent.[25]

Syndi-court also idealizes the culmination of disputes. The payment of monetary awards and settling of grievances is quick and efficient. Winners always get their money and never need to embark on the arduous journey of enforcing settlements. Losers always appear, and never need to be brought to court through service of process or suffer default judgments.

Additionally, significant legal nuances are lost, leading to misunderstandings of burdens, presumptions of guilt, and evidentiary issues. The inherent and often contrived "dramatization" of syndi-court contributes to a lay tendency to embrace absolutes and dichotomies—black or white,

20 People v. Jamieson, 47 N.Y.2d at 883–84.

21 People v. De Jesus, 42 N.Y.2d 519, 520 (1977). There, the trial court responded to the testimony of an alibi witness by saying "It is not good enough … and you know better," and commented "Let's not be playing any games," "I don't need any help from you," and "Oh, come on.

22 This can suggest that the court is skeptical of the witness's testimony. People v. Carter, 40 N.Y.2d 933, 934 (1976).

23 Editorials, New Jersey Lawyer, March 27, 2000, at 6.

24 Sherwin, When Law Goes Pop, The Vanishing Line Between Law and Pop Culture 8 (2000).

25 Cox, Judicial Watchdog Agency Wants to Protect Public From TV "Judges," Fulton County Daily Report, June 9, 2000.

right or wrong, guilt or innocence—which retards their ability to comprehend subtle analyses. Viewers may conclude that the justice system obfuscates issues, denies justice, and that judges are complicit in this injustice.

A model for litigant behavior. Finally, with repeated viewing, viewers may begin to model their behavior to comport with what they have witnessed on syndi-court. Hence, Judge Judy tutors viewers to present their cases in a real court, be it the trial, mediation, or small claims level. Litigants might, therefore, alter their behavior when appearing in court, attempting to play out what they have repeatedly seen on TV.[26]

Frequent viewers may also be inclined to represent themselves pro se. After all, though they may not be lawyers, they've seen it all on TV. Syndi-court presents average people litigating their own disputes without the aid of a lawyer, almost half of whom win. Thus, viewers may come to believe that either pro se representation is not very difficult or that pro se representation still ensures a 50 percent likelihood of success. It may also cause viewers to believe that judges will assist them, as this is what occurs on television. Indeed, there is evidence suggesting this interaction between frequent viewing of syndi-court and litigant behavior. This, in turn, might contribute to litigiousness, as one impediment to bringing suit is the expense of retaining a lawyer.

Additionally, by bringing a courtroom into the homes of viewers, it might make the real courtroom seem more accessible, and, therefore, litigation a more viable option. Some citizens who have legitimate legal gripes will forgo assertion of their legal rights because they cannot afford an attorney or, where that complaint is appropriate for the no-lawyers-allowed forum of small claims court, or were afraid to represent themselves.

Thus, by demonstrating the nature of disputes appropriate for and litigant preparedness of syndi-court, courtroom-shy litigants may increase their comfort level with the small claims court. Though this might produce a benefit of providing access to some who may have otherwise foregone enforcement of their rights, it might produce litigiousness in others. By showcasing all nature of disputes, however menial, as worthy of court action, syndi-court might promote litigiousness in American society.

Proposals

As with other attempts to connect television imagery with viewer behavior, this study cannot identify causation. The results may prove that frequent viewing of syndi-court teaches or cultivates in viewers a particular view of judges, or merely report that people who already hold such views are frequent viewers of such TV fare. Results may also speak to socio-economic status: a particular group of people may seek out these shows or may be the ones who are at home during the day and early evening to watch them.

Nevertheless, causation aside, the study demonstrates that a significant number of jurors walk into the courthouse with syndi-court experience. Indeed, a majority are frequent viewers. Furthermore, these frequent viewers possess a number of beliefs about judges and the justice system that, in many ways, are contrary to reality. And, regardless of how those beliefs were formed, they may improperly impact the delivery of justice and perceptions of the bench. Accordingly, court administrators, advocates, and judges should implement corrective actions to

---

[26] An assistant court executive in California related an exchange with one pro se litigant who explained that he and his wife obtained all of their information about the courts from watching Judge Judy. Carter, *Self-Help Speeds Up*, 87 ABA J. 34 (July 2001).

these potential influences. This is particularly warranted, since there is no evidence that prior court experience, such as jury service or being a witness or litigant, immunizes viewers against the effects of syndi-court.

Correcting the misimpressions borne of syndi-court and displacing them with the appropriate manner and etiquette of the courtroom should begin as soon as potential jurors enter the courthouse. Though all vicinages order jury duty differently, all share one thing: at some point, all prospective jurors sit in a room and wait. This is an opportunity to orient prospective jurors to the correct process and gently address the juxtaposition of syndi-court.

One method is a short (5–7 minute) video played on a constant loop in the juror "waiting room." In addition to explaining the basics of jury service, this information should also include reference to syndi-court, explaining that syndi-court's representation of judges is "dramatized" for effect, and that the judges that jurors will encounter in the courtroom will not and should not act like those on TV. It might also include video snippets of real trials with real judges in action—or, rather, inaction—with a voice over noting the differences. Many courthouses already have juror orientation programs in place; adding syndi-court cautions is relatively simple.

Attorneys might address the imagery of syndi-court through either instructive or investigative voir dire much like voir diring prospective jurors on any pertinent issue in the news, bias, or propensity toward police testimony. Counsel might ask the panel neutral questions pertaining to familiarity with, viewing habits of, and preference of judges on syndi-court. She can then shift to a more instructive tone, posing a series of leading questions designed to impart that syndi-court judges are not real, their behavior is uncommon, that judges typically are not to ask questions, that a judge who is quiet is not a judge who agrees, and even that the procedure or burdens (and testimony) will be different.

In conjunction with a voir dire strategy, counsel should request an instruction regarding syndi-court or an enhanced instruction that the jury is not to look to the court for an opinion regarding the outcome of the case. This will be more or less important depending on the personality of the court or whether it has been particularly quiet or talkative in response to certain aspects of the trial.

Regardless of counsel's actions, a court should also take precautions by instructing the jury. For example, when the slate of prospective jurors is first brought into the courtroom, as well as when the preliminary instructions are delivered to the impaneled jury, the court could simply explain to jurors that what they may have seen on syndi-court is incorrect, that judges are not to speak, that the court truly has no opinion, and that jurors are not to assume, look for clues to, or infer the existence of one. It is important to address these perceptions as soon as possible, otherwise a bias borne of syndi-court might take root that will be difficult to later remedy.

A similar instruction should be repeated in the main charge. Although final charges typically instruct that the judge has no opinion, where frequent viewers imbue the inactive behavior of "no opinion" with meaning, such an instruction remains impotent against the syndi-court effect: where juror pre-conceptions about the law differ from what judges state in their instructions, jurors are more likely to follow the instructions if the judges explicitly address the preconceptions, explaining how the law differs. Consequently, the naked "no bias, no opinion" instruction will likely be an ineffective remedy in contrast to an explicit instruction referring to syndi-court.

The law has long been fictionalized on television, but recently the reality programming of syndi-court has gained significant popularity. For many citizens, syndi-court is their only connection with the justice system. Thus, its representations of judges and law become unopposed reality. Unfortunately, the reality of syndi-court often diverges from the reality of the justice system, and imparts in frequent viewers beliefs about judicial behavior and demeanor that are illegitimate and even damaging to the system. This study demonstrates that a majority of prospective jurors are "frequent viewers," and thus the potential for damage is significant. Consequently, the justice system should implement strategies to disabuse jurors of misperceptions borne of syndi-court.

SECTION FOUR SUMMARY

Key Discussion Sessions

1. What are the primary findings of Deutsch and Cavender's article "*CSI* and Forensic Realism"? Do you believe that the issues regarding the television show *CSI* covered in their article have an impact on the public's perceived understanding of the criminal justice system and forensic evidence in particular? If so, how and if not, why not? Some claim that there is a *CSI* effect, suggesting that the *CSI* show has impacted what jurors might expect in regard to evidence presented in a trial. Others argue that any change is an increased understanding of technology while some claim there has been no change in expectations. Which of these perspectives do you believe to be true, and what is your supporting evidence? Lastly, did *CSI* or other crime dramas impact your decision to major in criminal justice or criminology or to take a class in this area of study? If so, which shows? If you are from another country, what impact do you believe such depictions might have on international perceptions of the United States criminal justice system?

2. Both Ray Surette, in his article "Media, Echoes: Systemic Effects of News Coverage," and Kimberlianne Podias, in her article "Should We Blame *Judge Judy*? The Messages TV Courtrooms Send Viewers," address real world effects of media. Which of these effects do you believe would have a larger impact on the courts? Explain your answer and discuss if you believe race, socioeconomic status, and/or education level might play a role and why. If you are from another country, do you believe similar effects take place in your country? If so, can you give examples?

Public Consumption Exercises

Remember, the public consumption exercises in this text build upon each other. You must have completed the exercises in Sections 1, 2, and 3 to complete the current exercises.

Exercise 5: Blog Posts and Press Release Lengths

Now that you have experience with identifying the specific findings of articles and how to paraphrase in short paragraphs, it's time to expand discussions to the average size of a blog post and press release.

Article Choose the article from this section you believe would be of the most interest to the student body of your university or members of your organization given the demographic data you gathered on this group in Section 1. Indicate which article you chose and why you believe this to be the best article.

Findings Paragraphs and Writing Level Identify consecutive paragraphs (no less than three) from the findings or results section of the article that contain the largest portion of key findings and retype them in a word document; make sure the wording is exact. Follow the instructions in Appendix C to calculate the writing level of the paragraphs. Does the writing level match the average literacy level for your university or organization? If it is written at a higher level than the average, how many grade levels must the authors of the piece reduce the writing to be easily read by the students at your university or by members of your organization?

Bulleted Facts Utilizing the bulleted fact exercise from Section 2, create a set of bulleted facts from both the literature review (trends in previous research, historical facts, etc.) and the entire results or findings sections of the article.

Blog Post While the average length of a blog varies, for this text we are going to use a limit of 500–600 words. Follow the instructions in Appendix D and write a 500–600 word blog post about the facts you pulled from the literature review and research findings. Write the piece at the average literacy level of your university or organization. (For help with paraphrasing, see the following website or other similar sites: https://owl.english.purdue.edu/owl/resource/563/1/.)

Press Release Next, review the instructions for writing a press release in Appendix E. Remember, a press release should not exceed 200–300 words. Copy your blog post and paste it under the **Press Release** heading in your paper. Follow the press release instructions in Appendix E, and edit your piece down to less than 300 words while maintaining the key findings and necessary background information. Remember, it is okay to use bulleted statements in a press release. Write the piece at the average literacy level of your university or organization. (For help with paraphrasing, see the following website or other similar sites: https://owl.english.purdue.edu/owl/resource/563/1/.)

Corrections and Punishment

A CULTURAL APPROACH TO CRIME AND PUNISHMENT, BLUEGRASS STYLE

by Kenneth D. Tunnell
School of Justice Studies, Eastern Kentucky University

Introduction: A Brief History of Bluegrass Music

The roots of Southern American music can be found in the music of the English, Irish, and lowland Scots who migrated to North America in the eighteenth century. As some settled in Appalachia, and particularly in the Blue Ridge Mountains and Cumberland Gap, they brought with them, among other cultural attributes, songs that had been a part of their oral histories and traditions for centuries.[1] While some of these early mountain songs have been found outside the Appalachian region, that area, with its mountains and highlands, "acted as a giant cultural deep freeze, preserving these old songs and singing methods better than in other parts of the country"[2] In fact, the Appalachian region and its Euro-American residents remained isolated until after the Civil War, and as recently as 1916, in rural Tennessee and Kentucky, English ballads were still being sung much as they were when first brought there.[3] The long period of isolation combined with the eclectic cultural assimilation gave rise to a unique blend of musical styles that today is known as bluegrass music.[4]

As important as European cultures and their musical traditions were in shaping mountain or bluegrass music, other forces played a part. Since the South historically has been biracial, the predominant cultural influences on Southern music have been both Anglo-American and African American.[5] In the U.S., rural Southern blacks and whites, although segregated by law, shared a similar cultural milieu and exchanged cultural characteristics. Their ways of life, similar in that both races were rural, poor, often isolated, and dependent on agriculture, were reflections of their cultures and their social classes. As bluegrass music emerged from the union of these cultures, it was given shape by the dominant themes, values, and traditions specific to them.[6] Although bluegrass is Anglo, it also is blues—blues borrowed from African American culture and applied to the often mournful and lonesome folk ballads of Anglo-Americans' history.[7] Even the recognized "father of bluegrass" himself, Bill Monroe, recognizes the significance of African American music, saying, "Bluegrass music is a field holler, just like blues."

The commonly shared ways of life and social class among Appalachian mountain dwellers are important for understanding not only the early formative stages of bluegrass music but also its growing popularity. Just as European whites migrated to Appalachia during the eighteenth century, their descendants—poor. Southern whites—began their migration from the Appalachian region to the urban north during World War II and the years immediately following. And like their ancestors, these former Appalachians brought with them their cultural traits, including their music. As bluegrass music was removed from its insular setting and exposed for the first time to a wide variety of urban dwellers, it soon was embraced by many non-Southerners, largely because of its inherent Anglo and African American folk heritage and values expressed in song.[8] Such values arc represented in bluegrass songs that address various issues, lifestyles, and actual historical events detailed from the perspective of rural mountain dwellers. These values have emerged as the dominant themes in bluegrass lyrics—themes that address not only the importance of family, home, and loved ones, but those that speak to the dark side of life, to violent crime and punishment in the community.

As the industrial working class evolved into a multicultural work force during the 1940s and 1950s, bluegrass music was on its way toward becoming a nationally recognized musical form. And it was during this period that bluegrass experienced its first real "take-off," as newly formed groups began performing on various radio shows and as studios began, in earnest, recording and marketing various bluegrass bands. Today bluegrass music has emerged from its Appalachian isolation; but, although not as regionally based as it once was, it still is primarily a class-based genre, appealing to both the Southern and Northern industrial working class.[9]

The Bluegrass Sound

While bluegrass music is growing in sales and concert attractions, it is not a major component of the music industry. Its fans and followers are small in number, and its profits pale in comparison with those of mainstream country and pop music. Thus, some readers may be unfamiliar with bluegrass music, its sound, and its essential elements. Bluegrass has been defined as

> polyphonic vocal and instrumental music played on certain unamplified instruments based on music brought from the British Isles to Appalachian regions and refined by additions of negro and urban music. Vocal lead parts are rendered in the high-pitched style of traditional British balladry, with chorus harmonies added by a high tenor sung a third or fifth above the lead, and lower baritone and/or bass lines.[10]

Bluegrass is the sound that comes together with particular acoustic stringed instruments (namely, the fiddle, banjo, guitar, bass, mandolin, and occasionally dobro) and with a particular timing, pitch, and vocal arrangement. Before 1940 string-band music, later to be called bluegrass, was rough-hewn; but Bill Monroe added elements of both jazz and blues to the country or hillbilly string sound.[11] Although Monroe first appeared on the Grand Ole Opry in 1939, the essential elements of what later came to be defined as bluegrass did not come together until 1940 in Monroe's band as "sacred and secular, black and white, urban and rural, combined to form an altogether new strain of American music."[12]

An essential element of bluegrass music, the singing, has come to be called "the high lonesome sound" because the lead and especially the tenor parts are pitched rather high, giving the song, along with its typically sad lyrics, a haunting, mournful, and lonesome sound. Like the songs themselves, this high lonesome sound may be the product of a centuries-ago singing style rooted in the oldest form of Christian worship—the psalm song. The psalm song, now known as the long-meter hymn and found predominantly in African American churches, may be a forerunner to the high lonesome sound of bluegrass music.[13] Again we see evidence of African American cultural influences on the sound of this musical genre. Although bluegrass singers may be unaware of, and thus unable to articulate, the significance of this heritage to bluegrass music, Monroe, an instrumental architect of the high lonesome sound, credits black blues music for giving shape to the high lonesome singing style. Monroe himself has said, "I would sing kindly the way I felt. I've always liked the touch of the blues, you know, and I put some of that into my singing. I like to sing the way ii touches me."[14]

The union of black and white music is not unique to the bluegrass sound, for jazz shares characteristics of each musical form. But bluegrass, with its eclectic blend of blues, black-face minstrelsy, and Celtic musical forms, was transformed into something greater than the sum of its parts as it made its sojourn into Appalachia, was preserved there, and then, like some anomaly from the past, was spread throughout the country and into various parts of the world. Both the musical forms that gave bluegrass its shape and sound and the dominant themes found in the music, shaped by songs from the old world and songs from the new, transformed bluegrass into a uniquely appealing musical form.

Attention is now turned to the dominant themes found in bluegrass lyrics, with particular attention to the theme of violence.

Themes in Bluegrass Music

Today the words *bluegrass music* conjure up certain images in the minds of even mildly interested or informed listeners. Songs that inspire such images as mountain cabins (e.g., "Cabin Home on the Hill"), close-knit families ("Calling My Children Home"), loving mothers ("If I Could Hear My Mother Pray Again"), a God to fear ("God Who Never Fails"), highways ("Wreck on the Highway"), graveyards ("Snow Covered Mound"), wayfarers ("Wayfaring Stranger"), maidens ("Georgia Rose"), rogues ("Roving Gambler"), and longing for a home that is no longer there ("Mother No Longer Awaits Me at Home") exemplify dominant themes in bluegrass music. Bluegrass songs are ripe with visions of an "idyllic world to which the singer either longs to return or expresses his intention to return."[15] The singer typically represents one in exile who "can't go home again," and one who experiences the "contrast of memory and experience" (e.g., "The Old Home Place").[16]

Still other dominant themes in bluegrass include unrequited love (e.g., "Sweet Thing" and "Old Love Letters"), the deceit of urban women ("Girl in the Blue Velvet Band"), being orphaned in the city, ("I Was Left on the Street"), one's own impending death ("The River of Death"), the death of a loved one ("No Mother or Dad"), the love between parent and child ("Little Girl and the Dreadful Snake"), and the belief in an eternal life where loved ones shall never part ("Heaven" and "How Beautiful Heaven Must Be").[17]

Many of these songs aggrandize home, spiritual life, family values, and home-spun tradition (e.g., "Where No Cabins Fall" and "I'm on My Way Back to the Old Home"), while some bemoan their disintegration ("If I Had My Life to Live Over," "The Old Home Town," and "Georgia Mules and Country Boys"). Such themes-in-song were openly accepted and loved by rural mountain whites and later (immediately following World War II) by those Appalachian whites who migrated north in search of employment and a better way of life than they could expect by remaining in Appalachia.[18]

Given such dominant themes, bluegrass performers and aficionados contentedly claim that bluegrass music is clean family music representing wholesome themes—unlike those found in more widely accepted mainstream country' music (themes such as infidelity, drinking, gambling, and divorce). Bluegrass performers take pride in offering clean, family entertainment, not only in their recorded music but also in their live performances. Some performers, for example, proudly claim that they play for the entire family and refuse to play where alcohol is served. Likewise, nearly all bluegrass festivals prohibit the audience from possessing and consuming alcoholic beverages.[19] Although a strong argument could be made that bluegrass music *is* to a large extent "wholesome," little is said about those themes that are neither wholesome nor family-oriented, and less is said about the oft-found violence in bluegrass music.

An Analysis of Bluegrass Murder Ballads

To understand violence found in bluegrass songs, I conducted a lyric analysis of bluegrass murder ballads. The base of bluegrass songs from which a sample could be drawn is voluminous. Yet the base of bluegrass murder songs is actually few in number, and as a result, sampling for this study was not necessary. Rather, I attempted to analyze the entire known universe of bluegrass murder ballads. Although few in number, these songs are essential elements to a bluegrass repertoire, not necessarily because murder songs are being written and recorded by bluegrass performers, but because they are still performed by both old-time and contemporary bluegrass bands at countless live bluegrass shows and festivals.

Because there is no universal list of murder ballads, I was left to my own devices to discover those songs representing units of analysis for this study. I used a variety of somewhat unconventional methods to compile a list of bluegrass murder ballads. First, I perused bluegrass song books, thematic books on bluegrass, and discographies that listed murder ballads.[20] Second, I questioned two long-time bluegrass fans and music collectors about such songs and also contacted two disc jockeys who host weekly bluegrass radio programs. From these four well- informed individuals, I learned of murder ballads that I could not have otherwise known. Third, I visited three record stores that specialize in marketing country and bluegrass recordings. From these visits I not only perused bluegrass recordings but informally learned of murder ballads by conversing with the shopkeepers. Fourth, I relied on my own personal knowledge, experiences, expertise, and bluegrass record collection. From these various sources of information, I discovered fifteen songs that give accounts of murder. The murders-in-song were then analyzed, revealing a disturbing latent content among the dominant themes.

Three distinct patterns emerged from this analysis. First, in almost every case, the murder occurs between acquaintances and nearly always involves a man killing a woman. Second, the woman's death is nearly always a violent one, with her body cruelly disposed of. Third, the murders depicted in song are characterized by either a lack of explanation for the violent acts or an explanation based on the man's jealousy and desire to possess the woman. And, as will be discussed subsequently, these lyrical patterns can in turn be contextualized within broader social, historical, and cultural explanations. These themes of violence in bluegrass music, and their larger context, are explicated in the remainder of this chapter.

Crime of Murder—Punishment of Death

The most popular British-derived murder ballad, "Pretty Polly" (c. 1750), originally known as "The Gosport Tragedy" and a mainstay among bluegrass songs, allegedly is based on a true story of a premeditated murder. In the song Polly discovers she is pregnant, and the child's father, her lover, kills her next to a grave that he had earlier prepared for her interment. Although there are several versions of the song, the most popular American version, oddly enough, focuses only on the murder and omits any mention of a courtship, seduction, and pregnancy:[21]

Oh Polly, pretty Polly, come go along with me
Polly, pretty Polly, come go along with me
Before vve get married some pleasures to see.

He rode her over hills and valleys so deep
He rode her over hills and valleys so deep
Pretty Polly mistrusted and then began to weep.

Oh Willie, oh Willie, I'm afraid of your ways
Willie, oh Willie, I'm afraid of your ways
The way you've been acting, you'll lead me astray.

Oh Polly, pretty Polly, your guess is about right
Polly, pretty Polly, your guess is about right
I dug on your grave the best part of last night.

She knelt down before him, pleading for her life
She knelt down before him, pleading for her life
Please let me be a single girl if I can't be your wife.

He stabbed her in the heart and her heart's blood did flow
He stabbed her in the heart and her heart's blood did flow
And into the grave pretty Polly did go.

He went to the jailhouse and what did he say
He went to the jailhouse and what did he say
I killed pretty Polly and tried to get away.

Oh gentlemen and ladies, I bid you farewell
Gentlemen and ladies, I bid you farewell
For killing pretty Polly my soul will go to hell.

From the song, we learn that this murder obviously occurred between acquaintances, with the man killing the woman. The punishment for such an act of premeditated murder is death. But the punishment is farther-reaching in its consequences than simply a formal punishment of death; for in this case, Willie anticipates a never- ending punishment as his soul spends eternity in hell. Just as he can do nothing to change Polly's demise, he can do nothing to change his own fate. The logic of this message is causal—Willie killed Polly, thus he will die and his soul forever suffer. This represents a simple yet punitive ideology about misdeeds—one based on "an eye for an eye"—which mandates that Willie's life too should perish.

While the background facts of the case reveal the historical ins and outs, they are impossible to learn simply from the song. This component of violence in bluegrass songs is troubling, for while murder ballads in bluegrass music more than likely are based on true stories, often little is learned about the characters and their relationships from the songs themselves. The violence toward women in bluegrass songs has been recognized by others who make the claim that the most common motif in murder ballads is one where the woman becomes pregnant, is stabbed by her lover, and is promptly thrown into a river.[22] While it is true from these songs of murder that the most common motif is one where the woman's lover kills her and throws her into a river, it is *not* clear that pregnancy or immorality has anything to do with the murders in most of these songs.

"Down in the Willow Garden" (also known as "Rose Connally"), a murder ballad that may have descended from Ireland, again illustrates how the woman is killed by her lover. Three possible explanations emerge for this murder: the act may have been a desperate attempt to avoid marriage; the murderer may have anticipated monetary rewards as a result of her death; or the murderer may have felt compelled, based on his own father's prodding, to do the killing. The crime and ensuing punishment are described in the first person by the slayer.

> Down in the willow garden
> My love and I did meet,
> And there we sat a-courting
> My love dropped off to sleep.
>
> I had a bottle of burgundy wine
> My young love did not know,
> And there I poisoned that dear little girl
> Down by the banks below.
>
> I stabbed her with a dagger
> Which was a bloody knife,
> I threw her in the river
> Which was a dreadful sight.
>
> My father had always told me
> That money would set me free
> If I would murder that sweet little miss
> Whose name was Rose Connally.
>
> He's sitting now by his cabin door
> A-wiping his tear-dimmed eyes.
> He's mourning for his own dear son
> Who walks to the scaffold high.

My race is run beneath the sun.
The devil is waiting for me.
For I did murder that dear little miss
Whose name was Rose Connally.

From these lyrics wc learn, as in "Pretty Polly," that the woman is killed by her lover. Her lover's punishment is death, as he and the scaffold confront one another. The most severe formal punishment that the state can impose is accompanied by informal sanctions—both his own guilt and recognition that his father is deeply troubled by his crime and impending death. He is overcome by the realization that he has ended a life and caused his father immense pain and suffering. While the slayer anticipates the most severe formal punishment, he also realizes clearly what grave consequences befall his family as a result of his own actions.

Again this depiction of violent murder in bluegrass songs reveals little about the characters and their connections and even less of what might explain why one punishment is imposed over another. Although capital punishment is described in bluegrass songs, just as often, the killer is punished by being confined to prison for a number of years.

Crime of Murder—Punishment of Imprisonment

No doubt, the majority of murder ballads are characterized by some form of man killing woman. One such song that does incorporate the depiction of a man murdering his pregnant lover is "Omic Wise," based on a true story and named for the victim, Omie, who is pregnant with the killer's child. He deceives her into believing that he will marry and care for her, when his real intention is to murder her in order to harbor the secret of their illegitimate child:

Oh listen to my story I'll tell you no lies
How John Louis did murder poor little Omie Wise.
He told her to meet him at Adam's Spring
He promised her money and other fine things.
So fool like she met him at Adam's Spring
No money he brought her nor other fine things.

"Go with me little Omie and away we will go
We'll go and get married and no one will know."
She climbed up behind him and away they did go
But away to the river where deep waters flow
"John Louis John Louis will you tell me your mind
Do you intend to marry me or leave me behind?"
"Little Omie little Omie I'll tell you my mind
My mind is to drown you and leave you behind."

"Have mercy on my baby and spare me my life
I'll go home as a beggar and never be your wife."
He kissed her and hugged her and turned her around

Then pushed her in deep waters where he knew she would drown.
He got on his pony and away he did ride
As the screams of Little Omie went down by his side.

Two boys went a fishing one fine summer day
And saw little Omie's body go floating away.
They threw their net around her and drew her to the bank
Her clothes all wet and muddy they laid her on a plank.
Then sent for John Louis to come to that place
And brought her out before him so that he might see her face.
He made no confession but they carried him to jail
No friends nor relations would go on his bail.

Although the punishment for this particular act is unclear (an anomaly in bluegrass crime ballads), we do learn from the song that John Louis is taken to jail. Furthermore, this crime clearly shocked and outraged the community. His family and friends were perhaps outraged and ashamed to the extent that they refused to bail him out of jail. In other bluegrass songs we sometimes learn that the jailed criminal has no friends or relations in a particular town. But in this song, Louis has both; they simply refuse to come to his aid. Today in rural Appalachia (where Omie Wise was murdered), murderers are often left in jail awaiting trial because their family and friends refuse to help them when all evidence points to their guilt. Families are disappointed and ashamed of such violent actions and of the "bad name" with which they are socially labeled because of a single family member's misdeeds.[25] This song, unlike others, is narrated in the third person, as a story of oral tradition where this awful deed, no doubt, has been recounted time and time again.

Still other songs are mysteries that offer no explanation for the murder. For example, "Little Sadie" begins with the woman's murder but then turns to the killer's flight, capture, trial, and punishment and well illustrates the absence of any explanation for Sadie's death. Unlike those songs mentioned earlier, here the penalty is not death, but a prison sentence of forty-one years and forty-one days. It also is interesting, and somewhat unusual for this genre, that in this song, the killer, who narrates the story line, confesses to his crime:

I went out last night for to make a little round
I met Little Sadie and shot her down
Went back home, got into bed
44 pistol under my head.

Woke up the next morning at half-past nine
The hacks and the buggies all standing in line
Gents and gamblers gathered round
To carry Little Sadie to the burying ground.

Well I began to think of what a deed I'd done
Grabbed my hat and away I run
I made a good run but a little too slow
They overtook me in Jericho.

I was standing on the corner reading the bill
When up stepped the sheriff from Thomasville
Said, "Young man ain't your name Brown
Remember the night you shot Sadie down?"

I said, "Yes sir but my name is Lee
I shot little Sadie in the first degree
First degree and second degree
If you got any papers won't you read 'em to me."

Well they took me downtown and dressed me in black
And put me on the train and started me back
All the way back to that Thomasville jail
And I had no money for to go my bail.

The judge and the jury took the stand
The judge held the papers in his right hand
41 days and 41 nights
41 years to wear the ball and stripes.

This song is typical of murder ballads in bluegrass music, except that the punishment is not "an eye for an eye," but time in prison for taking the life of Sadie. No explanation is offered for either Sadie's murder or the imposition of this punishment rather than death.

Another song with similar victim-victimizer relationships is "Poor Ellen Smith," a ballad allegedly composed by the murderer, Peter DeGraff, who was convicted of killing Ellen Smith in Winston-Salem, North Carolina, in August 1893.[24] While no explanation is offered for the murder, this particular song is unusual, for there is a sexual component to the crime that does not appear in other songs. Apparently, Ellen was sexually assaulted. The killer, who narrates the story in song, is apprehended by a posse, convicted by a jury, and serves twenty years in prison. While his punishment is less than that of Little Sadie's killer, it has other dimensions than simply time in prison. We learn that his punishment is also an informal one, for he suffers immense guilt for his act.

Poor Ellen Smith, how she was found
Shot through the heart, lying cold on the ground.
Her clothes were all scattered and thrown on the ground
And blood marks the spot where poor Ellen was found.

They picked up their rifles and hunted me down
And found me a-loafing around in the town.
They picked up her body and carried it away
And now she is sleeping in some lonesome old grave.

I got a letter yesterday and I read it today
The flowers on her grave have all faded away.

Some day I'll go home and say when I go
On poor Ellen's grave pretty flowers I'll sow.

I've been in this prison for twenty long years
Each night I see Ellen through my bitter tears.
The warden just told me that soon I'll be free
To go to her grave near that old willow tree.

My days in this prison are ending at last
I'll never be free from the sins of my past.
Poor Ellen Smith, how she was found
Shot through the heart, lying cold on the ground.

Perhaps one of the most graphically violent bluegrass songs of man killing woman was brought to this country by English settlers. In England it appeared as "The Wittam Miller" and "The Berkshire Tragedy," and in America as "The Oxford Girl," "The Bristol Girl," "The Wexford Girl," "The Lexington Girl," and most recently as "The Knoxville Girl." The man's desire to possess "his" woman appears to be the explanatory dimension of this crime. It appears that Willie did not completely possess the Knoxville girl's attention, for she, according to the murderer, had "roving eyes." The killer, who sings the song, is apprehended and sentenced to life in prison. He, like the murderer of Ellen Smith, reports suffering enormous guilt because of killing the woman he loved:

I met a little girl in Knoxville,
A town we all know well,
And every Sunday evening
Out in her home I'd dwell,
We went to take an evening walk
About a mile from town,
I picked a stick up off the ground
And knocked that fair girl down.

She fell down on her bended knees,
For mercy she did cry,
"Oh Willie, dear, don't kill me here,
I'm unprepared to die."
She never spoke one other word,
I only beat her more,
Until the ground around me
With her blood did flow.

I took her by her golden curls,
I dragged her round and round,
Throwing her in the river
That flows through Knoxville town,
Go down, go down, you Knoxville girl

With the dark and roving eyes,
Go down, go down, you Knoxville girl,
You can never be my bride.

I went back to Knoxville,
Got there about midnight,
My mother she was worried,
And woke up in a fright.
Saying, "Son, oh Son, what have you done
To bloody your clothes so?"
I told my anxious mother
I was bleeding at my nose.

I called for me a candle
To light my way to bed
I called for me a handkerchief
To bind my aching head.
I rolled and tumbled the whole night through
As trouble was for me
Like flames of hell around my bed
And in my eyes could see.

They carried me down to Knoxville,
They put me in a cell
My friends all tried to get me out
But none could go my bail.
I'm here to waste my life away
Down in this dirty old jail
Because I murdered that Knoxville girl,
The girl I loved so well.

In the following song, "99 Years and One Dark Day," the killer tells his tale of killing "his woman" and now spends his time laboring in prison. In this song, no reason is given for his slaying of his woman, and no reason for his receiving this particular punishment over another.

I've been in this prison 20 years or more
Shot my woman with a 44,
I'll be right here till my dying day
I got 99 years and one dark day.

Well the free days pass and the beds are hard
I spend all day breaking rocks in the yard,
Well there ain't no change it's gonna stay that way
I got 99 years and one dark day.

Ain't no singer can sing this song
To convince this warden that I ain't wrong,
It's my fate it's gonna stay that way
I got 99 years and one dark day.

Didn't learn to read I never learned to write
My whole life has been one big fight,
I never heard about the righteous way
I got 99 years and one dark day.

I committed a crime many years ago
Shot my woman with a 44,
I'll be right here till my dying day
I got 99 years and one dark day.

The murder of a woman by a man in some bluegrass songs is intertwined with love and marriage plans. Although the motive is still unclear, marriage does seem to have something to do with the murder in some of these songs. "Banks of the Ohio," one of the most popular folk-bluegrass songs, illustrates this theme in murder ballads:

I asked my love to take a walk
Just a walk a little way,
As we walked along we talked
All about our wedding day.

And only say that you'll be mine
And our home will happy be
Down beside where the waters ilow
On the banks of the Ohio.

I held a knife close to her breast
As into my arms she pressed,
She cried, "Oh, Willie dear, don't murder me.
I'm not prepared for eternity."

I took her by her lily white hand
Led her down where the waters stand,
There I pushed her in to drown
And watched her as she floated down.

I started home, 'tween twelve and one
Thinking of the deed I'd done
I killed the girl I love you see
Because she would not marry me

The very next day, bout half past four
Sheriff Smith knocked on my door
He said, "Young man, come now and go
Down to the banks of the Ohio."

The man's jealousy and his desire to possess "his" woman explain still other murders found in bluegrass music. For example, "Little Glass of Wine," a once very popular bluegrass song, tells the story of how a jealous lover poisons his Molly. Marriage is a part of this song and part of the explanation for the crime. It appears that Willie wanted to get married, Molly did not, and Willie resolved that if he could not have her, nobody would. The following is a portion of the song:

Come little girl let's go get married
My love is so great how' can you slight me,
I'll work for you both late and early
And at our wedding my little wife you'll be.

Oh, Willie dear, let's both consider
We're both too young to be married now,
When we're married, we're bound together
Let's stay single just one more year.

He went to the bar where she was dancing
A jealous thought came to his mind,
I'll kill that girl, my own true lover
'Fore I let another man beat my lime.

He went to the bar and he called her to him
She said, "Willie dear, what you want with me?"
"Come and drink wine with the one that loves you
More than anyone else you know," said he.

While they were at the bar a-drinking
That same old thought came to his mind,
He killed that girl, his own true lover
He gave her poison in a glass of wine.

As earlier researchers have observed, punishment for capital crimes varies considerably among a few explanatory variables (with the exception of race, which is not relevant here).[25] As in reality, the punishments in song also vary, as some murderers receive sentences of death and others sentences of life or a few years less. Although it is difficult to account for the use of prison as punishment in lieu of death, interestingly, the prison sentences are rather lengthy, ranging from twenty to ninety-nine years. This may indicate that judicial responses to these crimes, perhaps some of the most senselessly violent of their era, disallowed plea bargaining a murder charge to a less serious charge. But beyond this, what broader social and cultural patterns account for the presence of these violent crimes in bluegrass music?

Violent Crime in Bluegrass Music: A Cultural Explanation

Although songs that describe property crimes (e.g., "I Just Got Tired of Being Poor"), outlaws as heroes ("Pretty Boy Floyd" and "Jesse James"), women killing men ("Barbara Allen"), the confining life of prison ("Sad Prisoner's Lament," "Old Richmond Prison," and "Doing My Time"), murder as revenge ("Hills of Roane County"), crimes of disorderly conduct ("Six Months Ain't Long"), and even victimless crimes ("In the Jailhouse Now") emerge in bluegrass lyrics, the violent crime of man killing woman dominates crime stories found among bluegrass songs.

Though firmly entrenched in the culture of the old world, the genre of these songs has evolved into a truly American phenomenon. As art imitates life, we are left to wonder what factors might explain the emergence and persistence of such violent songs—songs that relate stories of specific violent acts and that often reflect violence in the broader society. These songs, their emergence and historical persistence, can be situated within at least four larger explanations: (1) as a result of oral tradition and communication, (2) as representative of the functions that crime has served and continues to serve in American society, (3) as a reflection of a subculture of violence, and (4) as an indication of historically held punishment ideologies for capital murder.

First, these songs of murder and punishment often represent historical facts, or some version of history, that individuals put to music. The violent acts depicted in these songs were no doubt shocking to the rural mountainous community and represented actions that could not go untold. To both communicate and preserve these stories, they were put into song form, passed on to others in the community, and passed down through the years, becoming a part of oral tradition and what we now call bluegrass music. These songs of violent crime and punishment became a part of the history of the region immediately affected by such violent acts and reflected, for the most part, actual historical incidents preserved in song form. Early in the history of these songs, the telling and singing of acts of violence were modes of communicating what was of interest to nearly everyone—shockingly violent crime. Later, with mass communication and the recording and marketing of these songs, they continued to be popular, as these stories of violence fell on new ears. Today these songs certainly are not recorded by bluegrass bands as often as they once were, but they remain fundamentally important to many a bluegrass band's repertoire and can be heard at nearly every live bluegrass show. Thus, within the rhythms of oral history and tradition, we today hear stories of violent crimes and subsequent punishments that have survived 100 years or more.

Second, these songs can be explained, in part, by the function that crime served at the time of the songs' inception and by the function that crime continues to serve. Americans' interest in crime may be functional, serving to reinforce conduct norms.[26] Social theorists have commented that Americans (among other societies) need crime to wonder about, to be shocked about, to reinforce socially approved norms and values, and to gaze in awe and disdain at the criminal who does what most cannot and would not do.[27] Americans historically have made folk heroes of criminals; today, in the midst of a growing crime-control industry, crime stories fill the daily newspapers, the nightly news, top-selling magazines, political rhetoric, and everyday conversation, as Americans consume crime, crime stories, and crime-related commodities.[28] Violent crimes such as those described here certainly are not desired by the community. However, as they occur, the subtle differences between normal and abnormal behavior become more clearly delineated within the shocked community. The parameters of official behavior, marked sharply by the shockingly violent behavior occurring beyond moral boundaries, arc symbolically strengthened as the community shares its mutually held values and standards for normative behavior. These songs of violent crime and punishment act to further bolster conduct norms and consensual forms of punishment.

The third potential explanation, and perhaps the most telling, is subcultural. Although the South and Appalachia have received the attention of social scientists, the subculture of violence has only recently been alluded to. These songs certainly fit within what we know about that culture and its historical levels of violence. From the various attempts at understanding this phenomenon, both the attributes of a subculture and individuals' integration into it have emerged as potentially useful components of an explanation. Earlier researchers, focusing on subcultural explanations for aggregate murder rates, found that

> the highest rates of homicide occur, among a relatively homogeneous subcultural group ... . Similar prevalent rates can be found in some rural areas. The value system of this group, we are contending, constitutes a subculture of violence. [T]he greater the degree of integration of the individual into this subculture, the higher the probability that his behavior will be violent in a variety of situations.[29]

These statements suggest that such a proclivity toward violence in rural areas may be explained by the cultural acceptance and reproduction of such behavior. Thus, for the fairly homogeneous and well-isolated rural area of Appalachia, such an explanation for a subculture with a wide acceptance of violence seems likely.

Violent behavior is explained not only by cultural differences but by social class. Research shows that lower-class young boys are more likely to be socialized into relying on direct expressions of aggression than middle-class young boys. This finding is related to, among other things, the types of punishment meted out by parents of different social classes and the various roles and responsibilities of fathers among different social classes. As compared to middle-class mothers, lower-class mothers report that their children are more likely to be struck, and the fathers in lower-class households often play a less-important role in the family than fathers in middle-class households.[50] As youngsters become integrated into a culture where violence is considered a viable option, violence as a way of resolving life's matters becomes socially reproduced.

These dimensions of both culture and social class are analytically useful when applied to Appalachia. The South, and especially Appalachia, not only has its own unique subcultural values but historically has been a very depressed area where poverty and disease have run rampant, while educational, occupational, and financial opportunities have been limited. The distribution of social classes in Appalachia, where many of these songs originated and are still revered, is clearly skewed toward the lower class.

The South, some historians posit, has been addicted to violence at nearly every level in society since long before the Civil War.[31] Violence in the name of one's honor has been considered acceptable behavior in Southern culture. From such a culture, Appalachians, especially men, who have relied on a "frontier" mentality have developed an ideology of independence.[32] The tendency for violence became a part of the Southerner's frontier existence and development. The Southern character, and especially the Appalachian, was (and is) entrenched with individualism and back-country pride. Throughout history, and even today, the Southerner "would knock hell out of whoever dared to cross him."[33] As a result Appalachian men have independently handled their own affairs, taken the law into their own hands, refrained from meddling in other people's business, and disciplined their children and their women however they saw fit, with full knowledge that their neighbors did not dare interfere. After all, in the cultural history of Appalachia, such behavior has been considered normal rather than deviant. It may well be that as eighteenth-century culture, stories, and songs were preserved in the southern Appalachian area, so were primitive attitudes about discipline, gender, and violence.

As part of conquering their environment with both frontier independence and machismo, Appalachian men have developed an attitude of dominance over women and have expected women to be subservient. In Appalachia clearly delineated and articulated gender differences have been imposed on youngsters early in life. Clear gender roles (e.g., the man as ruler of the household) have been reinforced and socially reproduced in the isolated area of Appalachia, where such ideologies were preserved as they went undisturbed by more enlightened outside forces.[34]

This frontier mentality and dominance over women are exemplified among themes found in Southern literature and bluegrass music—music that is almost entirely dominated by men.[35] Such themes have the latent effect, at least, of terrorizing women, further subjugating them, making them more dependent on males, threatening them by suggesting that murder is a viable alternative within interpersonal relationships, and propagating the independence of the Appalachian male. Art, after all, intertwines with life, and bluegrass music reproduces, among other things, the dark and violent side of Appalachian mountain life.

Beyond these social explanations, the crimes and punishments described in song reflect something of the historical period in which they were conceived. They certainly reflect the singing styles and traditions of centuries ago. But just as important, they inform us of the then-held ideologies on punishment for capital crimes—ideologies that, just as today, vary on the fundamental issues of capital punishment as retribution, capital punishment and imprisonment as deterrence, and incapacitation policies.

Retribution, as ideology, places the state in the role of executioner, to do what the victim's immediate family wants to do and wants to have done—to take the life of the one who takes. Although retribution in the form of state-sanctioned capital punishment offers a social response rather than a familial one, the response is the same—social vengeance, which is evident in many of these bluegrass murder ballads.

Deterrence ideologies are also present in these songs. When the murderer narrates the story of his crime and punishment, whether it be his own impending death or years in confinement, he does so to warn others of the terrible consequences for such behavior. The murderer's telling the story of his deed and his doom is a powerful medium, for through a dark tale we learn of the emotions of both the victim and the victimizes. We learn of the act itself and, just as important, of the killer's capture and punishment. His telling of the story serves as a warning as much as a story—a warning to avoid similar misfortunes. His punishment and words of insight are designed to affect society. In other words, the social hope is that his punishment deters at least some future violence. A punishment of death has other powerful implications for the community. Death is a symbolic punishment and the murderer a symbolic common enemy. His death punishment reaffirms conduct norms that were violated and also, ideally, sends a warning to others.

Support for incapacitation as punishment is evident in some of these songs where retribution in life is not levied, but rather a lengthy prison sentence is designed to isolate the murderer from the community. This policy undoubtedly represents a more progressive response to capital murder than a penalty of death. This shift in punishment types, reflected in song, may indicate fluctuating support for capital punishment. As public support for death as punishment waned and as lengthy prison sentences rather than death were meted out, murder ballads reflected those broader social changes.

These murder ballads reveal the historical culture of their inception. They tell stories of violent, senseless crimes that no doubt shocked communities, angered residents, and all but destroyed victims' families. They indicate some of the details of the murders, some of the reasons for the violence, and often some sense of the killer's capture or escape. But as with any good story, they also often end with a moral—a moral that serves as closure for the song and as important instruction about acceptable behavior and the consequences of deviance and crime.

Notes

This chapter is a revision of two of the author's previous publications and is reprinted here by permission: "Blood Marks the Spot Where Poor Ellen Was Found: Violent Crime in Bluegrass Music," *Popular Music and Society* 15 (1991): 95–115; "99 Years is Almost for Life: Punishment for Violent Crime in Bluegrass Music," *Journal of Popular Culture* 26 (1992): 165–81.

1. Bob Artis, *Bluegrass* (New York: Hawthorn Books, 1975); Steven D. Price, *Old as the Hills: The Story of Bluegrass Music* (New York: Viking Press, 1975). The Blue Ridge Mountains, the eastern range of the Appalachian Mountains, extend from southern Pennsylvania to northern Georgia; they constituted a formidable barrier during western migration. The Cumberland Gap is a natural passage through the Cumberland Mountains near where Virginia, Kentucky, and Tennessee meet; this passage served as Daniel Boone's Wilderness Road. Today, as then, subsistence farming is readily found throughout that area.

2. Charles Wolfe, *Kentucky Country: Folk and Country Music of Kentucky* (Lexington: University Press of Kentucky, 1982), 5.

3. Charles Wolfe, *Tennessee Strings* (Knoxville: University of Tennessee Press, 1977). The Appalachian region commonly includes the hilly and mountainous areas of ten states: Kentucky, Tennessee, Georgia, Alabama, North Carolina, South Carolina, Virginia, West Virginia, Ohio, and Maryland.

4. Fred Hill, *Grass Roots: Illustrated History of Bluegrass and Mountain Music* (Rutland, VT: Academy Books, 1980); Bill C. Malone, *Southern Music. American Music* (Lexington: University Press of Kentucky, 1979). Although I use the term *bluegrass*, bluegrass music itself did not evolve as a distinct genre until about 1950. Before then mountain string or hillbilly music had been simply *country music*. There was no separate bluegrass music category until Bill Monroe and his Bluegrass Boys brought the elements and dynamics together into a new sound that we today, in respecting Monroe and his home state of Kentucky, call bluegrass music. For simplicity, I use the term *bluegrass* throughout this chapter.

5. Bill C. Malone, "Music," in *Encyclopedia of Southern Culture*, ed. Charles R. Wilson and William Ferris (Chapel Hill: University of North Carolina Press, 1989), 985–92.

6. Not only did the people of this region experience a cultural integration of music, stories, and themes, they also shared and exchanged musical instruments. The banjo, an essential element of bluegrass music today, is African in origin. And the guitar, an instrument that was introduced relatively late to the Appalachian region and is essential to bluegrass music, was first played with skillful finesse by African Americans.

7. Although black music (ragtime, blues, country blues, minstrelsy, spirituals, and jazz) in this country has enjoyed wide exposure since the mid-nineteenth century, white folk music was "discovered" relatively late in the history of traditional American music. In fact, hillbilly music was not discovered until 1916 and was first recorded in the 1920s. The two most famous discoverers of folk music—John A. Lomax and Cecil Sharp—made very significant contributions toward both popularizing and preserving Appalachian folk music (Malone, "Music"). While Lomax collected and profited from what he mistakenly believed were racially homogeneous white cowboy songs. Sharp, with his assistant Maud Karpeles, traveled through the states of Kentucky, Virginia, Tennessee, North Carolina, and West Virginia during the years 1916–1918. They often stayed with local mountain people and encouraged them to play and sing their songs. As they did, Sharp wrote musical notes for what he heard as Karpeles wrote the lyrics in shorthand. They collected hundreds of songs and found that many, as a result of generations of oral tradition, had numerous versions and were widely known within their narrow region of observation. They collected the bulk of their material in the region between Tennessee and North Carolina, for, according to Sharp and Karpeles, it "was in this region that the most primitive conditions prevailed." As a result of their research and discovery, they published a book of 274 songs with 968 tunes. Later, Francis Child did likewise by publishing a multitude of English and Scottish ballads along with an analytical commentary of them. See Cecil Sharp and Maud Karpeles, *English Folk Songs from the Southern Appalachians* (London: Oxford University Press, 1932), xv; Francis J. Child, *The English and Scottish Popular Ballads*, Volume 5 (New York: Dover, 1965).

Still later, during the 1920s, the Okeh Recording Company sent Ralph Peer to locate mountain musicians to record. As Peer made his way into fairly isolated areas, he advertised in local newspapers for musicians. As pickers and singers came out of the mountains and hollows. Peer recorded them. The record company sold their records primarily to mountain dwellers, and country music experienced its first golden era during the years 1925–1935; see Artis, *Bluegrass*.

8. Neil V. Rosenberg, "Bluegrass," in *Encyclopedia of Southern Culture*, 993–94; Neil V. Rosenberg, *Bluegrass: A History* (Urbana: University of Illinois Press, 1985).

9. Robert Cantwell, *Bluegrass Breakdown: The Making of the Old Southern Sound* (Urbana: University of Illinois Press, 1984).

10. Price, 2.

11. Actually, the label *country music* was not applied to the hillbilly string band musical form until sometime after 1940. Rather, the more common labels were *mountain music, old-time music,* and *hillbilly music.* See Charles Wolfe, "Bluegrass Touches: An Interview with Bill Monroe," *Old Time Music* 16 (1975): 6–12. Most Southern musicians at that time had no use for the label *hillbilly* because of the many negative implications. This dislike is easy to understand, given commonly accepted definitions of the term by non-Appalachian residents. For example, the *Neu' York Journal* in 1900 defined a "hill-billie" as "a free and untrammelled white citizen of Appalachia who lives in the hills, has no means to speak of, dresses as he can, talks as he pleases, drinks whiskey when he gets it, and fires off his revolver as the fancy takes him"; see Archie Green, "Hillbilly Music: Source and Symbol," *Journal of American Folklore* 78 (1968): 204.

  Bill Monroe was asked, during an interview, about the use of the word *hillbilly.* He responded, "I have never liked the name, the word 'hillbilly'. It seemed like maybe another state out west would call you hillbilly if they thought that you'd never been to school or anything. I've never liked that and I've never used it in my music" (Wolfe, "Bluegrass Touches," 6). Like Monroe, most country music performers and country people have found *hillbilly* offensive.

12. Cantwell, xi. Monroe, during his early performances on the Grand Ole Opry, had Dave "Stringbean" Akeman playing banjo with him. Akeman played clawhammer or frailing style rather than the three-finger style. It was this element, the three-finger style, popularized by Earl Scruggs, that ultimately redefined the music that Monroe played as bluegrass.

13. Cantwell, *Bluegrass Breakdown.*

14. Charles Wolfe, "Bluegrass Touches," 7.

15. Cantwell, 226.

16. Cantwell, 228; Thomas Wolfe, *You Can't Go Home Again* (New York: Harper, 1940).

17. Ivan M. Tribe, "The Hillbilly versus the City: Urban Images in Country Music," *JEMF Quarterly* 10 (1974): 41–51.

18. This lack of hope was epitomized in a scene from *Coal Miner's Daughter,* a film about the life of country music star Loretta Lynn. The scene is a classic, where Doo, the man Loretta lalcr married, bemoans the fact that since his return from military service, he has found little work available in the mountains of home. A local moonshiner offers some bleak words of advice by saying, "Hell, Doo, up here there's only three things a man can do—coal mine, moonshine, or move on down the line." This scene vividly captures the limited alternatives available for improving one's lifestyle and material conditions in Appalachia.

19. Bluegrass festivals arc outdoor events typically held over a three-day weekend where at least a dozen acts perform. Festivals have dramatically increased in number in the past ten to fifteen years, giving bluegrass performers a steady circuit during the spring, summer, and fall, and giving the fans ample opportunity to hear bluegrass music. Fans usually camp at the site for the duration of the festival and the entertainers come and go in their touring buses. If not for bluegrass festivals, bluegrass performers, more than likely, would go hungrier than they already do.

20. Wayne Erbesen, *Backpocket Bluegrass Songbook* (New York: Pembroke Music, 1981); Rosenberg, *Bluegrass: A History;* Happy Traum, *Bluegrass Guitar* (New York: Oak Publications, 1974); Peter Wernick, *Bluegrass Songbook* (New York: Oak Publications, 1976).

21. Wolfe, *Kentucky Country.*

22. Erbesen, *Backpocket Bluegrass Songbook.*

23. Terry C. Cox and Kenneth D. Tunnell, "Competency to Stand Trial or the Trivial Pursuit of Justice," in *Homicide: The Victim-Offender Connection,* ed. Anna Wilson (Cincinnati: Anderson, 1993), 415–40.

24. Erbesen, *Backpocket Bluegrass Songbook.*

25. Ruth D. Peterson and William C. Bailey, "Murder and Capital Punishment in the United States: The Question of Deterrence," in *Criminal Law in Action,* ed. William J. Chambliss (New York: Wiley, 1984), 435–48; Marvin E. Wolfgang and Marc Riedel, "Race, Judicial Discretion, and the Death Penalty/' in *Criminal law in Action,* 449–61.

26. Emile Durkheim, *The Division of Labor in Society* (New York: The Free Press, 1984).

27. Karl Menninger, *The Crime of Punishment* (New York: Viking, 1966).

28. Nils Christie, *Crime Control as Industry* (London: Routledge, 1993); Kenneth D. Tunnell, "Film at Eleven: Recent Developments in the Commodification of Crime," *Sociological Spectrum* 12 (1992): 293–313.

29. Marvin E. Wolfgang and Franco Ferracuti, *The Subculture of Violence: Towards an Integrated Theory in Criminology* (Beverly Hills: Sage, 1982).

30. Wolfgang and Ferracuti, *The Subculture of Violence.*

31. Raymond D. Gastil, "Violence, Crime, and Punishment," in *Encyclopedia of Southern Culture,* 1473–76.

32. Although other nations have their own histories of the frontier (e.g., Canada and Australia), they do not have histories or current levels of violence like those found in America, and especially in the rural South.

33. Wilbur Joseph Cash, *The Mind of the South* (New York: Random House, 1941), 44.

34. Cantwell, *Bluegrass Breakdown.*

35. Richard Hofstadter, "Reflections on Violence in the U.S.," in *American Violence,* ed. Richard Hofstadter and Michael Wallace (New York: Vintage, 1970), 3–43. Also, the works of Jesse Stuart, Tennessee Williams, and James Agee well illustrate this mentality among Southern and Appalachian males.

THE NEWSWORTHINESS OF EXECUTIONS

By
Joseph E. Jacoby
Bowling Green State University
Bowling Green, OH

Eric F. Bronson
Lamar University
Beaumont, TX

Andrew R. Wilczak
Bowling Green State University
Bowling Green, OH

Julia M. Mack
Bowling Green State University
Bowling Green, OH

Deitra Suter
Network Knowledge,
Springfield, IL

Qiang Xu
Indiana University South Bend
South Bend, IN

Sean P. Rosenmerkel
Federal Bureau of Prisons
Washington, DC

Introduction

Between 1976, when the U.S. Supreme Court's ten-year moratorium on executions was lifted, and at the end of 2007 a total of 1,099 people were executed in the U.S. Over the last three decades, the number of executions increased, reaching a maximum of 98 in 1999, and then decreased to 42 in 2007. The present study analyzes changes in news coverage of executions over this period.

News media coverage of crime has received extensive scholarly analysis (e.g., book-length treatments are offered by Barak, 1994; Howitt, 1998; and Surette, 1998). We know, for example: crime news comprises an average of seven percent of all the news reported in newspapers and 20 percent of local television news, crime-and-justice news consistently constitutes one of the five top newspaper subject categories, and crime news is read and remembered by a larger proportion (one-quarter) of newspaper subscribers than any other category of news

Joseph E. Jacoby et al., "The Newsworthiness of Executions," *Journal of Criminal Justice and Popular Culture*, vol. 15, no. 2, pp. 168-188. Copyright © 2008 by School of Criminal Justice, University of Albany, SUNY. Reprinted with permission.

(Surrette, 1998, p. 67). The operations of the criminal justice system are, however, seldom reported in the news, except as the background setting for a story. The court system then becomes the main focus of a particular story about the response to crime, causing the actual imposition of punishment to be largely ignored by the news media (Surrette, 1998, p. 70). This paper considers the news coverage of just one aspect of the criminal justice process, the execution of offenders.

This paper seeks to determine: (1) the change in news coverage of executions as they changed in frequency between 1976 and 2007, and (2) the characteristics of specific executions that rendered them newsworthy, while other executions received little or no news coverage. We hypothesize that the increase of execution frequency caused a decline in news coverage, and that executions in which characteristics of the crime, offender, or victim were unique received more news coverage.

Newsworthiness

Determining the news value of a particular story—its "newsworthiness"—is a subjective task with no universally agreed upon criteria (Lundman, 2003). Surrette (1998, p. 61) argued that two factors contribute to the newsworthiness of a particular story. The first is "periodicity"—the relationship of the time cycle of the event to the publication cycle of the medium. If the event's occurrence or cycle matches the scheduling needs of the organization, the event is more likely to be reported. Similarly, the timing and predictability of the story (i.e., whether the media can plan their coverage around the event) also effects its status as a newsworthy event (Fox & Van Sickel, 2001; Jewkes, 2004).

Another factor influencing an event's newsworthiness is "consonance"—how closely the event is connected to previously developed news themes, as well as established public images of, and explanations for, events. Determining the consonance of a given event often includes a reliance on specific themes that have a history of generating public interest. The ability of the media to focus on the dramatic or unusual aspects of an event generally tends to increase the news value of the event. While no consensus exists about which characteristics render an event consonant with the goals of the media, a basic pattern has been established (Fox & Van Sickel, 2001; Jewkes, 2004; Greer, 2006). Stories that incorporate violent conflict, involve well-known persons, include graphic imagery, and allow for the reinforcement of traditional cultural values are preferred over more complex stories that may challenge the reader to reconsider widely held beliefs. In combination these factors relate not only to the consonance of an event with the goals of the media, as suggested by Surrette (1998), but also to the overall entertainment value of the story (Fox & Van Sickel, 2001).

Crime as News

The vast majority of crime news stories "focus disproportionately on the most serious and violent crimes" (Greer, 2006, p. 85). This generalization applies to network television newscasts, as well as those in big cities and small towns (Maguire, Sandage & Weatherby, 1999). Jewkes (2004) also asserts that violence increases the newsworthiness of crimes. Furthermore, events involving characters that are easily polarized into ideal types—e.g., the cold-blooded, evil offender versus the innocent victim—where the deviant behavior is easily highlighted and the offender easily identified, are more likely to be considered newsworthy (Greer, 2006).

Crime that is easily explained is also likely to be covered. For instance, Jewkes (2004) argues that the simplicity of an event can affect its status as a newsworthy event. A criminal event that is easily explainable (e.g., a murder) and will not confuse the audience is more likely to become news than a more complex event where the guilty party is not easily identifiable (e.g., stock market manipulation). Simple events appeal not only to the audience, but also to news media personnel. Events that offer news outlets easy access to information and do not require them to do much work are likely to receive coverage. Media outlets have become increasingly reliant upon information from official sources—typically the police—so oftentimes only those events the police want to be covered will receive coverage (Doyle, 2003; Sacco, 2005).

A consonant event—one that fits into a noticeable trend (i.e., can be characterized as one of a series of incidents in a previously identified "crime wave")—is more likely to be covered than an event that does not fit into such a pattern. If a given "crime wave" has been receiving a great deal of coverage, however, an event that fits the pattern may not be covered if it does not offer a new twist on the story (Sacco, 2005). The impact of consonance on newsworthiness is one quality that illustrates the importance of context in determining which events are newsworthy. Other aspects of context will also be seen to affect newsworthiness.

Executions as News

Considering the factors that determine the newsworthiness of events in general and crimes in particular, executions would seem to be events that should always be newsworthy. While the dominant, contemporary method of execution (i.e., lethal injection) minimizes visible manifestations of suffering, executions result in rapidly induced death—they may, therefore, be considered inherently violent. They are scheduled events that are also part of a pattern of similar events. Finally, they feature the affirmation of positive social values through the punishment of an offender that often is depicted as the embodiment of everything that is wrong with society (Greer, 2006). Despite all of the characteristics of executions that enhance their newsworthiness, many executions receive little or no news coverage.

Greer (2006) suggests that the characteristics of the crime that is being punished may influence the coverage that an execution receives; crimes that received more coverage during the investigation and trial phases because of the violent nature of the act or the characteristics of the offender may also receive more coverage during the punishment phase. This hypothesis implies that executions are not in themselves newsworthy events, but become newsworthy as the final episodes of continuing news stories about particular crimes.

Research Methods

Data Sources

The independent variables in this study are characteristics of executions and the people executed in the U.S. between 1977 and 2007. All data on the independent variables—names of offenders executed, dates of executions, number of victims, and race of victims and offenders—were obtained from the Death Penalty Information Center website (retrieved on February 20, 2008, from http://www.deathpenaltyinfo.org/).

The dependent variable is news coverage of executions. The two sources of data for news coverage were network television news programs and newspapers. TV news is an essential data source for this study because it has such a large audience. In 2002, the NBC evening news broadcast averaged 6.3 million viewers, ABC 6.7 million, and CBS 6.2 million—a total of 19.2 million viewers (MediaMark, 2002).

The Vanderbilt *Television News Archive* (retrieved February 20, 2008, from http://tvnews.vanderbilt .edu/) provided the data on national TV news coverage of executions. This *Archive*, "the world's most available, extensive and complete archive of television news" contains an index of all news stories broadcast on the evening news programs of three major TV networks (ABC, CBS, NBC), beginning in 1968. Archival coverage of CNN began October 2, 1995; therefore the present analysis includes reports of executions on CNN beginning on that date. Coverage of FOX began only in 2004, too recently for inclusion in this analysis.

Six newspapers with large readerships constituted the second set of data sources for this study. *USA Today*, was selected based on its national coverage and readership. With an average weekday readership of 6.3 million (retrieved on February 24, 2008, from http://www.newspapermedia.com/ docs/Top100.pdf), *USA Today* is currently the most widely read newspaper in the United States. Publication of *USA Today* began in 1984; data collection for the present study from *USA Today* began in that year.

The *New York Times* is included because it provides extensive coverage of national news and has the third largest readership in the U.S.: 4.8 million readers on an average weekday (retrieved on February 24, 2008, from http://www.newspapermedia.com/docs/Top100.pdf). The *Wall Street Journal* has a larger readership than the *New York Times*, but the *Journal's* primary focus on business news renders it unsuitable for inclusion in the present study.

Most events—including executions—are typically more salient to the residents of the geographic areas where they occur, and more newsworthy to the news media serving that area, than to people and media in other parts of the country. The small number of executions in most states obviated the study of a pattern of *change* in coverage within those states. Three states—Texas, Florida, and Georgia—executed a total of 507 people (or 46 percent of all people executed in the U.S.) during the period of the study. These three states were selected for separate analyses because they executed enough people to permit analysis of change in state-based news coverage.

A fourth state, Michigan, which does not have the death penalty, was also included in this study so that news coverage a state that does not have the death penalty could be compared with news coverage of executions in states that execute people with some regularity. The *Detroit Free Press* news archive (retrieved on February 20, 2008, from http://nl.newsbank.com/nl-search/we/Archives?s_site=freep&p) was searched for all reports executions in the U.S. during the study period, to reflect news coverage in Michigan. The *Detroit Free Press* has an average daily readership of 1.1 million (retrieved on February 20, 2008, from http://www.newspapermedia.com/docs/Top100.pdf).

In each of the four states, one newspaper was selected based on having both a large circulation and a searchable, on-line World Wide Web archive. The *Houston Chronicle* has an estimated average weekday readership of 1.2 million (retrieved on February 24, 2008, from http://www.newspaper-media.com/docs/Top100.pdf). The *Houston Chronicle's* archive (retrieved on February 20, 2008, from http://search.chron.com/chronicle/archiveSearch.do searched for reports of executions in Texas.

The *Miami Herald* archive (retrieved on February 20, 2008, from http://www.miamiherald. com/) was searched for reports of executions in Florida. The *Herald* has an estimated weekday readership of 806,000 (retrieved on February 24, 2008, from http://www.newspapermedia.com/docs/Top100.pdf).

The *Atlanta Journal-Constitution* archive (retrieved on February 20, 2008, from http://stacks.ajc.com/) was searched for reports of executions in Georgia. This newspaper has a weekday readership of 994,000 (retrieved on February 20, 2008, from http://www.newspapermedia.com/docs/Top100.pdf).

Variables

The dependent variable *news reports of executions* was operationalized as follows: A news report was included only if it both (1) was published/broadcast during the week following an execution, and (2) included a report of a completed execution. News stories about crimes, trials, appeals, and similar issues were excluded unless they also included reports of completed executions.

The *quantity of coverage* was operationalized in three ways. It was first defined dichotomously—whether or not an execution was reported. The second indicator was the number of broadcasts or published reports about each execution. The third indicator of quantity was length, measured either as the duration (in minutes) of a TV news story, or the number of words published in a newspaper article. If several reports about a single execution were televised/published, the lengths of all the stories were added together to yield a summary measure of quantity for each execution.

The *prominence of coverage* was operationalized dichotomously for both newspapers and TV broadcasts. Newspaper prominence was determined by whether an article appeared on the front page of the paper, while the prominence of televised stories was measured by whether the execution story was the lead story of a broadcast. The logic of this definition is simply that articles printed on the front page are more likely to be seen and read than articles printed elsewhere in a paper, while the first news story of a broadcast has a higher probability of being watched. If several stories were published or televised about a single execution, coverage of that execution was considered "prominent" if any of the articles appeared on page one (or the TV report was broadcast first in a news broadcast).

Results

Proportion of Executions Reported

The three national television networks reported fewer than seven percent of the executions that took place between 1977 and 2007. The national newspapers *USA Today* and *New York Times* reported 20 percent and 48 percent, respectively, of the executions during that period. The lowest level of coverage was found in Michigan (the state without a death penalty); the *Detroit Free Press* reported only 11 percent of executions in the U.S. The *Atlanta Journal-Constitution, Houston Chronicle,* and *Miami Herald,* on the other hand, reported 100 percent, 94 percent, and 95 percent, respectively, of the executions occurring in the states where those papers are published.

Number of News Reports

TV news averaged 15 reports per 100 executions. *USA Today* averaged 28 articles per 100 executions. The *Detroit Free Press* averaged only 11 articles per 100 executions. The three newspapers whose reports of in-state executions were recorded for this study printed more articles about executions occurring in those states. The *Atlanta Journal-Constitution* averaged the most articles (2.5 per execution) followed by the *Houston Chronicle* (1.6 articles per execution) and the *Miami Herald* (1.3 articles per execution).

Length of Reports

Because the standard deviations of report lengths were very large, medians are reported here. The length of articles about executions followed a similar pattern across the TV networks and five newspapers. Typical television news reports of executions were brief. Excluding those executions that were not reported by any of the networks, the median length of *all* network TV news reports combined was 140 seconds per execution. Published reports were shorter in newspapers with national coverage than in newspapers where only coverage of in-state executions was analyzed. In *USA Today* reports of executions averaged 37 words, compared to 366 words in the *New York Times* and 605 words in the *Detroit Free Press*. Longer articles appeared in the *Miami Herald* (median = 1,278 words), the *Atlanta Journal-Constitution* (1,258 words), and *Houston Chronicle* (536 words) about executions that occurred in Florida, Georgia, and Texas, respectively.

Prominence of Reports

"Prominence" was recorded dichotomously—whether or not a published article appeared on the front page of the newspaper. When *USA Today* reported executions at all, only two percent were reported on Page One. The *New York Times* reported three percent of all executions on Page One; among executions that were reported in the *Times*, five percent of all reports were on Page One. Newspapers published reports of in-state executions far more prominently: Forty-four percent of executions in Texas were reported on Page One in the *Houston Chronicle*, 55 percent of executions in Georgia were reported on Page One in the *Atlanta Journal-Constitution*, and 57 percent of executions in Florida were reported on Page One of the *Miami Herald*.

Change in Reporting over Time

The number of executions carried out each year since 1977 has ranged from one execution in 1977 to 98 in 1999. Executions have also increased in frequency in Texas, but occurred at fairly stable rates in Florida and Georgia. These patterns of change and stability serve as a backdrop for the analyses that follow.

Change in Proportion of Executions Reported

Since nearly all executions occurring in their respective states were reported in the Texas, Florida, and Georgia newspapers, no analysis of change in proportions of executions reported will be presented. Variation did occur, however, in coverage by the TV networks and national newspapers.

Between 1977 and 1983, when only a few executions occurred each year, every execution was reported on at least one of the TV networks. In 1984, when the number of executions began to increase rapidly, the proportion of executions reported dropped off just as rapidly. Network TV news coverage continued to drop off, so that no more than seven percent of executions were reported by TV network news in any year of the last decade.

For this and subsequent analyses of change in coverage over time, each execution was assigned a sequence number, from 1 to 1,099, starting with the first execution in 1977 and ending with the last one in 2007. The moderate, negative bivariate correlation ($r = -.208$) between the sequence number of the execution and reportage by the TV networks confirms the decline in proportion of executions reported.

A similar decline occurred in coverage of executions by the *New York Times* and *USA Today*. The *New York Times* reported most executions until 1996, but has covered only about one-fourth of executions since then. The strong correlation between the sequence number and the proportion reported ($r = -.613$) in the *New York* Times reflects this drop-off. *USA Today*'s coverage of executions, which was consistently less exhaustive than the *Times'*, declined in recent years all the way to zero in 2003. The bivariate correlation ($r = -.373$) reflects this decline over three decades. Change in reporting by the *Detroit Free Press* was similar, with a significant, negative correlation between sequence number and proportion reported ($r = -.285$).

One peculiar characteristic of *USA Today*'s coverage is the importance of the day of the week an execution occurs for determining whether the execution is reported. *USA Today* is published only on weekdays. Whereas 22–39 percent of executions occurring on Mondays, Tuesdays, and Wednesdays were reported, only 7 percent of executions occurring on Fridays were reported in *USA Today*. This relationship between day of the week and proportion reported is statistically significant ($df = 6$, $F = 7.249$). Executions that occur at the end of each week evidently become "old news," no longer worthy of reporting in Monday's edition of *USA Today*. This finding is consistent with Surrette's (1998) assertion that the relationship between the timing of an event to the publication cycle of the news medium is an important factor in determining the newsworthiness of the event.

Change in Number of Reports

The decline in proportion of executions reported is paralleled by a decline in the mean number of reports per execution published in *USA Today*, as indicated by the correlation between sequence number of executions and number of news reports ($r = -1.60$). The mean number of reports was not significantly related to the sequence number for TV news, the *New York Times*, or the *Detroit Free Press*. Considering the newspaper reports of in-state executions, the mean number of articles in the *Houston Chronicle* and *Atlanta Journal-Constitution* did not change significantly over time. The number of articles per execution increased significantly with sequence number ($r = .493$) in the *Miami Herald*.

Change in Length of Reports

The third measure of coverage quantity is story length. The mean length of news reports varied over time and by source. The length of articles in *USA Today* and TV news increased with sequence number of executions ($r = .395$ and $.342$, respectively). Change in article length in the *New York Times* and *Detroit Free Press* was not significant. The *Houston Chronicle*'s articles became significantly shorter ($r = -.145$) with sequence number, while article length in both the *Miami* Herald and *Atlanta Journal*-Constitution did not change significantly.

Change in Prominence

In only four years (1989, 1992, 1998, 2001) was any execution reported on Page 1of *USA Today*. Between 1979 and 1982 the *New York Times* reported all executions on the front page; after that few reports received such prominent coverage. The correlation between execution sequence number and publication on the front page was, however, not significant over the 30-year study period for either *USA Today* or the *New York Times*. Neither was the correlation between execution sequence number and reportage of executions as the lead story on TV network news.

The prominence of coverage of in-state executions by the Texas and Georgia newspapers was strongly, negatively correlated with sequence number (r = −.730 and −.654). From 1977 through 1998 the *Houston Chronicle* reported nearly all executions in Texas on the front page; since then, however, only 10 percent were reported on the front page. The *Atlanta Journal-Constitution*, published all reports of executions in Georgia on the front page in the period 1983–1991, but subsequently placed 78 percent further back in the paper. The *Miami Herald* showed no significant change in prominence of coverage of Florida executions.

Newsworthy Executions

In recent years most executions received little attention in the press, but some were reported and a few received extensive coverage. As Halmari and Östman (2001) argue, the "discourse pattern" in coverage tends to change when something about the offender, crime, or execution itself is extraordinary. In this section we explore the characteristics that rendered particular executions newsworthy.

Multivariate Analysis of Offender and Victim Characteristics

The race/ethnicity of the offender(s) was significantly related to the proportion of executions reported in the *New York Times,* but not the *Detroit Free Press, USA Today,* or TV network news, but race had no effect on the length of the report. [The *Miami Herald, Atlanta Journal-Constitution, and Houston Chronicle* were excluded from this analysis because nearly all executions occurring in the states where these papers were published were reported.] The racial/ethnic category with the highest proportion of reported executions in the *New York Times* involved neither White, Black, nor Latino offenders, but offenders from foreign countries and "other" racial/ethnic groups. The number of murder victims was also significantly related to the likelihood that an execution would be reported by the *New York Times, Detroit Free Press*, and TV network news, but not by *USA Today*.

Table 1 presents the findings of a series of logistic regression analyses testing whether age of offender, race/ethnicity of victim and offender, and number of victims influence whether an execution is reported at all. The first model examines the association between these characteristics and whether an execution was reported in the *New York Times*. Here, case sequence number, the age of the offender, the presence of a black offender, and the interaction between black offenders and the number of victims are significantly related to coverage.

The odds of an execution receiving coverage are 1.02 times higher for each year increase in the age of the offender. The odds of an execution receiving coverage in cases involving a black offender decrease by a factor of .299. However, this negative effect is reduced, depending on the number of victims involved: a case where the offender is black and a large number of victims were killed is significantly more likely to be reported. Finally, a unit increase in the case sequence number reduces the odds of an execution receiving coverage in the *New York Times* by a factor of .995

Table 1. Logistic Regression of Any Execution Coverage on Case Characteristics

	New York Times		USA Today		Detroit Free Press		TV Networks	
	Model 1	Model 2	Model 1	Model 2	Model 1	Model 2	Model 1	Model 2
Case Characteristics								
Case Number	-.005***	-.005***	-.004***	-.004***	-.004***	-.003***	-.003***	-.003***
	(.995)	(.995)	(.996)	(.996)	(.996)	(.996)	(.997)	(.997)
White Victim	.221	-.191	.018	-.241	.171	.376	.512	.964
	(1.247)	(.826)	(1.018)	(.786)	(1.186)	(1.456)	(1.669)	(2.623)
Black Offender	-.066	-1.206***	-.177	-.506	-.029	.176	-.406	.516
	(.936)	(.299)	(.838)	(.603)	(.972)	(1.193)	(.666)	(1.676)
Offender's Age	.018*	.019*	.015	.015	-.003	-.003	.008	.007
	(1.018)	(1.019)	(1.015)	(1.015)	(.997)	(.997)	(1.008)	(1.007)
Number of Victims	.223*	-.006	-.060	-.084	.049	.022	.266*	.355
	(1.250)	(.994)	(.942)	(.920)	(1.050)	(1.022)	(1.304)	(1.427)
Interaction Terms								
Black Offender * Number of Victims		.575*		.011		.058		-.218
		(1.777)		(1.011)		(1.059)		(.804)
White Victim * Number of Victims		.144		.038		.005		-.069
		(1.155)		(1.038)		(1.005)		(.933)
Black Offender * White Victim		.543		.418		-.358		-.736
		(1.720)		(1.519)		(.699)		(.479)
r²GSC	.485	.490	.226	.228	.178	.178	.144	.146
Model chi-square	488.914***	494.937***	166.430***	167.379***	98.293***	98.750***	64.278***	65.386***

N = 1,099 for all models

Cell entries are regression coefficients (β) with odds ratios in parentheses.

+; p < .10

*; p < .05

**; p < .01

***; p < .001

The association between case characteristics and whether an execution received coverage in *USA Today*, *The Detroit Free Press*, and televised news are virtually identical, with the exception of number of victims for TV news. In each case, the only significant factor is the case sequence number; neither the race of the actors involved nor the number of victims contributed significantly to whether an execution was reported.

Table 2 displays the results of OLS regression analyses testing whether the race of the offender or victim as well as the number of victims influenced the amount of news coverage an execution received. Coverage is measured here by the length of all newspaper articles about the execution, or the duration of television reports. In addition to these case characteristics, three interaction terms are included. These terms are black offender by number of victims, white victim by number of victims, and black offender by white victim.

The first set of models; the case sequence number is negatively related to the amount of coverage in the *New York Times*, while the number of victims is positively related. None of the interaction terms is significantly correlated with the dependent variable. Executions receive more coverage when there are more victims, but more recent executions receive less coverage. Together, these variables account for only 5.2 percent of the variance in the amount of coverage in the *New York Times*.

The second set of models repeats these analyses for coverage in *USA Today*. Both the sequence number and the number of victims are significantly correlated with the dependent variable; however, in contrast with coverage in the *New York Times*, the case sequence number is positively associated with the amount of coverage and remains positively associated when the interaction terms are included in the model. This counter-intuitive finding is explained by the pattern of coverage in *USA Today*, which reported executions less consistently as time progressed, but the more recent executions that were reported received substantial coverage. The interaction terms are not significant, indicating that the race of neither the victim nor the offender significantly impacts the amount of coverage an execution received. Altogether, these variables account for 22.7 percent of the variance in coverage.

The third set of models repeats these analyses using the amount of coverage in the *Detroit Free Press*. Here, none of the variables in either model, including the interaction effects, is significantly associated with the amount of coverage, and the total explanatory power of the model is substantially weaker than in the previous analyses, accounting for only 1.2 percent of the variance in coverage.

The final set of models repeats these analyses using the duration of execution reports in TV network news. The number of victims is associated with more coverage. Of the interaction terms, white victim by number of victims is significant, indicating that cases involving multiple white victims receive less coverage than cases with multiple, non-white victims. The main effect of number of victims is also significant and remains positively associated with amount of coverage. Altogether, these measures account for only 3.1 percent of the variance in coverage. The next section of these analyses assesses the relationship between the case characteristics and the prominence of coverage. For the newspapers in this analysis, the dependent variable is whether or not the execution was covered on the front page. For television news coverage, the dependent variable is whether or not the execution was the first story covered during any broadcast.

The final quantitative analysis, summarized in Table 3, focuses on the prominence of news coverage. Beginning with the *New York Times*, none of the variables was significantly related to the likelihood that an execution would be reported on Page 1. Furthermore, since no cases with a black offender and white victim were reported on Page 1, this interaction term was removed from the model.

This analysis is repeated using prominence of coverage in *USA Today* as the dependent variable. Here, because no executions featuring white victims or black offenders were covered on the front page of

Table 2. OLS Regression of Amount of Coverage on Case Characteristics

	New York Times		USA Today		Detroit Free Press		TV Networks	
	Model 1	Model 2	Model 1	Model 2	Model 1	Model 2	Model 1	Model 2
Case Characteristics								
Case sequence number	-.123**	-.122**	.399***	.383***	-.01	-.012	.016	.017
White Victim	.037	.063	.041	.292*	.022	.075	-.032	.127+
Black Offender	.019	.106	-.016	.167	-.015	.098	.039	.003
Offender's Age	.0003	-.004	-.022	-.024	-.039	-.041	.034	.031
Number of Victims	.180***	.306*	.219***	.418*	.090	.234	.101**	.192*
Interaction Terms								
Black Offender * Number of Victims		-.153		.017		-.148		.116
White Victim * Number of Victims		-.100		-.274		-.124		-.187*
Black Offender * White Victim		.025		-.231+		-.022		-.074 F
F	5.24***	3.55***	11.06***	7.71***	0.22	0.16	3.20**	4.22***
r^2	.048	.052	.206	.227	.01	.012	.015	.031

N = 1,099 for all models
+: $p < .10$
*: $p < .05$
**: $p < .01$
***: $p < .001$

237

Table 3. Logistic Regression of Prominence of Coverage on Case Characteristics

	New York Times		USA Today		TV Networks	
	Model 1	Model 2	Model 1	Model 2	Model 1	Model 2
Case Characteristics						
Case Number	-.001	-.001	-.0002	—	.002	.002
	(.999)	(.999)	(1.000)		(1.002)	(1.002)
White Victim	1.087	1.555	—	—	.614	1.397
	(2.966)	(4.734)			(1.849)	(4.004)
Black Offender	-.195	.976	—	—	1.454+	2.078
	(.823)	(2.653)			(4.278)	(7.990)
Offender's Age	.018	.015	-.072	—	-.036	-.035
	(1.018)	(1.015)	(.930)		(.965)	(.966)
Number of Victims	.438**	.880	.891**	—	.266	.761
	(1.550)	(2.411)	(2.437)		(1.305)	(2.140)
Interaction Terms						
Black Offender * Number of Victims		-.775	—	—		-.432
		(.461)				(.649)
White Victim * Number of Victims		-.379	—	—		-.481
		(.684)				(.618)
Black Offender * White Victim		—	—	—		—
r²GSC	.076	.089	.150	—	.166	.171
Model chi-square	13.5*	12.746*	8.968*	—	7.36	7.605

N = 1,099 for all models

Cell entries are regression coefficients (β) with odds ratios in parentheses.

+: p < .10
*: p < .05
**: p < .01
***: p < .001

238

the paper, none of the interaction terms could be included in the analysis. Only the number of victims is significantly associated with prominence of coverage; each additional victim in a case increases the odds that it will receive coverage on the front page by a factor of 2.44.

These analyses were repeated again with prominence of coverage on TV news broadcasts as the dependent variable. Again, separation effects limited the analysis, because no cases involving a black offender and white victim were reported first in a news broadcast. That said, none of the independent variables in this analysis was significantly correlated with prominence of coverage. Therefore, across all of these analyses, the only factor that significantly influenced whether or not an execution received prominent coverage was the number of victims.

Qualitative Analysis of Offenders, Victims, and Executions

Most reports of executions in *USA Today* were included in brief notices in a section entitled "News from the States", where news from each U.S. state is reported in a single paragraph. Only 45 (or 4 percent) of all executions received 100+ words of coverage. Furthermore, only 11 (or 1 percent) were reported extensively, in at least 1,000 words. A close reading of all articles in *USA Today*, covering 220 (or 20 percent) of all executions carried out in the U.S. between 1984 and 2007 revealed some common characteristics of the most extensively covered executions. These characteristics were found to be distributed among five categories that describe personal, social, and historical contexts. Many cases had more than one of these characteristics, so these categories are not mutually exclusive.

Offenders' Personal Characteristics: In some cases, offenders' personal characteristics—sex, mental capacities, or age—render them different from most people that are executed, thereby making their executions newsworthy. Both Margie Barfield (executed in North Carolina on November 2, 1984) and Karla Faye Tucker (executed in Texas on February 3, 1998) were female, born-again Christians. These two characteristics, in combination, attracted a great deal of debate and media attention. Being female, by itself, was insufficient for the execution to become newsworthy, however—the eight other executions of women did not receive extensive coverage. The execution of Delaware's Willie G. Sullivan (Delaware, September 24, 1999) attracted much debate, because he may have suffered from both mental retardation (with an IQ of 70), and fetal alcohol syndrome. Kelsey Patterson (Texas, May 18, 2004) and James Hubbard (Alabama, August 5, 2004), both mentally ill, were executed despite the 1986 U.S. Supreme Court decision in *Ford v. Wainwright* (477 US 399, 1986), which banned the execution of mentally ill people.

Attention was sometimes roused by an execution of a non-citizen or a person born outside the United States, prompting international involvement and much international press coverage on behalf of the condemned. For example, the government of Paraguay appealed unsuccessfully to the World Court at The Hague to prevent the execution of Paraguayan citizen Angel Breard (Virginia, April 14, 1998). Similarly, the execution of Mir Aimal Kasi (Virginia, November 14, 2002), a Pakistani citizen who killed two CIA agents, attracted much coverage because it elicited fears of Middle Eastern retaliation against Americans.

The Mexican government has attempted several times, without success, to avert executions of Mexican citizens in the U.S. The executions of Irineo Montoya (Texas, June 18, 1997), Mario B. Murphy (Virginia, September 17, 1997), and Miguel Flores (Texas, November 9, 2000) were rendered newsworthy by the fact that they were either born in or citizens of Mexico.

Stanley "Tookie" Williams (California, December 13, 2005), founder of the Crips street gang, was sentenced to death in 1979 for the slaying of four people in Los Angeles. While in prison he was nominated for the Nobel Peace Prize and other awards for his attempt to end the gang violence that he helped start. The Governor of California, Arnold Schwarzenegger, denied Williams' clemency request because Williams failed to express remorse and inform on other members of the Crips. Willliam's notoriety, his transformation while awaiting execution, and Schwarzenegger's denial of clemency combined to make this execution one of the most extensively reported in decades.

Legal Claims: Claims of inadequate representation and questions of factual guilt occasionally result in increased media attention. The foreign-born men, Breard, Montoya, Flores, and Murphy, claimed that they were denied access to their consulates immediately after their arrests, as guaranteed by international treaty. Additionally, Willie Darden (Florida, March 15, 1988), Gary Graham (a.k.a. Shaka Sankofa, Texas, June 22, 2000), and Juan Raul Garza (Federal, June 19, 2001) claimed that they had been the victims of racial prejudice in their legal representation and/or jury selection. The conviction of Virginia's Roger K. Coleman was so vigorously contested that his picture was on the cover of *Time Magazine* prior to his execution (May 20, 1992). According to Coleman's attorneys, he had an alibi that did not give him enough time to commit the crime, and another man had bragged about killing the victim.

Circumstances of the Crime: In news reports of executions, coverage is typically given not to the execution itself, but rather to the circumstances of the crime and the reactions of victims' families (Haney and Greene, 2004). Some capital cases are so gruesome, the death tolls so high, and the ways in which victims were killed so horrific that extensive news coverage is assured. The executions of mass/serial murderers, Ted Bundy (Florida, January 24, 1989), John Wayne Gacy (Illinois, May 10, 1994), and Timothy McVeigh (Federal, June 11, 2001), were each covered in articles longer than 1,000 words that included vivid details of their crimes and witnesses' responses to their deaths.

The characteristics of victims also influence the extent of reporting of executions. The executions of murderers of children are noteworthy: Westley Dodd was executed (Washington, January 5, 1993) after committing atrocities against three children. Margie Barfield (North Carolina, November 2, 1984), Judy Buenoano (Florida, March 30, 1998), and Betty Lou Beets (Texas, February 24, 2000) were all convicted of killing their romantic partners or children.

Protocol Violations: Executions have rules of etiquette for observers, prison personnel, and prisoners. An execution may be rendered newsworthy when those rules are violated. Protocol requires that condemned prisoners are to accept their impending deaths with quiet resignation. In a few instances, however, they refused to comply, and instead fought the guards escorting them to the death chamber. Gary Graham (Texas, June 22, 2000) showed evidence of a recent struggle as he was secured with several more restraints than usual on the day of his execution. Daniel Thomas (Florida, April 15, 1986) brawled with guards as he was led "kicking and screaming" to the electric chair, in view of execution witnesses.

Protocol violations may also include technical errors and equipment malfunctions, resulting in visible harm to the body and evidence of intense suffering. Phenomena falling into this subcategory of protocol violations are typically called "botched executions." This term is commonly used in anti-death penalty rhetoric, because it conjures up emotionally charged images of mutilation and pain that are diametrically opposed to the emotionally neutral language of laws and procedures prescribing executions.

Greer (2006) argues that botched executions are more likely to receive coverage. Although no rigorous effort has been made to specify the characteristics of "botched" executions, a list of 40 such events, carried out between 1982 and 2007, has been compiled by Radelet (2007) and is posted on the Death Penalty Information Center (DPIC) website. This list "… is not intended to be a comprehensive catalogue of botched executions, but simply a listing of well-known examples" (Radelet, 2007). This list includes a broad range of incidents where execution protocol was violated, ranging from delays caused by technicians' difficulty in finding a usable vein for a lethal injection (e.g., Morin—Texas, March 13,

1985; Rector—Arkansas, January 24, 1992) to more horrific events, such as offenders' catching fire during electrocution (e.g., Tafero—Florida, May 4, 1990; Medina—Florida, March 25, 1997).

Of the 40 the executions on Radelet's list, 37 occurred during the period covered by the *USA Today* dataset. In order to test the hypothesis that botched executions are more newsworthy than others, *USA Today's* coverage of the botched executions obtained from the DPIC was compared with coverage of other executions. Eleven of the 37 executions (30 percent) labeled as botched were reported in *USA Today*, which is not significantly more than the percentage of other executions reported. The reports of these eleven executions all included some details of the violations in protocol listed in the DPIC report, but none of these executions was reported on Page One of *USA Today*.

Historical Precedent: The most common category of newsworthiness was a "first" for a state or the nation. Similarly, executions that constitute a "record" of some sort fall into this category. More than one-third (38 percent) of newsworthy executions earned this designation because of their historical context.

Examples of precedent-setting executions that received greater than average coverage include the following: Margie Barfield (North Carolina, 1984), was the first woman executed in the United States since the death penalty was reinstated in 1976. The execution in Arkansas of Hoyt Clines, Darryl Richley, and James Holmes (August 3, 1994) was the first triple execution since 1962. The execution of Wilford Berry (February 19, 1999) was Ohio's first since 1963. Timothy McVeigh and Juan Raul Garza (June 11 and June 19, 2001) were the first Federal prisoners to be executed in thirty-eight years. Larry Wayne White's execution (May 22, 1997) was Texas' fourth execution in one week. Paul Nuncio (June 15, 2000) was the 134th Texan— the largest number ever to be executed during the administration of a single governor. Texas' governor at that time was George W. Bush.

Contemporaneous Events: While some executions possess one or more characteristics that make them exceptional, the presence of these characteristics does not guarantee extensive news coverage. The reporting of executions does not occur in a vacuum; other, contemporaneous events compete with executions for news coverage. News editors decide which of many reportable events are newsworthy. The coverage of executions depends on the number and importance of "competing" regional, national, and international events. The newsworthiness of executions is determined, at least in part, in relation to the newsworthiness of other, contemporaneous events.

Timothy Spencer killed four people, and was the first person in the nation to be convicted using DNA evidence. Since it was a historical "first," Spencer's (Virginia, April 27, 1994) execution would have been considered newsworthy, yet it received a meager 20 words in *USA Today*, possibly because it occurred two weeks before the scheduled execution of serial killer John Wayne Gacy (Illinois, May 10, 1994). Due to the far more horrific details of Gacy's killings, Spencer's execution was overshadowed by Gacy's impending execution.

A similar phenomenon occurred in 2001. For many months after the attacks on the World Trade Center and Pentagon, the news was dominated by reports of those attacks and other terrorist activities. None of the 63 executions in 2001 carried out after September 11 was reported in *USA Today*. The editors assigned a higher priority to other matters, stripping all executions of their newsworthiness, although if they had occurred under other circumstances, at least some would likely have been newsworthy.

Discussion and Conclusions

When, after a ten-year hiatus, executions resumed in 1977 all executions received extensive, prominent coverage by the broadcast and print media. As the pace of executions increased, coverage declined.

Executions have disappeared almost entirely from network TV news—between 2001 and 2007 only 14 (3.3 percent) of the 416 executions carried out in the U.S. was reported by *any* of the major TV networks. During the same period *USA Today* reported only 2.6 percent of executions. The low salience of executions in Michigan, a state that does not have the death penalty, is reflected in the infrequent and brief coverage of executions (that occurred in other states) in The *Detroit Free Press*.

The *Houston Chronicle* consistently reports executions in Texas, the state that executes the most people. Over time, however, the *Chronicle's* articles have become shorter and less prominent. More recently only a few "unusual" executions received extensive, prominent coverage. In Florida the *Miami Herald* has continued to publish about one long article per execution, but these articles are not consistently printed on Page One. Even in Georgia, which has executed the fewest people among this small sample of states, the prominence and quantity of news coverage has declined. The *Atlanta Journal-Constitution* has consistently published about two, long articles per Georgia execution, but in recent years, those articles have no longer appeared on the front page. As the number of executions has increased, both across the U.S. and within states, executions have become less newsworthy.

The low level of network TV coverage of executions should be viewed in light of the small number of news stories in a typical newscast. A review of the archive of all the regularly scheduled news broadcasts on CBS, NBC, ABC, and CNN in a recent month (retrieved February 29, 2008, from http://tvnews.vanderbilt.edu/) revealed that a single broadcast contains only 8–10 stories. A huge number of national and international events occur each day from which TV news editors must chose no more than ten. Among these occurrences on a typical day would probably be bombings, accidents, or severe weather somewhere in the world resulting in many deaths, as well as political and economic events with important national and international consequences. In competition with news reports of such a large number of large-scale events, a news story about the death of a single criminal offender by lethal injection may, understandably, fail to survive an editor's cut.

We hypothesize that the local TV coverage of in-state executions would be comparable to local newspaper reporting of in-state executions. Whereas most executions that occur in distant states would not be especially interesting to a local TV audience, executions that occur closer to home would be of interest, and would receive more coverage on local TV stations. Unfortunately, the archives of local TV stations are not generally accessible to researchers, so this hypothesis would be difficult to test.

The differentials between national and in-state news reports of executions help to explain the pattern found in a previously reported (Jacoby & Bronson, 2004) national survey of public awareness of completed executions. Jacoby & Bronson found that the public sharply underestimated the number of executions actually carried out in the U.S. (during the year prior to the survey), but more accurately estimated the number of executions carried out in respondents' home states.

Based on these findings, given the recent pattern of executions, news coverage of executions appears to depend partly on the rate of executions in a geographic area. Within each state the extent of newspaper coverage is inversely related to the rate of executions within that state. Over time, even in states with low annual execution rates, the newsworthiness of executions declines.

On a national level the amount and prominence of newspaper and TV reporting of executions is quite low. The race of victims and offenders seems to be a much less important factor in the reporting of executions than in the legal processes that result in executions. Characteristics of particular executions—unusual qualities of the offense, offender, victim, or context—render some executions more likely to receive national news coverage. Predicting with precision which executions will receive extensive (or any) national news coverage is difficult, however, because editorial decisions to publish or broadcast particular news stories depend heavily on the relative newsworthiness of competing, contemporaneous events.

On the national scene crime *is* news, but punishment, including capital punishment, is not. Even when a crime resulting in execution is unusually heinous, and has therefore received extensive news coverage, the execution carried out as punishment typically occurs more than a decade later. The crime story, for which the execution constitutes a conclusion, may not be followed over such a long period by the news media, which is continually confronted with the challenge of determining which more immediate events to cover.

The significance of the failure of the national news media to report executions remains unexplored, but some consequences can at least be suggested. The only way the vast majority of citizens can become aware of executions is through the mass media. In the absence of mass media reporting of executions, the public remains unaware that they occur. Public ignorance of most executions, therefore, renders moot the long-simmering debate about the deterrent and/or brutalization effect of capital punishment. The behavior of prospective murderers cannot be influenced by executions about which they do not know.

Perhaps even more important, citizens cannot participate knowledgeably in policy discussions about capital punishment if they remain ignorant about current punishment practices. Ironically, the evidence presented in this study reveals that over the last 30 years, as executions became more frequent, reports to the public about them declined.

Endnote

1. Earlier versions of this paper were presented at the Annual Meetings of the American Society of Criminology in 1998 and 2004 and the Academy of Criminal Justice Sciences in 2000 and 2003. Daniel Kenel and Scott Stevens assisted in the data collection for this study. Address all correspondence related to this paper to: Joseph E. Jacoby, Department of Sociology, Bowling Green State University, Bowling Green, OH 43403, jjacoby@bgsu.edu.

2. The views expressed in this paper are those of the authors and may not represent those views of the Federal Bureau of Prisons or the Department of Justice.

3. Joseph E. Jacoby received his Ph.D. from the University of Pennsylvania in 1976. He is a Professor of Sociology at Bowling Green State University. His research interests include the reentry of mentally ill offenders and public opinion about punishment.

4. Eric F. Bronson received his Ph.D. from Bowling Green State University in 2002. He is an Assistant Professor of Sociology and Criminal Justice at Quinnipiac University. His research interests include inmate subcultures and violence on college campuses. His teaching areas include corrections, sociology of sport, and race, crime and justice.

5. Andrew R. Wilczak received his M.A. from Eastern Michigan University in 2007. He is currently a Ph.D. student in sociology at Bowling Green State University. His research interests are violence & victimization, corrections, and social inequality.

6. Julia M. Mack received her B.S. from Saint Francis University in 2007. She is currently a M.A. student in the sociology department at Bowling Green State University. Her research interests include crime, corrections and the relationship between reintegration and recidivism.

7. Deitra Suter received her M.A. from Bowling Green State University in 2005. She is the Membership Coordinator for Network Knowledge a group of three public television stations in Western and Central Illinois. Her research interests include gender and crime, the death penalty, and the effects and relationships between religiosity and other aspects of American life and culture, including crime.

8. Qiang Xu received his Ph.D. from Bowling Green State University in 2006. He is currently an Assistant Professor of Public and Environmental Affairs at Indiana University South Bend. His research interests include: quantitative research methods, life course perspective on criminal involvement, gender and race differences in crime, and applications of geographic information systems.

9. Sean P. Rosenmerkel received his M.A. from Bowling Green State University in 1999 and has pursued additional graduate training at the University of Maryland.. He is currently a Social Science Research Analyst with the Federal Bureau of Prisons in Washington, DC. His current research interests include: correctional staff and inmate mental health, sex offender treatment, sexual misconduct in prisons, and general inmate programming.

References

Atlanta Journal-Constitution. Retrieved February 20, 2008, from http://www.ajc.com/.

Barak, G. (1994). *Media, process, and the social construction of crime.* New York: Garland Publishing.

Death Penalty Information Center. Retrieved on February 20, 2008, from http://www.deathpenaltyinfo.org/.

Detroit Free Press. Retrieved February 20, 2008, from http://nl.newsbank.com/nl-search/we/Archives?s_site=freep&p.

Doyle, A. (2003). *Arresting images.* University of Toronto Press: Toronto, Canada.

Fox, R. L., & Van Sickel, R. W. (2001). *Tabloid justice: Criminal justice in an age of media frenzy.* Lynne Rienner Publishers, Inc: Boulder, Colorado.

Greer, C. (2006). Delivering death: capital punishment, botched executions, and the American news media. In: P. Mason (Ed.), *Captured by the media: Prison discourse in popular culture* (pp. 84–102). Devon, U.K.: Willan Publishing.

Halmari, H., & Östman, J. (2001). The soft-spoken, angelic pickax killer: the notion of discourse pattern in controversial news reporting. *Journal of Pragmatics, 33*, 805–823.

Haney, C., & Greene, S. (2004). Capital constructions: newspaper reporting in death penalty cases. *Analyses of Social Issues & Public Policy, 4*, 129–150.

Houston Chronicle. Retrieved February 20, 2008, from http://www.chron.com/

Howitt, D. (1998). *Crime, the media and the law.* New York: John Wiley & Sons.

Jacoby, J.E. & Bronson, E.F. (2004). More executions, less news, little public knowledge: News coverage and public awareness of executions in the U.S., 1977–2003. Presented at the Annual Meetings of the American Society of Criminology, Nashville, TN.

Jewkes, Y. (2004). *Media & crime.* Sage Publications: London, U.K.

Lundman, R. (2003). The newsworthiness and selection bias in news about murder: comparative and relative effects of novelty and race and gender typifications on newspaper coverage of homicide. *Sociological Forum, 18*, 357–386.

Maguire, B., Sandage, D., & Weatherby, G.A. (1999). Crime stories as television news: A content analysis of national, big city, and small town newscasts. *Journal of Criminal Justice and Popular Culture, 7*, 1–14.

Mediamark Research, Inc. (2002). *Mediamark Reporter.* New York: NOP World.

Miami Herald. Retrieved February 20, 2008, from http://www.miamiherald.com/.

New York Times. Retrieved February 20, 2008, from http://www.nytimes.com/products/timesselect/thearchive.html.

Radelet, M.L. (2007, May 24). Some Examples of Post-Furman Botched Executions. Retrieved February 20, 2008, from http://www.deathpenaltyinfo.org/article.php?scid=8&did=478.

Sacco, V. F. (2005). *When crime waves.* Thousand Oaks, CA: Sage Publications.

Surette, R. (1998). *Media, crime, and criminal justice: Images and realities* (2nd Ed.). Belmont, CA: Wadsworth Publishing.

USA Today. Retrieved February 20, 2008, from http://www.usatoday.com/.

Vanderbilt Television News Archive. Retrieved February 20, 2008, from http://tvnews.vanderbilt.edu/

LOOKING BEYOND *CAGED HEAT*

Media Images of Women in Prison

by Dawn K. Cecil
University of South Florida

W omen in prison are a vulnerable and invisible population; we rarely have the opportunity to hear their stories. These women are invisible despite the fact that in the United States there are currently 106,174 women incarcerated in state and federal facilities and an additional 94,571 estimated to be imprisoned in county jails (Harrison, 2006). Prisons and jails are closed institutions, and in the minds of the public and the media, they are an afterthought (Surette, 2007). According to Surette (2007), "it is a tenet of social constructionism that the more remote the subject, the more the public perception of it will be shaped by media imagery" (p. 152). Thus, the media images presented about women in prison are an important source of storytelling and information. The problem is that media images of women in prison are rare; therefore, each image is extremely vital to understanding these women and their lives.

Historically, Hollywood has been responsible for the main images of female prisoners received by people. With taglines such as "Women's prison U.S.A.—Rape, Riot, Revenge! White hot desires melting cold prison steel" (Corman & Demme's 1974 *Caged Heat*); "Women so hot with desire they melt the chains that enslave them" (Corman & Hill's 1972 *The Big Bird Cage*); and "Their bodies were caged, but not their desires. They would do anything for a man—or to him" (Corman & Hill's 1971 *Big Doll House*), one can imagine what must be imprinted in the minds of viewers. These "babes-behind-bars" films perpetuate highly sexualized images of female prisoners. These films "reinforce society's stereotypes about female prisoners: that they are violent, worthless, sex-crazed monsters totally unworthy of humane treatment" (Clowers, 2001, p. 28).

Entertainment-based images of women in prison may dominate media coverage, but other images exist. Programs purporting to deal with "real" images of incarcerated women especially are important because they appear to be more legitimate than portrayals in films and television dramas, which makes it vital to examine these nonfiction images. This type of research has not been conducted; therefore, the current study examines documentaries, news magazine programs, and talk shows focusing on women in prison to develop a better understanding of how women are portrayed. It examines the accuracy of the images presented as well as the underlying messages. Chesney-Lind (1999) believes it is important for the people who are most knowledgeable about female offenders to challenge incomplete and inaccurate media images by "actively seek[ing] ways to build alliances, and build credibility, with progressive journalists, to construct better coverage of crime issues" (p. 134); however, before we can challenge these images must understand the messages they are sending.

Media Images of Women in Prison

Images of prison life are gendered. Most feature men in prison and highlight the violent nature of these institutions, and when they concentrate on women, the imagery is sexualized (Britton, 2003). These images of women in prison are found in all facets of the media; however, most of the literature on the representation of female prisoners focuses on the entertainment media.

The most common and damaging of these images are produced by Hollywood. Rafter (2006, p. 175) states, "Until recently, if one wanted to see a film about women in prison, there were only two choices: *I Want to Live!* and soft pornography," the latter of which are commonly referred to as "babes-behind-bars" or "vixens in chains" films.[1] Films such as *Big Doll House* (1971), *The Big Bird Cage* (1972), and *Caged Heat* (1974) are notorious for their highly sexualized images of women in prison. Very little factual representation is contained in these films. It is Hollywood, after all; they do not necessarily seek to educate—instead they aim to titillate:

> These tales of vulnerable young things navigating a harsh prison are largely vehicles for money shot–style images that are the films' raison d'être: a roomful of women being hosed down by their sadistic warden as punishment (1971's *Big Doll House*) ... or a young reform-school inmate gang-raped with a plunger by her roommates (1974's *Born Innocent*). (Clark, 2005, pp. 37–38)

Because the correctional system is rarely depicted in the media, prison films such as these are extremely influential (Freeman, 2000); however, the images in "babes-behind-bars" films are detrimental in that they negate the issues surrounding women in prison. Even more serious films, such as *Brokedown Palace* and *Last Dance*, "do not in fact develop or sustain a women's point of view on incarceration; rather, they simply substitute women for men in order to broaden the movies' appeal without changing their basic nature" (Rafter, 2006, p. 175, see also Wilson & O'Sullivan, 2004). So even if on the surface these types of films appear to be more accurate, in reality, women in prison are still presented both stereotypically and inaccurately.

Images of women in prison are not limited to Hollywood representations; television producers also focus on these women in entertainment programs as well as in educational and news programs. In terms of entertainment television, not many dramas focus on prison life, let alone women in prison. Two women in prison dramas aired on British and Australian networks. In an attempt to educate viewers on the perils of women in prison, an Australian production company created *Prisoner Cell Block H*, also known as *Prisoner*, which aired in the 1970s (see Wilson & O'Sullivan, 2004). Although it was intended to be a serious drama about women in prison, Wilson and O'Sullivan (2004) comment that it quickly became "archetypical camped-up cliché" (p. 123), thereby losing its ability to educate and inform viewers. The second program is *Bad Girls*, which is currently in its eighth season on British television. Set almost entirely in a fictitious women's prison in South London, it is said to be a combination soap opera, cult TV program, and drama (Wilson & O'Sullivan, 2004). According to Wilson and O'Sullivan (2004), *Bad Girls* is popular because it plays to the audience's desire to be entertained, while at the same time making a conscious effort to bring prison issues to the forefront. In doing so, the program "generally concludes that, as far as women are concerned, for a surprising proportion of prisoners prison is not an appropriate response to their problems, or their offending behavior" (Wilson & O'Sullivan, 2004, p. 130). However, this program does not completely diverge from its film predecessors in that sexuality is a key issue (see Herman, 2003; Wilson & O'Sullivan, 2004). Although less common than images presented on the silver screen, those presented in these television dramas offer a more comprehensive look into the lives of female prisoners, which is probably due in part to the serial nature of these programs. One must remember, though, that the images are still fictionalized, thereby limiting the accuracy of the information presented.

The entertainment media may present us with most of our images of prison, but how does the news media present the issue of women in prison? In general, the news media are not very likely to focus on the correctional system (Surette, 2007). In the media's eyes, only riots, escapes, and other rarities are considered newsworthy (Chermak, 1998; Lipschultz & Hilt, 2002). Female prisoners are unlikely to cause a major disturbance (Mann, 1984; Pollock, 2002) or escape (Culp, 2005). They also make up a small percentage of the prison population; thus, they rarely make the news. So, although there has been research on how the news media portray the correctional system (e.g., Freeman, 2000; Welch, Weber, & Edwards, 2000), there has not been much research on how the news media specifically portray women in prison. Cecil's (2007) work, however, is an exception. She examined newspaper images of incarcerated women by focusing on articles pertaining to Martha Stewart's imprisonment. Findings indicated that the sexualized images of women in prison were absent; in its place was a highly feminized view of female inmates that focused on crafts, cooking, and leisure activities. Overall, the articles failed to offer information about other aspects of prison life. Although these findings are reflective of a specific prisoner, the main problem lies in the normalization of her prison experiences. The newspaper articles paint a picture of imprisonment based on one prisoner and fail to offer alternative views of or information about women in prison (Cecil, 2007).

The news media are not the only source of reality-based images of prison. Today, shows regarding crime can be found on many cable stations in the United States. Most of the shows that focus on the prison system examine the lives of male prisoners, but there are some specials depicting female prisoners. The current study delves into the images of women in prison perpetuated in nonfiction media sources such as documentaries, televised news magazines, and talk shows. Because these programs present real images, they can have a profound impact on viewers. In addition, they present more than a brief clip about the issue, allowing more information to be passed on to viewers. However, many crime-related reality programming can be classified as "infotainment," which means that it is vital to consider the nature of these programs before examining them.

Fact, Fiction, and Frames

When people watch women in prison films and television dramas, there is, on some level, recognition that these are fictionalized accounts of life behind bars. Yet when they watch reality crime programs, there is an assumption that they are viewing truthful images. This is not always the case; sometimes fact and fiction are blended or, at the very least, a highly edited version of reality is presented (Cavender & Fishman, 1998). Programs such as news magazines, talk shows, and even documentaries are meant to not only inform but also entertain. The creation and extreme popularity of reality-based crime programs, such as *Cops*, has contributed to a growing body of literature discussing these programs (see, e.g., Doyle, 2003; Fishman & Cavender, 1998). Reality crime programs "blur the line between news and entertainment; some even blur the line between fact and fiction," while claiming to present the unadulterated truth (Cavender & Fishman, 1998, p. 3). As these programs have developed, the line between fact and fiction has become less clear, combining news format with elements from crime dramas and even the horror genre (Cavender, 1998). Yet viewers are led to believe that they are presented with the facts; therefore, what they view must be true and complete.

Even though the images used in these programs are real, they do not depict actual circumstances. Instead, they present highly edited versions of reality that are adulterated at every step of the process, from filming to final production. Producers are at the mercy of prison administrators, whose goal is to maintain institutional control and safety. Once these images are filmed within the institutional setting, the editing process results in countless hours of film on the cutting-room floor, thus creating a highly edited version of prison life. The version that is presented is highly dependent on how producers decide to frame the issue at hand.

Frames are an important concept in understanding media representations; they "are the focus, a parameter or boundary, for discussing a particular event. Frames focus on what will be discussed, how it will be discussed, and above all, how it will not be discussed" (Altheide, 1997, p. 651). According to Tuchman (1978), frames used by news organizations are influenced, in part, by prior frames. Taking this into consideration, it is likely that the frames used by the producers of reality-based programs are influenced by frames used in previous representations of female prisoners. There was really only one source to look to for these frames—"babes-behind-bars" films. Sex and violence are the main frames utilized by the makers of these films; thus, it would not be surprising if producers of infotainment programs reproduced the same images by relying on these frames. This is further reinforced by the fact that the media tend to focus on the most unlikely offenses, particularly violent offenses (Garofalo, 1981; Lundman, 2003; Schlesinger, Tumber, & Murdock, 1991), as a way to set up the crime problem and create fear (Altheide, 2002).

Research indicates that the frames used affect the nature of the coverage (Cavender, 2004). If producers draw from specific frames, then the information that does not fit into these prespecified areas will fall to the wayside, thereby excluding potentially vital facts needed to fully understand the topic at hand. Focusing on sex and violence means that the real problems faced by female prisoners today will be overlooked, and reality crime programs will perpetuate myths about women in prison similar to those found in fictional portrayals.

The exact way that these reality-based programs portray female inmates is unknown; therefore, the current study examines various types of programs depicting real images of women in prison. The aim is to not only describe how these women are portrayed but also identify the messages and frames associated with these images. It is only once we are aware of this that we can know for certain how to help improve the focus of these shows by actively engaging with the media.

Method

As previously mentioned, three types of programs are included in this study—documentaries, televised news magazines, and talk shows—in order to analyze images of women incarcerated in the United States. Various sources were used to identify programs included in this study. Search engines on the Internet, such as Google, as well as searches of individual network Web sites, were used to identify potential programs. This study relied on the purposive sampling of suitable programs. Purposive sampling is a nonprobability sampling technique that allows the researcher to judge which items are the most representative or useful (Babbie, 2004). Although this means that these programs may not be a truly representative sample, the programs included do represent some of the main depictions of women in prison that are easily available for public consumption. Several programs were identified. Based on availability, a sample of 10 programs was examined in this study. The programs are specifically discussed in the next section.

Once the programs were screened for appropriateness, data were collected during additional viewings. Media studies commonly use content analysis, which involves "the study of recorded human communications" (Babbie, 2004, p. 314; see also Altheide, 1996; Berger, 1998; Zito, 1975). This method was utilized because it allows the researcher to examine the images that are presented, known as manifest content, as well as the messages inherent in these images, or latent content (Babbie, 2004). More specific, this study relied on ethnographic content analysis, which is more qualitative in nature than traditional content analysis (see Altheide, 1996). Data were collected using both dialogue and visual images, and included descriptions of the women interviewed on camera, as well as the issues presented in each program.

To determine whether these programs address the major issues facing female inmates, literature on women in prison was used to identify those issues, which are sexual and physical abuse, motherhood, substance abuse, HIV and other health issues (including mental illness), and sexual harassment in prison (Belknap, 2007; Chesney-Lind & Pasko, 2004; Morash & Schram, 2002; Pollock, 2002). The selected programs were examined to determine whether these issues were addressed and, if so, how they were approached. In addition, when applicable, the number of inmates discussing these issues was counted, and what they said about these issues was documented.

Additional data were collected on the prison routine and prison life, which allowed for the exploration of themes related to these areas. Taken as a whole, this information provides insight into the overall messages perpetuated by these programs. These data allow for descriptions of the women and their crimes and the determination of whether these programs reflect the true nature of the issues faced by women in prison. Once the themes and issues were identified, the way that women in prison are presented in reality-based programs was identified.

The Programs

When examining the programs included in this study, it is important to consider the purpose and format of each program, as these factors may influence the main issues depicted. Of the 10 programs selected, 4 were televised news magazines (refer to Table 1). The first, ABC's *Primetime Live* segment "Women Doing Time" (Sesnon, 1996),[2] featured the host, Diane Sawyer, who spent 2 days and 2 nights in a women's prison to explore how women's lives behind bars are different from those of men. Later, ABC aired another *Primetime Live* titled "The Women in Maximum Security" (Pearson, 2004). Here, Sawyer spent 24 hours in a maximum security institution for women in Atlanta. In her introduction, Sawyer states that the aim is to show the reality of the inmates' lives. Similarly, *CBS News* aired a special called "Women Behind

Table 1. Description of Programs

Title, Producer, and Year of Release	Type of Program	Institution	Focus
CBS News "Women Behind Bars" (Martin, 1999)	News magazine	Denver Women's Correctional Facility	Provides a view of women's imprisonment through the eyes of inmates, staff, and administrators.
"From One Prison" (University of California Extension Center for Media and Independent Learning, 1994)	Documentary	Unknown women's prison in Michigan	Features four inmates imprisoned for killing their abusers discussing their cases and institutional life.
A & E Investigative Reports "Women in Prison" (Kurtis, 1993)	News magazine	Central California Women's Facility and California Institution for Women	Bill Curtis examines the world of women's prisons and how they are different from men's prisons.
Oprah Winfrey Show "Lisa Ling Goes to Prison: A Shocking Report" (Harpo, 2005)	Talk show	Dwight Correctional Institution, IL	Oprah Winfrey sends three suburban moms to walk in the shoes of inmates for a day.
ABC's Primetime Live "Women Doing Time" (Sesnon, 1996)	News magazine	Louisiana Correctional Institution for Women	Diane Sawyer spends 2 days and nights in a maximum security institution.
ABC's Primetime Live "The Women in Maximum Security" (Pearson, 2004)	News magazine	Metro State Prison for Women, GA	Diane Sawyer spends 24 hours in a maximum security institution.
Released: Five Short Films about Women and Prison (Juhasz, 2001)	Documentary	N/A	Each of the films focuses on the issue of women and prison through discussions with ex-inmates and others.
PBS "Troop 1500" (Spiro, 2005)	Documentary	Hilltop Unit of Gatesville Prison, TX	Examines the lives of mothers and daughters involved in a Girl Scouts Behind Bars program.
The Tyra Banks Show (ANE Productions Inc., 2006)	Talk show	California Institution for Women, Chino	Examines why women end up in prison, including the role of the men in their lives.
"What I Want my Words to Do to You" (Katz, 2003)	Documentary	Bedford Hills Correctional Institution, NY	Examines the lives of female prisoners by depicting women who participated in a writing program taught by playwright Eve Ensler.

Bars" that sought to explore how women are treated differently from men in the prison system (Martin, 1999). The final news magazine program analyzed was A&E Television's *Investigative Reports'* "Women in Prison" (Kurtis, 1993). This piece featured two women's institutions in order to offer a glimpse into the secret world of women's institutions and to identify how their problems differ from those of their male counterparts.

Two programs examined were talk shows. Due to the nature of the talk show format, these 2 programs featured fewer prison images and more studio footage than the other shows. The first was an episode of *The Oprah Winfrey Show* titled "Lisa Ling goes to prison: A shocking report," (Harpo Productions, 2005). Only one segment of this episode focused on female inmates. Oprah conducted an experiment in which she sent three suburban housewives to trade places with three inmates. These women spent a day in prison experiencing the entire process before being released and meeting the inmates face-to-face. The second talk show, *The Tyra Banks Show* (ANE Productions, 2006), involved Tyra spending a day in prison to examine why women are incarcerated and what role men play leading up to the women's imprisonment. The program shows clips of Tyra being processed and participating in the prison routine, as well as several recently released inmates discussing their experiences.

The remaining 4 programs included in this study were documentaries. The first, *From One Prison* (University of California Extension Center for Media and Independent Learning, 1994), had a very specific focus: to examine the background and experiences of women incarcerated for murdering their spouses. The second was an independent documentary, *Released: Five Short Films About Women and Prison* (Juhasz, 2001). It tackled the issue of women and prison mostly through stories about women who had been to prison. Four of the five short films are applicable to this study—"Gram O'Pussy," "Sheltered," "Unyielding Conditions," and "Making the Invisible Invincible: Cheryl Dunye's Stranger Inside."[3] Each of these segments presented various issues pertaining to women and prison, ranging from lack of opportunities for success to the dangers of the system and the stories of the invisible women behind bars. The third documentary, *What I Want My Words to Do to You,* (Katz, 2003) aired on PBS and focused on women who participated in a writing program directed by playwright Eve Ensler. The women were given a series of writing exercises to examine their crime, their past, and their future. The purpose of this documentary was to provide a more complete picture of the women who are incarcerated in this country. The last documentary analyzed was *Troop 1500*, (Spiro & Bernstein, 2005). It aired on PBS and featured incarcerated mothers and their daughters involved in a Girl Scout troop. The documentary focused on the interactions between the girls and their mothers during their monthly visits, as well as how the girls coped when they were apart from their mothers.

Overall, the televised news magazines had a broader focus than did the talk shows and documentaries. Programs that offer an overview of women in prison provide a wider array of information on these women than a documentary such as *Troop 1500* (2005), which focuses on a specific program within the institution. However, because each program was filmed within the prison setting, even programs meant to address more specific issues still presented information on life behind bars. There are also themes that run throughout these programs, regardless of the main purpose of the show. These themes are the main analytical focus of this study.

Findings

The Women and Their Crimes

There were 98 female inmates featured in the programs sampled. These women were predominately White. Race or ethnicity was available for 85 of these females and was as follows: 52% ($n = 44$) White, 42.4% ($n = 36$) African American, 4.7% ($n = 4$) Hispanic, and 1% ($n = 1$) Native American. These programs overrepresented both White and African American inmates, while underrepresenting Hispanics and women from other racial and ethnic backgrounds. Recent national prison statistics on female prisoners show the distribution by race as 44% White, 33.4% African American, 16% Hispanic, and 7% Native Americans and other ethnicities (Harrison & Beck, 2005). The racial and ethnic inaccuracies depicted in these programs coincide with other media representations. The media tend to focus on White offenders in general (Surette, 2007), to overrepresent African Americans when focusing on street violence (Dorfman & Schiraldi, 2001), and in general, to underrepresent Hispanics and other minority groups (Larson, 2006).

The women featured in these programs were incarcerated for anything from shoplifting to murder; however, the main focus was on violent inmates. Offenses were given for 80 of the inmates depicted on these programs. Nearly 69% ($n = 55$) of these women were incarcerated for violent offenses, whereas the remaining 31.25% ($n = 15$) were incarcerated for nonviolent offenses, including both drug and property offenses; therefore, these programs focused on the most unlikely offenses. For example, in 2004, only 33% of the women incarcerated in our nation's prisons were imprisoned for violent offenses (Harrison & Beck, 2005). Approximately 54% of the women in the programs were incarcerated for murder, manslaughter, or attempted murder, whereas in actuality, 12.2% of imprisoned women are incarcerated for these offenses (Harrison & Beck, 2005). This finding is not surprising because it is also the trend for general media reports on crime—the media focus on the least common types of crime, which are violent crimes (Garofalo, 1981; Lundman, 2003; Schlesinger et al., 1991). Details on the murders committed by women in these programs were given in some cases and indicated that many of these women murdered people whom they knew (41.9% of female murderers). More specifically, they murdered men who had abused or raped them (30.2% of female murderers).

These programs, however, did not completely ignore the reality of the crimes women committed. For example, on *Primetime Live* (1996), Sawyer began the segment by stating, "It is a world unto itself—a lost continent of 637 women in prison for everything from forging prescriptions to murder. Twenty-two percent have killed someone." In her 2004 show, Sawyer reported that more than 15% of the women in this prison have committed murder, and she provided facts about women who have killed.[4] This statement should inform viewers that these inmates are not the norm; yet, the program focused predominantly on the violent female offenders. This was typical of the programs sampled. Two of the programs commented on the increasing female prison population, attributing it to the war on drugs and mandatory minimum sentences, which according to research, are the main reasons for the increased female prison population (e.g., Chesney-Lind & Pasko, 2004). Rather than focusing on these issues, the camera lens is turned to the violent offenders, and the focus is on women's stories that are likely to have the most significant impact to viewers.

There also were two ways that these programs reinforced the image of the violent female offender: first, with descriptions of the women made by the hosts, and second, by highlighting issues of institutional violence by women. For example (*emphasis added in all quotations*):

OPRAH WINFREY (2005): Dwight Correctional Center is no Camp Cupcake. It's where over one thousand *hard-core* female criminals and *murderers* are locked up ... . For the first time in their lives, they encounter *murderers*.

DIANE SAWYER (2004): And the guards say it is a new trend—young women being as *violent* as men. They call it being off the chain.

TYRA BANKS (2006) : I am talking about *hardened* criminals, and a lot of them are facing life sentences for *cold-blooded* murder.

These are just a few examples of the way these women were described to viewers. To illustrate the second reinforcing measure, *CBS News* (1991) features women discussing violence between inmates, including "blanket parties," which involve covering an inmate with a blanket and beating them so the assailants cannot be identified. When discussing institutional violence in this manner, women appear to be as violent as the male prisoners depicted in the media. Focusing on their use of violence within the institution further reinforces the image of violent women behind bars, despite the fact that research indicates that there is less violence reported in women's prisons than men's facilities (Wolff, Blitz, Shi, Siegel, & Bachman, 2007).

Motherhood

Research indicates that approximately two thirds of women in prison are mothers of minor children (Mumola, 2000). In all, only 33 (33.7%) of the women in the programs analyzed mentioned that they had children. Underrepresenting the proportion of women in prison with minor children is a critical error. As the percentage of women in prison has increased, so too has the number of children affected by maternal incarceration. The imprisonment of a parent, particularly a mother, increases the chances of displacement from the home, as well as the onset of several risk factors, including the risk of delinquency (see, e.g., Johnston, 2006; Mumola, 2000; Petersilia, 2003; Phillips, Erkanli, Keeler, Costello, & Angold, 2006). Although underestimating the percentage of mothers in prison, most of the programs analyzed addressed this topic. Programs offered statistics on mothers in prison (*Investigative Reports,* 1993; *The Oprah Winfrey Show,* 2005; *Primetime Live,* 2004), and some revealed information about programs for mothers in prison, particularly visitation programs (*Investigative Reports,* 1993; *The Oprah Winfrey Show,* 2005; *Primetime Live,* 2004; *Troop 1500,* 2005; *What I Want My Words to Do to You,* 2003). *Primetime Live* (1996) was the only program that did not mention the issue of children, despite the fact that it was intended to show how life in women's prison is different from men's prison.

When presenting the issue of mothers in prison, however, most of the programs focused on how the mothers feel about their children and the effect of imprisonment on both mother and child. *The Tyra Banks Show* (2006) featured the reunification of two mothers and their daughters. It focused on the daughters discussing the effect of their mothers' imprisonment on their lives. *The Oprah Winfrey Show* (2005) took a slightly different approach to the subject by sending three suburban mothers to a women's prison to walk in the shoes of incarcerated mothers. After spending the day there, the guests had very strong opinions about what it must be like for these women, as the following dialogue demonstrates:

OPRAH: Jenne says she'd rather be dead than give birth to a baby in prison. Is that true?

JENNE: I feel bad saying that for the women who are there, because I certainly don't want them to think that they don't have hope. But that notion of someone taking my child away from me—there is no worse way I could be punished. Take away my kids, and I am dead ... . I'm emotionally and spiritually dead. You've punished me in the worst way possible. So I can't imagine them having to do that.

Overall, the programs focusing on incarcerated mothers showed how difficult it is for *both* the mothers and the children. This was particularly true of one documentary—*Troop 1500* (2005).

Troop 1500 offered the most comprehensive look at the issue of incarcerated mothers and their children. This documentary focused on a Girl Scout troop containing girls whose mothers were in prison. The program seeks to maintain the mother-child bond in an effort to break the cycle of crime. Although the mothers were not involved in the girls' daily lives, the monthly visitation allowed them to stay connected. Because *Troop 1500* depicted the girls, visits with their mothers, and the lives of the girls on the outside without their mothers, it provided the most insight into mothers in prison, especially with respect to the impact of imprisonment on both the mothers and the children. *Troop 1500* did this by showing interviews the girls conducted with their mothers and scenes of the girls at home. The relationships and interactions that were depicted are not very different from what one would expect from nonincarcerated mothers and their children; however, these women are required to squeeze in a month of mothering during a 4-hour visit. The mothers recognize what this potentially does to their children. Kenya, a mother of two girls, stated, "Your mom gives you a sense of self. We're not there for that, so they are getting that from someone else." Susan says, "I am constantly reminded of the suffering that they are going through because of my choice. I don't know my children anymore." Overall, this program showed viewers that, at least in terms of their relationships with their children, women in prison are not monsters and are not very different from mothers who are not incarcerated.

The programs also questioned why mothers would risk losing their children by doing things that may result in incarceration. On *Investigative Reports* (1993), host Curtis stated the following about incarcerated mothers: "You might think that separation from children would be a strong enough deterrent to keep anyone from coming back here, but many women will return despite conditions that will test their mental and physical stability." Comments such as these ignore the realities faced by many of these women when they are released. Although most women hope to reunite with their children upon release (Bloom & Steinhart, 1993; Hagan & Coleman, 2001; Hairston, 1991; Koban, 1983), the obstacles they face, such as finding a place to live and a stable job, make it a monumental task to reunite with their children and to remain out of prison. Instead, comments remind viewers that these women are not good mothers because they did not put their children first.

Abuse and Health Issues

It is a well-known fact that women in prison have significant histories of physical and/or sexual abuse (see, e.g., Chesney-Lind & Pasko, 2004; Pollock, 2002). In addition, female prisoners are also more likely than male prisoners to have substance abuse problems, are HIV positive at higher rates, and are more likely to have mental health problems (Greenfeld & Snell, 1999; James & Glaze, 2006; Maruschak, 2005). The programs examined touched on these issues, but only superficially.

Although most of the programs (80%, $n = 8$) contained segments about abuse in the lives of female offenders, overall there was not a lot of information given on this subject. Of the 94 women depicted, only 6 (6.4%) admitted on camera that they were abused as children, and 12 (12.8%) discussed abuse during adulthood. In reality, research indicates that nearly 60% of the women incarcerated in our country have been physically or sexually abused (Greenfeld & Snell, 1999). Thus, there is a vast contrast between the reality of abuse in the lives of female prisoners and that shown on the programs. The most common way that abuse was approached was by connecting it to the crimes that these women committed—in most cases, murdering their abuser. *From One Prison* (1994) focused exclusively on four women who killed their abusers. Their stories of abuse and the killing, as well as of their prosecution and subsequent incarceration, constituted the bulk of this program. Three additional programs featured battered women who killed, mentioning their crimes without delving into their stories. *Investigative Reports* (2003) offered the most information on female prisoners and abuse. The program focused on inmates who talk about their abuse, if only briefly. The host and others presented statistics on abuse in this population of women, linking abuse to drug use and other crimes. Finally, the programs gave viewers a look into a treatment program for violent female offenders who survived abuse. Overall, though abuse is major issue for the women in prison, the focus in the programs tended to be on the crimes women committed without an examination of why women committed these offenses.

Even more neglected than the issue of abuse in the lives of female prisoners were the issues of substance abuse, mental illness, and HIV. Nine of the programs examined featured inmates discussing substance abuse in their lives or provided statistics on drug use; however, only 14 (14.9%) women featured on these programs admitted to using drugs and/or alcohol. In reality, it is estimated that more than half of the women incarcerated used drugs and/or alcohol while committing the crime for which they were incarcerated (Greenfeld & Snell, 1999). And, although drug treatment programs are common in women's prisons, *Investigative Reports* (2003) was the only show to feature a discussion of a therapeutic community (within the California prison system.)

Two female prisoners (2%) were identified as being HIV positive, which is similar to the national average (of 2.7%; Maruschak, 2005). Although this figure represents a small percentage of the total female prison population, it is higher than the proportion of male inmates with HIV (Maruschak, 2005). Only 3 programs examined mentioned HIV. For the most part, these programs highlighted the dangers for staff when working with inmates who are HIV positive. This message was conveyed by filming an image of a sign warning people that they are entering an area housing inmates who may have communicable diseases (*Investigative Reports*, 2003) and by including a discussion by the Certified Emergency Response Team on the dangers of responding to crises—particularly the threat of exposure to blood (*Primetime Live*, 2004).

Although it is estimated that 73% of female inmates incarcerated in state facilities have mental health problems (James & Glaze, 2006), only 3 inmates in the programs examined (3.1%) were shown to have some sort of mental illness. *Primetime Live* (2004) was the only program that delved into the subject. Sawyer stated:

> But there is something else very disturbing and new that we learned. Increasingly, America's hospitals are releasing mental patients who then end up warehoused in the prison system. Prison doctors are overwhelmed and the patients are often confined to white cells, with the only human contact a voice on the other side of the door.

This statement was followed by a vignette depicting the Certified Emergency Response Team physically medicating a psychotic inmate in her cell. Visuals were not shown, but screams and other dialogue were used. Prison doctors talked about the issue of being forced to treat women who should be treated in hospitals. They believe that if these women had been treated properly, then they would have never found their way into the prison system. Although drastic examples were used in this program, it is the only program to bring this issue to light.

Overall, the health and well-being of the female prisoners was not a central theme featured in the programs examined. The topics were not addressed at length, and these programs failed to address issues such as depression, self-injury, and suicide, which are also major health-related issues facing female inmates (Pollock, 2002). The focus of these programs appears to be more on the secret lives of these women while they are in prison than on a true understanding of the problems faced by them. This portrayal was particularly evident in programs that focused on prison life and routine.

Prison Life and Routine

In an effort to unlock the secrets of institutional life, these programs focused on the prison routine and the inmate social system. These programs provided insight into the intake process, including strip searches, fingerprinting, and the classification process (*CBS News*, 1999; *The Oprah Winfrey Show*, 2005; *Primetime Live* 2004; *The Tyra Banks Show*, 2006). What they did not show viewers is how women are affected by the process. For example, Pollock (2002) writes, "The process of entry involves a dehumanizing sequence of shedding one's outer identity and becoming a 'number.' ... For women who are not used to it, the procedures can be quite frightening and alienating" (p. 70). The only image to reflect this was comments made by Tyra Banks when she was being processed during her special on women in prison. She stated: "I felt violated... . Even though I was going through the motions, I know that I could not handle it if I was actually going to prison."

The shows also introduced viewers to the prison programs women were involved in—from work to drug treatment (*CBS News*, 1999; *From One Prison*, 1994; *Investigative Reports*, 1993; *Troop 1500*, 2005; *What I Want My Words to Do to You*, 2003)—by setting up the need for the treatment program within the institution, showing viewers program participants and interviewing the women about their experiences within the program. *What I Want My Words to Do to You* and *Troop 1500* delved deeply into the programs they highlighted, which were atypical programs. *Troop 1500* focused on Girl Scouts Behind Bars and depicted the mothers and their daughters participating in the program, as well as discussions of the history and goals of that particular treatment program. *What I Want My Words to Do to You* depicted a writing program directed by playwright Eve Ensler, who worked with 15 women for 4 years. During this time, she assigned them various writing projects that examined their crimes and their lives both inside and outside prison walls. As viewers listened to the stories women wrote, they also learned about other treatment programs available to women in Bedford Hills Correctional Facility, including puppies behind bars and the children's center. In *From One Prison* (1994), the women made an important point about treatment programs in women's prisons comparing availability. The women commented that they have few program choices compared to men's facilities and that many of the treatment programs available in women's prisons are not useful on the outside, especially in terms of securing employment.

A few of the television programs examined also focused on the use of segregation, where inmates spend 23 hours per day in their cells (*CBS News*, 1999; *Investigative Reports*, 1993). Viewers see the inside of these cellblocks, learn the rules, and meet the inmates who are held there, but they do not learn about the effects of solitary confinement on the inmates.

Even more than the prison routine, the programs on women in prison gave viewers insight into the inmate social system (*CBS News*, 1999; *From One Prison*, 1994; *Primetime Live* 1996, 2004). In the 1996 *Primetime Live* special, Sawyer stated:

> It is a place of strange rituals and complicated codes. A woman serving a life sentence puts
> Martha Stewart to shame whipping up something from crushed Oreos smushed [*sic*] with

> Snickers and hot water... . And there is something else that I am told you would never see
> in a male's prison... . the women form what they call play families.

Some of the programs highlight the rules inherent in the inmate social system. For example, the *CBS News* (1999) special discussed the code that must be followed (e.g., no friends in prison; do not be friendly with the staff) and revealed that new inmates are threatened and bullied to determine whether they can stand up to the rules. Viewers are privy to ways that inmates circumvent minor prison rules, for example, by shooting notes across the floor into other cells in maximum security (*Primetime Live*, 1996, 2004). The audience sees how inmates create things such as a cigarette lighter from batteries, staples, and a brillo pad (*Primetime Live*, 2004) and baked potatoes from chips bought in the commissary (*Troop 1500*, 2005). And, of course, inmates make their own weapons from locks stuffed in socks or from pencils and razor blades (*Primetime Live*, 2004).

Possibly influenced by "babes-behind-bars" films, an aspect of prison life that received a lot of attention was sexual relations between prisoners. Interestingly, it was the news magazine shows that were the most likely to tackle this issue. Sawyer introduced her 2004 show by saying that they are offering a "look into the secrets of sex and survival in prison." Only one documentary and none of the talk shows discussed this subject. Despite the fact that women incarcerated experience sexual misconduct at the hands of staff (Morash & Schram, 2002), only one program, *From One Prison* (1994), discussed this issue. The inmates shared their stories about being inappropriately fondled by male correctional officers during shakedowns and about being raped by a male staff member. The remaining discussions of sex focused on prison-based lesbian relationships. Although prison sex is against the rules and can land violators in segregation, the inmates reported that women have sex in various places throughout the prison, and a person called a pinner serves as a lookout for staff to ensure privacy (*CBS News*, 1999). An inmate featured on *Primetime Live* (2004) stated:

> I've seen people have sex in the classroom, in programs, I've seen people have sex in medical,
> I've seen them having sex in the kitchen. I've even seen them disrespect God and have it in
> the church. I've seen it all.

And it becomes clear that these sexual relations can cause problems within the institutions. For example, Sawyer stated, "We are told that a lot of conflict around here is about sex and that even if you wander into the shower it can mean big trouble" (*Primetime Live*, 2004).

The two *Primetime Live* specials suggested that nearly every inmate has sex while in prison. The inmates in the 1996 special claimed that more than 99% participate, whereas those in the 2004 special estimated 90%. The exact number of female inmates who engage in sexual relationships with other women while incarcerated is unknown (Hensley, 2000); however, it is a well-known fact that incarcerated women do have same-sex relationships while incarcerated and that some of these relationships do not contain a sexual component (Pollock, 2002). Despite this fact, it was the sexual nature of these relationships that was highlighted.

Overall, relationships were portrayed in two main ways. On one hand, the programs suggested that women enter into these relationships willingly and for comfort. The *CBS News* (1999) special commented that prison life is lonely for most women and after being separated from the ones they love, "in time many turn to sexual relationships with one another." Curtis, the host of *Investigative Reports*, (1993) stated: "Some inmates turn to homosexuality for emotional support." Although this particular program made a point of discussing that women are relationship oriented, most of the programs failed to address the relationship side of this issue, instead choosing to highlight the sexual nature of the relationships. Donna, an inmate in the *CBS News* special (1999), was the only inmate who admitted being in a long-term relationship with another inmate, whereas a few others called their lovers their wives.

On the other hand, both the *Primetime Live* specials (1996, 2004) and *CBS News* portrayed a much more sexually aggressive environment within these institutions. Inmates commented that sexual predators exist in prison and "they try to get the straight girls gay … a lot of them do get turned out" (*CBS News*, 1999). Another inmate recounted her first day in prison:"I said no I am not gay and she said well you will be before you leave" (*Primetime Live*, 1996). So, though most female inmates are not typically forced into sexual relationships (Hensley, Castle, & Tewksbury, 2003), the dialogue used suggested that women are commonly coerced into them. Overall, in the programs that contained information on sex in prison, it was highlighted in such a way as to take the forefront to all of the issues facing women in prison.

Beyond some of the problems faced by these women and these other elements of prison life, these programs do touch on some additional subjects but not at length. The programs analyzed also offered information about the institutions themselves, which was almost always maximum security. Viewers learned little about the challenges women would face upon release. Prison life is filled with many different activities ranging from educational and vocational programming to social activities and idle time. Yet many of the programs examined focused on a very limited aspect of prison life. These programs repeated the same formula by focusing on rare events and aspects of prison life to capture the audience's attention.

Discussion and Conclusion

The images that people receive about women in prison are important. Wilson and O'Sullivan (2004) argue that prisons still exist in their condition because the public underestimates the true nature of these institutions. They believe that if prison and prisoners are given a "voice," then people will listen and be willing to change the system. In particular, they state,"Women's experience of prison can have a particular significance for raising issues of the irrationality of prison" (Wilson & O'Sullivan, 2004, p. 121). If we are to rely on the plight of female prisoners to raise awareness, then we need to make certain that the images people receive are accurate and focus on the major challenges these women face.

Women in prison films focus on innocent women who enter brutal prisons where they are sexually violated and physically attacked, but in the end they are able to fight against the corrupt administration and the vicious inmates to escape—presumably to live happily ever after in the free world. In reality, women are harmed by their experiences in prison, and the challenges they face on the outside almost ensure that a significant proportion of these women will return to the cells from which they were once released. These women suffer from a host of problems that contribute to imprisonment and to the likelihood that they will be incarcerated again in the future. The public is blind to these issues, but not by their own fault; after all, prisons are closed institutions, with limited available information. Yet, Beth Richie, a renowned criminologist, also believes that part of this blindness is by choice. In an interview on the issue, she states:

> This country, especially the [general] public, is still unfamiliar with, and unwilling to become familiar with, the situations many incarcerated women face. Instead, they choose to embrace

and not challenge the highly sexualized stereotypical images we get. To really understand women in prison we have to look at issues of poverty, joblessness, and how this country has chosen to respond to substance abuse. Those are hard issues to look at. (Lydersen, 2005, p. 39)

The producers of the programs are not very different. Few of these hard issues are examined in detail in the documentaries, news magazine programs, and talk shows examined in this study. Instead, they frame women's imprisonment much like it is depicted in the infamous Hollywood films.

Like "babes-behind-bars" films, the nonfiction accounts of women in prison featured in the programs examined focus on violent women who have sexual relationships while in prison. Unlike these films, the programs also focus on these women as mothers. Thus, while presenting the audience with the secrets of prison life, these reality-based programs appear to frame the issue of women in prison around three main factors: violence, sex, and motherhood. Each of these three frames assures viewers that these women deserve to be behind bars.

The majority of the women presented in these programs were violent; a high percentage of them were involved in murder. Focusing on violent women is detrimental because they are the exception; presenting the majority of women in prison as violent has the potential to harden viewers. Women are not supposed to be violent. These women have stepped outside the boundaries of appropriate female behavior; therefore, they must have gotten what they deserve. These programs reinforce this image by replicating the highly sexualized images of women in prison already perpetrated by Hollywood producers. Women who step outside the boundaries of acceptable sexual behavior are also demonized, as has been demonstrated throughout the development of the criminal justice system (see Chesney-Lind & Pasko, 2004). Even the images of motherhood reinforce the idea that these women are bad. The media tell us that good women focus on their families (Wood, 1994); they do not risk their families by doing things that may land them in prison. By focusing on the nonconforming female, viewers can absolve themselves of responsibility and be content to watch these images while remaining unattached to the issue.

The manner in which female inmates are depicted in many of the sample programs does not diverge very much from other media constructions of "bad girls." Literature on female offenders in the media highlights the fact that these women are portrayed as violent and links this violence to either sexuality or motherhood (Bailey & Hale, 2004; Bond-Maupin, 1998; Cecil, forthcoming; Chesney-Lind, 1999; Inness, 1999; McCaughey & King, 2001). Thus, the programs examined in this study repeat a very familiar formula, thereby reinforcing these other images of female offenders.

The way in which producers of these programs frame the issue of women in prison creates a false sense of the challenges faced by these women. By overemphasizing violence and sex, issues such as drug abuse, their histories of sexual and physical abuse, and other problems faced by female prisoners are significantly downplayed. It is the secondary stories in these programs about some of the real issues faced by imprisoned women, including motherhood, abuse, and addiction, that should help viewers understand these women. Although each of these topics is depicted in the programs examined, motherhood garnered much more attention than did stories of abuse and addiction. Yet, as mentioned previously, the way that motherhood is approached negates the real issue at hand. By underrepresenting the actual percentage of mothers in prison, the audience may not get a true sense of the scope of the issue, despite the fact that almost every program touches on the subject of incarcerated mothers.

In particular, the stories told about mothers in prison have the potential to humanize these women more than any other element included in the programs. Viewers see that women behind bars are actually not very different from women in the free world. Leslie Acoca, a psychologist featured on *Investigative Reports* (1993), thought that inmate mothers would care less for their children but admits she was mistaken. The warden of the prison featured in this program reiterates this statement by commenting that these women care for their kids the same way as women on the outside do; they feel pain when they cannot be there for them. Documentaries such as *Troop 1500* (2005) show this particular aspect of female prisoners, thereby normalizing and humanizing them. This view allows the audience to feel some sympathy for these women because they can understand the plight of these mothers. Yet in the same breath they remind viewers that these women have failed their children by going to prison in the first place.

Viewers may better understand the plight of women behind bars if they understand the true circumstances surrounding their imprisonment, including the role of physical and sexual abuse as well as substance abuse, and how all of these factors are related to their criminal histories. The programs about women in prison only touch on these subjects briefly, making them appear to be less important than they actually are. Furthermore, when programs connect women's abuse only to the crime of murder and substance abuse to their current imprisonment, the impact of their stories may backfire for some viewers. If more attention were paid to these factors instead of to the issues of sex and violence, then the public would have a better understanding of many of the women incarcerated in our country, which in turn may influence some to look at the hard issues mentioned by Richie (see Lydersen, 2005). As it stands, media representations of female prisoners focus on atypical female inmates and the superficial aspects of life in prison while ignoring the reality facing most women incarcerated in our country. People are not likely to be outraged by most of the images presented. At the very least, however, they may be able to sympathize and possibly empathize with some of these women. But will that be enough to induce change?

Because there are so few real images of women in prison, these programs are important. By presenting nonfiction accounts of female prisoners, producers can begin to inform the public of the issues facing female prisoners. However, the framing of the issues and the limitations of reality crime programming discussed earlier are important considerations. Recognizing how these programs are filmed in these closed institutions and how they are edited would add to a deeper understanding of the images presented. Future research will tackle this question. This study is just a small step in understanding the images of women in prison, but it can help us begin to see the types of images and messages that are being spread about female prisoners. While continuing to examine these images, academics and practitioners alike should become active storytellers for these women. By giving voice to these women's stories, perhaps such storytellers can make the media and the public aware of the real issues these women face instead of continuing to rely on the titillating tales of sex and violence to which they have grown accustomed.

Notes

1. *I Want to Live!* (1958) is based on the true story of Barbara Graham, who was executed at San Quentin. This film offers a more realistic portrayal of women in prison than do "babes-behind-bars" films in its depiction of the story about a woman who is sent to the gas chamber for a crime that she did not commit (Rafter, 2006).

2. The media source is cited in the proper APA citation format for the first instance, which requires the producer and year be listed. After that, the source is referred to by its name and the year it aired to make it easier to read and follow.

3. The fifth, "Breathe," is a cartoon and therefore was not included in this analysis.

4. These statistics may reflect the institution that is featured in these programs, but they do not reflect the national averages. The hosts do not offer national statistics for comparative purposes.

References

Altheide, D. L. (1996). *Qualitative media analysis.* Thousand Oaks, CA: Sage.

Altheide, D. L. (1997). The news media, the problem frame, and the production of fear. *The Sociological Quarterly, 38*(4), 647–668.

Altheide, D. L. (2002). *Creating fear: News and the construction of crisis.* New York: Aldine De Gruyter. ANE Productions, Inc. (2006). *The Tyra Banks show.*

Babbie, E. (2004). *The practice of social research* (10th ed.). Belmont, CA: Wadsworth.

Bailey, F., & Hale, D. (2004). *Blood on her hands: Women who murder.* Belmont, CA: Wadsworth.

Belknap, J. (2007). *The invisible women: Gender, crime, and justice* (3rd ed.). Belmont, CA: Wadsworth.

Berger, A. A. (1998). *Media research techniques* (2nd ed.). Thousand Oaks, CA: Sage.

Bloom, B., & Steinhart, D. (1993). *Why punish the children? A reappraisal of the children of incarcerated mothers in America.* San Francisco: National Council on Crime and Delinquency.

Bond-Maupin, L. (1998). "That wasn't even me they showed": Women as criminals on *America's Most Wanted. Violence Against Women, 4*(1), 30–44.

Britton, D. M. (2003). *At work in the iron cage: The prison as gendered organization.* New York: New York University Press.

Cavender, G. (1998). In "The shadow of shadows": Television reality crime programming. In M. Fishman & G. Cavender (Eds.), *Entertaining crime: Television reality programs* (pp. 79–94). New York: Aldine De Gruyter.

Cavender, G. (2004). Media and crime policy: A reconsideration of David Garland's *The Culture of Control. Punishment & Society, 6*(3), 335–348.

Cavender, G., & Fishman, M. (1998). Televised reality crime programs: Context and history. In M. Fishman & G. Cavender (Eds.), *Entertaining crime: Television reality programs* (pp. 3–15). New York: Aldine De Gruyter.

Cecil, D. (2007). Doing time in "Camp Cupcake": Lessons learned from newspaper accounts of Martha Stewart's incarceration. *Journal of Criminal Justice and Popular Culture, 14*(2), 142–160.

Cecil, D. (forthcoming). Dramatic portrayals of violent women: Female offenders on prime time crime dramas. *Journal of Criminal Justice and Popular Culture.*

Chermak, S. M. (1998). Police, courts, and corrections in the media. In F. Bailey & D. Hale (Eds.), *Popular culture, crime & justice* (pp. 87–99). Belmont, CA: West/Wadsworth.

Chesney-Lind, M. (1999). Media misogyny: Demonizing "violent" girls and women. In J. Ferrell & N. Websdale (Eds.), *Making trouble: Cultural constructions of crime, deviance, and control* (pp. 115–140). New York: Aldine De Gruyter.

Chesney-Lind, M., & Pasko, L. (2004). *The female offender: Girls, women, and crime* (2nd ed.). Thousand Oaks, CA: Sage.

Clark, A. (2005, Winter). Jail bait: Rethinking images of incarcerated women. *Bitch, 27,* 37–41, 95.

Clowers, M. (2001). Dykes, gangs, and danger: Debunking popular myths about maximum-security life. *Journal of Criminal Justice and Popular Culture, 9*(1), 22–30.

Corman, R. (Producer), & Demme, J. (Writer/Director). (1974). *Caged Heat* [Motion picture]. United States: New World Pictures.

Corman, R. (Producer), & Hill, J. (Writer/Director). (1972). *The Big Bird Cage* [Motion picture]. United States: New World Pictures.

Corman, R. (Producer), & Hill, J. (Director). (1971). *Big Doll House* [Motion picture]. United States: New World Pictures.

Culp, R. F. (2005). Frequency and characteristics of prison escapes in the United States: An analysis of national data. *The Prison Journal, 85*(3), 270–291.

Dorfman, L., & Schiraldi, V. (2001). Off balance: Youth, race and crime in the news. Washington, DC: Building Blocks for Youth.

Doyle, A. (2003). *Arresting images: Crime and policing in front of the television camera.* Toronto: University of Toronto Press.

Fishman, M., & Cavender, G. (1998). *Entertaining crime: Television reality programs.* New York: Aldine De Gruyter.

Freeman, R. M. (2000). *Popular culture and corrections.* Lanham, MD: American Correctional Association.

Garofalo, J. (1981). Crime and the mass media: A selective review of research. *Journal of research in crime and delinquency, 18,* 319–350.

Greenfeld, L. A., & Snell, T. L. (1999). *Women offenders.* Washington, DC: Department of Justice, Office of Justice Programs, Bureau of Justice Statistics.

Hagan, J., & Coleman, J. P. (2001). Returning captives of the American war on drugs: Issues of community and family reentry. *Crime and Delinquency, 47*(3), 352–367.

Hairston, C. F. (1991). Mothers in jail: Parent-child separation and jail visitation. *Affilia, 6*(2), 9–27.

Harpo Productions, Inc. (2005). *The Oprah Winfrey show: Lisa Ling goes to prison—A shocking report.*

Harrison, P. M. (2006). *Prison and jail inmates at midyear 2005.* Washington, DC: Department of Justice, Office of Justice Programs, Bureau of Justice Statistics.

Harrison, P. M., & Beck, A. J. (2005). *Prisoners in 2004.* Washington, DC: Department of Justice, Office of Justice Programs, Bureau of Justice Statistics.

Hensley, C. (2000). Attitudes towards homosexuality in a male and female prison: An exploratory study. *The prison journal, 80*(4), 434–441.

Hensley, C., Castle, T., & Tewksbury, R. (2003). Inmate-to-inmate sexual coercion in a prison for women. *Journal of Offender Rehabilitation, 37*(2), 77–87.

Herman, D. (2003). "*Bad Girls* changed my life": Homonormativity in a women's prison drama. *Critical Studies in Media Communication, 20*(2), 141–159.

Inness, S. A. (1999). *Tough girls: Women warriors and wonder women in popular culture.* Philadelphia: University of Pennsylvania Press.

James, D. J., & Glaze, L. E. (2006). *Mental health problems of prison and jail inmates.* Washington, DC: Department of Justice, Office of Justice Programs, Bureau of Justice Statistics.

Johnston, D. (2006). The wrong road: Efforts to understand the effects of parental crime and incarceration. *Criminology & Public Policy, 5*(4), 703–720.

Juhasz, A. (Producer). (2001). *Released: Five short films about women and prison.* Available from http://www.cineclix.com

Katz, J. (Producer). (2003). *What I want my words to do to you.* PBS Home Video.

Koban, L. (1983). Parents in prison. *Research in Law, Deviance and Social Control, 5,* 171–183.

Kurtis, B. (Producer). (1993). *Investigative reports: Women in prison.* A&E Home Video.

Larson, S. G. (2006). *Media and minorities: The politics of race in news and entertainment.* Lanham, MD: Rowman & Littlefield.

Lipschultz, J. H., & Hilt, M. L. (2002). *Crime and local television news: Dramatic, breaking and live from the scene.* Mahwah, NJ: Lawrence Erlbaum.

Lundman, R. (2003). The newsworthiness and selection bias in news about murder: Comparative and relative effects of novelty and race and gender typifications in newspaper coverage of homicide. *Sociological Forum, 18,* 257–286.

Lydersen, K. (2005, Winter). Bar none: A conversation with Beth Richie. *Bitch, 27,* 39, 41.

Mann, C. R. (1984). *Female crime and delinquency.* Tuscaloosa: University of Alabama Press.

Martin, R. (Producer). (1999). *Women behind bars.* CBS News Archive.

Maruschak, L. M. (2005). *HIV in prisons, 2003.* Washington, DC: Department of Justice, Office of Justice Programs, Bureau of Justice Statistics.

McCaughey, M., & King, N. (2001). *Reel knockouts: Violent women in the movies.* Austin: University of Texas Press.

Morash, M., & Schram, P. (2002). *The prison experience: Special issues of women in prison.* Prospect Heights, IL: Waveland Press.

Mumola, C. J. (2000). *Incarcerated parents and their children.* Washington, DC: Department of Justice, Office of Justice Programs, Bureau of Justice Statistics.

Pearson, M. (Producer). (2004). *Primetime live: The women in maximum security.* American Broadcasting Company.

Petersilia, J. (2003). *When prisoners come home.* New York: Oxford University Press.

Phillips, S. D., Erkanli, A., Keeler, G. P., Costello, E. J., & Angold, A. (2006). Disentangling the risks: Parent criminal justice involvement and children's exposure to family risks. *Criminology & Public Policy, 5*(4), 677–702.

Pollock, J. M. (2002). *Women, prison & crime* (2nd ed.). Belmont, CA: Wadsworth Thomson Learning.

Rafter, N. (2006). *Shots in the mirror: Crime films and society* (2nd ed.). New York: Oxford University Press.

Schlesinger, P., Tumber, H., & Murdock, G. (1991). The media of politics, crime, and criminal justice. *British Journal of Sociology, 42,* 397–420.

Sesnon, A. (Producer). (1996). *Primetime live: Women doing time.* American Broadcasting Company.

Spiro, E., & Bernstein, K. (Producers). (2005). *Troop 1500.* PBS Home Video.

Surette, R. (2007). *Media, crime, and criminal justice: Images, realities, and policies* (3rd ed.). Belmont, CA: Thomson Wadsworth.

Tuchman, G. (1978). *Making news: A study in the construction of reality.* New York: The Free Press.

University of California Extension Center for Media and Independent Learning. (Producer). (1994). *From one prison.* (Available from Carol Jacobsen, 180 Alhambra, Ann Arbor, MI 48103).

Welch, M., Weber, L., & Edwards, W. (2000). "All the news that's fit to print": A content analysis of the correctional debate in the *New York Times. The prison journal, 80*(3), 245–264.

Wilson, D., & O'Sullivan, S. (2004). *Images of incarceration: Representations of prison in film and television drama.* Winchester, UK: Waterside Press.

Wolff, N., Blitz, C. L., Shi, J., Siegel, J., & Bachman, R. (2007). Physical violence inside prisons: Rates of victimization. *Criminal Justice and Behavior, 34*(5), 588–599.

Wood, J. T. (1994). Gendered media: The influence of media on views of gender. In J. T. Wood (Ed.), *Gendered lives: Communication, gender, and culture* (pp. 231–244). Belmont, CA: Wadsworth.

Zito, G. V. (1975). *Methodology and meanings: Varieties of sociological inquiry.* New York: Praeger.

Dawn K. Cecil is an assistant professor of criminology at the University of South Florida, St. Petersburg. She holds a PhD in criminology from the University of Maryland. Her current research focuses on media images of female offenders and of the prison system, as well as coparenting relationships between mothers and maternal grandmothers during incarceration.

SECTION FIVE SUMMARY

Key Discussion Sessions

1. What are the primary points covered in Kenneth Tunnells piece "A Cultural Approach to Crime and Punishment, Bluegrass Style"? Do you believe the issues covered represent just the regions where bluegrass music finds its roots? How do other genres of music address the culture of punishment and in what context (supportive, non-supportive, etc.)? If you are from another country, do you have similar themes in the popular music from your country?

2. As was stated in Section I of this text, the United States leads the world in incarceration. We also incarcerate a higher percentage of our black population than South Africa at the height of apartheid (Alexander, 2010). Additionally the United States is the only G8 country (Canada, France, Germany, Italy, Japan, United Kingdom, United States, and Russia) to perform executions. In 2013, the United States ranked 5th in number of executions in the world falling behind China, Iran, Iraq, and Saudi Arabia (Amnesty International, 2014). Given these rankings, what do you believe the findings of the Jacoby et. al. article "The Newsworthiness of Executions" might reflect regarding the citizens of the United States and its culture? Explain your answer and discuss if you believe race, socioeconomic status, religion, and/or education level might play a role and why. Ask these same questions regarding the findings of Dawn K. Cecil's article "Looking Beyond Caged Heat: Media Images of Women in Prison." If you are from another country, how do citizens in your country view the death penalty? How do citizens in your country view the United States' utilization of the death penalty?

Amnesty International (2014). Death Sentences and Executions 2013. London, UK: Amnesty International Publications.

Alexander, Michelle (2010). The New Jim Crow: Mass Incarceration in the Age of Colorblindness. New York: The New Press. p. 7.

Public Consumption Exercise

Remember, the public consumption exercises in this text build upon each other. You must have completed the exercises in Sections 1, 2, 3, and 4 to complete the current exercises.

Exercise 5: Blog Posts and Who is Reading Them

How often do you see blog posts passed along through social media and how often do you actually read the posts? In this section, you will write another blog post and research the readership of blog posts.

Article Based on the demographic data collected in Section 1, choose an article from this section that you believe would be of the most interest to the residents of the county in which your university or organization is located. Indicate which article you chose and why you believe this to be the best article.

Findings Paragraphs and Writing Level Identify consecutive paragraphs (no less than three) from the findings or results section of the article that contain the largest portion of key findings and retype them in a word document; make sure the wording is exact. Follow the instructions in Appendix C to calculate the writing level of the paragraphs. Does the writing level match the average literacy level for the residents of the county? If it is written at a higher level than the average, how many grade levels must the authors of the piece reduce the writing to be easily read by the residence of the county in which your university or organization is located?

Bulleted Facts Utilizing the bulleted fact exercise from Section 2, create a set of bulleted facts from both the literature review (trends in previous research, historical facts, etc.) and the entire results or findings sections of the article.

Blog Post While the average length of a blog varies, for this text we are going to use 500–600 words. Follow the instructions in Appendix D to write a 500–600 word blog post about the facts you pulled from the literature review and research findings. Write the piece at the average literacy level of the county in which your university or organization is located. (For help with paraphrasing, see the following website or other similar sites: https://owl.english.purdue.edu/owl/resource/563/1/.)

Blog Readership Conduct your own research and determine the answers to the following questions and provide sources:

How many followers does the average blog have? What percentage of the United States adult population does this number represent?

What is the average number of reposts for a blog?

Who reads blog posts (age, race, gender, education level)?

Based on your research, what percentage of the United States population does the average blog post reach? How many of those reached actually read the post?

Justice System

THE PORTRAYAL OF CRIME AND JUSTICE IN THE COMIC BOOK SUPERHERO MYTHOS*

by Scott Vollum
Cary D. Adkinson
College of Criminal Justice
Sam Houston State University

Introduction

For decades, young Americans have looked to the world of comic book superheroes for a sense of justice. Since the 1930s the mythos of comic book superheroes has pervaded adolescents' sense of crime, justice and order. Whether it was through the weekly dose of comic book reading or, more contemporarily, through television and movie viewing, youths in America have been fixated on "superheroes" and their battles for justice: good vs. evil, right vs. wrong. What do they learn about justice from these superheroes and the worlds they inhabit? What "perspective" are they gaining from such mythologies? These are the questions that this article, through an analysis of the portrayal of crime and justice in the stories of comic book superheroes, attempts to answer.

Through analyses of two of the earliest comic book superheroes, Superman and Batman, and the worlds they inhabit, this article examines the message that superhero mythologies transmit in regard to the social phenomena of crime and justice in America[1]. Superman and Batman were selected for analysis for two primary reasons: (1) they are two of the most consistently popular and pervasive comic book superheroes ever created, and (2) despite their similarities, each character offers a unique perspective by which to examine the superhero mythos within American culture. [2] Dating back to the late 1930s, titles featuring both Superman and Batman have persistently been among the top selling comic books (Wright, 2001). In the early 1940s *Superman* reached a circulation of over 1,250,000 per month (Wright, 2001); *Batman* was not far behind with sales figures that ranked second only to *Superman* and *Action Comics*, which featured Superman (Goulart, 2001). Over a span of more than 60 years, the popularity of Superman and Batman comic books has not waned (Wright, 2001). In fact, an examination of the current top 50 solicited comic book titles for January of 2003 demonstrates the ongoing popularity of both Batman and Superman. According to *Wizard: The Comics Magazine*, of the 50 top selling comic books for January 2003, 14% feature Batman and/or Superman (Top 50, 2003). In fact, of the core titles, *Batman* currently ranks number 1 and *The Adventures of Superman* (formerly, *Superman*) ranks 48th (Top 50, 2003). Add to this the obvious transition of both superheroes into many other forms of media such as television, film, books, and video games and there is little question that both Batman and Superman have permeated popular culture in America and that their images pervade the consciousness of many. In addition to the ubiquity and popularity of these two superheroes and their associated mythologies, we are presented with two similar but in many ways divergent perspectives of the superhero mythos in popular culture. By examining Batman and Superman, we are offered the unique opportunity to analyze two of the first iconic superheroes that were developed within similar historical and social contexts but who represent diverging aspects of American culture and, importantly, two different perspectives on the nature of crime and justice in America.

The article begins with a brief discussion of the historical context in which Superman and Batman and their stories were developed. The genesis and backgrounds of Superman and Batman are then examined—who they are, how they came to be superheroes, and what motivated them to become crime-fighters. This is followed by an assessment of the social context within which each superhero operates—the social structure of their society—specifically focusing on the worlds they inhabit. Next, the crime and the criminals that are pitted against the superheroes are analyzed. Subsequently, the crime-fighting superheroes themselves, and, specifically, their responses to such crime and criminals are examined. Finally, the "perspectives" of crime and justice represented in these superhero mythologies are considered, drawing comparisons with some of the dominant perspectives in the field of criminology and criminal justice. The article concludes with a discussion of what the comic book superhero mythos says about crime and justice in American society.

Historical Context of the Batman and Superman Mythologies

Any examination of the impact and enduring influence of Superman and Batman must consider the historical context which gave them life. Both products of the 1930s, their origins and subsequent mythologies owe much to the American cultural landscape following the Great Depression (Goulart, 2001). Movies, serials, and radio programs offered escape from the memories and lingering effects of the Depression and quickly became popular forms of fantasy entertainment. As a cheap and easily accessible medium, comic books offered an especially attractive form of escapist fantasy for youth. Furthermore, with the passing of the Depression came a reluctant optimism that the worst was over and America's best times were yet to come. Public works projects moved mountains, changed the flow of mighty rivers, and raised buildings that tickled the clouds. In many ways, it seemed as if anything was possible for Americans. At the same time, however, the Depression shattered the fantasy of America's invulnerability, and with this Americans awoke to a new cultural landscape characterized by the realities of urban decay, poverty, and crime.

These two heroes epitomize this apparent cultural paradox in distinct ways that have been constructed through their respective mythologies. With his immigrant beginnings, patriotic red and blue costume, almost unlimited super powers, and unwavering commitment to "truth, justice, and the American way" Superman represents the hope and idealism of post-Depression America. Batman, however, offers a much more realistic construction. Born of violence, Batman adopts the mantle of the bat to strike fear into street criminals like the one who murdered his parents. His dark gray and black costume, his reliance on technology, and his willingness to resort to violence to accomplish his ends suggest that the new face of crime in post-Depression America necessitates a more retributive, street level form of justice. By adhering to common themes of the hero mythology while offering distinct interpretations of American culture and the nature of crime in the wake of the Great Depression, Superman and Batman, respectively, epitomize both the idealism of justice and the realism of urban crime. Although both Superman and Batman have evolved along with the American cultural landscape over their more than 60 years of existence, their central characterizations have remained largely intact; and, both have remained rooted firmly in the times in which they were created—post-Depression America.

Who are These Guys? The Genesis of Superhero Mythology

No two names are more synonymous with comic book crime-fighters than Superman and Batman. Virtually every American can recall some image of these two superheroes, diligently fighting crime and preserving American justice. Indeed, Superman and Batman were thrust into the popular culture limelight in the late 1930s, almost immediately becoming pop icons. Through stories of Superman and Batman, the world was introduced to larger than life crime-fighters that would be the prototypes for a genre that would grow and thrive in the decades to come—comic book superhero stories. Since their inception, Superman and Batman have pervaded popular culture (Goulart, 2001; Wright, 2001). Through television and film, these superheroes are as big today as they have ever been. But who are these crime-fighting superheroes? Where did they come from and how did they become such powerful superheroes?

Like many of the superheroes that would follow in his footsteps, Superman was not originally from this planet—he was an extraterrestrial. Superman was born on the planet Krypton. He was sent, via a rocket with only enough space for a child, to Earth by his parents just as Krypton was on the brink of destruction. On Earth, John and Mary Kent, an elderly couple that had always dreamed of raising a child, found him. They adopted him and named him Clark. Clark would grow up on the Kent's farm in a small town named Smallville.

As he grew up on this foreign planet, Clark quickly learned that he was not the same as the other boys and girls. He found that he had super powers—abilities to do things normal humans could not. He had super strength, super speed, x-ray eyesight, impenetrably strong skin, and the ability to fly. As he continued to mature, he learned to use these powers for good. His father, on his deathbed, implored Clark to "become a powerful force for good" and warned "[t]here are evil men in this world … criminals and outlaws who prey on decent folk! You must fight them … in cooperation with the law!" (National Periodical Comics, 1971, p. 207). Orphaned for the second time, Clark moved to Metropolis and got a job as a reporter on a newspaper, which, he felt, would keep him in touch with those who need his help. He vowed to spend his days fighting crime and injustice, and helping those in need.

Batman's story began when he was eight years old. The young Bruce Wayne, son of wealthy social-ites, witnessed the killing of his parents during a botched robbery on the way home from the theater. Standing over his parents' graves, he proclaimed "I swear I'll dedicate my life and inheritance to bringing your killer to justice … and to fighting all criminals! I swear it!" (Batman #47, 1948 in Kane, 1988). Traumatized by the brutal death of his parents, Bruce Wayne devoted his youth to developing the strength and knowledge to fight crime and avenge his parents' senseless murder. Independently wealthy because of his sizable inheritance, Bruce Wayne was able to concentrate on becoming an expert in scientific criminal investigation and on training his body to "physical and athletic perfection" (Batman #47, 1948 in Kane, 1988).

Once thoroughly trained, Bruce Wayne decided he must take on an alternate identity. Inspired by a bat that flies through his window, he decided he would become a bat, a creature of the night, *The Batman*. Aided by an underground scientific lab dubbed the "batcave," Bruce Wayne is able to create all the tools he needs to fight crime. Most importantly, he is able to create the bat-suit that will protect him and make him nearly invulnerable. Driven by his vigilant desire to fight crime and avenge his parents' death, Batman becomes an "obsessed loner" (Pearson and Uricchio, 1991, p. 19), wandering the streets at night in search of criminals whom he can make pay for their crimes.

Social Structure

The social structure of the worlds within which Superman and Batman fight crime is central to their roles as superheroes. The social structure says as much about the superhero mythos as do the images of the superheroes themselves. In many ways, Superman and Batman are confined to the worlds in which they exist. Their actions are largely reactions to the world around them. The structure of law, order and justice in their respective worlds shape the way they react to crime and injustice. While Superman and Batman are products of their worlds they also, to a large degree, define the worlds they inhabit. As Uricchio and Pearson (1991) claim in the case of Batman, it is a "symbiotic relationship" where "the fluctuating image of Gotham City relates to the fluctuating nature of crime in Batman's world and has implications for the playing out of the Batman's hegemonic function" (p. 187).

Both Superman and Batman reside in generic metropolitan cities, reminiscent of modern American metropolises: Superman in the aptly named Metropolis and Batman in Gotham City. Both cities are full of colorful criminals, and crime seems to be the most crucial social problem on the minds of the citizens. In each city there is an ongoing battle between the innocent, law-abiding citizens and the criminals. The superhero is the champion of the law-abiding masses and fights to maintain order in his city.

The similarities of Metropolis and Gotham City end there, however. Metropolis is a city of hope and optimism, while Gotham City represents the darker side of American cities appearing almost as a post-apocalyptic landscape full of dark alleys, dangerous streets, and corruption. Metropolis, on the other hand, is presented as a bustling community of relatively happy citizens where there is a clear division between good and evil. In a way, Metropolis and Gotham City represent the dichotomous nature of the great American city: at once offering hope, order, and the American dream while at the same time threatening despair, danger, and anarchy. Metropolis represents more of the former while Gotham City represents more of the latter.

Although both superheroes fight for justice, attempting to protect and serve the powerless and innocent masses against threats of crime and criminals, justice is notably different in their respective worlds. For Superman, law and the justice system are bright and shining examples of "the good guys." Law and justice must always prevail and are always to be respected. The officials of law and justice act in the best interest of the citizens of Metropolis and represent value-consensus about what is good and what is evil. For Batman, things are not so clear-cut. The line between good and evil is blurred. Those representing law and justice are not always the good guys. In Gotham City there are corrupt officials and irresponsible law enforcement officers. It is no surprise that Batman feels compelled to work outside the confines of the law, while Superman works only within the bounds of the law. The nature of society in Metropolis is one of consensus regarding values and norms. Gotham City, on the other hand, represents a state of conflict in which good and evil spring from the same place and where what is right and wrong is not always agreed upon.

Crime and Criminals

The threats to the citizens of Metropolis, like their superhero, come from somewhere else, deriving from some point external to their community. The threats to the citizens of Gotham City, on the other hand, generally come from within, almost as if they were generated by the city. Both superheroes contend with many of the same types of criminals, however. Faceless, nameless "thugs" and "hoodlums" are common in both Metropolis and Gotham City. Stereotypical gangsters and members of organized crime groups are also common foes. The difference is that in Superman's world such criminals are represented as outsiders who threaten the peace and social order in Metropolis. In Batman's world such criminals are depicted as *products* of Gotham City, part of the social fabric in which those on both sides of the law exist.

Although Metropolis and Gotham City have certain types of criminals in common, they also each have some that are distinctly unique. The outsider/insider dichotomy represented by the differences between Superman and Batman's respective worlds can be seen in the different types of criminals they encounter. For example, Superman often encounters anti-Americans that threaten democracy and the "American way" (See, for example, National Periodical Comics, 1971, p. 64). Superman is also likely to contend with recurring foes from other worlds—even more of "outsiders" than those from "un-friendly" countries. Batman, on the other hand, often contends with corrupt politicians—members of the very system that is in charge of upholding law and justice in Gotham City. Many of Batman's recurring foes are members of the wealthy community that want to "control the world." Others are "freaks" that have risen up from the bowels of the city, products of a harsh society that in one way or another cheated them. These villains in Gotham City are often only trying to create disorder and anarchy. Much like Batman, they are often driven by a traumatic event and an obsession with revenge.

Responses to Crime

Both Superman and Batman claim to be champions of the oppressed and to fight for justice and order. However, the ways they go about fighting crime and protecting citizens are quite divergent. Superman works within the boundaries of the law and in cooperation with official law enforcement. Superman fights for justice as defined by lawmakers. As Eagan (1987) puts it, Superman is the "defender of truth, justice and the American way" (p. 88). Batman, on the other hand, works outside the boundaries of the law and considers himself an arbiter of justice. Distrustful of law enforcement, Batman takes it upon himself to uphold justice and fight crime. While he often cooperates with law enforcement, he refuses to accept their boundaries as defining what is and is not just.

From the very beginning it was clear that Superman would represent a value-neutral proponent of American justice. In the first Superman comic book (National Periodical Comics, 1971), he takes on a variety of criminals, among them a street thug, a female offender, and an organized crime gangster. He even saves an innocent person from execution. There would also be numerous times that Superman would put a stop to vigilantism even though the victim was a known criminal. When confronting a lynch mob about to attack a criminal, Superman simply proclaims "this prisoner's fate will be decided in a court of justice" (National Periodical Comics, 1971, p. 23) and in another instance "even this rat deserves a fair trial" (National Periodical Comics, 1971, p. 345) and puts a stop to the violence.

Batman provides a direct contrast to Superman's value-neutral crime-fighter. Batman is a vigilante himself and fights for justice on his own terms and in the context of what he considers to be just. Batman would not have stopped the aforementioned lynch mob; he would have looked the other way or maybe even have joined in. Batman is motivated by his own values and his obsession with vengeance, while Superman is motivated primarily by the American justice system and democracy. Both superheroes are fighting for the same things—justice and social order, but their methods in responding to crime could not be more different.

Perspectives of Crime and Justice

Sutherland (1934) proposed that three processes make up the "object-matter of criminology:" the making of law, breaking of law, and reaction to the breaking of law (p. 3). The superhero mythos provides us with examples of each of these processes in its portrayal of crime and justice. More importantly, the mythologies of comic book superheroes reflect certain perspectives regarding crime and justice in the real world. In the previous sections, the focus was on describing the superhero mythos and the images that it presents. The focus of this section turns to an interpretation of the extant superhero images in the context of the field of criminology. This is done loosely in the context of Sutherland's three proposed processes.

Representation of Law

In regard to the making of law, or the representation of law in general, there is a clear distinction between Superman and Batman. The law as Superman sees it is best represented by the five consensus oriented propositions outlined by Chambliss (1999, p. 18–19):

1. The law represents the value-consensus of the society.
2. The law represents those values and perspectives which are fundamental to social order.
3. The law represents those values and perspectives which it is in the public interest to protect.
4. The state as represented in the legal system is value-neutral.
5. In pluralistic societies the law represents the interests of the society at large mediating between competing interest groups.

Superman represents the state and what Durkheim (1893) referred to as "the collective conscience" as a rational, value-neutral "defender of truth, justice and the American way" (Eagan, 1987, p. 88). As previously mentioned, Superman works within the bounds of the law and in complete cooperation with law enforcement. The basis for Superman's morality, in fact, derives from the laws that the American government imposes.

It must be pointed out that Chambliss introduced the five aforementioned propositions as antitheses to his arguments. Chambliss, in fact, argues that such consensus-oriented propositions are false and that "there is no value-consensus that is relevant to the law" (1999, p. 21). Chambliss (1999) discusses law as a result of competing interests with some groups or individuals having more power and influence over the law-making process due to the unequal distribution of wealth. Batman would tend to agree with Chambliss' conflict-oriented perspective. Batman refuses to accept the official definition of law and takes it upon himself to become an arbiter of justice, deriving his sense of law from within himself. His defiance of the law and the fact that he is extremely wealthy is dual evidence of a conflict perspective. His purpose is to fight crime and protect the citizens of Gotham City, but he refuses to accept the official laws in doing so, thus indicating that there is not value-consensus regarding law. Furthermore, he uses his wealth to produce his own brand of justice in the context of his own moral code, supporting Chambliss' (1999) conflict-oriented proposition that those who control the resources exert more influence over what does and does not become a law.

There is another role of the comic book superheroes that must not be neglected—that of "champion of the oppressed." This is a role that both superheroes embrace. Superman's approach to this role is much like that of the child-saving movement of the early 1900s as described by Platt (1969). Reformers involved in the child saving movement assumed an absolute morality and felt that they could "cure" the anomalous delinquents. Superman's view, like that of the reformers', is positivistic. Superman would agree with the reformers that the only way to change the "criminal class" would be to save them from the forces that lead them to criminality and to reaffirm faith in the traditional American system. Both Superman and Batman also often provide help to those less fortunate through acts of charity: Batman through his extreme wealth and Superman through his use of his super powers. For example, in one story, Superman claims "I'll rebuild this area so people won't have to live in slums" (National Periodical Comics, 1971, p.199). Believing the assumption that socioeconomic status is correlated with crime (see Tittle and Meier, 1990), this is just one more way the superheroes can preserve social order.

Breaking of Law

The superhero mythos provides us with vivid depictions of criminals. The portrayal of different types of criminals and the processes by which they become criminal are often very colorful. The depictions are also often indicative of certain criminological theories and perspectives. In this section, what some of those theories and perspectives are and how they are represented in the superhero mythos will be discussed.

First, a variety of types of criminals are presented throughout the pages of superhero comic book stories. There are gangsters, faceless thugs, corrupt politicians, ingenious madmen, alien (outside) threats and freakish aberrations. As diverse as the criminals are, some general patterns among the criminals can be detected. They all represent a threat to social order, they are generally motivated by either money and/or power or by revenge, and they have generally become criminals through mythical processes paralleling those of the superheroes. The recurring villains are generally more interested in destruction and world domination, usually out of vengeance (e.g. Lex Luthor, The Joker, The Penguin), while the myriad, run-of-the-mill criminals are generally after financial gain.

What do the crimes and criminals of the superhero mythos tell us about the breaking of law? In many instances we are presented with rational criminals with rational goals. Tunnell (1992) investigates such rational behavior of criminals and the various reasons and motivations that criminals commit property crimes. While most simply want money, many commit their crimes for a sense of accomplishment, sport, or vengeance. All these reasons are prevalent throughout the pages of superhero comic books. While money always seems to be a goal, challenging the superhero (sport), gaining revenge, and gaining power are extant motivations of the villains.

But what, according to the superhero mythos, led these individuals to become criminal? The single representation that flows throughout the many representations of criminals and villains is a sense of deterministic causes that led these individuals to a life of crime. Like the superheroes, the criminals and villains are presented as beings who were thrust into their roles by forces beyond their control. The causes are varied and virtually span the array of criminological theories that might be applied to their criminality.

The representation of genetic mutants, deformed freaks, and even the distorted facial features of the average street thug can be interpreted in the context of the early biological theories of criminal behavior. Lombroso (1911) would classify many of the criminals represented in the superhero mythos as "born criminals." Akers (2000: 43) summarizes the physical characteristics associated with Lombroso's notion of the born criminal as "asymmetry of the face or head, large monkey-like ears, large lips, receding chin, twisted nose, excessive cheek bones, long arms, excessive skin wrinkles, and extra fingers or toes." It seems that the comic book artists knew what they were doing when they conceptualized the criminals—the criminals they drew almost seem to epitomize these Lombrosian characteristics. While, as Fishbein (1990, p. 27) points out, "biological criminology was eventually discredited," the biological perspective's depiction of criminals still exists in the superhero mythos.

Other theories can be drawn upon in attempting to interpret the crime and criminal behavior in Metropolis and Gotham City. Learning models such as Sutherland's (1947) differential association theory and, more currently, Akers' (1985; 1998) social learning theory are good explanations of the crime resulting from the level of social networking by the criminals in Metropolis and Gotham City. In the superhero's world there are the good guys and the bad guys. The bad guys stick together, often forming alliances, learning from one-another and reinforcing each other's criminal behavior. Sutherland would interpret the villains of the superhero's world as having "an excess of definitions favorable to violation of the law over definitions unfavorable to violation of the law" (1947, p. 6). Generally, the needs and values of the villains are the same as those of the superhero, but because of this "differential association" of definitions favorable or unfavorable to breaking the law, the villains become criminal while Superman and Batman become superheroes.

The representation of crime on the societal level, particularly in regard to Gotham City, can best be interpreted in the context of social disorganization perspectives such as those of Shaw and McKay (1941) and, more recently, Bursik and Grasmick (1993a; 1993b). The urban decay and social disorder of Gotham city is an integral image in the development of its criminal sub-class. This image of Gotham city clearly approximates Shaw and McKay's original conception of "the zone in transition," and the crime in Gotham City reflects the effects of such disorder. As mentioned before, the criminals in Gotham City, like Batman, are integral parts of the social landscape. They seem almost to be formed from the bowels of the city. It seems as if the chaos and social disorganization of the dark and deteriorated Gotham City generates the criminals. It is the pervasive goal of the superhero to retain social order in the city and to eradicate crime.

Reaction to the Breaking of Law

The primary message regarding the reaction to the breaking of law in the superhero mythos is that, as indicated in the previous section, law and order must be maintained and certain behavior must be controlled. Eagan (1987) claims that the Superman mythos derives from the traditional American presumption that "the purpose of government is to maintain law and order, to police" and "to regulate behavior" (p. 91). These presumptions are integral to both Superman's and Batman's roles as crime-fighters.

What, though, do these superheroes represent as crime-fighters? The best interpretation can be made through Klockars' idea of "voluntary avocational policing" (1992, p. 1465). Voluntary avocational policing is defined as being "done by private citizens not because they are obliged by a threat of punishment but because they, for their own reasons, want to do it" (Klockars, 1992, p. 1465). As previously discussed, both Superman and Batman have their own reasons for fighting crime. Batman's approach, more specifically, represents the subcategory of vigilante voluntary avocational policing. Both Superman and Batman's approach to fighting crime also supports Klockars' argument that coercive force is the single defining factor of policing (1992, p. 1466). Superheroes, in their roles as crime-fighters, not only use coercive force, but often take that force to extremes.

The Hegemonic Function of the Superhero Mythos

The superhero mythos depicts a fanciful world of perfect heroes and colorful villains but also depicts a world reflecting the dominant values of American society. Such a depiction is by no means unintentional. Take, for example, the comics code enacted by the Comics Code Authority in 1954:

- In every instance good shall triumph over evil and the criminal punished for his misdeeds.
- Crimes shall never be presented in such a way as to promote distrust in the forces of law and justice. ...
- All lurid, unsavory, gruesome illustrations shall be eliminated.
- All situations dealing with the family unit should have as their ultimate goal the protection of the children and family life. In no way shall the breaking of the moral code be depicted as rewarding.

(Comics Code Authority, 1954 as cited in Boichal, 1991, p. 13)

It is clear that the Comics Code Authority knew the impact that the superhero mythos might have on those who were exposed to it. In many of the Superman and Batman stories over the decades, the superheroes almost come straight out and say "CRIME DOESN'T PAY!" While the mythos of Superman and the mythos of Batman present different perspectives of the law (Superman tells us that the law is to be respected; Batman tells us that law is to be feared), they are ultimately saying the same thing: Don't break the law!

But what, specifically, does the superhero mythos tell us about crime and justice in American society? The representation of crime and justice in the superhero mythos is predominantly derived from a conservative or "right" oriented perspective (as evidenced in the aforementioned comics code). The best way to outline what we learn from the superhero mythos is in the context of Miller's thorough discussion of ideology and criminal justice (1973). In discussing the ideology of the "right" or conservative perspective of crime and justice, Miller identifies five "crusading issues": (1) "excessive leniency toward lawbreakers," (2) "favoring the welfare and rights of lawbreakers over the welfare and rights of their victims, of law enforcement officials, and the law abiding citizen," (3) "erosion of discipline and of respect for constituted authority," (4) "the cost of crime," and (5) "excessive permissiveness" (1973, p. 143). These "crusading issues" of the political "right" are virtually mirrored by the crusades of the superhero mythos.

The messages portrayed in the comic book superhero mythos are clear. We are being told that we must preserve the status quo, or, as Superman might put it, "democracy and the American way"; threats to the status quo must be extinguished. We are presented with a world in which there is clearly right and wrong, good and evil. Good must prevail and social order must be maintained. The dominant hegemony is safe in the hands of the comic book superhero.

Endnotes

AUTHORS' NOTE: The authors would like to thank the anonymous reviewers and the editors at JCJPC for their constructive suggestions. The authors would also like to thank Joe Krocheski for his generosity in supplying sources for the analysis as well as his helpful suggestions in the development of this article. Finally, we are grateful to Dennis R. Longmire for his encouragement and assistance in the early development of this article. Address correspondence to Scott Vollum, College of Criminal Justice, Sam Houston State University, Huntsville, TX 77341-2296; e-mail: stdsav12@shsu.edu.

1. It should be noted that our analysis is limited to the representation of these superheroes in comic books alone. Although both of these superheroes are icons that transcend this particular medium, they have their genesis in comic books and their central characters (which are the central focus of this article) developed therein. Although an analysis of other media representations of both Superman and Batman would add an important element to the understanding of the superhero mythos and its portrayal of crime and justice, it is outside the scope of the current analysis.

2. Although the primary sources for analysis were the original comic book stories of Batman and Superman, our analysis of Batman was supplemented by Frank Miller's (1989) quintessential depiction of Batman in his Dark Knight series of graphic novels. Although Miller's depiction of Batman is, as the title suggests, much darker and "edgier" than the original, it remains predominantly true to the original Batman mythos while at the same time adding important depth to the character. Furthermore, in *The Dark Knight Returns* Miller (1989) presents a future version of the DC Universe in which both the mythologies of Batman and Superman, discussed herein, are taken to their logical extremes.

References

Primary Sources:
Kane, B. (1988). *The greatest Batman stories ever told*. New York, NY: DC Comics, Inc.
Miller, F. (1989). *The complete Frank Miller Batman*. Stanford, CT: Longmeadow Press.
National Periodical Comics. (1971). *Superman: From the thirties to the seventies*. New York, NY: Bonanza Books.

Secondary Sources:
Akers, R. L. (1985). *Deviant behavior: A social learning approach* (3rd ed.). Belmont, CA: Wadsworth.
Akers, R. L. (1998). *Social learning and social structure: A general theory of crime and deviance*. Boston: Northeastern University Press.
Akers, R. L. (2000). *Criminological theories: Introduction and evaluation* (3rd ed.). Los Angeles, CA: Roxbury Publishing Company.
Boichal, B. (1991). Batman: Commodity as myth. In R.E. Pearson and W. Uricchio (Eds.), *The many lives of Batman: Critical approaches to a superhero and his media* (pp. 4–17). New York: Routledge.

Bursik, R. J. and Grasmick, H .G. (1993a). Economic deprivation and neighborhood crime rates, 1960–1980. *Law and Society Review, 27*(2), 263–283.

Bursik, R. J. and Grasmick, H. G. (1993b). N*eighborhoods and crime: The dimensions of effective community control.* San Francisco, CA: Lexington Books.

Chambliss, B. J. (1999). The state, the law, and the definition of behavior as criminal or delinquent in F.R. Scarpitti and A. L. Nielsen (Eds.), C*rime and criminals: Contemporary and classic readings in criminology* (pp. 18–24). Los Angeles, CA: Roxbury Publishing Company.

Durkheim, E. (1893). *Division of labor in society.* New York: The Free Press.

Eagan, P. L. (1987). A flag with a human face" in D. Dooley and G. Engle (Eds.), *Superman at fifty: The persistence of a legend* (pp. 88-102). New York: Macmillan Publishing Company.

Fishbein, D. H. (1990). Biological perspectives in criminology. *Criminology, 28*(1), 27–72.

Goulart, R. (2001). *Great American comic books.* Lincolnwood: Publications International.

Klockars, C. B. (1992). Police. In E.F. Borgatta & M.L. Borgatta (Eds.), *Encyclopedia of sociology, volume 3,* (pp. 1463–1471). New York: MacMillan Publishing Company.

Lombroso, C. (1911). *Criminal man.* New York: G.P. Putnam's Sons.

Miller, W. B. (1973). Ideology and criminal justice policy: some current issues. *The journal of criminal law and criminology, 64*(2), 141–162.

Pearson, R. E. and Uricchio, W. (1991). Notes from the batcave: An interview with Dennis O'Neil. In R.E. Pearson and W. Uricchio (Eds.), *The many lives of Batman: Critical approaches to a superhero and his media* (pp.18–32). New York: Routledge.

Platt, A. (1969). The rise of the child-saving movement: A study in social policy and correctional reform. *Annals of the American Academy of Political and Social Science, 381,* 21–38.

Shaw, C. R. and McKay, H. D. (1941). *Juvenile delinquency and urban areas.* Chicago, IL: The University of Chicago Press.

Sutherland, E. H. (1934). *Principles of criminology.* Chicago, IL: J.B. Lipponcott Company.

Sutherland, E. H. (1947). *Principles of criminology, 4th ed.* Chicago, IL: J.B. Lipponcott Company.

Tittle, C. R. and Meier, R. F. (1990). Specifying the SES/delinquency relationship. *Criminology, 28*(2), 271–299.

Top 50. (2003, May). *Wizard: The comics magazine, 140,* 140.

Tunnell, K. D. (1992). *Choosing crime: The criminal calculus of property offenders.* Chicago, IL: Nelson-Hall Publishers.

Uricchio, W. and Pearson, R. E. (1991). I'm not fooled by that cheap disguise. In R.E. Pearson and W. Uricchio *The many lives of Batman: Critical approaches to a superhero and his media* (pp. 82–213). New York: Routledge.

Wright, B. W. (2001). *Comic book nation: The transformation of youth culture in America.* Baltimore: The Johns Hopkins University.

CULTURAL CRIMINOLOGY AND KRYPTONITE

Apocalyptic and Retributive Constructions of Crime and Justice in Comic Books

by Nickie D. Phillips, St. Francis College, USA
Staci Strobl, John Jay College of Criminal Justice, USA

It isn't real ... you're being entertained. That's what I'm going for with this series folks. Entertainment. Plain and simple. Not a complex analysis of the causes of crime, not a portrait of one man's tragic descent into murderous psychosis, not an in-depth examination of the vigilante down the ages. (Ennis, 2001)

Although various media studies have focused on portrayals of crime depicted in television, literature, film, and music, comic books have traditionally been neglected (Creekmur, 2004). The recent resurgence in popular interest in comic books has led to a handful of studies by criminologists that focus narrowly on criminal justice depictions related to particular comic books, characters, themes, or historical periods (Newman, 1993; Williams, 1998; Lovell, 2002, 2003; Nyberg, 2003). However, understanding the medium's criminal justice themes holistically represents a new frontier. Using a cultural criminology framework, this study examines a wide cross-section of representations of criminal justice in contemporary American comic books.

Literature Review

Shazam! The Resurgence of Interest in Comic Books

Comic books are a highly regarded art form rich with representations of crime and justice (Wright, 2001; Weiner, 2003; McGrath, 2004). Since the first issue of *Action Comics* in 1938 featuring Superman, comic books have penetrated American consciousness. Even those who have never read a comic book are familiar with American superheroes such as Spider-Man, Captain America, Batman, and Wonder Woman, and understand that such heroes are devoted to fighting crime, punishing the bad guys, and ultimately, establishing a sense of justice.

In addition to mainstream popularity, comic books have received critical acclaim. Various comics' creators have earned the highest literary awards for their comics. For example, Art Spiegelman received a Pulitzer Prize in 1992 for *Maus*; Neil Gaiman and Charles Vess were awarded the 1991 World Fantasy Award for *The Sandman's A Midsummer Night's Dream*; and Alan Moore and Dave Gibbons received the Hugo Award in 1988 for *The Watchmen*.

Although some argue that comic books occupy merely a subcultural niche of the mass media, comic books have been the inspiration for countless Hollywood movies. In fact, comic book justice is increasingly influential for mass movie-going audiences. For example, according to the *Rough Guide to Superheroes*, movies based on comic books averaged approximately two a year between 1990 and 2002, but there were seven such movies in 2003 and six in 2004 (Simpson et al., 2004). Recent comic book-related commercial successes include *Sin City, Spider-Man 2* and *Constantine*. Additionally, comic books have inspired countless video and console games from *Spider*-Man to the *Fantastic Four*, with video games alone grossing nearly US $10 billion in 2004 (from http://gameinfowire.com/news.asp?nid=5650).

Cultural Criminology Confronts Popular Media

The current study examines representations of crime and justice in American comic books through the lens of cultural criminology. Cultural criminology is influenced by a variety of perspectives including postmodernism, labeling, and Marxism, among others (Ferrell and Sanders, 1995). Importantly, cultural criminology rejects the positivist notion of objectivity in favor of a focus on the meanings of symbols and styles within particular cultural and subcultural frameworks. This study falls within the burgeoning field of cultural criminological explorations of media.

The influence of postmodernist thought on cultural criminology is apparent as the 'reality' of the crime problem is constantly questioned. Cultural criminologists question media representations of crime and justice, specifically, any over-reliance on 'official' data derived from government sources (Ferrell and Websdale, 1999). Media studies have shown the importance of the ways in which media frame issues of crime and justice and, in turn, influence public discourse (Cavender, 2004). From a postmodern perspective, the media do not merely reflect social reality but, in a media-saturated world, increasingly constitute the social reality itself (Strinati, 1993). Justice and representations of justice, therefore, can be seen as resonating in a 'vast hall of mirrors' (Ferrell, 1999; Hayward and Young, 2004: 259), thereby producing a dialectic of reflections on, and constructions of, justice.

Cultural criminology also focuses attention on the role of power and social inequality. Through a critical eye, cultural criminologists note the crucial connection between media and legal authority (Ferrell and Sanders, 1995). Specifically, cultural criminologists have described how media may influence public perception of social problems, such as the creation of moral panics, and may, in turn, influence criminal justice policy (Sanders and Lyon, 1995; Cavender, 2004).

Indeed, cultural criminologists have turned their gaze toward the media's extensive use of the criminal justice system as the source for popular images and storytelling, which in turn may contribute to public support for tough-on-crime agendas by 'entertaining the crisis' of crime in society:

> *Intertwined with mediated moral panic over crime and crime waves, amplified fear of street crime*
> *and stranger violence, and politically popular concern for the harm done to crime victims, then, is*

the pleasure found in consuming mediated crime imagery and crime drama. To the extent that the mass media constructs crime as entertainment, we are thus offered not only selective images and agendas, but the ironic mechanism for amusing ourselves to death ... by way of our own collective pain, misery and fear. (Ferrell, 1999: 407–8)

For example, Epstein (1995) shows how serial killer themes have emerged as intensely popular themes with the movie-going public. Typically, the serial killer is portrayed as a 'mythic monster', often evil incarnate, with superhuman powers. Epstein (1995) notes one potential effect of this cultural obsession is that 'police have been known to release serial killers because they did not fit the mythic persona created by the media' (p. 77). The investigation into the DC snipers was hindered by the use of the stereotypic, lonely white male serial-killer profile—a profile which had taken on its own reality through the media's obsession with it (Cochran, 2006). Likewise, Ferrell (1999) writes of the influence of fictional programming: 'Contemporary policing can in fact hardly be understood apart from its interpenetration with media at all levels, including ... television programs shap[ing] public perceptions of policing and serv[ing] as controversial tools of officer recruitment' (p. 411).

Imagining Criminal Justice: Truth, Justice and the American Way

Like other fictional media, comic books provide an alternate social reality for the characters to occupy, which may mirror broader society. But their impact extends deeper than mere reflection because they also provide an entertaining vehicle for readers to symbolically and vicariously experience the moral and philosophical questions sparked by criminal justice themes. Comic books seduce readers into a dominant narrative of good triumphing over evil, while simultaneously allowing them to experience criminal transgressions voyeuristically from a safe distance (Kane, 2004). As Katz (1987) suggested, reading about crime serves as a 'ritual moral exercise' in which people can work out their own moral unease without having to engage in anything more than passive consumption. Yet, under this phenomenological understanding, crime media and entertainment—including comic books—become spaces in public life where the meaning of crime and punishment is created, consumed, and recreated. Consumption of media which appears passive may have an active role in shaping public consciousness. Examinations of crime and justice representations, then, become important for understanding the cultural raw material which interacts with and feeds into public attitudes and perspectives.

In a postmodern world of infinite mirrors, media involvement with crime themes reflects the political climate and vice versa. Sanders and Lyon (1995) state that one way in which 'media misrepresent illegal behavior is by focusing on crimes as simple and direct individual acts rather than as sophisticated activities engaged in by established groups' (p. 31). Fictional depictions of law enforcement and their response to criminals favor 'individualistic etiological explanations' and 'are dominant and often become the foundation for agency approaches' (p. 33). Likewise, Beckett (1997) found that public concern regarding the crime and drug problem is related to 'levels of prior political initiative' and media coverage of the issues rather than actual crime rates (p. 21).

American criminal justice policy emphasizes individual motivation and responsibility for criminal behavior and de-emphasizes pointing the finger at social structural causes. As in Reagan's 1985 inaugural address and later repackaged in *Contract with America* (United States Congress, 1994), crime is envisioned as a threat to the larger population by those who should be held individually responsible for their behavior. The tough-on-crime approach crossed party lines when Clinton enacted the 1994 Crime Control Act. These recent political and ideological tendencies represent a neo-classical approach to crime and justice, underpinned by the Enlightenment notions of free will and responsibility which have long characterized American philosophical thought. Despite social-scientific data on the socio-economic etiology of crime, the political climate in America remains one loyal to notions of individual culpability and responsibility (Currie, 1998):

> When all external causes of crime are rejected, individual punishment emerges as the only logical social response to crime while criminology is demoted from a quest for understanding to the pragmatic task of crime detection. Offenders are stereotyped as monolithic, pathological, and violent; crime is analysed from a simplistic prey–predator paradigm; and crime policy is fixated in a punitive defensive posture. (Kappeler et al., 1993: 249–50)

Dominant Notions of Justice

Constructions of justice in comic books frequently manifest in story arcs that reproduce the existing power structures of larger society. Wright (2001) describes major comic book publishers DC, Dell, and Charlton as affirming 'all the basic assumptions of an American Cold War consensus ... none questioned the state of American society or the meaningful place of individuals within it' (p. 199). As Fingeroth (2004) explains, the superhero mass market craves comics that embody the old *Superman* television slogan, 'Truth, justice and the American way' (p. 159). Patriotic story lines in comic books, reinforcing the political status quo, were common during the First World War and the Cold War, imagining justice as a form of community redemption which rejects foreigners as the evil enemy (Wright, 2001).

Since 9/11, the G.W. Bush administration has steadily worked to reinvigorate a sense of nationalism using rhetoric based on fear (Curtis, 2004). Specifically, understanding of the social world has been sharply divided and recast as '*pre*' and '*post*' 9/11 in which danger lurks at every corner and threats are graver than ever before (Fleisher, 2002; Rice, 2002). The solution is simply to rid the world of the 'evildoers' (Greenberg, 2004).[1] While simplistic, the nationalistic rhetoric resonated with citizens as Bush's approval ratings soared above 80 per cent (Polling Report, 2001–2). One way in which comic book creators responded to the events of 9/11 was by issuing numerous special issues such as Marvel's *Heroes* and *9–11: Artists Respond*, in which traditional superheroes saluted the 'true' heroes such as law enforcement officers, firefighters, and other rescue personnel.

Nostalgia for a Desired Social Order

Patriotic themes are presented as a form of nostalgia in many comic books. Anderson (1991) potently theorizes the deep relationship between nostalgia and nationalism through his elucidation of 'imagined communities'. National story lines based on nostalgic cultural symbols such as poetry, myth and legend become ideological tools employed by governments who construct an idealized past as a model for a hopeful future.

Comic creators appear to be expressing a similar political and social longing through nostalgic reveries that ultimately uphold conservative American values.[2] In comic books, the desired social order the protagonist strives to achieve is the mythic return of better days, allegedly characterized by infrequent crime and just punishment. In this imagined social order, individuals who threaten the peace are identified as the 'other' and swiftly neutralized. The archetypal setting for comics is a tranquil community, with strong family values, enviable social capital and equality—all threatened by overwhelming evil, usually in the form of criminal violence—which has destroyed a peaceful, historic status quo (Fingeroth, 2004). Only through the cleansing of criminality by the protagonist can the desired status quo return, much like the retributive end of days in Christian eschatology, where the chosen good are saved at the expense of those defined as unworthy by their evil deeds. As one online Christian magazine writer observed, 'The great Bible stories—such as Samson in the book of Judges—are packed with the epic visions and good-versus-evil absolutes that fill the pages of classic comics and their modern, supercharged siblings known as "graphic novels"' (Mattingly, 2004). Themes of the community redemption through the hero's crusade to justice are often overtly Christian. For example, Nightcrawler, in the *X-Men* series, often quotes the Bible and pontificates about sin, penance, and righteousness while engaged in his fight for justice.

Retribution

According to Fingeroth (2004), comic books, like other media, invoke a populist notion of punishment—that which is morally satisfactory to the majority of community members (see also Sanders and Lyon, 1995). Retribution as a philosophy of punishment has often been associated with populism because of its appeal to the larger public as a ritual which symbolically returns society to its original order (Von Hirsch, 1976). Retribution differs from the policy aims of deterrence, which promotes crime prevention as its main objective; rehabilitation, which focuses on crime as a disease and corrective treatment as the response; and incapacitation, which banishes the offender to prison. Retribution's function rests on a western, philosophical notion of moral symmetry in which an offender gets what is deserved—their 'just desserts' (Von Hirsch, 1976).[3]

Oldenquist (1988) argues that a community cannot achieve its full humanity without the rituals associated with holding others morally accountable for their acts. Retribution is justified, therefore, because it benefits the society psychologically. This echoes the Nietzschean notion that rituals of punishment are deeply embedded in the very essence of human nature. Nozick (1981) argues that retribution satisfies the community's need to communicate to the offender that what they did was wrong. The punishment is designed to send the message of just how wrong the offense was and becomes a means to reconnect the offender to the moral norms of the society: 'When [the offender] undergoes punishment ... correct values are not totally without effect in his life (even though he does not follow them) because we hit him over the head with them' (p. 375).

Retribution, as a cleansing social ritual for the community and a means of communicating moral norms to the offender, has been immensely popular with the American public and conceivably forms a crucial part of the 'ritual moral exercise' of crime and justice in modern times (Katz, 1987). Retribution-style rhetoric has often been invoked by lawmakers and politicians who have long realized the political value of being perceived as 'tough-on-crime' (Beckett, 1997). The public is susceptible to the influence of political speech emphasizing and promoting such an agenda. Beckett (1997) states, 'Indeed, it is unlikely that political elites—particularly those seeking re-election—would persist in their efforts to mobilize concern about crime and drug use if the public did not appear to be receptive to them' (p. 23).

For example, the success of Bush's rhetoric mobilizing public support for the War on Terror arguably was based on his ability to conjure up nostalgic imaginings of crime and justice which symbolically resonated with the public, even if the facts on the ground were something else altogether. In response to the terrorist attacks in 2001, Bush invoked sound bites such as 'I want justice, and there's an old poster out West ... I recall, that said, "Wanted, Dead or Alive"' (CNN, 2001). A year later, Bush succinctly described the foreign policy approach toward the accused terrorists as an effort to 'smoke 'em out' (CNN, 2002).[4] Such rhetoric richly imagines terrorists and those who fight them as Old West villains and their vigilante cowboy protagonists. Implied here is a nostalgic yearning for the strong-arm, extra-legal tactics which in the Old West were justified by the absence of legitimate law enforcement, a theme which also strongly resonates in fictional media like comic books.

Doing Retribution

According to the literature on comic books, retribution and restoration of the desired social order may be accomplished by the comic book protagonist through both legal means and/or extra-legal means (i.e. taking the law into one's hands). Legal approaches include story lines—often influenced or funded by the US government—which depict the effectiveness of legitimate law enforcement agencies and/or officials in combating crime. For example, during the 1930s, J. Edgar Hoover influenced the comic strip *War on Crime*, which depicted 'real life tales of the FBI' and portrayed a favorable view of law enforcement (Lovell, 2002: 335). In 1971, the Department of Health, Education, and Welfare approached the creator of *Spider-Man* to write a story arc illustrating the dangers of drug use (Green, 2000). In 1990, the government enlisted Captain America as a soldier in the drug war in the government-inspired special issue titled *Captain America Goes to War Against Drugs*. More recently, in 1998 the government provided Marvel Comics with US $2.5 million to portray the dangers of marijuana use (Green, 2000).

More often, extra-legal responses to crime are portrayed in comics as necessary adjuncts to legitimate enforcement, to be used in times of crisis (Newman, 1993; Lovell, 2002). Comic book plots move inevitably toward the position of last resort: retaliatory, technically illegal, actions that must be tolerated in a time of crisis. The inadequacy of legitimate law enforcement is often a critical component of the crisis, thus freeing protagonists—both superhero and non-superheroes—to resort to illegitimate avenues to restore justice. In fact, Newman (1993), described the 1990 *Batman* movie's over-arching message as one in which 'Law Enforcement may call on Batman at any time to do violence to criminals which the established law enforcement machinery seems unable to carry out' (p. 315). Other characters such as The Punisher and Daredevil also resort to vigilante violence to avenge injustice (History Channel, 2003). Vigilante-related plots are enthusiastically embraced by readers. Mike Baron, Editor and writer of *Punisher: War Journals*, attributed the popularity of *Punisher* to 'the average citizen's outrage at the failure of society to punish evil' (Wright, 2001: 275). As Simpson et al. (2004) explain:

> Superheroes appear more attractive than society's flawed heroes. Having superpowers, they can operate as a one-superbeing judicial system outside the laws of any nation state, while sticking to a moral code that has truth and justice, not the protection of any vested interest, at heart. (p. 261)

Despite the dominance of a conservative effort to restore the status quo, the pendulum briefly swung in a more liberal direction in the 1960s. During this era, story arcs reflected the social upheaval apparent in society and explicitly questioned authority. *Green Lantern*, for example, was portrayed as a radical leftist tackling social issues such as racism, poverty, and corruption with special issues devoted to the assassinations of Martin Luther King Jr. and Robert Kennedy (Wright, 2001; O'Neil and Adams, 2004; Simpson et. al., 2004). However, incorporating social issues, such as the civil rights movement, into comics was dismissed as 'well-meaning, but clumsy' (Simpson et al., 2004: 264) and the old plots returned.

This research contributes to the literature by positioning comic books, and their overwhelming emphasis on crime and justice, as a cultural medium worthy of analysis. We will examine the type of crimes depicted in comic books, the desired social order in the comic books' imagined community, the style of justice employed by the protagonist (legal or extra-legal), and whether the depiction implies a retributive policy message, thereby reproducing dominant American notions of justice.

Methodology

To the Batcave!

Kane (2004) describes media studies within the framework of cultural criminology as 'an experimental ethnographic space' in which culture can be explored through the characters as 'virtual inhabitants' (p. 316). Such an approach links social reality to the social artefacts analyzed and takes into consideration what Hayward and Young (2004: 259) refer to as the deep 'interplay' of media and reality in postmodernism.

In our study, a purposive sample of 20 titles was drawn from the top 210 best-selling comic books and trade paperbacks released in December 2003 as recorded by ICv2.[5] Each monthly comic book has an issue number and often a story 'arc', or episode, that extends over several issues. In order to sample entire story arcs, we followed the selected issues forward and/or backwards in time, from December 2003, in order to include the entire arc in our analysis. Trade paperbacks are compilation books of all the issues in a particular story arc, and thus are relatively self-contained sagas.

The selection of monthlies involved separating the top best-sellers into ranked groups of 15 titles. Within each group we purposively selected a comic book. Purposive sampling allowed for the avoidance of children's books, such as *Archie* and *Daffy Duck*. The sample also contains a mixture of superhero and non-superhero titles. By spanning the top 200 best-selling comic books and selecting one title from the ranked groups, we included in our sample the most popular comic books, as well as those published by alternative or independent publishers located further down the list. Titles included *Ultimate Spider-Man*, *Justice League of America (JLA)*, *Punisher*, *Wonder Woman*, *100 Bullets*, and *Lucifer*. See Table 1 for a complete list of sampled monthly titles.

Trade paperbacks were chosen from the ranked list of the top 30 best sellers. The list was divided into ranked groups of 10 from which 2 books were selected from each. The sample included *Dark Knight Strikes Again*, *Powers: Anarchy*, *Wolverine: The Brotherhood*, *Heaven's War*, *Violent Cases*, and *Sleeper: Out in the Cold*. Titles represented both superhero and non-superhero genres and children's books were avoided. See Table 1 for the list of sampled trade paperbacks.

Qualitative analyses can suffer from the validity problem of selection bias because they involve researchers selecting a sample in a non-random fashion in order to prove or disprove an *a priori* hypothesis (Neuman, 2004). Several measures were taken to counterbalance the selection bias associated with a purposive sample, including the use of a relatively large sample size, the selection of titles across the spectrum of top sellers, and the inclusion of superhero and non-superhero genres. As the historian Lustick (1996) reminds qualitative researchers, selection of sources should be a self-conscious endeavor which recognizes the variance of information within a 'normal distribution of implicit theoretical commitments' (p. 615). Thus, patterns can be discerned without ignoring competing narratives and confidence in results are increased as the size and narrative scope of a sample increases.

Comic books, unlike other literary media, provide juxtapositions between what is seen and what is read offering more possibilities for interpretation. Identifying manifest, or surface, content involved noting the explicit behavior of the characters and the social environment they occupy by following the interaction between the language and graphics. As McCloud (1993, 2000) notes, most American comic

Table 1. Comic books selected Monthly title

Monthly title	Issues	Publisher	Rank	Distribution*
Ultimate Spider-Man	51,52,53,54	Marvel	9	97
JLA	91,92,93	DC	21	58
Punisher	33,34,35,36,37	Marvel	43	38
Batman DC	788,789	DC	50	36
Wonder Woman	197,198,199,200	DC	67	29
Fables	19,20,21,23	DC	80	25
Rose & Thorn	1,2,3,4,5,6	DC	92	22
Superman Kansas Sighting	1,2	DC	120	18
100 Bullets	47,48,49	DC	128	17
Lucifer	141	DC	141	13
Losers	7,8	DC	154	12
Route 666	19	CrossGen	177	10
Sam & Twitch	1,2,3,4,5,6	Image	186	9
Queen & Country	21,22,23,24,25	Oni Press	207	6
Trade paperback title	Issues	Publisher	Rank	Distribution*
Dark Knight Strikes Again	—	DC	3	5.1
Powers Volume V: Anarchy	—	Image	5	5.1
Wolverine: Brotherhood	—	Marvel	14	3
Heaven's War	—	Image	17	2.8
Violent Cases	—	Dark Horse	22	2.4
Sleeper: Out in the Cold	—	DC	25	2.3

Source: ICV2 sales estimates based on 13 January 2004, data from Diamond Publisher (2004) comics distributors.
*Distribution is represented in thousands of copies.

books play on the differences between words and pictures, both of which contribute to the comic book's 'vocabulary' (McCloud, 1993:47). Although graphic depictions have become increasingly realistic with the advent of computer animation, comics still operate iconically—using pictures that are simpler than reality as symbolic cues for interpretation—which when coupled with well-crafted, yet sparse, narrative or dialogue can convey worlds of plot development in only a few frames.

If we dig deeper, we find the juxtaposition of words and pictures also contributes to latent, or underlying content, which is more relevant for answering the policy questions implied by the depictions of justice in the comic book. Denisoff (1975) cautions that social scientists conducting content analysis may find meaning that the author neither intended, nor the reading public perceived. Regardless, such underlying meaning arguably exists to be discovered provided that it has a foundation in the more obvious surface content. Inter-rater reliability in discovering latent content was accomplished by having two readers approach each comic book in the sample independently before joining forces in the analysis. On all but two comic books there was agreement on the themes represented. Regarding the two disagreements, further discussion settled the discrepancies.

Once the sample was compiled, a content analysis was conducted to systematically understand the crime and justice themes contained in the comics as social artifacts. Content analysis involves the study of messages and the meaning they convey (Maxfield and Babbie, 1998/2001). To examine the extent to which contemporary comic books reproduce dominant notions of justice, four main research questions were developed:

- What is the crime problem addressed in the comic book?
- What is the desired social order in the community of the comic book?
- How is justice achieved, legally or extra-legally?
- What is the implied policy message of the comic book?

To ascertain the dominant notions of justice revealed in the comic books, we must first address the crime problem depicted in the comic book. Based on the literature about comic books we examined, it is expected that the most frequent crime problem depicted in the comic books will be street crimes. As such, individual criminal intent, motivations and pathologies will be highlighted by the comic books with little concern for the social forces propelling the actor (Wright, 2001; Simpson et. al., 2004).

Moreover, as has historically occurred in American comics (Wright, 2001), it is expected that contemporary comic book story arcs will imagine nostalgic communities characterized by a desired social order which values a nostalgic patriotism and retributivism. These dominant notions of justice will be addressed by examining the responses to the crime problem and implied policy messages. Based on previous literature (Newman, 1993; Lovell, 2002), it is expected that protagonists will resort to extra-legal approaches in order to reassert the desired social order. Therefore, we hypothesize that these comic books explicitly or implicitly endorse retributive criminal justice policies.

Results

Holy Crime Problem, Batman!

Crime themes were separated into three categories: dominant crime problems, secondary crime problems and social problems (Table 2). The dominant crime problem represents the primary problem the protagonist faces in terms of criminal behavior and acts as the focus of the plot development. Secondary crime problems are depictions of crimes that happen along the way as the protagonist responds to the dominant crime problem. In essence, these are crime-related sub-plots. The social problems category relates to portrayals of social, but not necessarily criminal, ills such as environmental destruction and homophobia.

The crime themes which emerged from the sample included organized crime, government corruption, terrorism, violent street crime, domestic violence and war crimes, among others. In contrast to the expectation that street crime would be the dominant crime problem, organized crime was found most frequently. In *Violent Cases*, for example, a retelling of the Al Capone stories is juxtaposed with the protagonist's reflection on his boyhood loss of innocence. He comes to realize the scope of human depravity in the world through hearing stories of mob violence from Capone's former osteopath. Organized crime also comes to the forefront in *Fables, Ultimate Spider-Man, Wonder Woman* and *Sleeper*.

Government corruption is often depicted as a dominant and secondary crime theme. For example, *The Losers* are a group of rogue CIA agents who are betrayed and left for dead by an unknown operative.

Table 2. Crime themes

Crime theme	Dominant crime problem	Secondary crime problem	Total crime problems	Social problems
Organized crime	5	1	6	—
Government corruption	3	2	5	—
Terrorism	3	1	4	—
Psychopathic criminality	2	3	5	—
Violent/street crime including drug abuse	2	6	8	—
White-collar crime	1	0	1	—
Communism	1	0	1	—
Alien invasion	1	1	2	—
Cosmic battle of good vs. evil	1	0	1	—
CRJ System as oppressor	1	0	1	—
Geopolitical conflict/war crimes	0	5	5	—
Criminal exploitation of women	0	3	3	—
Other	0	3	3	6

The group, determined to identify the mastermind and avenge their betrayal, recall numerous historical instances of corruption perpetrated by the US government.

Another dominant crime problem is terrorism. *Queen & Country*, a British spy book, depicts an MI6-like operations chief lamenting the complications of 'the endless inquiries into off-shore accounts and wire transfers' that the War on Terror has spawned (*Queen & Country*, Issue 21; Figure 1). The image shows the operations chief swishing his wine glass in a show of power and cool sophistication that could only come from a veteran of the most secret intelligence operations. Yet, the image also implies that even the most sophisticated spies are becoming increasingly challenged by the complexity of the new age of terrorism, which is worthy of a deep sigh.

A less frequent dominant crime problem is psychopathic criminality, referring to plots featuring a villain whose primary motivation is a psychological need, brought on by some sort of psychosis, to hurt others. Of note is the world of *Sam & Twitch*, in which the detectives combat such offenders as pedophile clowns, vengeful 'Franken-women' and other criminals described as 'monsters' (*Sam & Twitch*, Issue 5).

Violent street crime emerges as the most prevalent secondary crime theme. For example, in *Sam & Twitch*, Twitch's daughter is kidnapped off the street by a criminal seeking revenge on Twitch, the detective who caught him after a prior offense (Figure 2). These panels evoke every parent's worst nightmare. The disguised predator lies in wait, dressed as a helpless elderly lady, as the young girl approaches. The attire of the young girl, her cheerleading skirt and turtleneck, portrays her innocence. Quickly, the predator violently abducts her and forces her into the trunk of his car.

Finally, several comic books illustrate social problems, but in general these problems provide background or sub-plot material. Global economic inequality is touched upon in *JLA*. *Queen & Country* explores homophobia in military institutions while *Wonder Woman* exhibits concern about the environment.

Figure 1. Dominant crime problem—terrorism

Source: Queen & Country (Issue 21). Image credit: Oni Press, 1305 SE MLK Blvd., Suite A, Portland, OR 97214, USA.

Returning to Smallville: Community Redemption

The crime problem represents a crisis for the community, or other idealized entity, in the form of a nation, planet, or universe. In the sampled comics, the following imagined social orders were identified: American hegemony, transnationalism/globalism, cosmic order, small-town America, intergalactic cooperation, and traditional England.

Most often, the comics reflect a need to maintain American hegemony, expressed as a longing for America as a bastion of freedom and democracy and as a superpower leading the world. This occurs in *Batman Detective Comics, Ultimate Spider-Man, Powers, 100 Bullets, Sam & Twitch, Route 666, Punisher* and *Rose & Thorn.* In *Route 666,* for instance, the Cold War is revisited and Cassie, the protagonist, has the superhuman ability to see the Communists for who they are: demons. Cassie must appeal to the government of Empyrean, a thinly-disguised America, to prevent the demons from taking over the country. As one of her allies states, 'If Cassie can make someone see one of these creatures the way she made us see 'em, then maybe we can organize a decent counterattack!' (*Route 666,* Issue 19).

Transnationalism or globalism are idealized in several crime books including *JLA, The Losers, Queen & Country, Sleeper* and *Dark Knight.* This category embodies the goal of international cooperation and the use of transnational governing bodies, similar to the United Nations, as a means of maintaining order. In *JLA,* Superman is called away from his post as a representative at the United Nations in order to respond, with his superhero sidekicks, to an alien invasion. Although this comic book has an

Figure 2. Secondary crime problem—street crime

Source: Sam & Twitch (Issue 1). Image credit: © 2005 TMP International, Inc. All Rights Reserved. Todd McFarlane Productions, Inc. owns the copyrights and trademarks in Spawn and all related characters. Sam & Twitch and the other marks and logos displayed are trademarks of TMP International, Inc.

interplanetary setting, the superheroes seek order among nations on planet Earth and do not generally cooperate with aliens. In addition, *Wonder Woman* works toward maintaining international balance as the United Nations representative of her Amazon island nation.

Small-town America is imagined in *Superman: Kansas Sighting* in which Superman returns to his mid-western American roots in Smallville. Small-town America is also idealized in *Wolverine: The Brotherhood*. In this story arc, Wolverine is avenging the murder of a small-town girl who escaped from a terrorist militia (which also operates as a female sex slavery cult) only to be hunted down and killed by the militia leaders. As Wolverine states during a denouement moment with his friend Elf (a.k.a. Nightcrawler), 'They were a cult. They'd broken a town. Made it afraid. They kidnapped women. Girls. And they used them up' (*Wolverine: The Brotherhood*, Issue 6). Exiled to New York City, the characters in *Fables* long for a return to their bucolic place of origin, Fabletown, a pseudo-America with democratic elections and a criminal justice system complete with rules of evidence and due process protections.

The cosmic battle of good versus evil reigns in *Lucifer* and *Heaven's War*. These plots imagine a community whose citizens always choose good over evil and fight against moral relativism and Satanism. The worldview in both comic books reflects a need to restore heaven and hell to their proper cosmic positions with the eventual defeat of hell in an apocalyptic age. By contrast, despite the focus on good and evil, *Violent Cases* reminisces about traditional England; the main character recalls his childhood in Portsmouth living with his maternal grandparents. Remembrances of custom-made tweed coats, a fifth birthday party at the Queen's hotel, adults drinking sherry, and grimy, rain-soaked streets are juxtaposed with instances of probable child abuse and stories of gangsters from Capone's former osteopath. *Violent Cases* ends with the protagonist commenting that 'Nobody seems to wear a hat these days'.

Gee Whiz! The Authorities Cannot Protect Us

Unfortunately, in the world of comic books, those entrusted with the job of maintaining an ordered community through public security are largely unsuccessful. The majority of the comic books depicted government and law enforcement as ineffective in the fight against crime. Often the police were characterized as either dim-witted or lacking the resources to wage the battle against the crime problem. In *Route 666*, the police are seen reclining in their station reading the crime news in a tabloid newspaper, ignorant of a dangerous plot brewing. In *Fables*, the mayor, Old King Cole, and the Wolf from Little Red Riding, who works as Fabletown's detective, argue about being unable to gain a conviction of Prince Charming for the murder of Bluebeard (Figure 3). Old King Cole blames it on the detective's inability to gather admissible evidence, but the detective faults Fabletown's convoluted rules of evidence and due process requirements.

Government and law enforcement corruption occurred in the plots of a majority of comic books, many of which paired corruption and ineffectiveness themes. In *Wolverine: The Brotherhood*, an ATF agent brutalizes a suspect in interrogation as a necessary means of gaining information about a dangerous right-wing cult. In *Dark Knight Strikes Again*, *The Losers* and *Rose & Thorn*, the original dominant crime problem involves government corruption which further complicates the response to crime. In these stories, the protagonists find that the authorities have themselves created the crime problem. *Dark Knight Strikes Again* is set in a society that has deteriorated into a police state, with a holographic President, news merging into entertainment, and Congress passing the 'Freedom *from* Information Act'. One of the superheroes arch-nemeses has gained control of the world and has, at least temporarily, suppressed all superheroes.

This Looks Like a Job for Superman: Extra-Legal Justice

The primary path to justice reflects extra-legal responses to crime, or taking the law into one's own hands. The plots reveal a continuum of support for extra-legal, or vigilante, paths to achieve justice. *Lucifer*, *Heaven's War* and the *Punisher* represent the most extreme abandonment of the rule of law in favor of extra-legal moral crusading. The Punisher, for example, never attempts to work within the legal system and immediately embarks on his vigilante mission in the opening pages of the story arc. Necessitated by the confluence of the geopolitical forces inciting organized and transnational crime and the inadequate and/or corrupt law enforcement responses, the plot inevitably moves toward the position of last resort: retaliatory, technically illegal, actions that must be tolerated in a time of crisis. The narrator in the *Punisher* explains, 'he judges them, he passes sentence, then he blows them away. Justice happens in the time it takes to pull the trigger' (*Punisher*, Issue 33; Figure 4).

Along the path to extra-legal justice, several additional themes emerged which suggest an apparent formula in comic books: justifications for the use of violence, framing the world starkly as good versus evil, building and cooperating as a team, responding to broken treaties, taking control of the media and soul-searching about the role of superheroes.

Figure 3. Institutional response to the crime problem—ineffectiveness

Source: Fables (Issue 19). Image credit: "Fables" #19 © 2004 Bill Willingham & DC Comics. All Rights Reserved. Used with permission.

A majority of the titles highlighted the crisis-justification for violence: disorder has gotten so out of hand that the protagonist must resort to violent solutions outside the law. For instance, in *Punisher*, although Spider-Man and Daredevil take issue with the extreme vigilantism, their perspective is drowned out by the triumphant extra-legal violence. In *Dark Knight Strikes Again*, Batman swoops down to save the citizens of Gotham only after legitimate law enforcement and other superheroes have failed to bring justice. In the context of the greater evil of the destruction of values such as public safety, democracy and individual freedom, violence outside the law for social good is depicted as a justifiable response.

Figure 4. The justice process—vigilantism

Source: *Punisher* (Issue 33). Image credit: Marvel Entertainment, Inc., 417 Fifth Avenue, New York, NY 10016, USA.

In most of the comic books sampled, good and evil are visually depicted with no shading in between. For example, in *Rose & Thorn*, the neighborhoods that form the backdrop to the story are either an idealized urban park landscape with technocolor foliage or a seedy, socially disorganized part of the city where crime is rampant. This mirrors the duality of the Dr Jekyll/Mr Hyde-like main character. As Rose, she is a sweet, law-abiding woman with bright blue eyes, but when she is Thorn, she is green-eyed, danger-ous, arbitrarily violent and a hyper-sexualized psychopath. Likewise, in *Heaven's War*, Charles Williams leads Christian dualists, C.S. Lewis and J.R.R. Tolkien, in a cosmic battle against the moral relativist, Aleister Crowley. In one scene, Williams is standing on a checkerboard, revealing the clear delineations of black and white and emphasizing the moral superiority of placing oneself firmly on a white square (Figure 5).

Other comic books are more ambiguous regarding the theme of good versus evil. For example, in the *The Losers*, the United States government has clearly betrayed a team of CIA agents, yet when the characters are reflecting on the litany of corruptive behaviors perpetrated by the government throughout history, the scenes are portrayed in a hazy blue/gray color, graphically revealing the shades of gray surrounding the conduct. Additionally, in over half of the comic books sampled, the protagonist assembles a team of allies to fight for justice. *The Losers* are a rag-tag team of rogue CIA agents working together to understand why they were betrayed by the government. *JLA* revolves around a cooperative theme in which Superman is called away from a United Nations meeting by Plastic Man in order to meet with team-members about an alien invasion (Figure 6).

Half of the titles explored the theme of broken treaties among rivals and broken contracts among partners. In the world of comic books, heroes and villains battle according to rules previously agreed upon by participants. The challenge for protagonists comes when either allies or enemies begin to play outside the rules. Antagonists often betray prior contracts, thus freeing up the hero(es) to also play dirty and become vigilantes. For instance, in *Lucifer*, the delegates of Hell explicitly broke the rules established by Lucifer when they inhabited the body of the protagonist, thus disturbing the balance between good versus evil and necessitating a cosmic battle.

Justice is also achieved by using the media to one's advantage. Avenues include utilizing cable talk shows (*Sam & Twitch*), penning a tell-all best-seller (*Wonder Woman*), and releasing surveillance

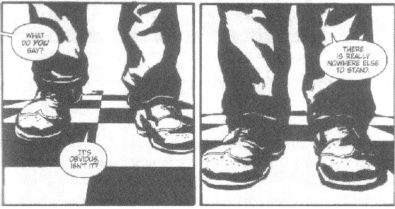

Figure 5. The justice process—framing the world as good versus evil

footage to news programmes (*Powers: Anarchy*). In fact, Miss Misery directly addresses the importance of media to her partner and states, 'pop culture is just another way to control the masses' (*Sleeper: Out in the Cold*).

Finally, over half the titles belonging to the superhero genre featured soul-searching moments during which the hero reflects on his/her role in society. Historically, the classic thoughtful, and perhaps reluctant, hero was Spider-Man. True to form, the *Ultimate Spider-Man* story arc shows a superhero ready to leave the hero circuit for a calm and settled life with Mary Jane. *Wolverine: The Brotherhood* follows the hero as he is plagued by the thought that by killing 27 people during his revenge sequence he may have turned into a mere animal himself. His friend Elf (a.k.a. Nightcrawler) consoles him: 'Were those men evil? Without question. By killing them in your rage are you evil? You are unique [Wolverine]. And I do not speak of what has been done to you. Is the wolf evil when it culls the sickness from the herd?' (Issue 6).

Deathworthiness: It's Clobberin' Time

Frequently, antagonists and even peripheral characters are killed as the protagonist travels the path to justice. However, not every character is morally 'deathworthy' in the eyes of the protagonist. In fact, three levels of deathworthiness, or justifiable victims the hero kills, were observed.

Figure 6. The justice process—building the team and initiating cooperation

Source: JLA (Issue 93). Image credit: "JLA" #19 © 2004 DC Comics. All Rights Reserved. Used with permission.

Most frequently, protagonists will only kill characters explicitly responsible for harms done to themselves or their family members. In *Batman Detective Comics*, a suspect falsely accused of a murder rampage turns murderously violent himself to avenge the wrongs done to him by the criminal justice system. The narrator states, 'Wrongly accused, wrongly imprisoned, Eddie Hurst's sudden madness, surely, was forgivable' (*Batman DC*, Issue 788). As the story arc unfolds, Batman openly sympathizes with the suspect's need for personal revenge. In *Sam & Twitch*, Twitch resorts to murder to avenge a crime against his daughter. The message of the story arc is that seeking revenge for crimes against one's family is a moral obligation, and may be rewarded rather than punished.

Furthermore, some protagonists kill anyone morally depraved, for any reason, whom they encounter during their fight for justice. Even criminals guilty of minor offenses may warrant an 'unofficial' death penalty. For example, a street junkie is blown away after informing the Punisher of the whereabouts of a sought-after criminal (Figure 7). As a street junkie, the informer is death-eligible under the Punisher's paradigm of ridding the community of all criminals, big and small.

Figure 7. Deathworthiness—anyone morally depraved

Source: The Punisher (Issue 33). Image credit: Marvel Entertainment, Inc., 417 Fifth Avenue, New York, NY 10016, USA.

Finally, in a minority of the comic books sampled, even innocents are eligible for death as part of a cosmic battle between good and evil. In *Lucifer,* a morally laudable John is nonetheless demonically possessed and ultimately killed as part of a larger battle between heaven and hell. When John asks the demon possessing him why he deserved his fate, the demon replies that it isn't deserved: 'You were just neutral ground, John,' the demon says (*Lucifer,* Issue 141).

Discussion

Cultural criminology suggests that media reflect and reproduce social reality. Popular media are replete with representations of crime and justice, and comic books are no exception. The extent to which comic books reflect dominant notions of justice is evident in the crime problems faced by protagonists, the imagined communities that promote American hegemony, the preference for retribution and the tacit approval of extra-legal means of achieving justice.

Our analysis revealed that contemporary comic books focus on organized crime and terrorism rather than on street crime and psychopathic criminality. The crime problems depicted in this sample are complex affairs involving multiple entities, often legitimate institutions gone bad, that operate in a variety of contexts transnationally, intergalactically and across cosmic dimensions. However, at the same time, when considering sub-plots, street crime is quite prevalent.

That the crime problem extends beyond the borders of the United States is most likely a reflection of the increasing awareness and concern regarding global issues in a 'post' 9/11 world. Terrorism and organized crime networks operating on a variety of fronts in a geopolitical struggle for power and control reflect current political dynamics. Further, the crime problem presents a formidable crisis for those who imagine their community otherwise. A plurality of comic books sampled seeks to maintain an imagined community of perfect order and safety in the context of an American, hegemonic, yet democratic, political entity. The imagined community is focused on an urban core, hoped to be swept of the dark vices that blight it, such as is the case with Batman's Gotham City. A notable minority of the comic books exhibit utopian yearnings for small-town America, like Superman's Smallville, and a remembered traditional England. These three categories together reflect a status quo-oriented goal for the protagonist who aims to achieve not a revolutionary new world, but a reactionary old order.

As expected, legitimate criminal justice institutions are either too corrupt, too ineffective—or both—to adequately respond to the challenges posed by the crime problem. Positive portrayals of legitimate authorities are rare, thus necessitating revenge-oriented, extra-legal justice. This represents a uniquely comic book-related theme which can be appreciated in contrast to popular American television crime dramas. In *CSI, Law & Order, 24* and *NYPD Blue* to name only a few, legitimate authorities are largely shown as sexy, clever and morally justified as they use their logical, physical and technological talents to bring down all manner of crime. Corrupt authorities surface in particular episodes, but they are eventually rooted out in these time-honored morality plays.

Retribution and revenge policy messages appear to dominate the comic book landscape. The message in *Ultimate Spider-Man* resonates within nearly half of the sample: the hero must be on the right side of the moral equation, but not necessarily on the right side of the law. Frequently, and ironically, the rule of law can only be defended by acting outside the law in order to restore an out-of-control world to balance. Extra-legality, then, gains a veneer of legality. Likewise *Rose & Thorn* suggests that vulnerable people—in this case exploited female mental patients—need to get in touch with their violent side. If harnessed effectively, their violent potential can be mobilized for the moral good.

The irony of comic books as a revenge fantasy is that evil is employed against evil in hopes of giving birth to good, a uniquely Judeo-Christian notion of apocalyptic redemption:

> There will be no more death, no more grief or crying or pain. The old things have disappeared ... whoever wins the victory receive this from me: I will be his God, and he will be my son. But cowards, traitors, perverts, murderers, the immoral, those who practice magic, those who worship idols, and all liars—the place for them is the lake burning with fire and sulfur ... (Revelation, 21: 3, 7–8)
>
> They shall be mine, says the Lord of hosts, my own special possession, on the day I take action. And I will have compassion on them, as a man has compassion on his son who serves him. Then you will again see the distinction between the just and the wicked; Between him who serves God, and him who does not serve him. For lo, the day is coming, blazing like an oven, when all the proud and all evildoers will be stubble, And the day that is coming will set them on fire, leaving them neither root nor branch, says the Lord of hosts. But for you who fear my name, there will arise the sun of justice with its healing rays; And you will gambol like calves out of the stall and tread down the wicked; They will become ashes under the soles of your feet. (Malachi, 3: 17–21)

Much like the book of Revelation and earlier prophetic narratives depict a symbolic return to the Kingdom of God lost to humans after the Original Sin, so too do comic books reflect violence as a hope-and-redemption strategy in the American cultural consciousness. As Greg Garrett opines in an interview about his book, *Holy Superheroes! Exploring Faith and Spirituality in Comic Books* (2004),

> the archetypal plot movement from despair to hope that the gospel narratives capture, and the archetypal American emphasis on individual self-reliance that we see in so many of our hero narratives from Franklin's Autobiography and Last of the Mohicans are all there in larger-than-life form in comics. (Yocum, 2006)

Our analysis indicates that for a return to paradise lost any number of revenge killings can be undertaken and a curious balance sheet ensues. To avenge one person's murder, Wolverine kills an additional 27 people. As the analysis of deathworthiness reveals, some characters' lives are just not as valuable as others. If the 27 people are morally depraved, then no harm in the larger sense has occurred. Victims of revenge violence are not the chosen ones during the apocalyptic battle against crime, and thus their demise in the metaphoric Lake of Fire restores balance, even if the number of people killed by the hero reflects a numeric imbalance. Indeed, retribution extends beyond utilitarian thinking. (Notably, there are a few indications of utilitarian-style deterrence policy messages in the sample.) Retribution as a policy goal seeks what is deserved (Von Hirsch, 1976)—in comic books, such a symmetrical response frequently involves numerous deathworthy characters whose lives are fundamentally devalued due to the characters.

In fact, loss of life is easier to tolerate when the loss is considered inevitable, as a necessary consequence of action. During wartime, the deathworthiness of innocent civilians is referred to as 'collateral damage' (CNN, 2003). In a December 2006 press conference, Bush indicated that he believed about 30,000 deaths of military troops and civilians had resulted from the War in Iraq. He then commented about the decision to go to war: 'Knowing what I know today, I'd make the decision again' (Boston Globe, 2005). In response to a question regarding the loss of civilian lives as a result of the War on Terror, Paul Wolfowitz, Deputy Secretary of Defense, stated simply that 'bad things happen in combat zones' (DoD, 2002). The political climate reflects the justification of mass violence that stems from the clear delineation of good and evil, and granting oneself as the moral executor of the abolishment of evil. Comic book protagonists are depicted as holding themselves similarly responsible for the moral and spiritual fate of the world:

> Violence is a staple of comics, as it is of American culture. Because superhero comics are action/ adventure stories, conflict is almost always worked out through violence, and I agree, in some cases it seems a little ridiculous: All right, we just met, so let's fight. Of course sometimes it's more justified as a plot element: the only way to stop the Joker/Bizarro/the Red Skull/etc. from killing a lot of people is to kick the crud out of him, and even people who oppose war will sometimes make exceptions … I'm not so naïve to think that, for example, Hitler and the Nazi state would have ever stopped killing people unless they'd been forced to stop. (Yocum, 2006)

Likewise, Bush called the War in Iraq the 'moral equivalent' of the Second World War and likened the Iraqi insurgents to the German and Japanese in that conflict (*Washington Post*, 2005). The nostalgia for the widely considered just-war actions of the Allies in the Second World War is utilized in order to garner support for the War in Iraq as a moral quest where the enemy is clearly evil and the motivations of Allied forces are morally necessary. Likewise, the nostalgia for the Second World War and the Cold

War are palpable in the American hegemony themes in the comic books sampled, most notably in *Route 666* and *Heaven's War*.

In contrast, nearly a half-dozen of the comic books reflect a deep sense of futility in which justice is completely outside the control of most humans and superhumans. According to the worldview depicted in *Sleeper: Out in the Cold*, oligarchic elites control all aspects of the political and social order and most humans are mere pawns in the game. The protagonist exhibits no hope that the social and political order can be changed and thus a fundamental injustice is the normative state. In *JLA*, terrorists, insurgents and fundamentalists are seen as ultimately unstoppable because there can be no criminal justice policy response for criminal acts of desperation. This particularly nihilistic view of the world is constructed in a minority of comic books and suggests one way the medium in some cases reflects an anti- or postapocalyptic consciousness.

Rehabilitation and Peacemaking: With Great Power Comes Great Responsibility

Our sample indicated that paths to justice exist on a broad continuum and alternatives to vigilantism and retribution—such as restorative justice/diplomacy and rehabilitation—are also depicted. As Williams (1998) discussed in an analysis of seven comic books, although it is tempting to make vast generalizations about comic books, there is enough variation in themes to warrant a more muted conclusion. Employing a Gramscian framework to discuss comic books as sites of hegemonic and counter-hegemonic discourse, smaller, independent comic books can be vehicles for counter-hegemonic themes of social justice (Williams, 1998). This study indicates, however, that a not-so-silent minority of top-selling comic books describe alternatives to extra-legal justice, including main staples like *Wonder Woman* and *100 Bullets*.

For example, peacemaking criminology is reflected in *Wonder Woman*. Wonder Woman prefers to talk through issues with her enemies whenever possible to restore order. As a representative of her home country in a transnational governing body, Wonder Woman envisions a kinder, gentler world. Rehabilitation is suggested by *100 Bullets* in a storyline in which criminals are likened to animals in cages; as the protagonist ceases his drug habit, he is shown freeing a tiger from a cage. The tiger leaves only a trace of footprints in the sand.

Limitations of the Study

As a starting point for the holistic study of comic books across genres, we took a broad approach which sought to underscore basic constructions of crime and justice. As a result, a detailed analysis of the interaction between themes of crime and justice and portrayals of gender, class and race, was beyond the scope of this study. Questions for future research include whether Wonder Woman's peacemaking ideology is acceptable to readers because she is female. Are stereotypes of women as nurturing and non-violent playing into her construction as the super-heroic diplomat? Another red flag is raised in regards to race and deathworthiness. Is it a coincidence that the morally depraved street junkie, deathworthy under the logic of the Punisher, is black? Is there a working-class logic underlying mainstream comics, in which street justice is the avenue of the economically powerless, disenfranchised from the halls of political power?

Conclusion

Although there are notable exceptions, contemporary mainstream comic books tend to fit into formulaic revenge fantasy plots in which protagonists respond to crime as a larger-than-life global or cosmic phenomenon. They are willing to act violently outside the law in order to restore the rule of law in a utopian American-style democracy. Retribution, and valuing some people's lives over others based on a Judeo-Christian moral balance sheet, is the underlying policy message conveyed by the medium.

Overly positivistic hype over the effects of comic books have created moral panics in the past, suggesting that comic books directly influence readers' behavior, causing juvenile delinquency (Wertham, 1954) and a retreat from Christianity (Fulce, 1990). However, our results show that mainstream comics push American values to their extreme in defense of status quo notions of preserving public safety in democracies and maintaining a Christian dualistic worldview. Comic books may not directly influence behavior, but they are a cultural resting place—perhaps a cultural sleeper cell—for an extreme paranoia about crime, fantasies about violent revenge and longings for a utopian American hegemony. Given the current rise of fundamentalist Christian ideology in mainstream politics and the suppression of the rule of law in a time of paranoia, it is no surprise that an increase in comic book-inspired Hollywood movies and interest in graphic novels is simultaneously palpable. Best-selling comic books are a cultural touchstone for conservative, reactionary values, such as criminal punishment as retribution, and reinforce the status quo with seductive and exciting storylines.

Notes

1. Greenberg (2004) writes in the *New Yorker*, 'Shortly after September 11, 2001, the President came across Proverbs 21:15: "When justice is done, it brings joy to the righteous but terror to evildoers." Soon, "evildoers" became his favorite term for Al Qaeda' (p. 92).

2. The nostalgia reaches meta-analytical proportions with the current boom in the comic books market as a nostalgia for a past nostalgia. Lovell (2002) describes the recent reprint of true-crime comics from the 1930s and 1940s (the 'golden age' of comic books) as a 'longing for things to be the way they were before everything changed' (p. 335) and a reminder of 'where we thought we once were, but also where we want to be' (p. 344).

3. The symmetry is Hegelian in that it is the restoration of the moral order after a moral negation. 'The annulment of the crime is retribution in so far as (a) retribution in conception is an "injury of the injury", and (b) since as existent a crime is something determinate in its scope both qualitatively and quantitatively, its negation as existent is similarly determinate' (Hegel, p. 101).

4. One political observer notes that Bush's foreign policy vision is 'less serious and more simplistic than an issue of Captain America' (from http://buffalobeast.com/91/50.htm).

5. ICv2 (Internal Correspondence version 2) 'provides news and information for pop culture retailers from "inside the world of pop culture products", with the only daily trade news, in-depth analysis, and product and sales information available anywhere' and is available at http://www.icv2.com/ index.html.

References

Anderson, B. (1991) *Imagined Communities*. London: Verso.

Beckett, K. (1997) *Making Crime Pay: Law and Order in Contemporary American Politics*. New York: Oxford University Press.

Boston Globe (2005) 'Iraqi Civilian Deaths Mount—and Count', 17 December.

Cavender, G. (2004) 'Media and Crime Policy: A Reconsideration of David Garland's *The Culture of Control*', *Punishment and Society* 6(3): 335–48.

CNN (2001) 'Bush: bin Laden "Prime Suspect"', 17 September.

CNN (2002) 'Bush Found Voice in Battle Against Terror', 8 September.

CNN (2003) 'Analysts: War Provides Textbook Case', 21 April.

Cochran, B (2006) 'DC Sniper Case: Lessons Learned', *Communicator* (December). Available at: http://www.rtnda. org/about/pres_Dec02.shtml

Creekmur, C. (2004) 'Superheroes and Science Fiction: Who Watches Comic Books?', *Science Fiction Studies* 31(2): 283–91.

Currie, E. (1998) *Crime and Punishment in America*. New York: Henry Holt/Metropolitan Books.

Curtis, A. (Director) (2004) *The Power of Nightmares: The Rise of the Politics of Fear*. London: BBC.

Denisoff, R.S. (1975) 'Content Analysis: The Achilles' Heel of Popular Culture', *Journal of Popular Culture* 9: 456–60.

Diamond Publishers (2004) 'News: Top 50 Graphic Novels Actual—December 2003'. Available at: www.icv2.com/ articles/home/4106.html

Department of Defense (DoD) (2002) 'Deputy Secretary Wolfowitz Town Hall Meeting at Bagram Air Base', 15 July. Available at: http://www.dod.mil/transcripts/2002/t07182002_t0717bab.html

Ennis, G. (2001) *The Punisher: Welcome Home, Frank*. New York: Marvel.

Epstein, S. (1995) 'The New Mythic Monster', in J. Ferrell and C. Sanders (eds) *Cultural Criminology*, pp. 66–79. Boston: Northeastern University Press.

Ferrell, J. (1999) 'Cultural Criminology', *Annual Review of Sociology* 25(1): 395–418.

Ferrell, J. and C. Sanders (eds) (1995) *Cultural Criminology*. Boston: Northeastern University Press.

Ferrell, J. and N. Websdale (1999) *Making Trouble: Cultural Constructions of Crime, Deviance, and Control*. New York: Aldine de Gruyter.

Fingeroth, D. (2004) *Superman on the Couch: What Superheroes Tell Us About Ourselves and Our Society*. New York: Continuum.

Fleisher, A. (2002) 'Press briefing by Ari Fleischer'. Available at: http://www.whitehouse.gov/news/releases /2002/05/20020517–6.html

Fulce, J. (1990) *Seduction of the Innocent Revisited*. Lafayette, LA: Huntington House.

Garrett, G. (2004) *Holy Superheroes! Exploring Faith and Spirituality in Comic Books*. Colorado Springs, CO: Navpress .com

Green, J. (2000) 'Holy Drug War, Batman!', *Playboy Magazine* (April). Available at: http://www.mapinc.org/drugnews/ v00/n400/a09.html?117

Greenberg, D. (2004) 'Fathers and Sons: George W. Bush and His Forebears', *New Yorker*, 12 July.

Hayward, K. and J. Young (2004) 'Cultural Criminology: Some Notes on the Script', *Theoretical Criminology* 8(3): 259–73.

History Channel (2003) *Comic Book Superheroes Unmasked*, 23 June.

Kane, S. (2004) 'The Unconventional Methods of Cultural Criminology', *Theoretical Criminology* 8(3): 303–21.

Kappeler, V., M. Blumberg and G. Potter (1993) *The Mythology of Crime and Criminal Justice*. Prospect Heights, IL: Waveland.

Katz, J. (1987) 'What Makes Crime News?', *Media, Culture and Society* 9: 47–75.

Lovell, J. (2002) 'Nostalgia, Comic Books and the "War Against Crime!": An Inquiry into the Resurgence of Popular Justice', *Journal of Popular Culture* 36(2): 335–51.

Lovell, J. (2003) 'Step Aside Superman … This Is a Job for [Captain] America! Comic Books and Superheroes Post September 11', In S. Chermak, F.Y. Bailey and M. Brown (eds) *Media Representations of September 11*, pp. 161–73. Westport, CT: Praeger.

Lustick, I. (1996) 'History, Historiography, and Political Science: Multiple Historical Records and the Problem of Selection Bias', *American Political Science Review* 90(3): 605–18.

McCloud, S. (1993) *Understanding Comics: The Invisible Art*. New York: Harper.

McCloud, S. (2000) *Reinventing Comics: How Imagination and Technology Are Revolutionizing an Art Form*. New York: Harper.

McGrath, C. (2004) 'Not Funnies: The Most Innovative Novels Being Published Now Just May Be Those of Some Seriously Strange Cartoonists', *New York Times Magazine*, 11 July.

Maxfield, M. and E. Babbie (1998/2001) *Research Methods for Criminology and Criminal Justice*. Belmont, CA: Wadsworth.

Mattingly, T. (2004) 'Comics Turn to Bible for Exciting Plots', *Good News Magazine* (March–April). Available at: http://www.goodnewsmag.org/magazine/2MarApr/ma04comics.htm

Newman, G. (1993) 'Batman and Justice: The True Story', *Humanity & Society* 17(3): 297–320.

Neuman, W.L. (2003) *Social Research Methods. Qualitative and Quantitative Approaches* (5th edn). Boston: Allyn and Bacon.

Nozick, R. (1981) *Philosophical Explanations*. Oxford: Oxford University Press.

NPD Funworld (2005) *The NPD Group Reports Annual 2004: U.S. Video Game Industry Retail sales*. Available at: http://www.npdfunworld.com/funServlet?nextpage/pr_body.html&content_ id=2076

Nyberg, A.K. (2003) 'Of Heroes and Superheroes', in S. Chermak, F.Y. Bailey and M. Brown (eds) *Media Representations of September 11*, pp. 175–85). Westport, CT: Praeger.

Oldenquist, A. (1988) 'An Explanation of Retribution', *Journal of Philosophy* 85(9): 473–6.

O'Neil, D. and N. Adams (2004) *Green Lantern, Green Arrow*. New York: DC Comics.

Polling Report (2001–2) 'President Bush: Job Ratings'. Available at: http://www.pollingreport.com/BushJob1.htm

Rice, C. (2002) 'National Security Advisor Holds Press Briefing', 16 May. Available at: http://www.whitehouse.gov/news/releases/2002/05/20020516–13.html

Sanders, C. and E. Lyon (1995) 'Repetitive Retribution: Media Images and the Cultural Construction of Criminal Justice', in J. Ferrell and C. Sanders (eds) *Cultural Criminology*, pp. 25–44. Boston: Northeastern University Press.

Simpson, P., H. Rodiss and M. Bushell (eds) (2004) *Rough Guide to Superheroes*. New York: Rough Guides.

Strinati, D. (1993) 'The Big Nothing? Contemporary Culture and the Emergence of Postmodernism', *European Journal of Social Sciences* 6(3): 359–75.

United States Congress, House of Representatives (1994) *Contract with America*. Available at: http://www.nationalcenter.org/ContractwithAmerica.html

Von Hirsch A. (1976) *Doing Justice*. New York: Hill and Wang.

Washington Post (2005) 'Bush Calls Iraq War Moral Equivalent of Allies' WWII Fight Against the Axis', 31 August.

Weiner, S. (2003) *Faster Than a Speeding Bullet: The Rise of the Graphic Novel*. New York: Nantier.

Wertham, F. (1954) *Seduction of the Innocent*. New York: Rinehart and Winston.

Williams, J. (1998) 'Comics: A Tool of Subversion?', in S.E. Anderson and G.J. Howard (eds) *Interrogating Popular Culture: Deviance, Justice and Social Order*, pp. 97–115. Guilderland, NY: Harrow and Heston Publishers.

Wright, B. (2001) *Comic Book Nation: The Transformation of Youth Culture in America*. Baltimore, MD: The Johns Hopkins University Press.

Yocum, M. (2006) 'Interview with Greg Garrett' *ComicCritique.com*, 9 January. Available at: http://www.comic-critique.com/st/interview_garrett.html.

NICKIE D. PHILLIPS, Assistant Professor, St Francis College, New York, USA.
Email: nphillips@gc.cuny.edu

STACI STROBL, Assistant Professor, John Jay College of Criminal Justice, New York, USA.
Email: sstrobl@gc.cuny.edu

HIP-HOP AND PROCEDURAL JUSTICE

Hip-Hop Artists' Perceptions of Criminal Justice

Kevin F. Steinmetz[1] and Howard Henderson[1]

Introduction

From its inception, hip-hop music (commonly referred to as rap) has been vehemently critiqued for its violent, misogynistic, and antipolicing rhetoric, all the while simultaneously being supported, by some, as an emergent mechanism in the furtherance of social justice.[1] The extant literature, concerning the relationship between hip-hop, deviance, crime, and the criminal justice system, posits that for the most part, hip-hop's culture and lyrical content have led to increased acceptance of aggression, derogatory perceptions of women, and disrespect for the criminal justice system, most notably the police (Bogt, Engels, Bogers, & Klooserman, 2010; Johnson, Adams, Ashburn, & Reed, 1995; Nisker, 2007). Hip-hop music is derived from a subculture disproportionality impacted by the criminal justice system, with findings consistently indicating that African Americans receive higher rates of arrest and more severe forms of punishment than all other racial/ethnic groups in the United States (Rocque, 2011). Despite numerous studies (Alridge, 2005; Cheney, 2005; Dennis, 2007; Kubrin, 2005a, 2005b; Martinez, 1997; Nisker, 2007; Quinn, 1996; Rose, 1994) that mention the criminal justice reality within hip-hop music, to date, mainstream criminal justice and criminology journals have yet to systematically examine the symbiotic relationship between criminal justice and hip-hop music.

1 Sam Houston State University, College of Criminal Justice, Huntsville, TX, USA
Corresponding Author: Kevin F. Steinmetz, Sam Houston State University, College of Criminal Justice, P.O. Box 2296, 816 17th St., Huntsville, TX, 77341, USA Email: kfs006@shsu.edu

The lack of hip-hop research in criminal justice and criminology journals is all the more perplexing, given the continual criminal justice "intra muros" entreat to measure public perceptions of the criminal justice system and its impact of such perceptions on behavioral outcomes (for example, see Gabbidon, Higgins, & Potter, 2011). Therefore, examining hip-hop's criminal justice relevant thematic content provides an alternative, contemporary avenue for assessing public portrayals of the system. As a result, situating our research within the broader body of knowledge focused on examinations of criminal justice perceptions, this study utilizes a systematic latent and manifest content analysis to assess hip-hop artist's portrayal of the criminal justice system.

Hip-hop music involves spoken word laid over a backing music track, typically with a prominent beat. Much like other musical art forms, hip-hop, from its inception, has served as a communicator of cultural messages to an audience that had few other socially acceptable accessible outlets for expression (Alridge, 2005). In the art form's early years, it was noted that "[h]ip-hop is like a CNN that black kids never had" (rapper Chuck D as quoted in Gates, 1990). While contemporary social media outlets threaten this once predominant avenue for expression and cultural transmission—with research showing African Americans are just as likely to use social media as other racial/ethnic groups (Smith, 2011)—hip-hop continues to provide an outlet of and for this artistic expression for a culture historically denied the benefits of the principles theoretically extended by the Bill of Rights. The music is a medium for the transmission of common experiences, struggles, and aspirations to other members of the hip-hop community and listeners from all strata of society: domestic and international. Given that this community also experiences an overrepresented reality within the criminal justice system, it is imperative that examinations of the perceptions of the system be assessed through the music.

Hip-hop emerged from economically, politically, and socially marginalized racial minority groups who have been disproportionately affected by the criminal justice system (Tonry, 2011). Research has demonstrated this same group has been disproportionately targeted by criminal justice policies, such as the "War on Crime" and the "War on Drugs" (Agozino, 2000; Tonry, 2011). As such, over the past 25 years African American men have faced incarceration rates five to seven times greater than those of White men (Tonry, 2011). Because criminal justice has an ever present reality within the hip-hop community, as a result of the disproportionate criminal justice experience of the African American population, the discipline's lack of hip-hop examinations is potentially overshadowing an intricate opportunity to understand the manner in which a cultural art form perceives institutionalized methods of social control (i.e., criminal justice system).

The disproportionate level of interaction between the hip-hop community and the criminal justice system gives the community more firsthand and vicarious experiences with the law enforcement apparatus, corrections system, and judicial process than many other groups. As such, the music generated by this population contains insights and narratives about criminal justice, which may be able to serve as a "report card" on the system and an alternative avenue by which to determine the public sentiment. In other words, the music of the hip-hop community may provide a unique lens in which to examine the impact criminal justice has on those under its purview—a perspective criminal justice and criminological researchers should not ignore.

In the current article, we contribute to the scholarship on hip-hop by conducting a latent and manifest lyrical content analysis. To date, this is the first systematic inductive content analysis of hip-hop portrayals of criminal justice conducted within those journals focused on criminal justice and criminology. The primary research question driving this study is centered on the manner and extent to which hip-hop lyrics portray criminal justice. To address this question, a random sample of 200 hip-hop songs was drawn from all platinum-selling hip-hop albums from 2000 to 2010. The lyrics within these songs provide an opportunity to examine the perceptions of hip-hop artists regarding the criminal justice system and its primary components. As noted in the review of the literature, vicarious experiences of the criminal justice system are as significant as actual; therefore, lyrical analysis of a music genre coming from a group so intertwined with the criminal justice system is pertinent. Research has shown that personal and vicarious experiences of injustices threaten the systems legitimacy and lead to a host of outcomes (i.e., noncompliance with law enforcement, delinquency, etc.). Examination of criminal justice portrayals through the lyrical content of hip-hop music subsequently offers a rare contribution to the extant literature on cultural influences and relevancy within criminal justice. In addition, this research simultaneously provides an opportunity to situate hip-hop research within the broader body of recent literature focused on the measurement of public perceptions of the system and the outcomes thereof.

We begin with a brief review of the previous literature comprising systematic and empirical analyses of hip-hop music, providing both the various foci of the research and their results. Then, a description of the methodology used in this content analysis will be summarized, which consists of a random sample of songs selected from platinum-selling albums utilizing a grounded theoretical-based coding approach. Lastly, the results of the analysis are provided which identify (1) various themes that emerged from the hip-hop lyrical portrayals of each component of the criminal justice system and (2) consistent underlying themes of unfairness and powerlessness which permeated the portrayals of criminal justice in rap.

Examining Hip-Hop

Despite hip-hop's position as one of the most popular and potentially influential music forms in contemporary popular culture, relatively little academic attention has been directed toward it within criminal justice and criminology journals. As such, this review of the literature broadens itself beyond the scope of immediate disciplinary publications and reviews specifically systematically conducted empirical studies examining hip-hop. Previous empirical research on hip-hop generally consists of content and legal analyses and behavioral outcomes. While there have been many notable essays and treatises written about hip-hop music (i.e., Dyson, 2007; Gilroy, 1993; Rose, 1994), the foci of this literature review remains limited to frame the state of systematic and empirical research on hip-hop. An exception to this rule is a brief mention of Butler's (2004, 2009) *Hip-Hop Theory of Justice* as it is one of the few theoretical pieces directly related to criminal justice and criminology.

Several studies have examined hip-hop for its effect on the behavior of juveniles. These studies found correlations between hip-hop music and youth acceptance of violence (Johnson et al., 1995; Johnson, Jackson, & Gatto, 1995), juvenile deviance (Mir-anda & Claes, 2004), and negative gender stereotypes (Bogt et al., 2010; Johnson et al., 1995). Each of these examinations found rap music or videos were associated with increased commission and acceptance of these behaviors. For example, Johnson, Jackson, and Gatto (1995) conducted a quasi-experimental study on a nonrandom sample of 46 adolescent African American males. In this study, they required one group to watch violent rap videos, one group to watch nonviolent videos, and a third control group which did not watch videos at all. After showing the videos and administering a vignette survey, the study found adolescents exposed to violent rap videos were more likely to accept violence in the vignettes than the other two groups.

Mahiri and Connor (2003) conducted a study that differed substantially from other behavioral outcomes studies that assume a simple causal link between exposure to hip-hop and negative outcomes.

Their study is unique in that it is a qualitative examination of the process youths go through while interpreting and internalizing their exposure to hip-hop's various messages. The authors examined a nonrandom sample of 41 middle-school students and found that instead of passively receiving the metaphorical messages conveyed through hip-hop, the youths were capable of critiquing, interpreting, and looking beyond hip-hop's ascribed negative features (i.e., hedonism and misogyny) to find the positive or pro-social messages in the music.

Like all research, hip-hop behavioral outcome studies are confronted with limitations. First, four out of five of these studies are limited by small sample sizes (n ≤ 60; Johnson, Adams, et al., 1995; Johnson, Jackson, et al., 1995; Mahiri & Connor, 2003; Miranda & Claes, 2004). Second, all of these studies utilized nonrandom samples. Third, two of these studies examined acceptance of violence without drawing connections between acceptance, commission, and willingness to commit violence (Johnson, Adams, et al., 1995; Johnson, Jackson, et al., 1995). Finally, four out of five of these studies assumed a simple causal link between exposure to hip-hop and negative outcomes rather than the dynamic process of internalizing and interpreting the art form (Bogt et al., 2010; Johnson, Adams, et al., 1995; Johnson, Jackson, et al., 1995; Miranda & Claes, 2004).

Numerous studies in hip-hop have derived conclusions based on a content analysis of hip-hop lyrics (Armstrong, 2001; Knobloch-Westerwick, Musto, & Shaw, 2008; Kubrin, 2005a, 2005b; Weitzer & Kubrin 2009) or music videos (Conrad, Dixon, & Zhang, 2009; Zhang, Dixon, & Conrad, 2010). Collectively, these studies deductively found support of hip-hop's violent endorsements, misogyny, materialism, colorism/afro-centrism, and nihilism which results from living in harsh, oppressive, and otherwise negative conditions. For example, Weitzer and Kubrin (2009) conducted a content analysis examining portrayals of women in a random sample of 403 gangsta rap songs in which they found that rap music "naturalizes certain alleged characteristics of men and women and, in accordance with these imputed differences, seeks to restrict, rather than broaden, women's proper roles and resuscitate male domination" (Weitzer & Kubrin, 2009, p. 24).

Hip-hop content analyses are not without limitations. First, these studies have largely focused exclusively on the perceptibly negative features of rap—that is misogyny and violence. By negative in the previous context we are referring to the nature of research drawing attention to the socially disapproved themes predominant throughout hip-hop, without spending any or much time (1) contextualizing the art form, (2) discussing any socially redeeming qualities of the music, or (3) examining the lyrics in such a way as to provide an avenue for the messages contained in hip-hop to be expressed in the artist's own words. As such, the research has been myopic in its examination of hip-hop lyrical content. Perhaps the only exception to this negative focus is Kubrin's (2005b) study looking at nihilism in hip-hop music. As described in this study, however, nihilism—while not necessarily a negative feature of hip-hop in-and-of-itself—may be analogous to a negative characterization because it is a result of "living in an environment filled with violence and limited opportunities" (Kubrin, 2005b, p. 441) and is conducive to or correlated with negative outcomes. Second, content analyses of hip-hop have been exclusively deductive. While not diminishing the importance of deductive research, inductive research is useful for (1) providing alternative interpretations of hip-hop and (2) allowing the words and meanings of hip-hop artists to be heard in the research.

Hip-hop has also been examined from a legal and theoretical-development perspective. For example, by examining the use of hip-hop lyrics in criminal proceedings, Dennis (2007) found that hip-hop lyrics composed by defendants were being unfairly used by prosecutors as criminal evidence. The courts were failing to contextualize the hyperbolic nature of hip-hop lyrics. Rather, lyrics were taken at face value and submitted as criminal evidence against a defendant. In short, Dennis (2007) unveils a disjuncture between courts and their interpretation of hip-hop culture. Understanding this disjuncture is important because of its implications beyond the court room. For example, hip-hop artist Common created a controversy recently as a result of being invited to the White House by President Obama to read poetry to inner city youth (Marikar, 2011). Critics asserted Common's lyrics incited violence and lacked artistic merit—an interpretation with a disjuncture similar to the one discussed by Dennis (2007). These critics chastised Common for a few violent lyrics while (1) ignoring the fact that most of his other lyrics are nonviolent and (2) not considering the context in which Common's work is situated.

One theoretical review warrants mention because of its direct relationship to the dynamic between hip-hop and criminal justice. Butler (2004, 2009), drawing from hip-hop music and culture, developed a hip-hop "theory of justice." He asserts that within hip-hop lyrics lies a theory of punishment, which values the individual while simultaneously supporting the idea of "just desserts." His scholarship represents the only academic attempt (known to the authors) to develop a theory of punishment premised on the cultural expressions of the hip-hop culture.

In sum, previous literature has predominantly been pessimistic toward hip-hop by primarily focusing on its perceived misogynistic, deviant, and violent undertones. In particular, studies which have focused on the relationship between hip-hop's lyrical/visual content and impact on behavioral outcomes have taken a jaundiced view toward hip-hop. Despite a few exceptions to this derogatory evaluative norm (Butler, 2004, 2009; Dennis, 2007; Mahiri &Connor, 2003), most empirical hip-hop research has fallen victim to the negative interpretive lens of examining the music.

The current study builds on the previous literature in multiple dimensions. Unlike most of the prior research, this study will utilize an inductive approach which allows the words and meaning of hip-hop artists to be expressed and synthesized into a cohesive framework rather than imposing a deductive framework onto the lyrics. More importantly, the current study builds upon the extant literature by being the first to examine hip-hop and its discussion of criminal justice for insights which could provide an alternative framework of understanding the hip-hop community's perspective on the criminal justice system. In short, the overall goal of this research is to provide guidance for researches and policy makers regarding future criminal justice interactions with this population, which has typically perceived the system as unjust (Rocque, 2011).

The Present Study

The purpose of this study is to conduct a content analysis of hip-hop lyrical portrayals of the criminal justice system. "Criminal justice" is operationalized as the three branches (i.e., law enforcement, corrections, and courts). Hip-hop lyrics were chosen as the unit of analysis for two reasons. First, as highlighted in the literature, limited research has been conducted specifically on hip-hop's perspective of the criminal justice system even though this art form has expressed opinions about social control and criminal justice since its inception (Butler, 2004). Despite the prevalence of criminal justice in hip-hop, scholars have yet to determine the nature and extent of these portrayals.

Our perceptions-based examination situates itself within the broader body of knowledge on the criminal justice system which involves surveys of the general public to assess their perceptions of the system's legitimacy (Henderson, Wells, Maguire, & Gray, 2010; Sunshine & Tyler, 2003; Tyler, 2006; Tyler & Huo, 2002). For this study, the lyrics provide the data for assessing hip-hop artists' perceptions and, as detailed further in the discussion, have implications for understanding the hip-hop community's perceived legitimacy of the criminal justice system.

Second, hip-hop lyrics were also chosen as the unit of analysis as a result of its position at the center of many controversies in public discourse. For example, hip-hop has been derided as an endorser of violence against the police (Hamm & Ferrell, 1998). Considering the controversial nature of hip-hop, its implied message, increasing popularity, and representation of a community so intimately associated with the criminal justice system, who also happen to have a less favorable view of the system, researchers interested in social and cultural processes should look into hip-hop as a potential object of study.

Methodology

Sample

Consistent with previous hip-hop research, the lyrics chosen for this sample were taken from 200 hip-hop songs randomly selected from 1,507 tracks on 87 platinum-selling hip-hop albums released between 2000 and 2010 using a random-platinum sampling procedure similar to those used by Kubrin (2005a, 2005b) and Weitzer and Kubrin (2009).[2] Platinum albums (1 million or more sold) were chosen to increase the likelihood of listenership. A lyric was operationalized as a single thought expressed through the words of the song. Due to their redundancy, "greatest hits" albums and soundtracks were excluded. Given that this research focuses on the perceptions of the American criminal justice system, the two platinum-selling European albums were also omitted.

Multiple sources were consulted in order to develop the sample. Platinum status was determined by referring to data from the Recording Industry Association of America (RIAA). Amazon.com was used to provide track listings. ARTISTdirect.com, an online resource with information on music artists and groups, was utilized to (1) decide which songs were classified as rap/hip-hop and (2) provide track listing information unavailable on amazon.com. lyrics from the randomly selected songs were obtained from The Original Hip-Hop/Rap Lyrics Archive (www.ohhla.com) with clarification of various slang terms provided by The Rap Dictionary (www.rapdict.org).

Plan of Analysis

The first level of analysis in the current study consisted of a latent content analysis which allowed for the inductive and systematic examination of the lyrics for the identification of common themes. Second, a manifest analysis was then used to develop frequencies for the latent themes so comparisons could be drawn between them. A song was considered to discuss criminal justice if it mentioned police, corrections, or courts in a literal and/or metaphorical sense. Below is a more detailed description of the inductive approach adopted in the current study.

Coding Procedure

Using a grounded theoretical approach (Charmaz, 2006), the qualitative notes derived from each lyric were initially coded based on the characterization or portrayal given by hip-hop artists regarding each branch of the criminal justice system.[3] A single word or phrase which best captured the characterization given by the artists was assigned to each lyric in this phase. In addition to reading each song's lyrics multiple times, every song was listened to at least twice. Listening to the music allowed for consideration of the lyric's musical context to ensure proper interpretation of hip-hop characterizations of criminal justice.

The next stage of coding involved finding patterns among the criminal justice characterizations. To avoid detachment from textual context, any possible patterns were checked against the song's lyrics to provide confirmation. The identified patterns constitute "thematic categories" of criminal justice portrayals. For example, in order to be categorized under policing, any lyric that characterized the police as "chasers" or "watchers" was coded as the thematic subcategory of *police as predatory*.

Once the process of developing thematic categories was complete, two general themes emerged from the data: (1) the unfairness of the criminal justice system, and (2) feelings of powerlessness in confronting this unfairness. In this study, unfairness is defined as the exercise of authority which differentially applies to individuals based on ascribed attributes such as race, class, or gender.[4] Premised on previous research (Geis & Ross, 1998; Thomas & González-Prendez, 2009), powerlessness involves a perceived loss of control, an inability to (1) access "valued resources," (2) overcome obstacles, and (3) seek resolutions. Drawing from this literature, we developed a definition of powerlessness which takes into consideration the criminal justice focus of the study. As such, we defined powerlessness as the perceived inability to seek resti-tutions and reparations through the legitimate legal apparatus and/or the inability to cope with challenges created by the imposition of authority.

Results

Table 1 presents the number of lyrical mentioning's relative to each specific branch of the criminal justice system (i.e., law enforcement, corrections, and/or courts). In this sample, 128 separate lyrics made a mention of criminal justice in some form or fashion. In addition, some lyrics would mention multiple distinct components of the criminal justice system. As such, this study distinguishes between lyrics (single thoughts expressed by the words of the song) and mentionings (each time a distinct component of the criminal justice is mentioned in the lyrics, with multiple mentionings occurring occasionally in a single lyric). Within the 128 lyrics that referred to criminal justice, there were 139 individual mentionings. Of these 139 mentionings, 81 (63.28%) mentioned law enforcement, 47 (36.72%) mentioned corrections, and 11 (8.59%) mentioned the criminal legal system. For purposes of this analysis, hip-hop portrayals of each branch are presented separately with their corresponding thematic categories. Example lyrics are pulled from the sample to provide illustrations of each theme. To ensure clarity of lyrical portrayals and to avoid miring the reader in excessive detail, only one or two lyrical examples of each theme are provided, as the utilization of more would not provide additional clarity.

As demonstrated in Table 1, of the three identifiable criminal justice themes, mentionings of law enforcement (58.27%) occurred most frequently. A chi-square test showed that mentionings of criminal

Table 1. Overall Criminal Justice Themes

Lyrical theme	N	%	χ^2
Law Enforcement	81	58.27	
Corrections	47	33.81	
Courts	11	7.91	
Total	139		80.69[***]

Note. Percentages will total more than 100% due to rounding.
[***]*p* < .0001.

justice were significantly more likely to be of law enforcement than the other two branches ($\chi^2 = 80.69$, $df = 3, p < .001$). This finding is supported by the reality that law enforcement is the branch of criminal justice most likely to be encountered by the citizenry.

Table 2 provides frequencies for the thematic categories under each criminal justice branch to provide an examination of the extent of these mentionings. The reader should note that because of the infrequency of lyrics relevant to the judicial system, thematic categories could not be adequately developed. Nonetheless, this data remains useful for the general conclusions drawn and will be highlighted in the discussion section.

Chi-square tests were run to determine the prominence of each respective subtheme within law enforcement and correctional mentionings. The results of the chi-square tests are discussed within their respective subthemes. These tests assess the significant likelihood of a particular subtheme portrayal within a lyric.

A Hip-Hop's Portrayal of Law Enforcement

The most discussed branch of the criminal justice system was law enforcement ($n = 81$; 58.27% of lyrics). There are three subthemes in law enforcement mentionings which emerged—*law enforcement as hunters, law enforcement as oppressors*, and *law enforcement as illegitimate*. A degree of conceptual overlap between these categories exists. For example, various aspects of law enforcement can be viewed as both oppressive and illegitimate, such as in a case of police corruption. As a result, rather than creating mutually exclusive categories, this analysis focused primarily on distinguishing the different qualities of the portrayals.

Table 2. Identified Subthemes of Criminal Justice Branch Mentioning's

Focus of criminal justice Branch mentionings	N	%	χ^2
Law enforcement			
as predatory	43	43.88	0.309***
as oppressors	20	20.41	20.753
as illegitimate	21	21.43	18.778
passive and indirect references	14	14.29	34.679
Total	98		
Corrections			
interferes with social ties	47	53.41	6.149***
conditions and effects	8	9.09	20.447
oppressive	13	14.77	9.383
punishment as appropriate	9	10.23	17.894
nondescript negative	5	5.68	29.128
passive and indirect references	6	6.82	26.064
Total	88		

Note. Percentages will not total more than 100% due to rounding.
***$p < .0001$.

Law Enforcement as Predatory

In the hip-hop lyrics within this sample, law enforcement officers are often described in a way that makes them seem predatory ($n = 43$; 43.88%). Of the law enforcement subthemes, discussing law enforcement, the chi-square test demonstrated that the category *law enforcement as predatory* was significantly more likely to be mentioned than any of the other themes within hip-hop discussions of law enforcement ($\chi^2 = .309$, $df = 4$; $p < .001$). Within this sample, rap artists often portrayed police as those who chase, stalk, watch, catch, and cage. Taken together, these portrayals characterize the police *as predatory*. Jay-Z provides an example of hip-hop's portrayal of law enforcement as predatory in "December 4th" (2003) where he raps, "Goodbye to the game all the spoils, the adrenaline rush/your blood boils, you in a spot, knowin' cops could rush/at you in the drop, you so easy to touch." In other words, the cops are portrayed as a lurking threat, as Jay-Z engages in a drug deal, he knows the police could be lurking out beyond his sensory range, ready to strike as he places himself in the vulnerable position of committing a crime.

Law Enforcement as Oppressors

Another way in which law enforcement is characterized by hip-hop artists is *as oppressors* ($n = 20$; 20.41%; $\chi^2 = 20.753$; $df = 4$; $p > .05$). Here, we find the oppression enacted by police officers taking two general forms. The first being in the form of *direct oppression* which involves law enforcement directly engaging in activities perceived as oppressive. Direct oppression is often lyrically expressed as cops acting in a way that impedes on hip-hop artist's upward mobility and the predatory behavior of law enforcement. Under direct oppression, the hip-hop artist's environment, sense of safety, and security are affected by the police. The second form is *indirect oppression*, in which law enforcement actions, while not necessarily oppressive in-and-of themselves, become oppressive as they contribute to an already negative or harsh environment hip-hop artists find themselves in. These portrayals involved a discussion of the negative features in their lives or environment such as poverty or violence in which the police were included as an additional negative feature.

Jay-Z expresses *direct oppression* by discussing the police as inhibitors of upward mobility. He notes, "You know why they call The Projects a project, because it's a project!/an experiment, we're in it, only as objects/and the object for us to explore our prospects/and sidestep cops on the way to the top—yes!" ("Kingdom Come," 2006). In this song, Jay-Z describes selling drugs as a means (of very few available) to achieving socioeconomic upward mobility. In the aforementioned lyric, the cops are portrayed as an obstacle that must be "sidestepped" to climb the socioeconomic ladder. We also find this example to be one of *indirect oppression* as well because "The Projects"—housing specifically built for the impoverished—is associated with poverty. As such, any actions by the police which must be "sidestep[ped]" as the artists "explore [their] prospects" are viewed as oppressive because it contributes to the negative lived experience of poverty (Jay-Z, "Kingdom Come," 2006).

Law Enforcement as Illegitimate

In this category, *police as illegitimate*, we find law enforcement portrayed as liars, manipulators, harassers, corrupt, violent, discriminatory, and impotent ($n = 21$; 21.43%; $\chi^2 = 18.778$; $df = 4$; $p > .05$). It is in this characterization where hip-hop focuses on portraying law enforcement as deserving of none of the legitimacy it currently holds. Law enforcement is stripped of its image of altruism and its order-protecting veneer. Hip-hop artists portray the police as defaulters on the notion of protecting and serving as opposed to preservers of the peace. *Law enforcement as illegitimate* has a great deal of overlap with *law enforcement as oppression* because some of the same police behaviors are described in both, such as in cases of police brutality. The important distinction between these two categories is that portrayals of *law enforcement as oppression* focuses on the police contribution to social and psychological distress experienced by hip-hop artists and the law enforcement intention to keep the hip-hop community in their current social position, while *law enforcement as illegitimate* focuses on the police contradiction to that very image that supposedly gives them legitimacy. As an example of this conceptual overlap, police corruption (like a police officer stealing drugs from a hip-hop artists/dealer) can simultaneously act to abuse hip-hop artists (*oppressive*) while eroding the image of law enforcement as just and righteous (*illegitimate*).

As mentioned previously, many topics are expressed by hip-hop artists that portray the police as illegitimate. Each one of these conveys an improper or poor exercise of police power and authority. For example, Snoop Dogg ("Set It Off") discusses police brutality when he raps, "It's somethin bout these motherfuckin' West coast G's/make that cheese, when the cops come you bet' not freeze/blast on 'em like the Genovese, they yo' enemies/lock you up and fuck you up/talk shit to you beat you down then cuff you up/and leave you in a cell stuffed (damn!)/I ain't got no money for bail, that's real as fuck (f'real)" ("Set It Off," 2000). Here, the police are said to imprison and brutalize people with the implication that the treatment is undeserved. As such, Snoop Dogg portrays the police as antagonists who need to be deterred from action through gunfire.

Passive and Indirect References

The final category for hip-hop discussions of law enforcement is the *passive and indirect references* category which serves as a "catch-all" including mentions of the police that do not fit into the aforementioned sections ($n = 14$; 14.29%; $\chi^2 = 34.679$; $df = 4$; $p > .05$). There are four types of lyrics which fall into this category. First are lyrics which provide a negative view of the police but do not provide enough detail to categorize the lyric as *law enforcement as predatory, oppression,* or *illegitimate*. For example, in "I'm With Whateva" (2005), Notorious B.I.G. states, "If you don't love yourself, I'll make you see your own heart/and we don't like the NARCs, stay away from the cell." Here, Notorious B.I.G. conveys the police ("NARCs") as negative but does not provide any other details to contextualize his portrayal. Second, this category includes lyrics which refer to the titles of other songs containing the words "cop" or "police." As an example, Snoop Dogg raps in his song "Pimp Slapp'd" (2002), "You're not able to compete with the heat that I drop/and I still ain't been paid for '1-8-7 on a cop.'" Here, Snoop Dogg is not talking about law enforcement per se but is only discussing a song with "cop" in the title. Third, neutral depictions of law enforcement are included in this category such as when the police are described as crime stoppers. Finally, this category also included lyrics that fit into other categories but also had a component that did not logically align with one of the main categories. For example, in Wyclef Jean's "Thug Angels" (2000) he raps "Police is in the news, watch yourself. Ya'll saw what they did to Diallo." Here, through the reference to police shooting victim Amadou Diallo, the police are recognized as possessing the ability to illegitimately exercise extreme force—placing this lyric into *police as illegitimate*. In the context of the rest of the song, however, this lyric also serves to continue Wyclef's argument that the police are generally a nuisance which is a characterization that does not necessarily fit into the main categories.

Summary

Hip-hop portrayals of law enforcement, according to this content analysis, generally take three forms. First, law enforcement can be portrayed as *predatory*, a characterization that was significantly more likely to occur than any of the other portrayals of law enforcement ($\chi^2 = 0.309$; $df = 4$). Officers are said to stalk, chase, catch, and cage hip-hop artists. Second, law enforcement is portrayed as oppressive.

Artists claim that law enforcement officers act to directly oppress them by taking advantage and preventing upward mobility. They also are portrayed as indirectly oppressing the artists by contributing to an already difficult and negative social environment. Third, hip-hop artists describe the police as an illegitimate arm of the government by acting in a way that does not fulfill the maxim of "protect and serve." In addition, while there were other types of portrayals within this sample, they were so few they could not reliably be condensed into thematic categories. The general characteristics of these portrayals, however, were negative or neutral (no indication was given in order to determine whether the artist favored or disdained the police in the particular lyric) and none were positive.

A Hip-Hop's Portrayal of Corrections

Within the hip-hop lyrics, portrayals of corrections were the second most mentioned ($n = 47$; 36.72%). Of the correctional portrayals, six subthemes emerged: *interferes with social ties, conditions and effects, oppression, punishment as appropriate, nondescript negative,* and *passive and indirect references.* In general, characterizations of the correctional system were negative with the exception of one category: *punishment as appropriate.*

Interferes with Social ties

The most prevalent portrayal of corrections presented in the sample focuses on corrections as an interferer of social ties ($n = 47$; 53.41%). A chi-square test indicated corrections as an *interferer of social ties* was significantly more likely to be mentioned than the other correctional subcategories ($\chi^2 = 6.149$, $df = 6$; $p < .001$). Here, hip-hop artists recognize the negative impact incarceration has on relationships within the community. The artists demonstrate that incarceration not only punishes the offender but also friends, family, and others who are socially connected to the offender/offenders. For example, Tupac ("Better Dayz," 2002) raps, "plus my P.O. [parole or probation officer] won't let me hang with the brothers I grew up with." Here, Tupac is describing how his probation officer, an agent of the correctional apparatus, prevents him from engaging with his friends. In this sense, the punishment is not only about *incarceration* (the denial of liberty) but also about the *separation from loved ones.* As expressed by the hip-hop artists, it seems punishment is inflicted on the offender, their friends, and family.

Conditions and Effects

In addition to the severing of social ties, hip-hop artists also describe the conditions of incarceration and their effects ($n = 8$; 9.09%; $\chi^2 = 20.447$; $df = 6$; $p > .05$). Lyrics in this category compose 17% of all lyrical mentions of corrections. Within the lyrics, prison conditions are often described as brutal, inhumane, filthy, degrading, and cruel. For example, the Ying Yang Twins and Bun B ("23 hour lockdown," 2005), in their appeal to have their friend released from prison, describe prison conditions as "23 hour lockdown/where they treat you like a ho/slide you a plate up under the door/Nigga have to shit in the middle of the floor/prison ain't a place that we need to go."

The effects of prison are described as dehumanizing, animalizing, and often as engendered negative emotions like anger, frustration, and despair. For example, the Ying Yang Twins and Bun B ("23 Hour Lockdown," 2005) describe these effects when they rap, "23 hours lockdown in a cell/can drive a nigga crazy as hell/looking at four walls/can do nothing at all/got you feeling like a dog in a cage/a monkey in a rage." Here, the artists use similes comparing the status of "prisoner" analogous to that of an "animal." The conditions are also said to drive a person toward anger and insanity.

Oppression

Similar to the discussion of law enforcement, hip-hop artists recognize the correctional apparatus as a source of oppression ($n = 13$; 14.77%; $\chi^2 = 9.383$; $df = 6$; $p > .05$). A lyric was considered to pertain to oppression if it described corrections as (1) interfering with upward social mobility; (2) a place where resistors are held (or as a place to resist); (3) the final stop after being victimized by the criminal justice system; or (4) housing for those failed by the collapse of other social institutions (i.e., schools, etc.). The underlying theme that unifies this category is that prison acts to secure people or populations into their current social position and also contributes to the victimization of hip-hop artists by other branches of the criminal justice system. For example, Tupac describes politicians as responsible for mass incarceration: "I shed tattooed tears and couldn't sleep good/for multiple years, witness peers catch gunshots/nobody cares, seen the politicians ban us/they'd rather see us locked in chains, please explain/why they can't stand us, is there a way for me to change?" ("Thugz Mansion," 2002). Here, incarceration is said to be an instrument of political force against Tupac and the hip-hop genre of music.

Punishment as Appropriate

It is important to remember that, despite all of this resistance, the hip-hop community is not opposed to the idea of punishment ($n = 9$; 10.23%; $\chi^2 = 17.894$; $df = 6$; $p > .05$). These artists seem to support the idea that "people who harm others should be harmed in return" (Butler, 2009, p. 133). For example, Mystikal advocates for the punishment of the man who murdered his sister: "fuckin' well right I got a grudge/on your Ma, and her lawyer, and the courts/and the jurors, and the judge/defenses, your immediate family members/I'm pissin on it and burning the district attorney/You stepped down on us/ shipped that coward out his fuckin' cell and let him skip town on us" ("Murderer III," 2000). Clearly, he supports the idea of punishment and retribution for the slayer of his sister through the means provided by the criminal justice system.

Nondescript Negative

Within this category are discussions of the correctional branch of the criminal justice system which do not adequately fit into the previous categories, but do provide a negative characterization ($n = 5$; 5.68%; $\chi^2 = 29.128$; $df = 6$; $p > .05$). These portrayals are difficult to characterize beyond the quality of "negative." As such, they are labeled as *nondescript negative*. With 5 lyrics falling into this category, we find that these lyrics portray corrections as something to avoid, where "snitches" send people (perhaps reflecting more poorly on the supposed "snitch" than the corrections system itself), and as a general inconvenience. For example, Notorious B.I.G. raps, "If you don't love yourself, I'll make you see your own heart and we don't like the narcs, stay away from the cell, hey, I'ma shoot it out if I'm facing the ail [jail]" ("I'm With Whateva," 2005). He indicates he does not want to go to jail but does not provide any other descriptions or reasons why. As such, jail is described as *negative* but this portrayal is *nondescript*.

Passive and Indirect References

Like the *passive and indirect references* category in the law enforcement section, songs which do not fall logically into other categories and which are not numerous enough to justify their own categorization are found here ($n = 6$; 6.82%; $\chi^2 = 26.064$; $df = 6$; $p > .05$). Fourteen percent of the lyrical mentions of corrections were placed here. Eminem provides an example of a lyric that mentions corrections that does not fit into one of the main categories when, in the song "I'm Back" (2000) he raps, "Manson, you're safe in that cell, be thankful it's jail." Here, jail is portrayed as a haven that deviates from most of the other lyrics concerning corrections.

Providing support for Anderson's (1990) "code of the street," which argues convict or ex-convict status can be empowering in street culture, three lyrics claim having friends in prison actually acts as a positive status symbol. For example, Jada-kiss (Eve, "Thug in the Street," 2001), while describing various aspects of his life associated with living in the ghetto, says "I got niggas in jail." Within the context of the rest of the song, this is meant to bolster his "street" status. Also, here are lyrics that had fit into another category described previously, like *oppression*, but also provided a reference to criminal justice that did not fit into any of the aforementioned sections. For example, in Tupac's "Mama's Just a Little Girl" (2002), he raps, "only functions at the pen, cuz everybody's in/paying back society, I'm guilty of a life of sin." Here, he recognizes the appropriateness of punishment ("I'm guilty of a life of sin") but also says something else about corrections by saying "everybody's in." While certainly we can infer what may have been meant, there is not enough detail to discern meaning which makes this lyric fall into the *passive and indirect references* category.

Summary

Within this sample, there were primarily five categorizations which typified the manner in which corrections were portrayed by rap artists. First, corrections were described as breaking apart social ties to family and friends. Second, the conditions of incarceration were described by hip-hop artists along with the associated effects. Third, the correctional apparatus was portrayed as oppressive. Descriptions of prisons or jails as impeding upward mobility, political weapons, contributors to past criminal justice system victimization, and a holding facility for those failed by other social institutions composed this category. Fourth, hip-hop artists—while denouncing corrections in general—upheld the idea of punishment's appropriateness. Finally, characterizations of the correctional system which were negative but did not provide any other details were described. In addition, while there were portrayals outside the scope of these aforementioned sections, they were not numerous enough to constitute their own category and were relegated to the *passive and indirect reference* section.

Portrayal of Criminal and Civil Courts

The court system personnel, primarily consisting of judges, prosecutors, defense attorneys, and the judiciary system, in general, is the least discussed branch of the criminal justice system by hip-hop artists ($n = 11$; 8.59%). It is beyond the scope of the data to determine why this would be the case but, this lack of portrayal may be emblematical of the reality that this is the area of the system that has the least amount of direct contact with persons as they are processed through the criminal justice system. Contact with police officers would happen more frequently than encounters with lawyers and judges and more time would be spent in jail or prisons than within a court room, and thus the lyrics may represent the degree of familiarity. Whatever the reason, the low level of discussion about the court system limits our ability to conduct logical inferences. Despite this limitation, we can still gleam relevance from what *is* mentioned about the judicial system by artists.

One way hip-hop artists describe various components of the court system are as instruments of control. In a rather gendered example, Cam'Ron raps, "Niggas don't listen to broads, they having you sitting in court/for kids that ain't yours, come home with me" ("Come Home With Me," 2002). As demonstrated by Cam'Ron, hip-hop artists sometimes describe the court system as a tool used by women to control them. Women are portrayed as dependent on the resources of the man and, to extract these resources, the court system is used.

While the court system is described as an instrument of control, hip-hop artists also describe how to resist this control through the use of defense attorneys. For example, Jay-Z recollects advice given to him, which involved keeping enough money to hire a lawyer if criminal activity should turn sour: "Old heads taught me, yung'un, walk softly/carry a big clip, that'll get niggaz off me/keep coke in coffee, keep money smellin' mothy/change is cool to cop but more important is lawyer fees" ("Never Change," 2001). In other words, to resist control imposed through the court system, one must fight it within the system itself through lawyers.

Hip-hop artists recognize a problem with trying to legitimately engage the court system, however, even with defense attorneys. The court system is portrayed as falling short of its promise to fulfill justice. In a lyric used as an example previously but still providing a powerful display of hip-hop's perceptions of the failures of the judicial process, Mystikal laments the court's treatment of the man who killed his sister: "fuckin' well right I got a grudge/on your Ma, and her lawyer, and the courts/and the jurors, and the judge/defenses, your immediate family members/I'm pissin on it and burning the district attorney/You stepped down on us/shipped that coward out his fuckin' cell and let him skip town on us" ("Murderer III," 2000). Here, Mystikal is asserting the court system failed to provide justice for him and his family by letting the killer go.

Summary

Hip-hop artists within this sample seldom discussed the court system. As such, prominent themes and categories did not emerge from the data. Regardless, there were three general ways the court system was described in the data. First, the court system was portrayed as an instrument of control. Second, hip-hop artists described the need to have a lawyer to avoid legal trouble. Finally, the court system was portrayed as falling short of its promise to serve justice. It should also be noted that none of the hip-hop artists had anything supportive or positive to say about courts; the discussion was pessimistic.

Discussion: Unfairness and Powerlessness

The extant literature on hip-hop and its relevancy to criminal justice and delinquency have focused primarily on its derogatory mentionings of women, police, and influence on deviant behavior (Armstrong, 2001; Conrad et al., 2009; Knobloch-Westerwick et al., 2008; Kubrin, 2005a, 2005b; Weitzer & Kubrin, 2009; Zhang et al., 2010). Given the intimate relationship between the hip-hop community and the American criminal justice reality, it is perplexing that to date no research has intentionally focused on the systematic examination of the criminal justice nature within discussions espoused in the music of hip-hop culture. Criminal justice's oversight of this community is all the more troubling, considering the extant literature that focuses on measurements of public perceptions and their influence on human behavior. Given that hip-hop is an expression of the predominantly African American community, our research has been premised on the notion that African American's have a unique world view as a result of their lived experiences (Feagin, 2010; Unnever & Gabbidon, 2011). Initially, we sought to examine the criminal justice mentionings within the lyrical content of hip-hop music and whether or not there was a greater likelihood of that mentioning categorization. After deciphering the criminal justice relevant mentioning, we examined the extent of those criminal justice mentionings. In other words, what was the nature of the criminal justice lyrical content? The results from our findings are consistent with the existing literature which has noted that feelings of unfair treatment result from perceived procedural injustices and threaten the perceptions of legitimacy within the minority communities, the very components of which have served as the basis for procedural justice and legitimacy theory (Tyler, 2006; Tyler & Huo, 2002).

Procedural justice and legitimacy theory, rooted in Weber's (1968) study on power's legitimacy and resurged by the works of Tyler (2006), hypothesizes that as authorities enact fair decisions, premised on facts, as opposed to conjecture, the citizenry will feel personally obligated to comply with the established rules and ultimately possess greater levels of trust. In other words, procedural justice and legitimacy theory notes that as perceptions of unfairness increase, so to do perceptions of injustice. Research has demonstrated perceptions of illegitimacy lead to a lack of willingness to work with the criminal justice system, noncompliance, an inability to maintain order, delinquency, and an overall inability of the system to control criminal activity. The idea of fairness (i.e., procedural justice) has been found to significantly influence the acceptance of decisions made by police (Tyler, 2006; Tyler & Huo, 2002), correctional officials (Henderson et al., 2010), and legal decisions (Tyler, 1984). Research has also demonstrated that procedural justice increases perceived legitimacy of authorities as well as impact behavioral outcomes of delinquency and order maintenance (Henderson et al., 2010; Sunshine & Tyler, 2003; Tyler, 2006; Tyler & Huo, 2002).

After examining the hip-hop portrayals of criminal justice in this research, two overarching themes emerged. The first theme is *unfairness*. In examining the various themes from law enforcement (*as predatory, as oppressors*, and *as illegitimate*) and corrections (*separates social ties, conditions and effects, oppressive, punishment as appropriate*, and *nondescript negative*) in addition to the findings for the judicial branch of the criminal justice system, many of the discussions portray the operations and actions of the system as patently unfair, which has ramifications from a procedural justice perspective (Tyler, 2006). The Wu-Tang Clan ("Let My Niggas Live," 2000) provide an example that clearly demonstrates the intersection between police brutality/lethal use of force and unfairness when they say, "I'm gon' be shot by some pig [police officer] who's gonna swear that it was a mistake/I accept that as part of my destiny!" Here, the artist is claiming to expect to die by a police officer shooting him and then lying about his intent. Consistent with research on public perceptions of the police, the before mentioned lyric echoes the notion of the unfairness of police actions, which may be detrimental to the legitimacy and acceptance of decisions made by law enforcement (Tyler, 2006; Tyler & Huo, 2002).

Along with the descriptions of unfairness is also an obvious lack of respect for the criminal justice system within these lyrics primarily as result of being the victim of unjust treatment. Tupac ("Crooked Nigga Too," 2004) provides an example that representatively characterizes the relationship between perceptions of unfair treatment and respect for the police when he raps, "Yo, why I got beef with police?/Ain't that a bitch that motherfuckers got a beef with me/They make it hard for me to sleep/I wake up at the slightest peep, and my sheets are three feet deep." Police action perceived as hostile and unfair engenders an equally hostile and indignant response from Tupac, indicating a tremendous amount of disrespect for the police. The relationship between perceptions of fairness and respect is consistent with research on procedural justice and legitimacy (Henderson et al., 2010; Sunshine & Tyler, 2003; Tyler, 1984, 2006; Tyler & Huo, 2002), which, as noted above, holds that as perceptions of unfairness increase (gained through direct or vicarious experience), so do perceptions of injustice. Research has demonstrated the subsequent increase in perceptions of injustice leads to an unwillingness to work with the criminal justice system, noncompliance, an inability to maintain order, delinquency, and an overall failure of the system to control criminal activity. The idea of fairness (i.e., procedural justice) has been found to significantly influence the acceptance of decisions made by police (Tyler, 2006; Tyler & Huo, 2002), correctional officials (Henderson et al., 2010), and legal decisions (Tyler, 1984). In addition, increased perceptions of fairness have also been shown to lead to an increase in the perceived legitimacy of authorities and the behavioral outcomes of delinquency and order maintenance (Henderson et al., 2010; Sunshine & Tyler, 2003; Tyler, 2006; Tyler & Huo, 2002). Within hip-hop, artists not only convey their own or others experiences but the art form also provides vicarious experiences of unfairness to others which, according to procedural justice and legitimacy theory, will likely decrease the hip-hop community's perceived legitimacy of the criminal justice system.

While the literature on procedural justice and legitimacy primarily focuses on perceptions of fairness and injustice, the current study also revealed a second major theme within the sample of hip-hop lyrics which is separate but related to unfairness—*powerlessness*. Hip-hop artists often portray the criminal justice system as an institution with an immense amount of power over their lives; an ever present reality which they must continually struggle against. Research has found that perceptions of powerlessness are linked to urban disorder (Geis & Ross, 1998)—relevant because hip-hop has historically been fostered in an urban setting—and may be conducive to feelings of anger and distress (Thomas & González-Prendez, 2009).[5] As such, it would be logical to postulate that perceptions of powerlessness and its associated negative effects can easily contribute to perceptions of unfairness and injustice. Jay-Z ("Pray," 2007) provides an example of perceived powerlessness and its implications for procedural justice when he raps, "The same BM ["big mover"—a drug dealer] is pulled over by the boys dressed blue/they had their guns drawn screaming, 'just move or is there something else you suggest we can do?'/He made his way to the trunk/opened it like, 'huh?'/A treasure chest was removed/cops said he'll be back next month/what we call corrupt, he calls payin' dues." In this scenario, the officers steal from the drug dealer without fear of repercussions because they have the legal authority. In essence, the drug dealer was powerless to stop the corrupt activity of the police as they took advantage of him. The situation involves a power dynamic in which the dealer was unfairly taken advantage of but was unable to seek redress.

Powerlessness is also demonstrated in other scenarios, such as when hip-hop artists describe resisting the criminal justice system or boast about overcoming it. On their face, these situations indicate a sort of empowerment for hip-hop artists. Acts of resistance and boasting represents struggles against power and may even demonstrate cracks in the veneer of authority. In describing these incidents, however, the artists are engaging in these acts of resistance or evasion *in the face of the power wielded by the criminal justice system*. In other words, there is still recognition the criminal justice system possesses a great amount of power to be overcome or opposed. For example, in his song "Lil' Homies," Tupac (2001) raps, "runnin' from these punk police, cause lil' niggaz run the streets (my fuckin' lil' homies)." Here, Tupac notes that these "lil' homies" (delinquent hip-hop adolescents) evade the police and acquire some control of their immediate environment (they "run the streets"). Despite this, the very act of running from the police indicates recognition of the power and authority wielded by law enforcement. Tupac also describes the police as "punk," which indicates a disdain, a possible by-product of the anger, frustration, and indignation developed from perceptions of powerlessness (Thomas & González-Prendez, 2009) and unfairness (Tyler, 2006).

Hip-hop, as a culture and a form of music, is vehemently intertwined with the minority communities who most frequently encounter the criminal justice system (Rocque, 2011). Within our sample, we found that hip-hop artists often describe the criminal justice system as an institution of unfairness and a powerful antagonistic force in their lives. Under procedural justice and legitimacy theory, hip-hop can be construed as a vicarious experience of injustice for the entire hip-hop community. In addition, hip-hop music, as an indirect experience, may build upon community member's previous direct or indirect experiences with criminal justice. As such, hip-hop may also affect the perceptions of legitimacy for the entire hip-hop community. Similar to John Locke's notion that legitimacy is contingent upon the "consent of the governed" (Ashcraft, 1991), if criminal justice policy makers seek to overcome the loss of legitimacy among the hip-hop community, two areas need to be addressed: (1) implementation of criminal justice duties—within every branch—need to be evaluated for procedural justice and (2) avenues of redress need to be opened up for those who believe that have been unjustly treated by the criminal justice system. If the implementation of criminal justice is made more perceptibly fair with opportunities for resolution, then members of the hip-hop community may confer more legitimacy onto the criminal justice system (Tyler, 2006; Tyler & Huo, 2002). According to procedural justice and legitimacy theory, legitimacy is a theory of social control and has serious criminal justice policy implications.

Limitations and Directions for Future Research

Despite the advances of this research, there are a number of limitations that must be recognized. First, this sample was drawn from top-selling, mainstream hip-hop albums and this is a common limitation among hip-hop studies. It is unknown whether nonmainstream albums have increased freedoms to engage in more intense or different expressions of the criminal justice system, which may not be contained in hip-hop that climbs to the top of the sales charts. As such, future research should include songs from nonplatinum-selling, underground, or local rap artists. Second, the current study is limited in its sample size ($n = 200$). More rich and detailed results may have emerged from a larger sample. Considering the inductive and grounded approach of this study, however, the sample size is adequate. Inductive studies are often more labor intensive than many quantitative studies and, as such, concessions must be made to allow the research to be manageable. Despite the given justification, future research could benefit from a larger sample size. Sizable samples allow for themes to be more easily extracted and also provide more support for those themes. For example, the inability to reliably extract themes within hip-hop portrayals of the court system may have been resolved by drawing a larger sample that may have included more references to the legal system. Third, while our content analysis did provide support for procedural justice andlegitimacy theory, future research would benefit from examining other sources of data, such as surveys/interviews of hip-hop listeners and artists to provide a more robust examination of hip-hop perceptions and their relationship to legitimacy. Despite the aforementioned limitations, this study explores a previously unexamined area of research and expands on the narrow scope of hip-hop music relative to the components of the criminal justice system.

Academic inquiry from criminal justice andcriminologyhave donea disservice to itself by dismally focusing on hip-hop,and whenso, conducting examinations primarily focused on the misogynistic or violent lyrical content and the music's impact on delinquency resulting from problematic method-ological inquiries. The current study serves as an exploratory investigationinto theinsights of hip-hop artists toward the criminal justice system. The hip-hop community is disproportionately affected by the operations of the criminal justice system—a reality expressed within their music. As academics, to miss what they have to tell us is to ignore the perceptions of a population that has experienced the (rather dire) consequences of our criminal justice system, inherently violating the theory of consent.

Acknowledgments

The authors would like to thank the reviewers for their invaluable and insightful comments and critiques. In addition, the authors would also like to thank the Graduate Standards and Admissions Committee of the College of Criminal Justice as well as the Graduate Office at Sam Houston State University for the summer fellowship which provided the opportunity to conduct the research presented in this manuscript.

Declaration of Conflicting Interests

The author(s) declared no potential conflicts of interest with respect to the research, authorship, and/or publication of this article.

Funding

The author(s) received no financial support for the research, authorship, and/or publication of this article.

Notes

1. For the sake of simplicity, the terms "hip-hop" and "rap" are used interchangeably. The authors, however, recognize hip-hop as a term that refers to a specific urban-based subculture, while rap music is recognized as the subculture's emergent music form.

2. There are many problems that confront the random-platinum method of sampling which should be noted. First, there is no guarantee that platinum-selling songs are the most influential or respected songs in the hip-hop community. Second, it serves as only a crude proxy to listenership. Considering the many ways music can be consumed—legal or otherwise—album sales can only capture one narrow sliver of potential listenership for a song. Third, this method does not pick up influential underground or nonmainstream artists. In short, this method only guarantees that we are selecting songs that have been heavily purchased. That said, this method has become standard in hip-hop studies because of the difficulty inherent in systematically and randomly sampling any other way. In other words, we are confronted with the challenge of theoretical objectivity mired by the subjective reality of research.

3. The data for this study was analyzed and coded by the first author. The practice of using one coder to analyze lyrics has been engaged in by other hip-hop scholars (Armstrong, 2001; Kubrin, 2005a; Kubrin, 2005b). In addition, intercoder reliability—ensuring coding by more than one coder is both consistent and reliable—was neither a concern nor an issue because only one coder was used. As such, there was no other coder to be inconsistent with.

4. The definition of fairness/unfairness used within this study is based on the procedural justice literature (i.e., Tyler, 2006; Tyler & Huo, 2002) and scholarship which applies components of procedural justice to the execution of criminal justice on minority communities (i.e., Unnever & Gabbidon, 2011; Rocque, 2011).

5. The study by Thomas and González-Prendez (2009) focused on a sample of African Amer-ican women. There is, however, little reason to believe that feelings of powerlessness would not engender similar emotions like anger and distress in males, of which hip-hop is dominated.

References

Agozino, B. (2000). Theorizing otherness, the war on drugs and incarceration. *Theoretical Criminology, 4,* 359–376.

Alridge, D. P. (2005). From civil rights to hip-hop: Toward a nexus of ideas. *The Journal of African American History, 90,* 226–252.

Anderson, E. (1990). *Streetwise: Race, class, and change in an urban community.* Chicago, IL: University of Chicago Press.

Armstrong, E. G. (2001). Gangsta misogyny: A content analysis of the portrayals of violence against women in rap music, 1987-1993. *Journal of Criminal Justice and Popular Culture, 8,* 96–126.

Ashcraft, R. (1991). *John Locke: Critical assessments.* London, England: Routledge.

Bogt, T. F. M., Engels, R. C. M. E., Bogers, S., & Kloosterman, M. (2010). "Shake it baby, shake it": Media preferences, sexual attitudes and gender stereotypes among adolescents. *Sex Roles, 63,* 844–859.

Bureau of Justice Statistics. (2010, December). *Bulletin: Correctional populations in the United States, 2009* (NCJ 231681). Washington, DC: L. E. Glaze.

Butler, P. (2004). Much respect: Toward a hip-hop theory of punishment. *Stanford Law Review, 56,* 983–1016.

Butler, P. (2009). *Let's get free: A hip-hop theory of justice.* New York, NY: The New Press.

Cam'Ron. (2002). *Come home with me.* On *Come home with me* [CD]. USA: Sony Records/Epic Records.

Charmaz, K. (2006). *Constructing grounded theory: A practical guide through qualitative analysis.* Thousand Oaks, CA: Sage Publications, Inc.

Cheney, C. (2005). In search of the "revolutionary generation": (En)gendering the golden age of rap nationalism. *The Journal of African American History, 90,* 278–298.

Conrad, K., Dixon, T., & Zhang, Y. (2009). Controversial rap themes, gender portrayals and skin tone distortion: A content analysis of rap music videos. *Journal of Broadcasting & Electronic Media, 51,* 134–156.

Dennis, A. (2007). Poetic (in)justice. *Columbia Journal of Law & the Arts, 31,* 1–41.

Dyson, M. E. (2007). *Know what I mean? Reflections on hip hop.* New York, NY: Basic Civitas Books.

Feagin, J. R. (2010). *Racist America: Roots, current realities, and future reparation.* New York, NY: Routledge.

Gabbidon, S., Higgins, G., & Potter, H. (2011). Race, gender, and the perception of recently experiencing unfair treatment by the police: Exploratory results from an all-black sample. *Criminal Justice Review, 36,* 5–21.

Gates, D. (1990, March 19). Decoding rap music. *Newsweek, 115,* 60–63. Retrieved May 31, 2011 from Academic Search Complete.

Geis, K. J., & Ross, C. E. (1998). A new look at urban alienation: The effect of neighborhood disorder on perceived powerlessness. *Social Psychology Quarterly, 61,* 232–246.

Gilroy, P. (1993). *The Black Atlantic: Modernity and double-consciousness.* Cambridge, UK: Harvard University Press.

Hamm, M. S., & Ferrell, J. (1998). Rap, cops, and crime: Clarifying the "cop killer" controversy. Reprinted In R. C. Monk (Ed.), *Taking sides: Clashing views on controversial issues in crime and criminology* (pp. 23–28). Guilford, CT: Dushkin/McGraw-Hill.

Henderson, H., Wells, W., Maguire, E. R., & Gray, J. (2010). Evaluating the measurement properties of procedural justice in a correctional setting. *Criminal Justice and Behavior, 37,* 384–399.

Jay-Z. (2001). *Never change.* On *Blueprint* [CD]. USA: Roc-a-Fella Records.

Jay-Z. (2003). *December 4th.* On *Black album* [CD]. USA: Roc-a-Fella Records.

Jay-Z. (2006). Do U Wanna Ride (feat. John Legend). On *Kingdom come* [CD]. USA: Rock-a-Fella Records, Def Jam Recordings.

Jay-Z. (2007). *Pray.* On *American gangster* [CD]. USA: Rock-a-Fella Records.

Johnson, J. D., Adams, M. S., Ashburn, L., & Reed, W. (1995). Differential gender effects of exposure to rap music on African American adolescents' acceptance of teen dating violence. *Sex Roles, 33,* 597–605.

Johnson, J. D., Jackson, L. A., & Gatto, L. (1995). Violent attitudes and deferred academic aspirations: Deleterious effects of exposure to rap music. *Basic and Applied Social Psychology, 16*, 27–41.

Knobloch-Westerwick, S., Musto, P., & Shaw, K. (2008). Rebellion in the top music charts: Defiant messages in rap/hip-hop and rock music 1993 and 2003. *Journal of Media Psychology, 20*, 15–23.

Kubrin, C. E. (2005a). Gangstas, thugs, and hustlas: Identity and the code of the street in rap music. *Social Problems, 52*, 360–378.

Kubrin, C. E. (2005b). "I see death around the corner": Nihilism in rap music. *Sociological Perspectives, 48*, 433–459.

Mahiri, J., & Connor, E. (2003). Black youth violence has a bad rap. *Journal of Social Issues, 59*, 121–140.

Marikar, S. (2011, May 11). Common's White House visit slammed by critics. *ABCNews.* Retrieved September 12, 2011 from http://abcnews.go.com/Entertainment/rapper-commons-white-house-visit-called-controversial-critics/story?id=13572464

Martinez, T. A. (1997). Popular culture as oppositional culture: Rap as resistance. *Sociological Perspectives, 40*, 265–286.

Miranda, D., & Claes, M. (2004). Rap music genres and deviant behaviors in French-Canadian adolescents. *Journal of Youth and Adolescence, 33*, 113–122.

Mystikal. (2000). *Murderer III.* On *Let's get ready* [CD]. USA: Jive Records.

Nisker, J. (2007). "Only god can judge me": Tupac Shakur, the legal system, and lyrical subversion. *The Journal of Criminal Justice and Popular Culture, 14*, 176–196.

Quinn, M. (1996). "Never shoulda been let out the penitentiary": Gangsta rap and the struggle over racial identity. *Cultural Critique, 34*, 65–89.

Rocque, M. (2011). Racial disparities in the criminal justice system and perceptions of legitimacy: A theoretical linkage. *Race and Justice, 1*, 292–315.

Rose, T. (1994). *Black noise: Rap music and Black culture in contemporary America.* Middle-town, CT: Wesleyan University Press.

Shakur, T. (2002). *Better dayz.* On *Better dayz* [CD]. USA: Interscope Records.

Shakur, T. (2002). *Thugz mansion.* On *Better dayz* [CD]. USA: Interscope Records.

Shakur, T. (2004). *Crooked Nigga too.* On *Loyal to the game* [CD]. USA: Amaru Records/Inter-scope Records.

Smith, A. (2011). *Why Americans use social media: Social networking sites are appealing as a way to maintain contact with close ties and reconnect with old friends.* Washington, DC: Pew Research Center. Retrieved February 21, 2012 from http://pewinternet.org//media//Files/Reports/2011/Why%20Americans%20Use%20Social%20Media.pdf

Snoop Dogg. (2000). *Set it off.* On *The last meal* [CD]. USA: No Limit Records/Priority Records/EMI Records.

Sunshine, J., & Tyler, T. R. (2003). The role of procedural justice and legitimacy in shaping public support for policing. *Law and Society Review, 37*, 513–548.

Thomas, S. A., & González-Prendez, A. A. (2009). Powerlessness, anger, and stress in African American women: Implications for physical and emotional health. *Health Care for Women International, 30*, 93–113.

Tonry, M. (2011). *Punishing race: A continuing American dilemma.* New York, NY: Oxford University Press.

Tyler, T. R. (1984). The role of perceived injustice in defendants' evaluations of their courtroom experience. *Law and Society Review, 18*, 51–74.

Tyler, T. R. (2004). Enhancing police legitimacy. *The Annals of the American Academy of Political and Social Science, 593*, 84–99.

Tyler, T. R. (2006). *Why people obey the law.* Princeton, NJ: Princeton University Press.

Tyler, T. R., & Huo, Y. J. (2002). *Trust in the law: Encouraging public cooperation with the police and courts.* New York, NY: Russell Sage Foundation.

Unnever, J. D., & Gabbidon, S. L. (2011). *A theory of African American offending.* New York, NY: Routledge.

Weber, M. (1968). *Economy and society*. G. Roth & C. Wittich (Eds.). Berkeley: University of California Press.

Weitzer, R., & Kubrin, C. E. (2009). Misogyny in rap music: A content analysis of prevalence and meanings. *Men and Masculinities, 12*, 3–29.

Wyclef, J. (2000). *Thug angels. On The ecleftic: 2 sides II a book* [CD]. USA: Sony Records.

Ying-Yang Twins. (2005). 23 hr. lock down. On U.S.A.: *United States of Atlanta* [CD]. USA: Tvt Records.

Zhang, Y., Dixon, T. L., & Conrad, K. (2010). Female body image as a function of themes in rap music videos: A content analysis. *Sex Roles, 62*, 787–797.

Bios

Kevin F. Steinmetz is a doctoral student at the College of Criminal Justice at Sam Houston State University.

Howard Henderson is an assistant professor within the College of Criminal Justice at Sam Houston State University.

SECTION SIX SUMMARY

Key Discussion Sessions

1. In recent years we have seen a variety of superhero movies become worldwide box office hits as well as superhero's turned into hit television shows. Virtually all of these superhero movies and television shows originated in comic books. Can you list movies and television shows that have appeared since 2000 that find their origins in comic books? If yes, what are they? What were the primary findings in Vollum and Adkinson's article "The Portrayal of Crime and Justice in the Comic Book Superhero Mythos" and Phillips and Strobl's article "Cultural Criminology and Kryptonite: Apocalyptic and Retributive Constructions of Crime and Justice in Comic Books"? Given the findings from both articles, why do you feel that the movies and television shows are so popular? Given the findings of both articles, what impact might this popularity have on societal views of different aspects of the criminal justice system? If you are from another country, what are your thoughts and observations regarding such films and televisions shows and American society?

2. In this final discussion you are asked to explain the lessons and policy implications put forth in the Steinmetz and Henderson (2012) article "Hip-Hop and Procedural Justice: Hip-Hop Artists' Perceptions of Criminal Justice" to another person. To do so, you will have to take some time to summarize your thoughts about the article's findings and limitations. Think about ways to effectively communicate these concepts. Be careful about whom you approach and how to begin that conversation. It is important to consider how the individual you choose may react and how to effectively deal with their questions and thoughts about the complex reality of the hip-hop culture and its criminal justice interaction. After you complete this conversation, you will share the experience in the class discussion session.

   - Find someone who is not familiar with the findings of the Steinmetz and Henderson piece; this person can be a family member, colleague, or friend. Then explain the policy implications covered in the article to them. Pay particular attention to their reaction and any clarifying questions they he or she asks.
   - Reflect on your experience and think about what you learned from explaining these findings and limitations.
   - Consider whether you would explain the concepts covered in the article differently next time, if you would emphasize different aspects of the hip-hop criminal justice interaction, and whether you think, based on the person's reaction, that his or her community would implement the policies you have put forth.

With these thoughts in mind:

Prepare a brief description of the explanation of the hip-hop criminal justice policy implications that you used for this week's discussion. Briefly describe the person you chose and their reaction. Finally, describe any difficulties you had in preparing for this final discussion and any insights you gained.

Public Consumption Exercise

Remember, the public consumption exercises in this text build upon each other. You must have completed the exercises in Sections 1, 2, 3, 4, and 5 to complete the current exercises.

Exercise 5: Press Releases and Maximizing Impact

As was stated in Section 1, the majority of Americans receive their news from local news. In this exercise, you will write press releases for the local press in the region where your home county is located and another press release for the local press in the region where your county from another region is located.

Article

Based on the demographic data collected in Section 1, choose an article from this section that you believe would be of the most interest to the residents of your home county (Article 1) and the county from another region (Article 2). Indicate which articles you chose and why you believe they are the best articles.

Findings Paragraphs and Writing Level for Article 1

Identify consecutive paragraphs (no less than three) from the findings or results section of the article that contain the largest portion of key findings and retype them in a word document; make sure the wording is exact. Follow the instructions in Appendix C to calculate the writing level of the paragraphs. Does the writing level match the average literacy level for the residence of the county? If it is written at a higher level than the average, how many grade levels must the authors of the piece reduce the writing to be easily read by the residence of the county?

Findings Paragraphs and Writing Level for Article 2

Repeat the above process for Article 2.

Bulleted Facts Article 1

Utilizing the bulleted fact exercise from Section 2, create a set of bulleted facts from both the literature review (trends in previous research, historical facts, etc.) and the entire results or findings sections from Article 1.

Bulleted Facts Article 2

Repeat the above process for Article 2

Press Release for Local Paper and Television News Article 1

Next, review the instructions for writing a press release in Appendix E. Remember, a press release should not exceed 200–300 words. Write a press release for Article 1 (home county) and a press release for Article 2 (other region). Remember, it is okay to use bulleted statements in a press release. Write the piece at the average literacy level of the designated county. (For help with paraphrasing, see the following website or other similar sites: https://owl.english.purdue.edu/owl/resource/563/1/.)

Press Release for Local Paper and Television News Article 2

Repeat the above process for Article 2

Local Newspaper Readership and Television News Viewership

Conduct your own research and determine the answers to the following questions and provide sources:

1. Identify the primary local newspaper for your home area. Look up or contact the newspaper and determine what its readership is for its daily paper (not counting Sunday papers).
2. Identify the primary local newspaper for your other region. Look up or contact the newspaper and determine what its readership is for its daily paper (not counting Sunday papers).
3. Choose a local television station from your home area (CBS, NBC, ABC, or FOX). Look up or contact the local television station and determine what its viewership is for its evening news broadcasts.
4. Choose a local television station from the other region (CBS, NBC, ABC, or FOX). Look up or contact the local television station and determine what its viewership is for its evening news broadcasts.

APPENDIX A

List of Over 200 Journals Publishing Crime and Media Research

The following list represents peer-reviewed journals that have published at least one crime and media research article since 2004. This list is not to be considered exhaustive, but rather it is intended to demonstrate the wide range of journal options that crime and media researchers have to choose from given the broad scope of media influence. Many more journals probably exist that are open to crime and media research but have simply not received submissions.

20th Century British History
Addiction
Addictive Behavior
Adult Education Quarterly
African Journal of Criminology and Justice Studies
Aggression and Violent Behavior
Aggressive Behavior
American Behavioral Scientist
American Business Law Journal
American Communication Journal
American Journal of Criminal Justice
Archives of Sexual Behavior
Asian Journal of Criminology
Australian & New Zealand Journal of Criminology
Australian Feminist Studies
Berkley Journal of Gender, Law & Justice
British Journal of Community Justice
Canadian Journal of Communication
Canadian Journal of Criminology and Criminal Justice
Canadian Journal of Women & the Law
Canadian Review of American Studies
Child Maltreatment
Clinical Law Review
Clinical Pediatrics
Communication & Society
Communication Research
Communication Research Reports
Communication Reports

Communications Lawyer

Computer Speech & Language

Conflict Resolution & Negotiation Journal

Connecticut Law Review

Contemporary British History

Contemporary Justice Review

Crime & Delinquency

Crime, Law and Social Change

Crime, Media, Culture

Criminal Justice and Behavior

Criminal Justice and Popular Culture

Criminal Justice Policy Review

Criminal Justice Review

Criminal Justice Studies

Criminology and Criminal Justice

Critical Criminology

Critical Discourse Studies

Critical Studies in Media Communication

Current Sociology

Death Studies

DePaul Law Review

Developmental Psychology

Deviant Behavior

Discourse & Society

Drugs: Education, Prevention & Policy

European Journal of American Studies

European Journal of Communication

European Journal of Criminology

European Journal of Cultural Studies

European Journal of Political Research

Feminist Criminology

Feminist Media Studies

Feminist Theory

Film Quarterly

Florida Communication Journal

Gender and Society

Genders

Global Crime

Government Information Quarterly

Homicide Studies

Howard Journal of Communications

Howard Journal of Criminal Justice

Information & Communications Technology Law

Information Culture

Interdisciplinary Comic Studies

International Criminal Justice Review

International Journal of Criminal Justice Sciences

International Journal of Crime, Justice and Social Democracy

International Journal of Cultural Studies

International Journal of Cyber Criminology

International Journal of Legal Profession

International Journal of Media & Cultural Politics

International Journal of Offender Therapy and Comparative Criminology

International Journal of Police Science & Management

International Journal for the Semiotics of Law

International Review of Victimology

Journal of Aggression, Maltreatment & Trauma

Journal of American Culture

Journal of Applied Journalism & Media Studies

Journal of Applied Social Science

Journal of Black Studies

Journal of Broadcasting & Electronic Media

Journal of Communication

Journal of Communication & Culture

Journal of Communication Inquiry

Journal of Contemporary Criminal Justice

Journal of Crime and Justice

Journal of Criminal Justice

Journal of Criminal Justice and Law Review

Journal of Criminal Justice Education

Journal of Criminal Law

Journal of Drug Issues

Journal of Ethnicity and Criminal Justice

Journal of Family Violence

Journal of Gender Studies

Journal of Graphic Novels and Comics

Journal of Health Communication

Journal of Human Rights

Journal of Intercultural Communication Research

Journal of International Criminal Justice

Journal of Interpersonal Violence

Journal of Language & Social Psychology

Journal of Mass Media Ethics

Journal of Media & Cultural Studies

Journal of Mixed Methods Research

Journal of Police Science and Administration

Journal of Popular Film and Television

Journal of Popular Television

Journal of Public Health Policy

Journal of Psychoactive Drugs

Journal of Psychiatry & Law
Journal of Qualitative Criminal Justice and Criminology
Journal of Quantitative Criminology
Journal of Research in Crime & Delinquency
Journal of Risk & Uncertainty
Journal of School Violence
Journal of Sociology
Journal of the History of Sexuality
Journal of the Institute of Justice & International Studies
Journal of Theoretical and Philosophical Criminology
Journal of Urban Affairs
Journal of Vacation Marketing
Journal of Youth & Adolescence
Journalism
Journalism & Mass Communication Quarterly
Journalism Practice
Justice Quarterly
Language & Literature
Law & Contemporary Problems
Law, Crime & History
Law, Culture and the Humanities
Law & Humanities
Law Review
Law and Society Review
Loyola of Los Angeles Entertainment Law Review
Loyola of Los Angeles Law Review
Mass Communication & Society
Media, Culture & Society
Media Development
Media History
Media Psychology
Media, War & Conflict
New Media & Society
Newspaper Research Journal
Police Forum
Police Quarterly
Policing
Policing: A Journal of Policy & Practice
Policing: An International Journal of Policy Strategies and Management
Policing & Society
Policy Studies Journal
Political Communication
Political Psychology
Prison Service Journal
Probation Journal

Psychology, Crime & Law
Psychology & Law
Psychology of Music
Public Opinion Quarterly
Punishment & Society
Quarterly Journal of Speech
Race and Class
Race and Justice
Radical Criminology
Seton Hall Journal of Sports & Entertainment Law
Sexual Abuse: A Journal of Research and Treatment
Sex Roles
Social Forces
Social Justice: A Journal of Crime, Conflict & World Order
Social Problems
Sociology of Crime, Law and Deviance
Sociological Perspectives
Southwestern Mass Communication Journal
Space and Culture
Studies in Conflict & Terrorism
Studies in Hispanic Cinemas
Studies in Latin American Popular Culture
Studies in Law, Politics & Society
Studies in Literature & Language
Substance Use & Misuse
Surveillance & Society
Terrorism & Political Violence
Text & Talk
The British Journal of Criminology
The Columbia Journal of Law and the Arts
The Journal of Gang Research
The Journal of Popular Culture
The Judges' Journal
The Prison Journal
The Sociological Quarterly
The Yale Law Journal
Theoretical Criminology
Theory, Culture & Society
Tourist Studies
Trauma, Violence, & Abuse
UCLA Entertainment Law Review
Urban Studies
Violence Against Women
Visual Communication Quarterly
Western Criminology Review

Western Journal of Communication
Widener Law Review
Women & Criminal Justice
Women's Studies in Communication
Youth Violence and Juvenile Justice

APPENDIX B

Brownbag or Round Table Session

The type of session your class or group chooses will be dependent on the time of day, class size, whether the course is an undergraduate or graduate course, and the venue. **Brownbag sessions** are generally set to take place around lunchtime where individuals bring their own lunch or food may be provided, depending on the resources available. Further, there does not have to be a limitation to the number of people attending the session. **Roundtable sessions**, on the other hand, generally do not have a preferred time of day, and the number of attendees tends to be no more than 20 people. Therefore, a roundtable session may be more conducive to just class members while a brownbag session could be opened up to other students and faculty. The point of conducting either of these sessions, or any other type of session, is to create a venue for getting specific feedback, having in-depth discussions, and determining how criminologists and media personnel can work together to create a more informed public.

Session: Criminologists and the Media

For this session, students or instructors will have to establish the type of session, the venue, and time for the session early in the semester. Second, they will need to invite four to six members of the local press (e.g., newspapers, television, radio) who cover criminal justice related topics to take part in a session designed to determine how criminologists (i.e., those who study crime and the criminal justice system) can better be utilized as experts in media coverage of crime and justice issues. You will want to let participants know ahead of time what the topic is and also if there are time limits on their responses to topics raised. Remember, this session is designed to build bridges between the two groups, so criticisms should be held to a minimum. The point of the session is to find common ground and move toward a more informed citizenry. Some suggested questions to guide the session are provided below:

1. Do you know what criminology and criminal justice professors do? Specifically, do you know what their expertise entails? (Prior to the session, prepare explanations with your professor to provide to the panel if they do not know or have misconceptions of what criminology and criminal justice professors do. An example might be: "Criminologists study social, psychological, economic, and cultural factors, among others that impact law making, law breaking, reactions to laws, and reactions to law breaking.")

2. How many times have you been approached by criminology and criminal justice professors about reporting the findings of their research? If so, what was your honest experience?

3. Have you ever asked to use a criminology or criminal justice professor who has a Ph.D., to comment on a news piece? We emphasize "with a Ph.D." given that this is the highest level of education in this field, and these individuals are the ones most actively conducting research.

4. If a panel member answers "yes," ask them "what was your experience?" If a panel member answers "no," ask them why they have not used a criminologist given their level of expertise.

5. If you were approached about doing a piece on a local professor's published peer-reviewed research or ongoing research on such topics as:

   - Methamphetamine or crack cocaine user depictions and the impact of such depictions on real world sentencing
   - How African American or female police officers are depicted in cop films and the potential impact on public perceptions
   - How television news viewers perceive the race of offenders and police officers
   - The potential impact crime shows, such as *CSI*, might have on juror expectations
   - The potential role court TV programs such as *Judge Judy* may play on juror expectations
   - Rap/hip-hop lyrics and attitudes toward domestic violence
   - How rap music depicts the criminal justice system and why
   - How one high-profile case in the media changes the way similar cases are processed

   Would you be interested in such topics?
   Do you foresee any particular barriers to reporting on such studies?

6. Last questions: In the field of criminology and criminal justice, crime and media studies in particular, frustration exists because news programs rarely use those who study crime and justice issues. Frustration also stems from the lack of discussion regarding social issues that could serve as better crime prevention methods than focusing on the traditional "get tough on crime" perspective. Why do you think so few criminologists and other social scientists are utilized? Why do you think the "get tough" message is so often relied upon?

   It is often suggested in criminology and academia, in general, that the ownership of the media outlet prevents academic experts from appearing in the news. Do you think this is the case?

   End your session by opening the floor for additional questions.

APPENDIX C

Checking Writing Level

Word 2007:

1. **Open Microsoft Word**
2. In the top left corner you will find a round button. **Click on the round button**.
3. After clicking on the round button, a menu should appear. Go to the bottom of the menu and click on **Word Options**.
4. In the left-hand menu click **Proofing**
5. In the menu titled "Check Spelling and Grammar in Word" check the box **Show Readability Statistics**.
6. Lastly, click **OK**.

Word 2010:

1. **Open Microsoft Word**
2. In the top left corner click on **File**.
3. At the bottom of the menu click **Options**
4. In the left-hand menu click **Proofing**
5. Under the header **When Checking Spelling and Grammar in Word** check the box **Show Readability Statistics**. If the box is already checked, don't change the setting.
6. Lastly, Click **OK**

After you have set up the Readability Statistics for Word, you can determine the writing level for each assignment by doing the following:

1. Place your cursor at the start of the first paragraph of the material you wish to check.
2. Left-click your mouse and hold it down. Drag your cursor down until you have highlighted the material you wish to check.
3. Next, leaving the material highlighted, click on the "Review" tab on the top of Word.
4. Next, click on "Spelling & Grammar." This will take you through an examination of your spelling and grammar. If you are pulling from an article, make sure that before you say OK to suggested changes that the wording actually differs from what was in the original text.
5. When that process is complete, a box will pop up with your readability statistics. You will want to record the Flesch-Kincaid Grade Level.

NOTE: It is important to note that grade levels are not static. Someone in the 12th grade may read at a 7th grade level while a student in the 7th grade may read at a 12th grade level. Similarly, peer-reviewed research writing levels can vary from publication to publication and from section to section. The key is determining the average literacy rate of your target audience and the writing level of the research findings you wish to convey so that you know how many grade levels you need to come down to at least meet the average for the audience. If the material from an article already meets the level, try to reduce it by two more grade levels.

APPENDIX D

Writing a Blog

The following piece gives you an example of a blog. It then proceeds to answer some common questions about blogs, and suggests how to write a blog post. While blog posts are very organic and do not have the structural limitations of a peer-reviewed paper, peer-reviewed book, or press release, please make sure you follow the limitations placed on the assignment instructions, specifically the length of your blog.

Sunday, June 10, 2012

I've been thinking, again, about the weather. This time, though, I mean the external meteorology, climate change, not the solipsistic this-is-how-it-looks-inside-so-that's-how-I-see-the-outside stuff. I know I've written about things climatic before, at least tangentially, but it's getting harder to deny that we're entering a strange new world unless you're a multi-billionaire already, someone who's made your fortune on environmentally-degrading endeavors and wants still way more money and so you spend barrels of cash on having "experts" plant the seeds in the minds of average people that this whole climate-change thing is a hoax and no, this isn't a run-on sentence, just a lengthy and barely-controlled one.

But really, is there any plausible deniability left? David Letterman started his TV career as a weatherman in Indianapolis and once said that there were hailstones the size of canned hams falling in his broadcast area. I don't guess that's accurate even now, but as Jackson Browne said, "Don't think it won't happen just because it hasn't happened yet." We've had at least 3 hailstorms in the last couple weeks in this area, some quite damaging; I certainly can't remember belonging to the hailstorm-of-the-week-club ever in the past. And in case you're wondering, I got a great deal on hyphens on E-bay recently, so I've got plenty to use willy-nilly (see?).

I know, too, that I mentioned Kurt Vonnegut's *Cat's Cradle* a while ago, so I'm sure I've given you all a chance to reread it. As you'll recall, then, the book's basic premise is that, the US military, grown tired of being mired in swamp after swamp in their various wars, have (that may be a more British verb form there, the "have" rather than "has," "military" for them being a collective noun rather than a single entity, thus "they have" rather than "it has," leading to the awkward-sounding, to our ears, use of the singular v--oh, never mind) commissioned their scientists to come up with something that dries up any mud they might encounter. The result is something called "Ice Nine" (Jerry Garcia named his music publishing company "Ice Nine," for what it's worth). It works great, essentially freeze-drying the water in the mud and allowing their vehicles to ride atop the suddenly hard ground.

The problem, of course, one which no one considered, is that Earth is a closed system and all water on the planet is ultimately connected to all other water. Hence, the entire planet becomes a rime-covered waterless uninhabitable desert. Oops! As Vonnegut describes it: There was the sound like that of the gentle closing of a portal as big as the sky, the great door of heaven being closed softly. It was a grand AH-WHOOM.

I opened my eyes--and all the sea was ice-nine.

The moist green earth was a blue-white pearl.

The sky darkened … the sun … became a sickly yellow ball, tiny and cruel. The sky was filled with worms. The worms were tornadoes.

When my kids were babies and I'd stop in their rooms to kiss them one more time on my way to bed, I often took the opportunity to apologize to them (they were asleep--I wasn't trying to give them nightmares. What kind of person do you think I am, for chrissakes?) for having brought them into this world. The only reasons, it seems to me, to have kids intentionally are the biologically-encoded drive all organisms have, to propagate to ensure the continuation of the species (hardly necessary in our case, what with seven billion others around to handle that) and ego: the need to ensure a specific genetic line's continuation, or to attempt to ensure one's own immortality, or whatever other socio-psychological theory is currently in vogue about that issue. But I don't think it's 'cause we think we're giving these new beings a slice o' paradise.

Maybe the sky's not falling, maybe it won't soon be filled with worms of tornadoes, though I bet there are people in this country who'd say it already has been. But it sure seems to me that we're at least dipping our toes into waters we know nothing about. We're changing the sky above us with greenhouse gases and the very ground beneath us with our hydrofracking experiments to feed our fossil fuel dependency which will then put more gases into the atmosphere which will then, you get where I'm going. I guess what baffles me most is this: where do the Koch Bros. and all of the other billionaire anti-climate-change propagandists and fanatical, dissembling environmental deregu-lators think they're gonna go if cataclysmic events caused by our behaviors do happen? Are they so insulated by money and privilege that they think they're somehow immune? Must be, but wow. And what of their children and children's children?

All of this sparked by a few hailstones--what a whackjob I must be. But the music'll be good: lots of weather-related stuff--"Stormy Weather," "Bless the Weather," "Earthquake Weather," "Hail, Hail, Rock 'n' Roll," and many "nowhere" songs, 'cause we don't really know where we are anymore and there's nowhere else to go, and Bruce Cockburn's "The Trouble With Normal." Join me Tuesday, noon-till-two, won'tcha? And "Hi," Rybie!

"Pay attention to the open sky/You never know what will be comin' down … ."

Questions about the example:

1. Unlike the author of a printed book, whose work has been approved by editors and reviewers, a blogger has not been reviewed by anyone, and a blog can be as fanciful and false as the writer wants to make it. How does Edson establish his authority on the subjects he's discussing?
2. How did you feel when you got to the end and realized that Edson also has a radio show?
3. Do you like reading someone's strong personal feelings, or would you appreciate a more "objec-tive" or balanced presentation?
4. Do you imagine that writing a post like this makes the writer feel better? Here's how blogger/contractor/ex-writing teacher Edson answered that question: *Weirdly, yes, I do feel better, though I'm not sure I can really say why. There's all of this anger and outrage and bafflement and bemusement and sadness spinning around inside of me and being able to put it down and out seems to assuage it if only*

briefly. I've always just wanted people to get me and know what a wonderful and valuable and amazing person I am and carry on accordingly, which is to my mind simply the flip side of screaming, gnawing, nearly-debilitating-at-times insecurity. I also like to think that, while I'm not ever gonna change anything significantly, maybe someone will think differently about something I write about, or just think about it, or maybe realize there are others who think similarly. And some of it's just a chance to show off stuff I've got that others maybe don't. It ain't pretty between these ears on the inside, either.

Questions about Blogs

1. **What are its purposes?**
    The purposes for which someone starts or contributes to a blog are as diverse as the subjects of blogs themselves. Some blog, certainly, in the hopes of making money. But most bloggers also spend the time and energy to express themselves, to make the point THEY want to make about basketball statistics or race relations. Some bloggers want readers; others don't seem to care about an audience. But they DO care about making their point. Mark Edson clearly wants to make himself heard about climate change. What other purposes does his blog serve?

2. **Who are its audiences?**
    The answer to that question seems to change by the day, as more and more people find blogs useful sources of ideas, useful outlets for expression, or both. Bloggers seldom know who might read what they write, though most have a core readership. Beginning bloggers imagine a readership and write for it … and sometimes it materializes.

3. **What's the typical content?**
    Most blogs contain a large measure of opinion. Many also contain information, though that information usually hasn't been checked by anyone and should therefore be considered less reliable than information from most printed sources and even wikis.

4. **How long is it?**
    As long as the blogger wants to make it.

5. **How is it arranged on the page?**
    Most blogs scroll straight down but they may highlight or downplay the text and the surrounding material. People writing for someone else's blog don't usually have much control over how their words appear.

6. **What pronouns are used?**
    Most bloggers use "I."

7. **What's the tone?**
    It depends on how the blogger wants to be perceived and can range from purposefully obscure or offensive to business-like and formal.

8. **How does it vary?**

Literary journal editors always say "read an issue before submitting a piece to us," and that advice is probably even more true for bloggers. You don't ant to blog in a tuxedo about gardens if others are blogging in cutoffs about Dr. Seuss.

Suggested Moves for Writing a Blog

Creating your own blog is just about as easy as opening a new document in a word-processing program. Use something like Google's Blogger, tailored for newcomers. It will take you step by step through the process that results in your blog becoming available on the Internet. For free. A slightly more complex process involves downloading software like WordPress and then finding a web host for your blog. (One of WordPress's favorite hosts is Laughing Squid.) Or you may be able to use social media as a blogging tool.

1. Discover.
   First, **Shut up the critic**. Your first attempt at a blog will likely feel awkward, as does any new genre. **Freewrite** about what motivated you to blog in the first place or about what you know about the subject of the blog. If you're supposed to blog as an assignment, **Inventory**. There's bound to be something in those lists that you want to tell the world about. Consider **Creating a persona**. Is there a particular aspect of your character or your opinions that you'd like to give voice to? It can be fun and liberating to write as someone else. Early in the process, **Share your story**.

2. Develop.
   The next generation of bloggers may blog in textspeak, but many writers today approach writing a blog as they would approach an essay. Follow the **Accordion Principle**. Write your ideas out in full the first time, not worrying about word count. Then go back and save the good parts. You need to consider your multiple potential audiences and how they might read your blog. **Brainstorm a list of contexts**. Your audience may see your ideas in a context you never imagined. People may not be able to hear the virtues of the golf course you're proposing if all they're thinking about are potential wild parties at the clubhouse. As soon as you've got a draft to work with, **Explain your code words**.

3. Gather.
   Try **Memory joggers** and **Brainstorm songs and song lines**. Finding a song that connects to your post can both help your thinking about it and give you a way to hook your readers.
   Even if you've chosen a subject you know a lot about, you may need to do traditional research. You don't want to spread inaccuracies to a potentially huge audience.

4. Integrate.
   Your ability to **Summarize** may be important at this stage. Can you quickly and fairly boil down a book or an interview into a couple of sentences? Can you take a paragraph of your own and turn it into a single sentence? **Integrate your own ideas**.

5. Focus.

   It's up to you—and perhaps the blog's traditions—whether your blog has the same kind of focus and point you'd want in a personal essay. Try **Filling in the blanks** to come up with potential focal points. If that doesn't work, **Find the problem/tension/conflict**. And once you've got some kind of direction, **Brainstorm leads**. You only have seconds to catch the eye of hyperactive Internet readers. If you haven't yet systematically considered all your possible audiences, **Focus for different audiences**.

6. Organize.

   A blog post may not need as tight a structure as a formal essay, but you should still **Answer readers' questions**. If you're interested in communicating with readers, not just in expressing yourself, make sure you're **Writing reader-based prose**. Is your post long and complex? **Use headings and subheadings**.

7. Revise.

   Imagine that your post is to be read by thousands. Make it as good as possible. **Revise your process**. To make sure that the whole thing holds together, **Make ends meet**. Be sure to **Share**.

8. Present.

   You may not have much control over how your post looks, but you can look at other posts on the blog and try to imagine how you can use its color scheme and highlighting techniques.

APPENDIX E
Basics of Writing a Press Release

Utilize the following instructions to help construct your press release. Some of the terms are generic and are meant to apply across all situations. For the purposes of your assignment, the term "Event" would be the publication of the research and the journal in which it appears; "Where" would be the department and university associated with the authors. Additionally, you do not need to meet all the "News Value" and "Newsworthy" criteria. These are just examples; pick the criteria that best fit the findings of the study you are using.

Writing for the Media

News releases are designed for both broadcast and print media. Whether sent in digital or print form, they are intended to be published or "picked up" by a news outlet such as a newspaper, radio station, magazine, or television news broadcast. Therefore, it is imperative that any news release is **newsworthy**. Yet there is a difference between the content in a news release and actual news. News releases are carefully crafted messages that promote a company's point of view, whereas news, in theory, must be more objective.

The news release must catch the eye of the editor with its newsworthiness and objectivity while also promoting the company's perspective. Newsworthiness is made up of two elements. The first are the **news values or five Ws and one H**—who, what, where, when, why, how—and are familiar to many people. Each of the news values is defined in Table 1.1. The second element of newsworthiness is seen in the criteria listed in Table 1.2. Writers use one or several of these elements or **angles** to emphasize newsworthiness.

When using a news release, the editor may reprint it as is or use the release as a starting point by assigning a reporter to follow up on the information provided in the release.

Style, Tone, Objectivity

Because news releases are written for the media, they must appeal to that discerning audience. First, a news release must never appear to be advertising—no editor wants to give free publicity! This means that the writing voice and tone should be objective rather than persuasive. As you compose a news release, think about a skeptical, cranky editor going through dozens or hundreds of these potential news items every week. Your job is to appeal to this editor's need for news to fill holes in

Table 1.1. News Values

News value	Definition
Who	Exact names and titles of people involved in an event
What	Major action or event stated in one sentence—often includes lesser actions or events related to major event
When	Time of event clearly stated
Where	Location of event
Why/how	Explanation of event including its context

Table 1.2. Elements of Newsworthiness

Newsworthy element	Explanation
Timeliness	Events are only newsworthy just before or directly after they occur
Prominence	Prominent fi gures and celebrities help publicize anything
Proximity	Local angle is a great "hook." (Editors say that if it happens to *our* community, it's news.)
Significance	Number and type of people who will be affected can make an item newsworthy
Uniqueness	Any bizarre or odd event will capture an editor's eye
Human interest	People like to read about other people, so this angle is also used to create interest
Newness	"Free" and "new" are key words that help generate interest in a news item

the publication. Your need—to secure free publicity—is moot if your release does not make it past the editor's discriminating eye.

To appeal to the editor, keep the following in mind:

1. Keep word choice neutral and accurate. Avoid overblown adjectives and instead rely on strong nouns and verbs to make your point. Be factual, clear, and succinct.

2. Be correct. Writing for the media also means you must pay special attention to correctness. People in the media consider themselves writers, so news releases must be well written and tightly edited. Typos, misspellings, grammatical errors, or incorrect format will turn off an editor and minimize your chance of achieving your writing objective. The style guide the media uses (and consequently the style guide with which PR writers need to be familiar) is *The AP Stylebook*.

3. Decide if the release is hard news or more of a feature news story. News releases can be written in either a hard- or soft-news style. Hard news is timely and has immediacy. Soft news focuses on people or issues that affect people's lives. A soft news release (also called a *feature*) might take the form of a story about a child whose life was saved by a new drug, with the issuing company being the drug manufacturer.

News Release Submissions

News releases may be sent in hard copy or as an email. For optimal pick up, you should investigate how the organization you hope will use your news prefers to receive its releases. Many media outlets have guidelines for submitting a release.

Hard copy. Some organizations may prefer to receive news releases in hard copy format. Hard copy releases can run one to three pages, but most editors prefer concise releases of no more than two pages or three hundred words. If you are sending the release to multiple sections of a newspaper, be sure to include a note to each section editor that you have done so. When sending a hard copy release, issue it on company letterhead. Double space your text and indent each new paragraph.

Email. The majority of news releases today are sent electronically. These news releases are shorter than print news releases and generally fit on one or two screens. However, they adhere to the same rules as print releases except for the following:

1. The subject line of the email should contain the main idea of the release.
2. The release should not be an attachment; it should be contained in the body of the email.[1]
3. Company name (because it may not appear on letterhead) and contact information appear at the top of the electronic release and again at the end of the message. Some electronic news releases include an image such as the company logo at the top.
4. There should be one space above and below the headline.
5. Body copy is single-spaced with double-spacing between paragraphs, flush left.

Elements of the Hard News Release

The basic elements of a hard news release are as follows and are illustrated in Figure 1.1.

Headline ("head") and subhead. The purpose of the headline ("head") is to concisely capture the main idea of the release. Headlines are written with present-tense verbs and omit the articles "a," "an," and "the." The headline in a news release is crucial because if it does not clearly appeal to the editor and get the message across that an item is newsworthy, the release will be ignored. It is, in essence, the "sales pitch," although it must be worded to avoid sounding like an advertisement.

Consider the difference in these two headlines. The first is overly persuasive, and the second is more objective.

1. *New Herb Guarantees Safe Weight Loss and Money-Back Guarantee*
2. *New Study Shows Herb's Effectiveness as Weight Loss Tool*

Headlines use clear, concrete language, avoiding vague, unspecific words. For best search engine optimization (SEO), the headline should contain key words that are repeated strategically throughout the release that echo the essence of the message. The headline should not mimic the lead paragraph; it should use different wording to get across the main idea of the release.

Secondary head. The secondary head ("subhead") is often a complete sentence that uses a full verb and the articles that are frequently omitted from headlines. The subhead assumes the presence of the headline and gives additional information that provides another layer of detail. It should not repeat the first headline and is not mandatory. Notice how the following subhead builds on the previous headline example.

Researchers find that thermogenic herbs rid the body of excess fluids.

Lead. The lead, or first paragraph, is the most important part of the release. Although many lead styles exist, the most common is the summary lead, which includes as many of the five Ws and one H as can fit without sounding awkward. In the lead we stress the release's news value, and we focus on an angle to make it newsworthy. (Refer to the previous list of newsworthy angles.) The order of information related in a lead should reflect the company's goal in writing the news release, but it must also keep in mind the needs of news organizations. Leads can be as many as 30–35 words, as long as they are clear.

Body (inverted pyramid style). The body of most news releases is one to two pages (occasionally up to three.) The body features relatively short paragraphs, although too many short, choppy paragraphs are discouraged. Like any good writing, the body of the document should be concise, clear, and accurate. Sentences should be varied and have good rhythm. However, news releases also possess the qualities of good journalism and use journalism's "inverted pyramid" style of writing. This means that the body is organized in descending order of importance; the most important elements are placed at the top, and the least important are placed toward the bottom. Editors use this style because, when deciding how much space or time to devote to an item, they cut from the bottom. By writing in the inverted pyramid style, we are helping the editor.

After the lead paragraph summarizes the release's newsworthiness, the second paragraph contains the next most important part of the news. What follows in subsequent paragraphs is less important, and so on. After all the points of the release have been covered, many releases add a paragraph that contains background information the reader may need to fully understand the significance of some aspect of the preceding story.

Quotations. Most news releases contain a quotation from someone in the company in the third or fourth paragraph. For example, if the release is about a new hire or a promotion, the division manager may be quoted. If the release is about a new product, some other company offi-cial will make a statement that is quoted in the news release. Oftentimes these quotes are created by the public relations professional (in which case the quote is *always* approved by a superior.) The purpose of using a quote is to combine information the organization wants to impart with a more personal perspective.

Quotations, which can be direct or paraphrased, add life to a story that a disembodied statement does not.

When quoting, the following should be taken into consideration:

1. Use the exact spelling and title of the person being quoted.
2. Use the first and last name the first time a person is named. Use only the last name thereafter.
3. Put commas and periods inside quotes.
4. Put other punctuation marks within the quotation marks if they are part of the quote. (Example: XYZ company spokesperson Jane Doe said, "Would we be willing to ship this package without worry? Yes, we would!")
5. Attribute each quote.
6. Introduce each person quoted. (Example: Mark Elliot, recipient of this year's award, said, "I am grateful for the opportunity to serve my community.")
7. Use "said" rather than "laughed," "snorted," and the like in news releases.
8. Use "according to" when referring to an inanimate source, not when referring to a person.
9. Use an indirect quote only when the speaker is inarticulate.

Boilerplate. The final paragraph of most news release is the "boilerplate." The boilerplate paragraph is a short summary (often including the company mission) that provides background information about an organization and may be 50–100 words. It may include what the company produces, the number of employees or outlets it has, its stock-trading information, or its corporate philosophy.

Document Design

News releases include the following information and stylistic elements:

1. **Company address**: Name, street, city, zip code, phone number, fax, and website.
2. Words "**News Release**" typed in upper case figured prominently under company name.
3. **Contact name**: Name of person to whom questions about the release may be directed as well as the individual's phone number, email address, and fax.
4. **Release date**: If the release is meant to be distributed upon receipt, write "**FOR IMMEDIATE RELEASE**." If the release is to be embargoed, write, "**EMBARGOED UNTIL 1–1–20XX**." Releases are embargoed only when the issuer does not want that news to precede an announcement or, in the case of a scientific study, that study's publication in a peer-edited journal. Use caps and boldface for both immediate and embargoed release dates.
5. **Date of distribution**: The date the release is prepared. The date of distribution appears either under the release date or as part of the dateline.
6. **Headline**: Upper case, underline, and boldface are preferred.
7. **Dateline**: City and state of event's location followed by a dash that goes directly into the lead paragraph.
8. **Bullets**. Use plain bullets rather than numbers for lists or to itemize facts. Use bullets sparingly.
9. The word "**more**" must appear at the bottom of each page unless the release is only one page. A **page slug** (page 2 of 2) should appear at the top of the subsequent page, flush left.
10. Type in 12-point Times New Roman.

11. **Boilerplate**. Should appear after the news.
12. Use **end marks** "# # #" or "–30–" to indicate the end of the release.
13. **Visuals**. Photos that illustrate an element of your release are optional. If you include a photo, write a caption that explains what the photo illustrates.

Refer to the "News Release Checklist" at the end of this chapter as a guide when you compose your news release.

Conclusion

News releases have been labeled the workhorse of the PR professional. Although the media is in a state of flux, the news release is still a key ingredient in any public relations mix.

Figure 1.1. News Release Checklist

✓	News Release Item
	Complete contact information included: name, phone, email, address
	Headline is objective, tightly written, newsworthy; omits articles
	Subhead, if used, does not repeat news in headline; adds another layer of information and is written in a complete sentence
	Lead includes news values and main point of release; contains about 30 words
	Body is in inverted pyramid style, with more important news higher in story and details of news lower in story
	Quotations are not fl uff but actual news put into the mouth of an appropriate company offi cial. Quotations follow guidelines and punctuation rules
	Boilerplate contains enough information to adequately identify company scope, mission, and size
	Hard copy document is formatted correctly. Includes company letterhead with logo, contact information, release date, date of distribution, headline in caps and underlined/centered, dateline; body is double-spaced with indented paragraphs two and beyond; page numbering follows guidelines; uses end marks at end of release
	Electronic submission is formatted correctly. Includes email subject line with main idea of release. Release is cut-and-pasted into the body of the email. Contact information appears both at top and bottom of release. Company logo (optional) appears at top with one space above and below headline. Body copy is singlespaced with double-spacing between paragraphs